AND WEAPONS FOR ALL

AND WEAPONS FOR ALL

WILLIAM D. HARTUNG

A hardcover edition of this book was published in 1994 by HarperCollins Publishers.

HarperCollins books may be purchased for educational, business, or sales promotional use. For information, please write: Special Markets Department, HarperCollins Publishers, Inc., 10 East 53rd Street, New York, NY 10022.

First HarperPerennial edition published 1995.

Designed by George J. McKeon

The Library of Congress has catalogued the hardcover edition as follows:
Hartung, William D.
And weapons for all / William D. Hartung.—1st ed.
p. cm.
Includes index.
ISBN 0-06-019014-0
1. United States—Military policy. 2. Arms transfers—United States. I. Title.
UA23.H368 1994
355'.0355'73—dc20 93-29213

ISBN 0-06-092641-4 (pbk)
95 96 97 98 99 ❖/ RRD 10 9 8 7 6 5 4 3 2 1

Contents

Acknowledgments

This book has been seven years in the making, and I have many people to thank for helping me along the way.

First and foremost, I want to thank my agent, Sydelle Kramer of the Frances Goldin Literary Agency, for sticking with this project at a time when many in the publishing world thought that the end of the Cold War had rendered a book on this subject obsolete, and for helping me to conceptualize the book. I am grateful to Aaron Asher for bringing this project to HarperCollins under his imprint, and I owe a special debt of gratitude to my editor at HarperCollins, Joy Johannessen, both for her encouragement while I was writing the book and for helping me to vastly improve its readability and logic.

My appreciation goes to all of the staff at the World Policy Institute at the New School for Social Research, where I have been based during the final stages of production and editing, but in particular to the director, Sherle Schwenninger, who gave me extremely useful feedback on how to frame the argument of the book, and to my associate Rosy Nimroody, who helped with last-minute research tasks. Much of the analysis that informs the book was developed in articles that I wrote for the *World Policy Journal*, and I would like to thank all of the editors I have worked with, including James Chace, Susan Berfield, Richard Caplan, Adrienne Edgar, and Sherle Schwenninger.

I would also like to thank the editors at my other favorite publication, *The Bulletin of the Atomic Scientists*, for giving me the opportunity

to analyze the arms trade in their pages on numerous occasions over the past seven years. The idea for this book began with a two-part series I did for the *Bulletin* in 1987 during Len Ackland's tenure as editor, and for each of the past two years I have had the pleasure of working with Mike Moore and Linda Rothstein on feature articles on the state of the trade.

When I started the book, I was working as an assistant to New York State attorney general Robert Abrams. I would like to thank Bob Abrams and my supervisor, Timothy Gilles, for allowing me the flexibility to take time off to work on this project during 1991 and 1992, as well as all of my friends at the attorney general's office who were so supportive when I first took on this daunting project.

From the outset, I have had the assistance of an entire community of researchers working on issues of military spending and the arms trade. I'd particularly like to thank David Gold, who first encouraged me to write a book on this subject when we were working together at the Council on Economic Priorities, and who passed along invaluable insights and information once I actually got down to the writing. Michael Klare's work on American arms transfer policies first inspired me to take up this subject, and I have benefited from his advice and support during the course of this project. My friend and fellow investigative writer George Winslow gave me feedback on the manuscript at every stage. Paul Ferrari of the Investor Responsibility Research Center was particularly generous in sharing files, sources, and contacts, as was Lora Lumpe of the Federation of American Scientists, who also reviewed the manuscript and provided me with a researcher's home away from home during my visits to Washington. Lee Feinstein of the Arms Control Association and Natalie Goldring of the British American Security Information Council were both extremely helpful in giving me their perspectives on emerging issues and passing along timely information.

It's not possible to mention everyone who provided useful background, but I would be remiss if I did not at least acknowledge the following friends and colleagues who helped make this book possible: Nicole Ball of the Overseas Development Council, Greg Bischak and Jim Raffel of the National Commission on Economic Conversion and Disarmament, David Brooks and Jim Cason of La Jornada, Chuck Call of the Washington Office on Latin America, Bruce Chafin and Pete Stockton of the Subcommittee on Investigations of the House Committee on Energy and Commerce, Bob and Beth DeGrasse, Anne Detrick and Caleb Rossiter of the Project on Demilitarization and

Democracy, Burt Glass and Mark Sternman of Peace Action, Sandra Ionno of the British American Security Information Council, Stephen Goose of the Arms Project at Human Rights Watch, Richard Grimmett of the Congressional Research Service, Richard Knight of the American Committee on Africa, Ann Markusen of the Project on Regional and Industrial Economics at Rutgers University, Lucy Mathiak of the University of Wisconsin, Andrew Pierre of the Carnegie Endowment for International Peace, Joe Stork of *Middle East Report*, and Cora Weiss.

I conducted more than one hundred interviews while I was researching and writing this book, with government policymakers, corporate officials, congressional staffers, and independent experts, and I would like to thank all of them for squeezing me into their busy schedules.

There is no simple way to track U.S. arms transfer policy, because it touches on overlapping issues of foreign policy, economics, and military strategy. However, there are a few journalists whose consistent, in-depth reporting on various aspects of the subject have made it much easier to piece together this story, including Alan Friedman of the *Financial Times*; Jeff Gerth of the *New York Times*; Ralph Vartabedian, Douglas Frantz, and Murray Waas of the *Los Angeles Times*; Peter Grier of the *Christian Science Monitor*; Thomas Flanagan of the Lancaster, Pennsylvania *Post-Intelligencer*, David Morrison of the *National Journal*; and Peter Stone, first at the *Legal Times* and then at the *National Journal*. Some of the best investigative pieces on the elaborate underside of the arms trade have been done on television, and I have drawn on the excellent work done by ABC News *Nightline* and the Public Broadcasting System's *Frontline* series.

While I was working on the book, I received a research and writing grant from the Program on Peace and International Cooperation of the John D. and Catherine T. MacArthur Foundation on the subject of "Future Directions for U.S. Arms Transfer Policy." The results of that work are reflected throughout the book, but particularly in the recommendations for changes in policy that appear in chapter 13. I would also like to thank the Compton Foundation, the S. H. Cowell Foundation, the John Merck Fund, and the Ploughshares Fund for their ongoing support for my work on the control of the international arms trade at the World Policy Institute at the New School, without which I would not have been able to stay so closely in touch with new developments in this field.

Most important, I would like to thank my wife, Audrey Waysse, for seeing me through all of the highs and lows that come with an ambitious project of this kind. She served as my reader, adviser, and supporter at every step of the way, and she also came up with the title.

The interval between the release of the hardcover and paperback editions of this book was marked by the birth of our daughter, Emma Waysse Hartung, an event far more momentous for me than anything described in these pages. This edition is dedicated to Emma.

William D. Hartung
New York, N.Y.

1

The $134 Billion Question

It would be tragic if the nations of the Middle East were now, in the wake of war, to embark on a new arms race.

—U.S. PRESIDENT GEORGE BUSH, IN HIS ADDRESS TO A JOINT SESSION OF CONGRESS AT THE CONCLUSION OF THE GULF WAR, MARCH 6, 1991

I expect to review our arms sales policy and to take it up with the other major sellers of the world as part of a long-term effort to reduce the proliferation of weapons of destruction in the hands of people who might use them in very destructive ways.

—U.S. PRESIDENT-ELECT BILL CLINTON, AT A CAPITOL HILL NEWS CONFERENCE, NOVEMBER 20, 1992

On the evening of January 12, 1993, one week before Bill Clinton took his oath of office as the forty-second president of the United States, Pfc. Domingo Arroyo was killed by a sniper's bullet on the streets of Mogadishu.

The twenty-one-year old marine was the first U.S. military casualty of the six-week-old intervention in Somalia. In the Elizabeth, New Jersey, neighborhood where Arroyo had spent his teenage years, acquaintances remembered him as a good kid who always wanted to serve in the military. His cousin said that he was the kind of person who "wanted to help others," and the local congressman described him simply as "a hero." The tragedy of his untimely death was balanced by a sense that he was a brave young man who had risked his life for a purpose, to help feed starving people.[1]

But the death of Domingo Arroyo also highlighted a problem that will confront Bill Clinton and other U.S. presidents with increasing regularity in the years to come: Arroyo was killed in a country whose military forces had been armed and trained by his own government. From 1977 until the outbreak of full-scale civil war in Somalia in 1989, the United States supplied nearly $300 million in military aid to Somali dictator Siad Barre. When Barre was overthrown in 1991, a portion of his stockpile of U.S.-supplied military trucks, armored vehicles, antitank weapons, rifles, and ammunition found its way into the hands of the armed gangs that U.S. forces were later sent to Somalia to deal with. While no one knows for sure whether the rifle that killed Domingo Arroyo was made in the U.S.A., there is no question that the rival warlords that have torn Somali society to shreds have plenty of U.S. equipment.[2]

This "boomerang effect," in which U.S. forces face U.S. weapons in battle, has become a routine occurrence in the post–Cold War era. The last four times the United States has sent substantial numbers of troops into conflict—in Panama, Iraq, Somalia, and Haiti—its opponents have been armed with U.S. military technology. And the chances are better than even that the next time U.S. troops are sent into a war zone, U.S. arms will be aimed at them again: during Bill Clinton's first year in office, the United States entered into agreements to supply over $32 billion in arms and training to more than 140 nations. Even worse, of the forty-eight nations in which ethnic warfare was under way in 1993, thirty-nine of them had received weaponry from the United States in the period leading up to the conflict.[3]

Beyond the potential threat it poses to U.S. military personnel, the legacy of U.S. arms trafficking is fueling violence and disorder throughout the globe, often in ways that were never intended when these weapons were originally transferred. In Afghanistan, the U.S. Central Intelligence Agency (CIA) has been desperately trying to recover hundreds of shoulder-launched Stinger antiaircraft missiles that it supplied to anticommunist rebel forces during the 1980s. The Stinger has been described by Sen. Dennis DeConcini of Arizona as "the ultimate terrorist weapon" because of its capacity to shoot down civilian airliners; DeConcini was understandably reluctant to yield control over the missiles to groups that might turn around and sell them on the world market.

According to Edward Juchniewicz, the CIA's associate director for covert operations during the Reagan administration, DeConcini's worst fears have now been realized:

> The Iranians have already captured or otherwise obtained some Stingers and continue to accumulate them. I understand why people are exercised. I wouldn't want one to hit the airplane I'm on.

As of July 1993, the CIA had spent more than $10 million trying to get the Stingers back from Afghan rebel commanders, with only modest success. U.S. government agents found themselves in a bidding war with rebel groups, terrorist organizations, and foreign governments willing to pay $60,000–70,000 per missile—more than three times the original price. In response to this problem, the CIA simply upped the ante, budgeting an additional $55 million to purchase as many of the remaining Stingers as it could.

The irony of the U.S. government having to beg, borrow, and buy sophisticated weaponry that it originally gave away as covert military aid is apparently lost on the officials who were responsible for this policy. As Juchniewicz put it, "One makes the assumption when one goes to battle that one's equipment will be captured by the enemy. So unfortunately, we lost some Stingers, and now our enemy has one of our best weapons." But his matter-of-fact reaction obscured a key point: the problem wasn't that the Stingers were captured in battle by an enemy, it was that they were being sold to the highest bidder by Afghan factions who had been considered friends.[4]

The armed mischief and mayhem supported by the CIA's former clients in Afghanistan extends far beyond the sale of deadly missiles. The agency's most dangerous export might not be weapons but rather the people it has trained to use them. Throughout the war against the Soviets right up to the present, the Afghan factions have been running an open-ended arms bazaar and weapons training camp for Islamic fundamentalists from around the world. *Washington Post* columnist Jim Hoagland quoted an Algerian official as saying that this "floating army" of Islamic fighters that was so painstakingly created with U.S. assistance during the Afghan struggle will "come back to haunt the Saudis" and other U.S. allies. The consequences may have already come home to roost in the United States itself: among the more prominent students at the Afghan rebel camps have been Ramzi Ahmed Yousef and Ahmad M. Ajaj, two of the suspects in the 1993 bombing of the World Trade Center. Sheik Omar Abdel Rahman, the alleged inspirational leader of the men who organized the Trade Center attack, served as a recruiter for the Afghan rebels during the 1980s, and there have been allegations that the CIA's decision to let him enter the United States may have been a payback for his assistance in building the Afghan resistance. David Whipple, the former head of counterterrorism at the CIA, has made it clear that these are not isolated cases: "Some of the same people who are actual or potential terrorists in this country are former guerrilla fighters in Afghanistan." If the CIA is successful in its $55 million Stinger buy-back plan, it will have swelled the coffers of the Afghan rebels and their fundamentalist network, providing them with more money to build their so-called floating army.[5]

Unfortunately, the Somali and Afghan examples are not the only cases of U.S. arms trading gone awry. In Angola, Jonas Savimbi's National Union for the Total Independence of Angola (UNITA) forces put their ample collection of U.S. weaponry to work in an effort to defy the results of United Nations–sponsored elections and shoot their way into power. In Pakistan, the main conduit for U.S. supplies to the Afghan rebels during the 1980s, large parts of the country have degenerated into an open-air weapons market, complete with private armies and gunrunning into the neighboring Indian province of Kashmir. In Latin America, U.S. arms have been poured into Peru, Colombia, and Ecuador, further militarizing the complex struggles among government forces, drug traffickers, and left-wing guerrilla movements and undermining prospects for peaceful, democratic development in the Andean region.

These examples pale in comparison with what may be yet to come. Military leaders in Pakistan have already indicated that their U.S. F-16 aircraft are the most likely delivery vehicles for that nation's proposed arsenal of nuclear weapons, and a continuation of hostilities between India and Pakistan could put that plan to the test. A change in government in Saudi Arabia or one of the other Persian Gulf sheikdoms would immediately bring tens of billions of dollars' worth of top-of-the-line weaponry into play in the Middle East in new and destructive ways. Last but not least, the weapons production technology that U.S. companies have so generously provided to customers in Turkey, Taiwan, South Korea, and other nascent weapons-exporting nations could eventually develop into an alternative supply line for outlaw nations and movements that are seeking to circumvent U.S. or UN embargoes.[6]

The cumulative evidence indicating that the arms sales practices of the past twenty-five years have helped fuel terrorism and war on four continents should give the Clinton administration ample warning of the risks of conducting business as usual in arms transfer policy. In 1991, mindful of the consequences of unconstrained arms trafficking, world leaders pledged to rein in the weapons trade that had fueled the Gulf War. Now those promises are a distant memory, as presidents, prime ministers, and diplomats spend more time promoting weapons exports than they do attempting to control them. Given the obvious dangers of the disorderly world of the 1990s—where alliances, governments, and even borders can change in short order—the need to control arms trafficking is even more urgent now than it was three years ago.

To understand why the post–Gulf War pledges of restraint were never implemented, it is necessary to observe the mind-set of the international arms merchants at work.

The Talk of Paris: How Our Weapons Won the Gulf War

At first glance, the bustle of activity at Le Bourget airport in advance of the June 1991 Paris Air Show looked like the preparations for any other trade show, only on a grander scale. Scores of carpenters and electricians were rushing to put up displays in the main exhibition hall, shouting instructions back and forth over the buzz of electric saws. Temporary money exchanges, refreshment stands, and even a haircutting salon were being set up to accommodate the tens of thousands of visitors expected to attend the daily sessions. A small army of caterers and florists ferried provisions to the long rows of corporate entertainment "chalets" that were being built specially for the occasion to wine and dine potential clients. Invitations had already gone out for the dizzying round of luncheons, receptions, and parties in and around Paris that had become an integral part of the air show experience.

For all its outward similarities to other trade shows, there was one critical difference at Le Bourget. The most important business at hand wasn't hawking bed and bath supplies or marketing the year's new car models—it was selling weapons. And despite George Bush's lofty rhetoric about reining in the arms trade, it would soon become apparent that the most effective weapons salespersons at the 1991 air show were not the company lobbyists or free-lance arms brokers who were there in force but rather the representatives of the U.S. government.

A quick tour of the grounds offered the first indications that this was no ordinary industrial exposition. The main exhibit hall was a giant airplane hangar, several football fields in length, punctuated with huge overhead signs reading "Lockheed," "Dassault," "British Aerospace," "United Technologies," "Deutsche Aerospace," "Martin Marietta," and hundreds of other names of the most important companies in the world's military-industrial establishment. On the floor below, workers were prying open a crate filled with frighteningly realistic plastic copies of surface-to-air missiles. At another display, tiny helicopters were propped on wooden sticks, like insects mounted on pins in a high school science project. Across the aisle, under a neon sign that said "Guerre Electronique" ("Electronic Warfare"), a glass case held a 3-D display of model soldiers in the heat of battle, armed with laser-guided weapons and shoulder-fired missiles.

Outside the hangar, on the tarmac leading to the main runway, there were no more models, no aura of a museum or high-tech toy store, just real weapons. A Patriot missile launcher, fresh from an avalanche of positive publicity in the Gulf War, was being unpacked and assembled. Twenty yards farther on sat a British Tornado fighter plane, with a mouthful of razor-sharp teeth painted on its side, along with the words "Gulf Killer." Beyond that was a fenced-off area that would soon host a corral of U.S. planes and helicopters used in the recent war against Iraq, including a nasty-looking Stealth fighter plane, all angles and dark colors, guarded by military police in combat camouflage.

Arrayed up and down the runway and inside the surrounding buildings was a virtual United Nations of world weaponry: missiles, planes, and helicopters from more than three dozen nations, including Britain, France, the former Soviet Union, China, the United States, Israel, Germany, and Indonesia. There were passenger airliners and commercial space vehicles on display as well, but they were only of passing interest. It was clear from the outset that in Paris in 1991, the weapons would be the stars of the show.

With all these elaborate preparations in place, expectations were high for the biggest, most heavily attended Paris Air Show ever—and perhaps the most controversial as well.

Just three months earlier, the same weapons that were on display on the tarmac at Le Bourget had played a part in killing tens of thousands of people in the war to drive Iraqi military forces out of Kuwait, one of the bloodiest conflicts in the long, violent history of Middle East wars. Editorialists, legislators, and the general public in most of the major arms supplying nations had begun a steady drumbeat of criticism over the role of corporate and government arms traders in building up Saddam Hussein's arsenal. The public outcry was so great that even the presidents and prime ministers of the leading arms supplying nations had been moved to act. Less than two weeks prior to the Paris Air Show, in a speech at the U.S. Air Force Academy in Colorado Springs, George Bush had pledged to pursue a Middle East arms control initiative. Working in parallel with Bush, Pres. François Mitterrand of France announced that he would be hosting a meeting in July of the world's five leading weapons-exporting nations—the United States, the Soviet Union, France, the United Kingdom, and China—with the aim of devising a plan to limit the flow of armaments to the Middle East and other regions of conflict. For the first time in over a decade, curbing the international arms trade was becoming a priority item on the world's political agenda.

But while many observers saw the war with Iraq as compelling evidence of the dangers of the arms trade, the industry executives and military officers gathered in Paris saw it as an unprecedented opportunity to tout their latest products and aggressively expand weapons sales. The tone for the entire event was set at the initial press briefing when Serge Dassault, the commissioner general of the air show and the chairman of France's top arms exporting firm, Dassault Aviation, shrugged off a reporter's question about how political discussions on limiting arms sales to the Middle East in the wake of the Gulf War might affect future military exports to the region: "If people in the Middle East want to buy helicopters and airplanes they will buy them, won't they? It's a fact that there is a big market in the Middle East, and hopefully that will continue." Dassault was clearly irritated that anyone attending the air show would even suggest the possibility of limiting arms sales. He seemed to consider the question an example of poor etiquette, as if the journalist who asked it had broken some unstated taboo by linking the shiny new weapons at Paris to the human devastation of the Gulf War.

The message Dassault and his colleagues wanted people to bring back from Paris was that this was the time to stock up on new weapons systems, not cut back. They were proud of the performance of their weapons in the war with Iraq, and they were in no mood to accept any political limits on their marketing efforts. In fact, the favorite sales pitch at the 1991 air show was, "How our weapons won the Gulf War," as one American executive put it.

The Gulf War theme was struck early and often, but no nation harped on it as persistently or effectively as the United States. Offering the chance to see the planes of the Gulf War up close was just one aspect of a multimedia marketing strategy to highlight the role of these weapons in the conflict and win new clients for U.S. arms makers. The General Electric booth featured a photo display entitled "GE Power in the Gulf," with pictures and descriptions of all the Desert Storm aircraft that had GE engines; Grumman's glossy brochure for its new J-Stars radar aircraft touted it as "the eyes of the Storm"; and the LTV corporation was handing out wall posters showing "LTV in the Field," with action shots of the company's weapons systems on one side and newspaper quotes about their performance in the Gulf War on the other.

Video was definitely in. Many of the U.S. exhibitors had put together their very own "greatest hits" tapes. The McDonnell Douglas press center had continuous screenings of an elaborate video on the Apache helicopter, featuring shots of a squadron taking off at dusk to the strains of "Amazing Grace" and then heading out to destroy Iraqi tanks and take Iraqi soldiers prisoner. The upstairs dining room in LTV's entertainment chalet had a TV screen set into the wall, silently showing footage of the firm's Multiple Launch Rocket System (MLRS) firing furiously in the Gulf, followed by shots of convoys of LTV "Hummers"—the all-purpose military truck that replaced the jeep—on patrol in the desert.

The most sophisticated video display at Le Bourget was an interactive terminal set up by the U.S. Air Force, where passersby could choose from a menu of U.S. aircraft: at the press of a button, the viewer would be treated to scenes ranging from a test flight of the new advanced-technology fighter (ATF) to combat footage of the Stealth fighter making "pinpoint" bombing runs in Iraq. In a mirror image of much of the press coverage of the war, all the bombs in the air force video were on target, and there was no footage of anyone being killed or wounded by this high-tech onslaught. The only inkling of the true consequences of the bombing came in the middle of the Stealth tape, when a truck could be seen racing across a bridge just as a bomb was taking it out. One air force general was so pleased with this sequence that he urged his guest to "watch this," and gleefully traced his finger across the screen, following the path of the truck to its destruction.

The posters and videos were supplemented by hundreds of free souvenirs. Adults and children alike were clamoring for lapel pins depicting everything from a Stealth fighter plane to a GE aircraft engine. Desert Storm bumper stickers and coasters were being handed out at every turn, complete with company logos. McDonnell Douglas came up with the tackiest giveaway item of all, a sturdy plastic Desert Storm drinking cup with pictures of F-15s, Apache helicopters, and Tomahawk cruise missiles adorning the sides. A McDonnell Douglas public relations person assured me that the company had "tried to be subtle" in its Gulf War–related promotions because they "didn't want to be seen as going over the line, trying to capitalize on the war."

While most of these marketing techniques were readily exploited by the French, the British, the Germans, and other weapons manufacturers displaying their wares at Le Bourget, U.S. companies had one decisive edge on the competition: an unprecedented level of marketing and public relations assistance from the Pentagon. This new, aggressive posture was first revealed in a memo by Paul Wolfowitz, the undersecretary of defense for policy, in which he directed the Department of Defense to do everything in its power to show "a positive U.S. presence" at the 1991 air show in support of U.S. industry. Ironically, these marching orders for the Pentagon to help promote U.S. arms sales in Paris were handed down on March 6, 1991, the same day that President Bush was telling a joint session of Congress that one of his four key post–Gulf War goals was to *limit* the transfer of advanced armaments to the Middle East. This gross divergence between public rhetoric of arms sales restraint and behind-the-scenes actions was to emerge as the dominant theme of the Bush administration's post–Gulf War arms sales policy.

The 1991 air show marked the first time that the U.S. Air Force, Navy, and Army each had their own booths in the U.S. pavilion, staffed by technical experts and weapons program officers who could field questions about the characteristics of particular U.S. systems as visitors watched the weapons perform on videotape. The air force had the most impressive display, built around the theme of the prominence of air power in the Gulf conflict. The display itself was supplemented with several lectures by Maj. Gen. Robert Rankine ("the Air Force's senior technologist [on] Air Force systems and technologies that made their debut in Operation Desert Storm") in which he extolled the virtues of such wartime innovations as the new GBU-28 bomb, which can allegedly burrow hundreds of feet underground to destroy enemy command bunkers.

The Pentagon's most significant contribution to the U.S. presence at Le Bourget was to bring twenty-one Desert Storm aircraft to Paris, complete with pilots and crew—all at taxpayers' expense. The aircraft, which formed part of an overall U.S. display, were flown in by active-duty U.S. military pilots on so-called training missions to Paris. This creative bureaucratic maneuver on the part of the Pentagon saved U.S. defense contractors hundreds of thousands of dollars in leasing fees and transportation costs that they would normally have been expected to pay to display these systems at the air show.

Even more valuable from a pure marketing standpoint than the aircraft themselves were the scores of air force, navy, and army personnel in uniform—the first time the U.S. government had ever provided such a coordinated military presence at Le Bourget. In all, nearly 150 U.S. military personnel were assigned to the show—not only pilots and crew members but security police to stand guard over the aircraft.

The pilots were the toast of Le Bourget, standing next to the planes and helicopters they flew in the Gulf and telling war stories about how the aircraft performed in the heat of battle. In many instances, military personnel would appear on the tarmac with representatives of the aircraft's manufacturer, providing an extremely effective one-two sales pitch. While members of the public and the press were limited to posing questions from behind a metal railing that surrounded the U.S. aircraft display, potential customers were brought inside the fence to meet the pilots up close, inspect the aircraft, and sit in the cockpits. Pilots were also available to support company press conferences about particular weapons systems, as well as for literally hundreds of one-on-one interviews with members of the international press corps.

If there were any doubts about the propriety of using active-duty military personnel as virtual salespersons for the arms companies, no one was voicing them in Paris. In response to a question about why the Department of Defense had chosen to play such an unprecedented up-front role at Le Bourget, air force public affairs officer Lt. Col. John Kirkwood asserted that Secretary of Defense Dick Cheney "felt it was appropriate" for the military services to participate because "the image of the U.S. as a leader in aerospace at this point in time is primarily carried by the military" as a result of the air war in the Gulf.[7]

The most enduring image of the United States that was put forward in Paris was that of an arms merchant desperate to make the next sale. The blatant efforts by U.S. military personnel and corporate executives to capitalize on the Gulf War were in direct contradiction to President Bush's pledge, given just two weeks prior to the air show, to take steps to halt the proliferation of weapons to the Middle East. Indeed, the military delegations from Saudi Arabia, Kuwait, the United Arab Emirates, and other oil-rich Persian Gulf sheikdoms were actively pursued by U.S. government and corporate personnel throughout the ten days at Paris in the hopes of setting the stage for multibillion-dollar arms packages that would keep U.S. military firms busy for years to come.

The Plan at Dayton: Dominating the World Arms Market

It's hard to imagine a sharper contrast to the flash and bright lights of Paris than the colorless, antiseptic atmosphere of a conference room at the Stouffer Inn in downtown Dayton, Ohio. But in some ways the meeting in Dayton on July 17–18, 1991, on "Defense Exports in the Post–Desert Storm Environment," offered a better glimpse of the mind-set that has made the United States arms merchant to the world than did the dazzling round of parties and flight demonstrations in Paris. Paris was a celebration of the arms industry's performance in the Gulf, while Dayton was more like a marketing meeting, the kind of dull but necessary follow-up needed to gauge the prospects of turning the industry's windfall of publicity from the Gulf War into long-term sales opportunities.

Even more directly than the Paris Air Show, the Dayton meeting underscored the degree to which U.S. government personnel and agencies charged with regulating the arms trade viewed themselves as partners with industry in promoting U.S. arms sales. The gathering in Dayton also unveiled the U.S. government's new, post–Cold War rationale for aggressive sales of U.S. armaments abroad. The narrow bureaucratic outlook that sees only the alleged strategic, economic, and political benefits of multibillion-dollar arms sales while ignoring the very real dangers of runaway weapons trafficking was starkly on display.

The Dayton symposium, organized by the Pentagon's arms sales branch, the Defense Security Assistance Agency (DSAA), in conjunction with the American Defense Preparedness Association, an industry trade group, brought together nearly two hundred executives of weapons-exporting companies with their government counterparts in the Pentagon, the Departments of State and Commerce, and the Congress to strategize about how U.S. arms firms could best capitalize on the aftermath of the Gulf conflict to dominate world weapons markets in the 1990s. The conference was held in Dayton because it is the home of the Defense Institute for Security Assistance Management (DISAM, pronounced "die-sam"), a sort of school for government arms brokers run out of the nearby Wright-Patterson Air Force Base. DISAM is responsible for training the thousands of Pentagon bureaucrats and military personnel who negotiate, implement, and consummate the billions of dollars' worth of U.S.-government-sponsored arms sales that are carried out on behalf of U.S. military contractors every year.

The proceedings were opened on an optimistic note by U.S. Army Col. Jackson Todd, deputy commandant of DISAM, who spoke approvingly of "the big surge in demand for U.S. military hardware" over the past year. Todd made no bones about the fact that the Gulf War offered the best possible advertisement for U.S. weapons, noting that "CNN TV really did a good job for us televising U.S. equipment in Desert Storm."

After acknowledging a few little problems on the horizon, such as "congressional pressure for reductions in arms sales," Colonel Todd reminded the assembled arms industry representatives to hurry and submit their materials for the Pentagon's newly developed "Catalog of U.S. Defense Articles and Services," a Bush administration innovation designed to make it easier for U.S. government personnel overseas to promote the sale of U.S. weaponry. The catalog came in a three-ring binder, divided into helpful categories like "ammunition/propellants," "fire control/target acquisition," and "missiles/rockets." Companies were encouraged to send a picture and description of any military item they wanted to sell abroad to any and all of the U.S. government's security assistance offices located in seventy-four countries throughout the world. To manufacturers, Todd touted the catalog as "a means to make your product known to our overseas personnel." A memo contained in each participant's registration packet was even more explicit: "We at DSAA are encouraged by the enthusiasm this project is engendering. We believe that its success or failure will be determined by the quality and volume of information made available and the interest we can generate within the potential customer countries."

The idea that a U.S. official in Saudi Arabia, Pakistan, or El Salvador could just whip out a handy illustrated catalog of U.S. weaponry to impress the local military men seems like a parody from an overwrought novel about merchants of death. But Colonel Todd's only regret seemed to be that the Pentagon hadn't thought of it sooner.

Lest anyone think that the colonel's dedication to marketing U.S. weapons was the result of a parochial Pentagon outlook, his brief remarks were reinforced by Sinclair "Sandy" Martel, an assistant secretary of state who had been delegated the task of presenting the Bush administration's perspective on military assistance and arms sales. He picked up where Todd left off, declaring unequivocally that "Desert Storm vindicated the approach we've been taking to security assistance over the past 25 years and more." Martel went on to paint a picture of U.S. military assistance as one giant quid pro quo, giving detailed examples of how the nations that receive 90 percent of American arms aid—Israel, Egypt, Portugal, Greece, Turkey, and the Philippines—had done America's bidding in the Gulf War: "Without the full unstinting support of these governments, we would not have had the success we enjoyed in Operation Desert Storm. . . . The network of relationships, commonality of equipment, and understanding of U.S. military doctrine that we have developed over the years have served us well in a time of real national need." In short, Martel implied, being a global policeman means being a global arms merchant.[8]

After a ringing endorsement of the strategic merits of selling U.S. arms with relative abandon, the U.S. State Department representative proceeded to explain to his industry audience, with no apologies to Dickens, that it was a best-of-times, worst-of-times period for arms exports:

> Best of times—the West won the Cold War without firing a shot. Worst of times—the very defense industries, which contributed so much, face contraction and consolidation because military budgets are being slashed by 25 percent. Good news—the Gulf War was won primarily by American technology and arms. The demand for American goods is at a peak. Bad news—at the same time, there are calls for a moratorium on arms sales to the Middle East region.

And on he went, despite his involvement in President Bush's widely touted initiative to curb the arms trade, each time indicating as a "plus" any change that relaxed regulations on military technology transfers and as a "minus" any new controls. But the industry need not worry, Martel seemed to be saying, because the people in charge of implementing President Bush's arms curbs were as much in favor of exports as ever. They weren't about to do anything that would cut into the arms industry's lucrative foreign markets.

Now that the Pentagon and State Department representatives had made it clear that they were squarely in industry's corner, it was time to hear "congressional concerns," as the program put it, from Ivo Spalatin, the staff director of the Subcommittee on Arms Control, International Security, and Science of the House Foreign Affairs Committee. Spalatin had been the point man for Congressman Dante Fascell's proposal for a moratorium on U.S. arms sales to the Middle East in the wake of the Gulf War, a "pause" that could be used to build momentum for controlling the flow of weaponry into the region. It was the only plan on the table that might actually do anything concrete to restrain the mad rush to rearm the Middle East, and the industry hated it.

The stage seemed set for a confrontation, or at least a healthy back-and-forth on the issue of arms transfer controls. But a funny thing happened on the way to the debate. Spalatin tried to take industry's side as well. He asserted that U.S. industry could actually make *more* sales under a multilateral restraint regime, which would inhibit European suppliers while leaving U.S. firms with basically the same rules they were playing under already. Under a multilateral regime the U.S. defense industry would "do better in terms of arms sales than [it did] in the 1980s," Spalatin assured the executives.

As for the dreaded moratorium, Spalatin reminded industry personnel that the proposed legislation allowed the president to lift it as soon as he could certify that any other major supplier had made a sale to the Middle East. Spalatin volunteered his own estimate that if a moratorium passed Congress it would last only 60, 90, or, at the outside, 120 days. Without saying it in so many words, he was acknowledging that the proposed congressional moratorium on weapons exports was a symbolic gesture that would put only the smallest of dents in the arms business.

Despite Spalatin's best efforts, the arms traders weren't buying his conciliatory message. A buzz of skepticism and laughter greeted his claims about the moratorium, with people yelling out comments such as, "It's been violated already!" and "It's a dead issue!" At that point, Spalatin blew up. The conciliatory tone went out the window. He started lecturing the crowd, blurting out at one point, with reference to the Gulf War, "You people are always saying that we need security assistance to prevent war. . . . Well, it didn't work this time, we had to go to war anyway."

Now that the flak from the crowd had wounded Spalatin's ego, he made a much more impassioned defense of the need for at least some minimal form of arms trade controls, asserting that the real point of the moratorium was to "jump start the process" and "kick the president in the ass" to force him to negotiate meaningful restrictions with the other arms supplying nations. He closed with his own variation on the lessons of the Gulf War: "If there is a post–Gulf War message, it's that you've got to have an international coalition. It takes an international coalition to go to war, and it's going to take an international coalition to deter war."

Spalatin's bottom line—that a system of multilateral controls might trim the Middle East arms market from the $200 billion level of the 1980s to $170–185 billion in the 1990s—was more than the industry representatives could take. They wanted to get going *now* on cornering the Middle East arms market, and the more sales the better. As the symposium broke for lunch, most of the participants were shaking their heads and chuckling, as if Spalatin's modest arms control proposal had been sent from another planet.

The speakers who followed Spalatin in the afternoon only served to underscore the message that now was the time for U.S. suppliers to make their move if they wanted to dominate world arms markets in the years to come. But it was a whole new world, where more than just U.S. weapons were for sale. The hidden message of the Gulf War was that U.S. troops could be had as well, if the price was right. Henry Rowen, who was about to leave his post as the assistant secretary of defense for international security affairs, gloated that Operation Desert Storm had been the "world's biggest fund-raiser, which raised $60 billion for U.S. military forces alone." That U.S. troops in the Gulf had played what in effect was a mercenary role—bought and paid for by Saudi Arabia, Kuwait, Japan, Germany, and other countries with more ready cash on hand than the United States—was being portrayed as a point of pride. As the Soviet Union became more and more absorbed in its own internal problems, depriving the United States of its favorite superpower rival, the massive U.S. interventionary capacity that had been built up during the Cold War was in search of a mission, available for hire to the highest bidder. The Bush administration now seemed to be proposing that U.S. forces play global rent-a-cop rather than global policeman.

In addition to the direct cash benefits of lending U.S. troops to allies like the Kuwaiti and Saudi monarchies, Rowen cited a longer-term benefit, the prospect that countries "might reallocate their defense budgets to accommodate the kind of systems that were so successful in the Gulf War." In Rowen's view, U.S. troops in battle were the ultimate advertisement for the products of America's arms industries, and if their exploits in the war zones of the world pumped up the market for U.S. weaponry, so much the better.

A subsequent speaker, Col. Robert LaTourrette, who handles weapons transfer issues for the U.S. Central Command, the body that directed U.S. military efforts in the Gulf War, revealed that Rowen's hopeful projection of an arms sales bonanza was already coming to fruition. LaTourrette was happy to report that there had been $34 billion in requests for U.S. armaments from countries in the Middle East and the Persian Gulf since the beginning of Operation Desert Shield in August 1990; and, in LaTourrette's opinion, that was "just the tip of the iceberg." Industry lobbyist Joel Johnson reinforced Colonel LaTourrette's point later in the day when he predicted that in the wake of the Gulf War "we're going to see the U.S. move up willy-nilly to about 50 percent or more of the world's arms markets." While Johnson acknowledged that this surge in U.S. exports "could lead to embarrassing sound bites about merchants of death," he presented it as a positive and natural state of affairs that would bring the U.S. share of the world weapons market to "about the same as our aerospace share."

And so it went through the course of the two-day symposium. While George Bush was promising the nation that he was going to do his best to curb the arms trade, the message from Paris and Dayton, from government bureaucrats and industry executives alike, was that it was time for the United States to capitalize on the favorable publicity generated by the Gulf War to recapture its title as the world's number one weapons-trafficking nation.

Paris 1993: Change? Or Business as Usual?

On the surface, the 1993 Paris Air Show appeared to be dramatically different from the post–Gulf War exhibition that had occurred two years earlier.

The most obvious difference was that the world's leading arms supplying nation, the United States, had a new president, and a new approach. Clinton's deputy secretary of defense, William Perry, had issued a memorandum in April that prohibited direct Department of Defense participation in the 1993 air show. Military personnel could attend only as observers, and companies would have to pay leasing fees for any combat aircraft they wanted to display. The change in the U.S. exhibits was dramatic: there were no pilots on the tarmac singing the praises of U.S. combat aircraft, and there were no army, navy, or air force "technologists" in the U.S. pavilion standing ready to answer questions about the capabilities of U.S. weaponry. The twenty-one Desert Storm aircraft that had been arrayed on the tarmac two years earlier were replaced by a more modest collection of seven or eight military planes and helicopters.

One administration insider claimed that Perry chose to keep the Defense Department out of the Paris show to avoid the appearance of giving a "handout to industry" at a time of tight budgets. In the past, these costs could have just been hidden away in the multibillion-dollar Pentagon budget. But that was no longer an option. After the use of U.S. pilots from Desert Storm to hawk weapons at the 1991 air show was revealed, Congressman Howard Berman of California sponsored legislation requiring the Pentagon to charge contractors for the weapons they exhibited at international air shows and to report on the costs of sending pilots to such shows on "training missions." Reporting these subsidies could have been extremely embarrassing at a time when everyone from senior citizens to children in poverty were being asked to sacrifice in the name of deficit reduction, so Perry decided to let the arms contractors foot the bill. Pentagon spokesperson Bob Hall also cited "proliferation concerns" as a factor in the decision to limit Defense Department participation, but he undercut his own point by noting that the policy was going to apply for the Paris Air Show only.[9]

U.S. arms exporting firms were disappointed, to put it mildly. They had hoped to make the 1993 show a repeat of 1991. An industry lobbyist told me about a plan to set up "two corrals of aircraft highlighting the post–Cold War role of the U.S. military." One, focused on the "humanitarian mission," would have featured U.S. helicopters and transport planes that had been used during the UN intervention in Somalia. The second grouping would have struck the theme of "enforcing international agreements," using fighter aircraft that were employed to police the "no-fly zones" in Iraq and Bosnia. This ambitious marketing scheme had been scuttled by the Pentagon's shift in policy, but the industry wasn't giving up. The lobbyist told me that he hoped to convince the Clinton administration to support a display along these lines at the next major international exhibition, the spring 1994 air show in Singapore. (That effort was ultimately successful, as we will see in Chapter 13.)

In the meantime, U.S. companies were doing their best to make up for the lack of direct military involvement at Paris. Lockheed sponsored daily demonstration flights of its F-16 fighter, a hot export item that had already been sold to over fifteen foreign air forces. The company followed up with scores of formal and informal briefings at its entertainment chalet, where prospective customers could dine on place mats adorned with photos of F-16s and Stealth fighters. McDonnell Douglas held a continuous round of press conferences to show how the company planned to maintain its "dominant position" in a shrinking marketplace for military combat aircraft. Company vice president Bob Trice scoffed at suggestions that it might be time for military-oriented firms to develop commercial product lines: "There are a lot of people in the world who don't want to see a defense industry—they'd like to see us building washing machines." Trice assured his audience that that would never happen, because of McDonnell Douglas's strategy of actively pursuing U.S. and foreign military contracts, knocking "weaker competitors" out of business along the way. Lockheed and McDonnell Douglas were joined at Le Bourget by over 350 other U.S. companies, selling everything from spare parts to surface-to-air missiles. But despite U.S. industry's best efforts, there was no question that the high-profile, gung-ho atmosphere that had characterized the U.S. exhibitions in 1991 was missing.

In fact, the U.S. was arguably outperformed by other exhibitors who had learned the wonders of Western marketing techniques by observing the tactics of U.S. and European firms. Officials of the Moscow Aircraft Production Organization (MAPO) handed out free

MiG-29 fighter lapel pins to journalists attending its briefings on the aircraft; a slick promotional flyer for the plane showed a MiG in a steep climb, with the slogan "The Guarantee of a Peaceful Sky." In their zeal to make a sale, Russian industry officials even put out a sign next to the plane entitled "Proposals for Updating MiG-29 Aircraft Export Variants," listing new features such as updated radar and laser-guided missiles that customers could mix and match as they pleased.

Israel caused a stir with two intriguing new products that were displayed side by side: an upgraded Northrop F-5 fighter called the "F-5 Plus" and a modified Romanian MiG-21 called the "MiG-21-2000." Israel's push to take on both U.S. and Russian companies in the lucrative "upgrade" market is a bold move, particularly when one considers that much of the technology and expertise it is using to do so was supplied by the United States. But when the reigning industry ethos is to beat the other guy to the punch, the Israeli marketing strategy seems perfectly in keeping with the policies of the other major exporting nations.[10]

The decision to get the Pentagon out of the weapons marketing business could have been an extremely positive signal if it had been linked to a larger policy of promoting multilateral controls on the arms trade. But in the face of vigorous promotional efforts by its potential competitors, and in the absence of an overarching policy to justify its decision to keep the Pentagon home from the 1993 air show, the Clinton administration risked looking like it was merely dropping the ball in the race for foreign sales.

Into this policy vacuum stepped Secretary of Commerce Ron Brown, the Clinton administration's salesman par excellence. Brown came to Le Bourget as President Clinton's personal representative, and in his three days in Paris he tried to single-handedly make up for the lack of a Pentagon presence there. At the official opening ceremonies for the U.S. pavilion, standing confidently at a podium that was right next to an F-16 fighter plane, Brown made it clear that the administration's top priority would be meeting the needs of the aerospace and defense industries: "The president is committed to moving beyond the arm's-length relationship that has too long existed between the public and private sectors. . . . We will work with you to help you find buyers for your products in the world marketplace, and then we will work to help you close the deal." Brown pledged to meet with every single U.S. exhibitor at Le Bourget, and to find out what the administration could do to help them. He also promised ongoing personal involvement by high-ranking Clinton administration officials to make the industry's case with potential foreign customers: "If President Mitterrand and Chancellor Kohl can get on an airplane at a moment's notice and fly to distant parts of the world to advocate the interests of French and German business and industry, the U.S. government should do no less. . . . We are going to be much more aggressive." To underscore the fact that this commitment to exports extended to military as well as commercial products, Brown reminded a reporter from the *Wall Street Journal* that he had traveled to Saudi Arabia in early 1993 to "urge that country to buy military equipment made by U.S. manufacturers." At Le Bourget itself, Brown was aggressively lobbying foreign officials to buy U.S. weaponry, including a visit with representatives of the Malaysian government during which he urged them to buy the McDonnell Douglas F/A-18 fighter plane. [11]

In the absence of a major pronouncement on its approach to arms sales, the Clinton administration's performance at Le Bourget provided a preview of the forces that will influence its policy in this area. Concerns about weapons proliferation and fear of public criticism of government-funded arms trafficking will be weighed against the desire to promote exports and jobs in the defense industry. Unlike George Bush, who had a stated policy of pursuing arms export restraint that was repeatedly violated in practice, Bill Clinton has taken great pains to avoid making a clear statement of policy on arms sales. As a result, even when he does the right thing, as he did in pulling back U.S. pilots from the Paris Air Show, it's hard to know whether he's doing it for the right reason or, more important, if he'll do it again the next time he faces a similar situation. If Paris 1993 is any guide, arms sales policy under the Clinton administration is up for grabs. Its final shape will be determined by who pushes harder—the advocates of restraint or the proponents of unrestricted weapons exports.

However it chooses to tackle the problem of conventional arms sales, the Clinton administration will be dealing with a big business. In the 1980s alone, the United States sold $134 billion in weapons and military services to more than 160 nations and political movements, far outstripping any other nation in the diversity of its customer base and the range of military goods and services it had to offer.[12] The trend has accelerated during the 1990s, as the disappearance of subsidized Soviet sales has combined with the public relations boost given to U.S. systems by the Gulf War to place the United States in a position of unrivaled dominance in the world arms market. In 1993, the United States controlled nearly 73 percent of the weapons trade to the Third World.[13]

This surge in orders has made weapons exports an important factor in the national economy, accounting for roughly 5 percent of all

U.S. exports and supporting several hundred thousand jobs. The stakes are even higher for particular companies. Major arms manufacturers like McDonnell Douglas, Lockheed, and Raytheon now rely on foreign military sales for up to one-third of their total revenues, and communities like St. Louis, Fort Worth, Boston, and Los Angeles, where these firms operate, have become economically dependent on weapons exports.[14]

The economic weight of the arms export sector translates into political clout as well. During the presidential campaign, Bill Clinton displayed a penchant for supporting controversial sales like the F-15 fighter deal with Saudi Arabia and the F-16 aircraft package for Taiwan on pork barrel economic grounds (see chapter 13). So far he has been no better at resisting these pressures as president.

This book addresses the urgent question of how the world's leading democracy has also become the world's number-one arms merchant. It analyzes the combination of flawed strategic vision, political opportunism, and plain old-fashioned greed that has produced an aggressive arms sales policy on the part of the U.S. government, despite the clear and growing dangers of such an approach for the security of the citizenry and the maintenance of a democratic foreign policy.

As the end of the Cold War offers new possibilities for reducing tensions in the Third World, and as regional conflicts underscore the dangers of unrestrained arms trafficking, it is more important than ever to analyze the forces driving the United States to export advanced weaponry. It is time for a full-scale public debate on this subject, in which citizens demand an accounting of whom their government is arming in their name, and why. It is the aim of this book to foster that necessary and long-overdue debate now, while there is still time to bring America's multibillion-dollar arms trade under control.

2

The Nixon Doctrine: Roots of the Arms Sales Addiction

The current U.S. role as the world's leading arms merchant was quietly inaugurated on July 25, 1969, with a few off-the-cuff remarks by Richard Nixon to a group of reporters at the Top o' the Mar Officers' Club in Guam. The president and his entourage were in Guam for a refueling stop on the first leg of a whirlwind eight-nation tour that would take him from Vietnam to Romania.

Nixon was in a remarkably upbeat mood on this, the second major foreign trip of his presidency. He had kicked off the trip with a public relations coup when he personally welcomed Apollo astronauts Neil Armstrong and Buzz Aldrin back from their historic mission to the moon. Typical of the president's high spirits was his comment that the U.S. moon landing marked "the greatest week in the history of the world since the Creation." *Newsweek* observed that Nixon seemed intent on "setting records for hyperbole" at every stop, citing as further examples the president's assertions that the Vietnam War was "one of America's finest hours" and that U.S.-backed South Vietnamese dictator Nguyen Van Thieu was "one of the four or five most capable politicians in the world."[1]

In contrast to this high-profile cheerleading on behalf of America's political wisdom and technological prowess, Nixon's remarks to the press corps in Guam were surprisingly low-key. The thrust of his somewhat rambling commentary was that although Vietnam had been "terribly frustrating," this was no time to throw in the towel; the United States must "continue to play a significant role" in Asia after the war. But in the future, Nixon argued, "problems of internal security" and "problems of military defense, except for the threat of a nuclear power involving nuclear weapons," should be handled by "the Asian nations themselves." The United States would provide military and economic assistance to allied regimes, but "the objective of any American administration would be to avoid another war like Vietnam any place in the world."[2]

With these few comments, made on background, the "Nixon Doctrine" was born. The announcement of this significant shift in global strategy took most of the president's advisers, including Nixon press secretary Ron Ziegler, completely by surprise. As veteran Nixon watcher Tad Szulc has pointed out, "Unlike the other important foreign policy pronouncements of the Nixon era, the doctrine was neither researched by the NSC [National Security Council] staff nor even put down on paper in a coherent way."[3]

Nixon clearly had his reasons for elevating arms transfers to a prominent position in his foreign policy, even though his new doctrine had not been vetted by the bureaucracy. First and foremost, the policy of "sending arms instead of sending troops," as one Pentagon official described it, offered the Nixon administration a way to exert military influence throughout the Third World without taking on the political risks or paying the economic costs involved in direct military interventions like the one in Vietnam. Despite talk of Nixon as a foreign policy innovator, his doctrine was firmly rooted in the Cold War mind-set that put combating the Soviet Union and its allies (real or imagined) at the top of the U.S. international agenda. Nixon was simply searching for a cheaper, less politically contentious way to maintain the U.S. role as global policeman, fighting the spread of socialist and nationalist regimes in the Third World in the name of containing the Soviet Union.

In the process of cobbling together this new strategic design, very little thought was given to whether the United States could in fact control the purposes for which its weapons were used once the arms trade was running full-speed ahead. And, at least at the outset, neither Nixon nor any other observer could have possibly foreseen the degree to which economic motives like bailing out U.S. defense contractors and counterbalancing OPEC oil price increases would emerge to overwhelm the original strategic rationale for Nixon's new arms sales policy.

None of these larger issues were on the public agenda at the time of Nixon's Guam speech. The most immediate response to his comments, both from the media and from many of the president's own staff, was puzzlement at the unexpected nature of his apparent strategic shift. The one associate who was not surprised by the substance of Nixon's remarks in Guam was his national security adviser and political alter ego, Henry Kissinger, who claimed credit for formulating the outlines of the new doctrine in a series of discussions with the president prior to his trip to Asia.

Barely six months into Nixon's first term, Kissinger had already emerged as the principal player in the formation of the administration's foreign policy. It was Nixon's firm belief that "the president makes foreign policy," and Kissinger was his partner in that task, preempting many of the powers and responsibilities normally reserved for the secretary of state and the secretary of defense. Historian Robert Litwak has commented on the "unprecedented centralization and secrecy" that characterized "the Nixon–Kissinger foreign policy style," and it was already clearly in evidence at this early stage of the Nixon presidency.[4]

But for all his privileged access to the president, even Kissinger was taken aback by the timing of Nixon's announcement, noting in his memoirs that "to this day I do not think that Nixon intended a major policy pronouncement in Guam; his original purpose had been to make some news because of the empty period produced by crossing the international dateline."[5]

The press, the public, and the Congress were slow to grasp the full import of Nixon's statement in Guam, interpreting it primarily with respect to its implications for the prosecution of the war in Vietnam. Some political analysts regarded it as a face-saving way to pull U.S. troops out of Vietnam without appearing to be "weak" or "vacillating." Antiwar activists took a more critical view, seeing it not as a step toward ending the war but as part of a cynical strategy for blunting domestic criticism while continuing the war by other, more brutal, means, including an intensified bombing campaign.

Kissinger gave weight to this more critical interpretation when he indicated that the new strategy was simply a way of ensuring that "Asian boys will fight Asian boys," limiting U.S. casualties and domestic political fallout in the process. If there were lingering doubts about whether this new approach represented anything more than a convenient tactical maneuver, Kissinger put them to rest a few years later when he snapped back in response to arguments that the escalation of the war into Cambodia violated the spirit of the Nixon Doctrine: "It's his doctrine and he can damned well do what he wants with it."[6]

As the debates raged on about how Nixon's policy would affect the conduct of the war in Southeast Asia, there was very little discussion of its worldwide implications. Under the guise of seeking peace, the Nixon/Kissinger strategy proposed to flood the Third World with advanced implements of war. The dangers inherent in putting sophisticated U.S. military technology in the hands of a string of undemocratic and unstable regimes were overlooked in the interests of a new grand design for combating the Soviet Union and keeping the Third World safe for U.S. investment and trade.

In essence, the Nixon Doctrine was an attempt to salvage a global interventionary role for the United States in the face of the political, strategic, and economic limitations that had become so painfully evident as a result of the war in Vietnam. As Nixon himself had noted a year earlier in an article in *Foreign Affairs*, the war had "imposed severe strains" and sown "bitter dissension" domestically, producing "a deep reluctance to become involved once again in a similar intervention on a similar basis."[7] These domestic political obstacles to direct U.S. military intervention were compounded by the immense costs of sustaining a massive overseas troop presence and the strategic impossibility of conducting simultaneous military engagements on behalf of the dozen or so U.S.-backed regimes in the Third World that were threatened by guerrilla insurgencies.

The Nixon Doctrine promised a leaner, meaner strategy for exerting global U.S. military influence by recruiting key regional powers to serve as junior partners in a U.S.-dominated anticommunist coalition. These military surrogates would receive unprecedented levels of U.S. arms and training in return for doing the U.S. government's military bidding in their area of responsibility. Candidates for the surrogate role included the regimes in Brazil, Zaire, Indonesia, and—last but not least—Iran.

Not only was the size of U.S. arms transfers about to increase at a phenomenal pace under the Nixon/Kissinger strategy, but the composition of U.S. exports was going to change dramatically as well. Prior to the Nixon administration, most U.S. overseas arms shipments involved secondhand equipment transferred through military aid programs. This trend was initiated during World War II with the Roosevelt administration's Lend Lease program, which provided over $50 billion in armaments, food, and other supplies to U.S. allies. Harry Truman carried this wartime practice into the Cold War era when he pushed through $1 billion in economic and military aid for Greece and Turkey from 1947 to 1950 in the name of "fighting communism."

This pattern of handing out U.S. equipment to the anticommunist ally of the moment held firm until the early 1960s, when Kennedy administration secretary of defense Robert McNamara began to emphasize selling arms instead of giving them away, as a means of improving the U.S. balance of trade. Despite McNamara's efforts to turn weapons into a "cash crop," it wasn't until Nixon came along that the balance of U.S. arms exports shifted decisively away from aid toward sales. This important change was barely noticed at this early stage of the Nixon policy, when the focus of attention was on his newly proposed strategic rationale for accelerating U.S. weapons exports.

The president's men presented the Nixon Doctrine as the most viable means of getting U.S. troops out of Vietnam, but journalist Anthony Sampson has rightly observed that it was in fact "a gamble of extraordinary rashness, for it assumed that the allies who had this new freedom to buy arms . . . would use them wisely, in the Western interest." And at no point did the United States gamble more heavily or lose more spectacularly than when it decided to feed the Shah of Iran's insatiable appetite for advanced weaponry.[8]

Whatever questions might be raised about the wisdom of arming the shah or any of a dozen other dictators who beefed up their arsenals under the Nixon Doctrine, Nixon himself saw virtually no risk to peace or security flowing from his freewheeling arms sales policy. Years after he had been driven from office by the Watergate scandal, in a book entitled *The Real War* Nixon lamented that "some Americans have an almost theological aversion to having the United States sell arms abroad." Nixon argued that these critics "ignore one very important point. There is almost no case on record since World War II in which arms provided by the United States have been used by the country receiving them for purposes of aggression. Soviet arms are the ones that are constantly used to break the peace."[9] Despite dozens of examples to the contrary, Nixon's almost mystical belief that U.S.-supplied arms could never be used aggressively was to persist within the foreign policy bureaucracy, surfacing during the Bush administration as a rationale for massive sales to the Middle East even after the Soviet Union had ceased to exist.

The actual record of U.S. arms transfers under the Nixon Doctrine disproves the former president's absurd claim. Not only did the overall volume of U.S. arms sales explode (from less than $2 billion per year in the late 1960s to $17 billion per year by the mid-1970s), but many of the nations receiving the largest increases in U.S. weaponry were precisely those engaging in the most egregious cases of aggression against neighboring territories or their own citizens. In

Indonesia, the Suharto regime received a record $52 million in U.S. military equipment in 1975, the year it decided to invade neighboring East Timor, with a green light from President Ford and his secretary of state, Henry Kissinger. Indonesia's illegal occupation continues to this day. In Morocco, U.S. approval of $243 million in arms transfers in 1975 emboldened King Hassan to annex the neighboring territory of Western Sahara, an illegal action that the United Nations is still trying to reverse eighteen years later. And in Chile, Augusto Pinochet's military junta, which came to power in a 1973 coup engineered with the help of Kissinger and the CIA, ordered over $80 million in U.S. arms in 1974, a fivefold increase over levels received just one year earlier. These arms served Pinochet well in an eighteen-year reign of terror and repression against his own people.[10]

The Nixon Doctrine gave the arms trade a bad name, and for good reason: it spawned an unprecedented spree of U.S.-supplied violence and repression on the part of despots on three continents. But neither Nixon nor Kissinger showed any signs of caring about these harsh consequences of their arms sales policy, preoccupying themselves instead with its pivotal role in their new grand design for containing Soviet influence and keeping revolutionary and nationalist movements at bay. Both men saw the Nixon Doctrine as a convenient way to exert global military influence without having to consult Congress or the public, a feature that appealed to their penchant for secrecy in the conduct of foreign relations. Their fascination with these apparent benefits of the new policy blinded Nixon and Kissinger to its most obvious drawback: the surrogate strategy would only be as reliable as the surrogates chosen to carry it out.

The Shah as "Model" Surrogate

The most telling example of the flaws inherent in the Nixon Doctrine was not to be found in Chile, Indonesia, Morocco, nor any of the scores of other nations whose weapons purchases from the United States soared during this period. All these cases pale in comparison to what happened in Iran. Mohammed Reza Pahlavi, the shah of Iran, Richard Nixon's old friend and staunch anticommunist ally, was to provide the ultimate test of the surrogate strategy. Throughout the 1970s, he bought more U.S. military hardware, employed more U.S. technical experts, and undertook more aggressive military action at the behest of the United States than any other foreign beneficiary of the Nixon arms sales policy.

Nixon and Kissinger's embrace of the shah was prompted initially by a 1968 British decision to withdraw militarily from the Middle East, leaving a power vacuum that they felt obliged to fill to ensure that the fragile, pro-Western, oil-rich monarchies of the Persian Gulf region would survive and continue to offer U.S. petroleum companies favorable access to their resources. Even more important, the U.S. arms supply relationship with Iran became the same kind of measure of U.S. "resolve" and "determination" to stand by its allies, however ill chosen, that had produced one policy fiasco after another in Vietnam. Just as Vietnam had been a test case of the policy of direct U.S. intervention, Iran was to become a test case of the viability of the surrogate strategy—with equally disastrous results.[11]

The shah had long harbored a desire to amass an arsenal of U.S. weaponry that would make Iran the dominant military power in the Middle East and Southwest Asia. The steady supplies of military aid offered by the Eisenhower, Kennedy, and Johnson administrations, averaging out to about $100 million per year, fell far short of his ambitious plans. To the shah's delight, Nixon's emphasis on arming regional allies changed all that. In 1969, the year of Nixon's remarks at Guam, Iranian purchases of U.S. armaments increased to nearly a quarter of a billion dollars.

This impressive increase in the quantities of U.S. weapons available to Iran was followed a few years later by an even more radical, qualitative shift. While most U.S. arms transfers to the Third World in the post–World War II era had involved older systems that were being retired from service by U.S. forces, Nixon decided that Iran would be given access to the latest in U.S. military hardware, hot off the production lines.

The shah's blank check to purchase virtually anything in the U.S. arsenal was personally delivered by Nixon and Kissinger in a May 1972 stopover in the Iranian capital of Teheran on their way back from the first U.S.–Soviet summit meeting in Moscow. Even more so than in Guam three years earlier, the president and his principal adviser were riding high when they reached Iran. Within a four-month span, they had engineered the first visits by a U.S. president to the communist capitals of Moscow and Beijing. And they had come away with concrete results: an agreement to move toward normalizing U.S. relations with China and the SALT I strategic arms treaty with the Soviet Union. Compared with this heady diplomacy, their meeting with the shah seemed almost an afterthought.

In typical Nixon/Kissinger style, they held their two working meetings with the shah in private, leaving the undersecretary of state for the region, Joseph Sisco, behind in his hotel room. The main subject was the supply of U.S. arms to Iran in support of the shah's new role as the U.S. military surrogate in the Persian Gulf. Ignoring Pentagon warnings not to offer unlimited access to top-of-the-line U.S. systems, Nixon quickly agreed to the shah's request to purchase either the air force's F-15 or the navy's F-14 fighter aircraft, the two newest planes in the U.S. arsenal. This marked an abrupt departure from past practice: each of the planes was still in development and had not even been deployed with U.S. forces yet. Never before had a Third World leader been offered first crack at sophisticated combat systems of this kind.

Having dispensed with this unstated tenet of U.S. arms transfer policy in a few brief words, Nixon went on to assure his friend that *any* Iranian request, short of asking to purchase U.S. nuclear weapons, would be approved, bypassing the usual State Department and Pentagon review procedures. Throughout the 1970s, Kissinger was to serve as the bureaucratic enforcer of this policy, periodically providing blunt reminders to Pentagon and State Department officials with qualms about the shah's arms buying binge to keep their doubts to themselves. In return for providing the Iranian dictator with unrestricted access to the U.S. arsenal, Nixon reiterated his request that the shah serve as a pro-U.S. policeman of the Gulf region, protecting the flow of oil and preventing the emergence of progressive regimes that might offer it to the United States and its allies on less favorable terms. At one point in the meeting, Nixon reportedly looked directly at the shah and asked him to "protect me."[12]

It was a dream come true for the shah, an amateur pilot and avid reader of *Aviation Week and Space Technology* whose passion for advanced military hardware was exceeded only by his ambition to build the most powerful nation in the Persian Gulf and Southwest Asia. After the meetings, when the shah's ambassador to Washington asked him if he got what he wanted, he replied without hesitation: "Yes, more than I wanted, more than I expected."[13]

Spurred by OPEC's quadrupling of oil prices in the wake of the 1973 Arab–Israeli conflict, the shah quickly assembled a weapons shopping list that included 80 Grumman F-14 fighter planes; more than 100 General Dynamics F-16 fighters; 108 McDonnell Douglas F-4 fighter jets; hundreds of helicopters, bombs, and advanced missiles; and an entire modern naval force built around U.S. Spruance-class destroyers and high-tech British Hovercraft. At one stroke, he ordered 800 British Chieftain tanks, more than the British army itself possessed. Columnist and longtime supporter of the shah Arnaud de

Borchgrave marveled at how "Teheran's brass has been buying up military hardware from the U.S. the way most people stock up on a week's supply of groceries at a supermarket."[14]

The Iranian ruler's multibillion-dollar shopping trips highlighted the extent to which the Nixon Doctrine was being transformed from a strategy for maintaining global military influence into a policy driven by powerful economic motivations. By the end of the 1970s, major military producers like McDonnell Douglas and Northrop were getting between one-third and one-half of their business from foreign sales, and they devoted considerable time, effort, and money lobbying Congress and the executive branch to approve and broker these deals on their behalf.[15] These economic factors—along with the obvious flaws in Nixon and Kissinger's original notion that the United States could reliably use arms sales to influence and control events halfway around the world—drove U.S. arms sales policy out of control.

The shah's new freedom to spend almost at will on U.S. weapons was good news for American defense contractors, who were frantically seeking markets to compensate for cutbacks in Vietnam War spending. Spending on the war had peaked in 1969, and major defense contractors like Boeing, Lockheed, General Dynamics, and McDonnell Douglas were facing shutdowns of major weapons production lines and layoffs of tens of thousands of workers. Lockheed's widely publicized troubles in its commercial and military programs had already led to a controversial $250 million government bailout, and layoffs at Boeing in Seattle had prompted someone to post a billboard, only partly in jest, that said, "Would the last person out of town please turn out the lights." The prospect of unimpeded access to new foreign markets under the Nixon Doctrine offered a much needed financial shot in the arm to the titans of military industry.[16]

Added economic impetus for arming Nixon's favorite client came from the need to recapture some of the billions of dollars that were flowing out of the country to pay for OPEC's oil price increases, in a process known as "recycling petrodollars." Henry Kissinger was the strongest proponent of this additional rationale for selling the shah and other Third World oil states the finest, most expensive weapons money could buy, although his views were also shared by many other key officials in the Nixon and Ford administrations.

It was estimated that by the end of 1974, Iran and Saudi Arabia alone would accumulate cash reserves of over $40 billion as a result of OPEC price increases, with the potential to wreak havoc in the international banking system and drastically change power relations between these Mideast oil states and the developed nations that had dominated their economies for decades. As one Pentagon official summarized the issue, "The biggest long-range problem facing the United States is finding a way to get the Arabs to spend their dollars without letting them get control of our economy." In keeping with this concern, the Nixon administration had appointed an interagency task force headed by Undersecretary of Defense William Clements to seek out new arms business in the Middle East for U.S. contractors. These efforts paid off handsomely, as the United States sold over $4 billion in arms to Saudi Arabia, Iran, and Kuwait in 1973–74 alone.[17]

Former U.S. ambassador to Saudi Arabia James Akins has indicated that the arms-for-oil connection went a step further, suggesting that Henry Kissinger may have actively encouraged the shah to press for increased oil prices as a way to fund his purchases of U.S. armaments under the Nixon Doctrine. Kissinger vehemently denies the charge, but his actions were certainly consistent with it: he acquiesced in Iranian oil price increases with barely a diplomatic protest while rapidly approving any and every weapons request the shah sent his way. Whether or not there was an explicit U.S. government decision to link high oil prices and massive arms sales as a way to underwrite the Nixon Doctrine, the trading of arms for oil money proceeded apace. Dollars out for oil, dollars in from arms sales, and presumably the U.S. balance of payments would come out all right—or so the thinking went.[18]

What these massive sales might do to the balance of power in the Middle East was another question. There had barely been a moment to breathe at the conclusion of the 1973 Arab–Israeli war, which had brought the superpowers dangerously close to the brink of a direct confrontation, when a new round of arms sales to all parties to the conflict was set in motion. The Nixon Doctrine, for all of its self-assured strategic rationales, was rapidly evolving under the pressure of powerful economic forces into an uncontrolled race for position in a multibillion-dollar Third World arms market.

While Pentagon analysts had qualms about giving the shah free rein, Nixon had complete confidence in his old friend and ally. They had first met more than two decades earlier when then–vice president Nixon went on a 1953 fact-finding tour of Iran. The visit came just a few months after an American/British-backed military coup had restored the shah to power and overthrown the democratically elected prime minister, Mohammed Mossadegh. The coup had been engineered by a handful of Americans of impeccable political lineage, including Teddy Roosevelt's grandson Kermit, a CIA operative, and Gen. H. Norman Schwarzkopf, whose son was to serve as commander of U.S. forces in the Gulf War thirty-eight years later.[19]

Nixon took an immediate liking to the thirty-four-year-old Iranian ruler and was strongly supportive of the shah's ambition to serve as a bulwark against communism in the region. President Eisenhower did not share Nixon's unqualified enthusiasm for the occupant of Iran's Peacock Throne, and he frequently cut back on the shah's extensive military aid requests. But Nixon continued to cultivate close personal ties to the shah, visiting Iran four times during his own period of political inactivity in the early and mid-1960s. Perhaps because of their common ideological instincts, or their equally fierce and overriding desires for unchecked political power, Nixon was blinded to the fatal flaws of the man he had entrusted with the keys to the U.S. arsenal.

Probably the most glaring indication that the shah had become a dictatorial, power-hungry egotist who was out of touch with the needs of his own people came in 1971 when he threw a $200 million party to mark the twenty-five-hundredth anniversary of the founding of the Iranian empire by Cyrus the Great. Held in a hillside tent city constructed for the occasion next to the ruins of the ancient Iranian city of Persepolis, the festivities were attended by "a reigning Emperor (Haile Selassie of Ethiopia), nine Kings, five Queens, 13 princes, eight princesses, 16 Presidents, two Governor Generals, two Foreign Ministers, nine sheiks and two sultans." As if borrowing a page of rhetorical overkill from his friend Richard Nixon, the shah described the scandalously expensive party as "the most wonderful thing the world has ever seen."[20]

Not everyone agreed with this assessment, least of all the average Iranians who were excluded from the event. While the shah's three thousand guests dined on quail eggs, caviar, and rack of lamb prepared by Maxim's of Paris, millions of Iranians were going hungry. There was a famine in progress that extended into the same province where the anniversary celebration was being held. Thousands of political dissidents had been rounded up and jailed by the shah's secret police in advance of the events at Persepolis, and a United Press International report described "helicopters ceaselessly patrolling the hills on guard against urban guerrillas who threatened a bloodbath during the celebration."[21]

The sense of tension between the shah's artificial show of national unity and prosperity and the real conflicts wracking Iran penetrated inside the carefully guarded festivities as well. *Newsweek* reported that "100 potted banana trees in the banquet hall abruptly died after being yanked out of their pots by security guards looking for bombs."[22]

A number of leaders of the Iranian revolution that overthrew the shah in December of 1978 point to the shah's orgy of excess and self-congratulation at Persepolis as a turning point in their decision to oppose his regime. Ayatollah Khomeini himself sent a stern message from exile denouncing the shah for hosting this luxurious spectacle while Iranians were literally dying of hunger, asserting that "we do not want to celebrate over people's corpses."[23]

The shah testily dismissed all the criticisms of his international coming-out party in tones worthy of Marie-Antoinette: "Why are we reproached for serving dinner to 50 heads of state? What am I supposed to do, serve them bread and radishes?"[24]

The shah's tastes in weaponry were, if anything, even more extravagant than his preferences in haute cuisine. His goal was to build an army second to none in the region, a more capable and sophisticated air force than those maintained by former Middle East colonial powers Britain and France, and a navy capable of patrolling not only the Persian Gulf but the Indian Ocean as well. He was committed to a rapid expansion of Iran's network of military bases, from a helicopter production and testing facility at Isfahan staffed by ten thousand to a new Indian Ocean naval port at Chah Bahar on the Gulf of Oman. When he was asked whether his ambition was for Iran to become the strongest country in the area, the shah simply smiled and said, "It is not an ambition. It is inevitable." But his visions of Iranian power were not limited to the Persian Gulf—he regularly boasted that by the early 1980s, Iran would be a military and economic powerhouse "the equal of France or West Germany."[25]

As the newly anointed military surrogate of the United States, the shah was eager to flex his military muscle on behalf of his patron and arms supplier, in keeping with the role that had been explicitly laid out for him by Nixon and Kissinger in their May 1972 meeting. The shah's first priority, combating "subversion" in the oil-rich sheikdoms of the Persian Gulf, dovetailed neatly with Nixon and Kissinger's vision of U.S. interests in the region. They were intent on propping up these corrupt monarchies at the expense of radical and democratic forces based on the theory that the existing regimes would offer better guarantees of continued Western investment in and control of the region's oil resources. The shah himself had granted U.S. oil companies generous terms on the refining and marketing of Iranian oil after the 1953 CIA coup that had put him back in power, and he had no intention of letting radical or even nationalist democratic forces gain a foothold in any of the other oil monarchies of the Gulf region. His role as "guardian of the oil lanes" had more to do with putting down internal rebellions against the sheikdoms of the Gulf area than it did with protecting against the much less likely prospect of a Soviet invasion or takeover of the oil fields.

In his first major test as a military surrogate, the shah sent a naval task force, thousands of ground troops, and scores of helicopter gunships to help put down a leftist rebellion in the Dhofar province of neighboring Oman, an ultimately successful intervention that ground on for five years, from 1971 to 1976. In 1973, about thirty Iranian Chinook helicopters helped put down a rebellion in the Pakistani province of Baluchistan. Beyond these regional "policing duties," the shah reached far outside the Gulf region to lend F-4 fighters to the embattled Thieu regime in South Vietnam, send planes to Morocco, and provide troops to the Mobutu regime in Zaire to help suppress an insurgency in Shaba province. British Middle East expert Fred Halliday argued persuasively in the late 1970s that "no Third World state has a record of intervention outside its frontiers comparable with Iran's."[26] The shah had taken up his role as America's "regional gendarme" with a vengeance.

Not all rebellions were deemed illegitimate in the shah's eyes, however. Throughout the mid-1970s Iran served as a conduit for CIA arms to Kurdish rebels fighting against Saddam Hussein's Ba'athist regime in Iraq. Kissinger and the CIA were strong advocates of arming the Kurds, not out of any principled support for Kurdish independence but because they felt that the rebel forces would tie up Iraq's military forces and keep them from making common cause with the other Arab military forces of the region against Israel. Unfortunately for the Kurdish movement, once the objective of weakening Hussein's regime and diverting its attention from the Arab confrontation with Israel had been accomplished, the shah made a deal with the Iraqi leader and cut the Kurds off cold, with Kissinger's full support. As a result, the Kurdish rebellion was abruptly put down by Iraqi forces, and thousands of Kurds were expelled from Iran to face torture or death at the hands of Hussein's regime.

The note of cynical calculation behind the U.S. decision to assist the shah in the arming of the Kurds was revealed in a CIA memo published by *New York Times* columnist William Safire: "Iran, like ourselves, has seen the benefit in a stalemate situation . . . in which Iraq is intrinsically weakened by the Kurds' refusal to relinquish its semi-autonomy. Neither Iran nor ourselves wish to see the matter resolved one way or the other." But once the shah decided he could do without the Kurds and resolve his disputes over borders and oil resources with Iraq directly, there were no regrets among U.S. policymakers, least of all Kissinger. His response to critics of this sellout of the Kurdish resistance was to assert that "covert action should not be confused with missionary work."[27]

As Kissinger and Nixon well knew, the shah was no saint in his domestic policies either. Their undiminished support for the Iranian dictator despite his increasingly repressive policies served as a model for the Nixon Doctrine's approach to scores of other dictatorships throughout the Third World. Nixon and Kissinger made it clear that they were far more interested in propping up anti-Soviet, anticommunist regimes and reaping the economic benefits of unrestrained arms sales than they were in encouraging their weapons clients to observe the niceties of human rights or democratic procedure. In the case of the shah, they made this point quite explicitly.

At the same May 1972 meeting where Nixon had given the green light for arming Iran to whatever level the shah desired, he also advised him to ignore "our liberals' griping" about his dismal human rights record and do whatever he felt was necessary to stay firmly in control. The period of the shah's U.S.-supported military meddling beyond Iran's borders also saw the most severe internal repression of his two decades in power. His earlier governing formula of mixing some social and political reforms with hard-line repressive tactics gave way to an unrelenting crackdown on domestic dissent, with the hated Savak intelligence service and the U.S.-trained Imperial Iranian Gendarmerie as its principal tools. Apart from the U.S. role in the 1953 coup that restored the shah to power in the first place, nothing did more to sow enmity and hatred for the United States in Iran than the active collaboration of the CIA in training and supplying the shah's intelligence and internal security forces. Iranian opposition leaders charged that the shah was holding over one hundred thousand political prisoners; and torture had become a routine aspect of government policy. By 1975 the secretary general of Amnesty International could bluntly declare that "no country in the world has a worse human rights record than Iran."[28]

Richard Nixon and Henry Kissinger had a kinder, more forgiving view of their friend and partner, despite his systematic abuses of human rights. While Nixon did acknowledge that the shah "did not provide as much progress in political rights as most Americans would have wished," Kissinger refused to go even that far. Even after the 1978 revolution that drove him from power, Kissinger staunchly defended the shah as a "dedicated reformer" and "that rarest of leaders, an unconditional ally," implying that whatever "failings" he may have had as a leader of the Iranian people were more than made up for by his loyalty to the U.S. strategic agenda.[29]

Not everyone in the U.S. defense and foreign policy establishment was as convinced as Nixon and Kissinger that the shah's unregulated U.S.-arms-buying spree was serving the best interests of either the United States or Iran. James Schlesinger, a hard-liner and Cold Warrior par excellence who served as secretary of defense during the Nixon and Ford administrations, tried to put the brakes on runaway sales to Iran, but he continually ran into a stone wall put up first by Nixon and then, after his resignation, by President Ford's secretary of state, Henry Kissinger.

Schlesinger was not opposed to arming Iran per se, but he was concerned that the pace at which the shah was gobbling up complex U.S. weapons systems might actually weaken Iran's military forces. The defense secretary was not alone in his belief that Iran lacked the trained personnel needed to operate and maintain this high-tech hardware and that the shah might end up with huge stockpiles of expensive weaponry that his military forces would not be able to use for years, if at all. As a result, as Schlesinger warned a congressional inquiry, the unrestrained transfer of advanced weapons systems to nations like Iran that were unable to operate them effectively without extensive U.S. technical support could "erode long-run confidence in the Department of Defense as the main agent for U.S. arms sales."[30]

It wasn't that Schlesinger wanted to end the Pentagon's role as middleman for sales of major U.S. combat systems. He just wanted to promote the department's image as a "responsible" arms merchant to the Third World, an "honest broker" that would give overseas clients objective advice about the pros and cons of a given sale. But even this moderately militaristic line on the problem was more restrictive than Kissinger could tolerate.

Schlesinger's attempt to inject a note of "truth in advertising" into the U.S. government's arms sales efforts was destined to meet with stiff resistance. With respect to sales to Iran, the shah's word was law, and "His Imperial Majesty" had yet to meet an arms purchase he didn't like. The official policy throughout the Nixon/Ford years remained that weapons requests from the shah "should not be second guessed" by the U.S. foreign policy bureaucracy, no matter how ill advised a particular sale or the overall pattern of sales might seem. Kissinger had made this point crystal clear in a memo issued shortly after the May 1972 meeting that initiated the carte blanche policy toward Iran. Not only had the president decided that it was up to the shah to decide when he was ready to buy the F-14 or F-15 fighter aircraft, but this same "Shah knows best" approach would apply to *all* U.S. arms sales to Iran:

> The President has also reiterated that, in general, decisions on the acquisition of military equipment should be left primarily to the Government of Iran. If the Government of Iran has decided to buy certain equipment, the purchase of U.S. equipment should be encouraged tactfully where appropriate, and technical advice on the capabilities of the equipment in question should be provided.[31]

Kissinger has since tried to minimize the importance of Nixon's blank-check policy by claiming that it was thwarted by the Defense Department and State Department bureaucracies and forgotten once Nixon left office. But Kissinger clearly remembered it when it suited his purposes. For example, when the shah visited Washington in 1975, Kissinger dashed off a briefing memo to President Ford reminding him of the policy in no uncertain terms: "After President Nixon visited Teheran in May 1972, we adopted a policy which provides, in effect, that we will accede to any of the Shah's requests for arms purchases from us." The memo made it sound like Kissinger was the one making policy, while Ford was simply being informed of what the policy was, as if he were a new member of Kissinger's staff. If Schlesinger was to achieve even a modest reorientation of U.S. arms sales practices toward Iran, he was going to have to outmaneuver Henry Kissinger.[32]

Finally, in September 1975, after commissioning an independent assessment of the Iranian arms program, Schlesinger sent President Ford a copy of the study with a memo indicating his "doubt whether our policy of supporting an apparently open-ended Iranian military buildup will continue to serve our long-term interests." Schlesinger requested an interagency review of arms transfer policy toward Iran, but his request was sidetracked at Kissinger's behest, surfacing in a much diluted form only after Schlesinger had left the administration, replaced as secretary of defense by Donald Rumsfeld.[33]

Greed Takes Over: The Scramble for Contracts

While efforts from within the Nixon and Ford administrations to exert some minimal control over the U.S. arms trade with the shah were thwarted, Congress could not be silenced quite so easily. In July 1976 the Subcommittee on Foreign Assistance of the Senate Foreign Relations Committee released a report entitled "U.S. Military Sales to Iran," a scathing indictment of the Nixon/Kissinger policy. The key finding was that "for at least three years U.S. arms sales to Iran were out of control." Furthermore, the report argued, "the 1972 decision by President Nixon to . . . let Iran buy anything it wanted, effectively exempted Iran from arms sales review processes in the State and Defense Department . . . [and] created a bonanza for U.S. weapons manufacturers, the procurement branches of the three U.S. services, and the Defense Security Assistance Agency."[34]

The Nixon/Kissinger "anything goes" approach had generated an atmosphere of intense competition among major U.S. contractors and even branches of the U.S. military to see who could sell the most to the shah's regime. The Senate report noted that "between 1973–75, the activities of U.S. arms salesmen, official and private, were not closely supervised by Executive Branch officials charged with doing so." The Senate report even revealed the emergence of a new form of interservice rivalry, based on which branch of the armed forces could do a better job of selling weapons overseas:

> Each of the U.S. services, particularly the Air Force and Navy, was trying to sell equipment for its own reasons, usually to lower per unit costs of its own procurement or to recoup part of prior research and development investment. On occasion, the services fiercely competed with each other for sales to Iran, e.g., the Air Force and Navy to sell the F-15 and F-14 respectively.[35]

To illustrate the militarization of U.S.–Iranian relations, the subcommittee published a list of visits to Iran by senior U.S. military officials from 1973 to 1976, as compared with visits by high-level State Department officials. An astounding 118 U.S. delegations headed by generals, admirals, and other high-ranking military officers had visited Iran during the first three years of the Nixon/Kissinger military surrogate policy, in many cases to push new arms sales or follow up on existing deals. In a telling contrast, only a handful of State Department officials of senior rank (eleven) went to Iran during this same period; and for two years there was no visitor to Iran from the State Department's Bureau of Politico-Military Affairs, the agency charged with overseeing arms sales programs. The military men on both sides clearly had the upper hand in shaping the character of U.S.–Iranian relations, while the diplomats appeared to be going along for the ride.

But the fastest-growing and most potentially problematic U.S. presence in Iran was not military but civilian—thousands of employees of U.S. military contractors had come to help build, maintain, and service the shah's high-tech weaponry. This influx had several troubling implications. First, as the Senate report noted with alarm, most informed observers felt that the new levels of sophisticated weaponry being purchased by the shah could not be operated by his forces for at least five to ten years without "increasing numbers of American support personnel," both military and corporate technical personnel who had come to be known as "white-collar mercenaries." Tens of thousands of American personnel and their families would have to be stationed in Iran to keep pace with the unchecked growth of the shah's arsenal, and there was serious concern that they could themselves become targets of hostage taking or terrorist attacks, as had already happened once, in 1975, when three Rockwell International employees were run off the road and murdered right in the middle of Teheran (they had been working on the top-secret IBEX communications project, which many Iranian activists felt was going to be used for domestic spying purposes by the shah's internal security and intelligence forces). Far from removing U.S. citizens from the line of fire by sending arms instead of troops, it appeared that, in Iran at least, the Nixon Doctrine was just putting a new breed of military technocrat at risk in place of uniformed soldiers.[36]

Whatever the risks, U.S. defense firms like Bell Helicopter, General Dynamics, Northrop, McDonnell Douglas, and Grumman sent scores of technical and sales representatives to Iran to tout their weapons systems. With Vietnam War orders in a tailspin, several firms were literally staking their survival on foreign sales, and Iran was by far the most lucrative market. Northrop had gotten a jump on the competition by putting Kermit Roosevelt, a longtime friend of the shah who had organized the 1953 CIA coup that restored him to power, on retainer at a fee of $75,000 per year to act as their sales representative in Iran.[37]

But Roosevelt was far from alone on the Iranian sales circuit, which was clogged with former military and intelligence men employed by U.S. companies to make their case to the shah and his generals. Three months after his retirement as chairman of the Joint Chiefs of Staff, Adm. Thomas Moorer turned up in Teheran as a consultant for Stanwick International, a ship repair firm. Several former chiefs of U.S. Military Assistance Advisory Groups (MAAGs) in Iran had signed on with U.S. companies such as Rockwell International and Philco-Ford to sell military equipment to their contacts in the Iranian armed forces. In addition to playing the connections of their agents and lobbyists for all they were worth, U.S. contractors also paid millions of dollars in bribes through middlemen, money that ended up enriching key officials like Iranian chief of procurement General Hassan Toufanian, not to mention numerous members of the Iranian royal family.[38]

The payoffs to Iran were part of a much larger pattern of corrupt overseas business practices that were spawned by the Nixon Doctrine's aggressive promotion of arms sales. Investigations by the Senate Subcommittee on Multinational Corporations and the Securities and Exchange Commission (SEC), prompted by the Watergate special prosecutor's discovery of a multimillion-dollar political "slush fund" maintained by the Northrop Corporation, revealed that bribery and political influence peddling were rampant in the overseas operations of U.S. business. The SEC found evidence that during the 1960s and 1970s, nearly four hundred U.S. companies had engaged in questionable sales practices or made questionable payments overseas worth hundreds of millions of dollars. But while it was evident that companies in many lines of business were making payoffs, it was also clear that military contractors were leading the pack. Northrop admitted paying bribes and "commissions" of more than $30 million in connection with its efforts to sell fighter planes to foreign customers between 1971 and 1975, while Lockheed grudgingly owned up to over $200 million in improper payments abroad, to officials in Turkey, Indonesia, Saudi Arabia, Italy, Japan, and West Germany.[39]

Nixon and Kissinger's strategy of arming surrogates to fight on behalf of U.S. interests had degenerated into a mad scramble for multibillion-dollar contracts, where greed outstripped common sense and the economic incentives to sell far outweighed any concerns about the strategic dangers of continuing to arm unpopular and unstable regimes like that run by the shah of Iran.

The culture of corruption and insider dealing in Iran was so insidious that even those who had been charged with cleaning it up soon fell prey to the allure of quick and easy profits. The prime example was Richard Hallock, a retired U.S. Army colonel who was sent to Iran in 1973 as Secretary of Defense Schlesinger's personal representative, for the purpose of bringing the burgeoning Iranian sales program under control. Hallock's brief was to provide the shah and Toufanian with independent, objective assessments of the scores of weapons proposals they were fielding from U.S. contractors and military representatives. Schlesinger hoped that Hallock's advice would help the shah and his military men sort through the misleading claims and unrestrained hype of contractor representatives who were desperate to make a sale, any sale, regardless of its appropriateness to Iran's military requirements. Hallock was also supposed to monitor the overall U.S. sales program in Iran and inform Schlesinger of any irregularities or problems that emerged.

Whatever Schlesinger's original intention was in sending Hallock to Iran, it soon became evident that his watchdog was more interested in profiting from the arms trade with Iran than in regulating it. By September 1974, Hallock had formed his own consulting firm, Intrec, and hired himself out as an adviser to Toufanian and the shah in return for a multimillion-dollar contract. At the same time, Hallock's consulting firm was apparently representing Northrop, E Systems, and Teledyne in their efforts to win contracts in Iran. As Middle East analyst Barry Rubin pointed out, this put Hallock in "the enviable position of advising the Shah on what to buy, advising the United States government on what to recommend to him, helping the arms supply company to close these deals, and overseeing the program under which all these transactions were being made."[40] Hallock was forced out of government service in 1975 when the Defense Department's Criminal Division started an investigation into this complex web of business and government dealings.

This new determination on the part of the U.S. arms industry to export at all costs was probably the most enduring legacy of the Nixon Doctrine, and no company more clearly exemplified it than the Grumman Corporation. The Long Island–based aircraft firm had relied for most of its corporate life on building aircraft for the U.S. Navy, but its latest contract—for the swing-wing, supersonic, multiweapon F-14 Tomcat fighter—looked like it could be its last. By 1971, the plane's cost had skyrocketed to nearly $15 million, a figure that at that time made it the most expensive fighter ever built. And Grumman stood to lose hundreds of millions of dollars on the new aircraft under a fixed-price contract negotiated at the end of Robert McNamara's tenure at the Department of Defense. The F-14 was not going to make it on Pentagon funding alone. Grumman needed a wealthy foreign benefactor to help bail out its financially troubled program.

Grumman's new CEO, John Bierwirth, a savvy, cosmopolitan marketing man who had been recruited from National Distillers, saw the company's salvation in exports. To Bierwirth, there was apparently little difference between selling whiskey and selling weapons, and he decided to spare no expense in aggressively promoting sales of the Tomcat overseas. An in-house Grumman forecast projected a worldwide market for over one thousand of the new planes, but there would be no sales if the company couldn't come up with a quick infusion of cash to get the program off the ground and pull the company out of the red. Grumman executives were convinced that the shah of Iran would be their savior—and they were right. Iran ultimately contracted for eighty F-14s at a total cost of close to $2 billion. The Shah even helped Grumman with financing, engineering a $75 million loan from the Melli Bank of Iran to tide the firm over its cash-flow crisis.[41]

But in their eagerness to make a deal, it appears that Grumman's overseas sales force cut more than a few ethical corners. An investigation by Sen. Frank Church's Subcommittee on Multinational Corporations revealed that Grumman had paid $28 million in commissions to Iranian "agents" close to General Mohammed Khatami, the shah's brother-in-law and the head of the Iranian Air Force, and to General Toufanian, the shah's right-hand man. While there was no direct proof that the money found its way into the shah's pockets, there was strong circumstantial evidence that some of it ended up with members of the royal family.

One of Grumman's agents, an Iranian middleman named Houshang Lavi, engaged in an astounding colloquy with Jack Blum, counsel to the Church committee investigation, regarding the purpose of the "agents' fees" Grumman paid in Iran. The questioning centered on how Lavi's Iranian contact, a retired Iranian colonel named Assari, had spent $3 million in Grumman funds forwarded to him to help promote the sale of the F-14 in Iran:

> BLUM: What was he supposed to do for you?
>
> LAVI: He was supposed to be conduit and, at the time the Grumman representatives would go to Iran, he was supposed to accommodate them.
>
> BLUM: Well, you said that he was supposed to be a conduit. What was he supposed to be a conduit for?
>
> LAVI: Well, take them to the hotel, show them the rounds, introduce them to the Iranian general staff.
>
> BLUM: And that was all he was supposed to do?
>
> LAVI: Yes, sir.
>
> BLUM: You assigned him a payment of $3 million at one point.
>
> LAVI: Yes, sir.
>
> BLUM: Was that to be his fee for making hotel reservations?
>
> LAVI: Part of it. No, sir, not only hotel reservations, but as I told you he was also advising the Grumman representatives how to, what to do in Iran, you know.

After a bit more beating around the bush, Lavi finally admitted that Grumman's fees went through a middleman into the hands of Toufanian and Khatami. The Iranian government denied Lavi's charges.[42]

Whether or not these giant fees were in fact hidden payoffs, they were only a small part of a comprehensive and aggressive Grumman sales campaign in Iran. Interestingly enough, the company started pitching Iran on the F-14 more than two years before Nixon and Kissinger gave the shah the go-ahead to buy it, while the plane was still in development. This aspect of Grumman's sales technique was of particular concern to Senator Church. He wanted to know "whether the cart gets in front of the horse" in marketing U.S. arms abroad, so that "by the time the national policy decision is made, forces have come into play that largely predetermine the decision." Church's query was a diplomatic way of asking whether, under the umbrella of the Nixon/Kissinger policy, private companies had in effect used salesmanship and questionable payments to take control of sensitive foreign policy decisions that should have been the province of the president and the Congress.

Grumman's first man in Iran was an Australian archaeology buff and alleged intelligence operative named Colin Jupp, who just happened to be in Iran on a dig during the 1953 coup that brought the shah to power. Jupp was an old acquaintance of the shah and a number of influential Iranian military men, and he was employed by Grumman to get an early hearing for the F-14 in decisionmaking circles in Iran. He looked for every opportunity to do so: for example, Jupp managed to attach himself to Vice President Agnew's delegation to the gala 1971 celebration of Iran's twenty-five-hundredth anniversary, where he allegedly gave a scale model of the F-14 to General Khatami.

Later that year, Jupp prevailed upon an old friend, Colonel Mansfield, the U.S. military attaché in the Soviet Union, to brief General Khatami on the Soviet air threat to Iran and to make the case that the Grumman F-14 was the only plane that could shoot down the top-of-the-line Soviet fighter, the MiG-25. The Iranian attaché in Moscow, General N. Payrow, reported the details of this briefing directly to the shah. And in April 1972, the month before the Teheran meeting at which Nixon and Kissinger gave the shah the okay to buy F-14s, the peripatetic Mr. Jupp reported meetings with "at least thirty aides" in the White House, including Nixon assistants Charles Colson and Bob Haldeman (of Watergate fame), to plead the case for foreign sales of the plane.

Jupp's considerable efforts were just part of Grumman's full-court press for the F-14. The company spent over a quarter of a million dollars to support a navy demonstration of the Tomcat at the 1973 Paris Air Show, which was attended by all the top brass of the Iranian military establishment. And the company managed to maneuver behind the scenes to get the shah to see a "fly off" between the F-14 and the McDonnell Douglas F-15 fighters during one of his frequent visits to the U.S. The Grumman plane did a series of nifty stunts and sharp ascents that had the shah literally tracing its movements with his hands. McDonnell Douglas officials were miffed, as the F-15 they had sent to show the shah was a development model that was not ready to perform the kind of acrobatics that Grumman used to get His Imperial Majesty's rapt attention.[43]

While the shah's largess may have been at least temporarily good for Grumman, Northrop, McDonnell Douglas, and the scores of other U.S. arms firms that struck deals with him, it was not so clear that the companies' products were good for Iran, or for the stability of the shah's regime. George Ball, a veteran diplomat and statesman who had served in the Kennedy and Johnson administrations and as a consultant on a special review of Iranian policy for President Carter, was convinced that Nixon's open-ended sales policy had hastened the shah's decline and fall:

> I think it clear that in anointing the Shah as the guardian of Western interests in the whole Gulf area, Nixon inadvertently encouraged the megalomania that ultimately contributed to the Shah's downfall. Permitting him free access to the whole range of advanced items in our military arsenal was like giving the keys to the world's largest liquor store to a confirmed alcoholic.[44]

Ball's perspective on the role of the Nixon/Kissinger policy was reinforced by an aide to the shah, who was interviewed by author William Shawcross: "Persepolis was his [the shah's] blastoff into the heavens. After that he was refueled by Nixon and by oil. He never came back to earth."[45] A similar assessment could be made of the Nixon Doctrine itself—propelled by anticommunism and an effort to salvage a global interventionary role for the United States in the wake of the Vietnam fiasco, refueled by oil-rich clients and pork barrel politics, Nixon and Kissinger's weapons-trading impulses never came back down to earth and never allowed them to take a realistic view of the consequences of their arms sales policies.

The shah's conspicuous spending on arms at the expense of more urgent needs such as agricultural development drove an even greater wedge between the haves and have-nots of Iranian society. While two-thirds of Iran remained illiterate and many Iranians survived on a diet of bread and vegetable oil, the shah was busily purchasing multibillion-dollar weapons and heavy industrial plants along with the high-priced Western technical talent needed to run them. As one influential Iranian leader with contacts at the top levels of the nation's business and government elite noted during the peak period of the shah's mammoth, military-driven investment plans, "They are childish, totally unrealistic. Look at our miserable villages and even the streets of this capital [Teheran]. There's enough practical work for us to do without such nonsense."[46]

The ubiquitous presence of U.S. military personnel and corporate employees in Iran further fanned popular resentment, while implicating the U.S. government with a man that most Iranians had come to see as a brutal and corrupt dictator. While his police state tactics would not have been tolerated indefinitely in any case, the shah's military spending binge unquestionably hastened his demise, delivering billions of dollars of U.S. arms into the hands of a hostile revolutionary regime in the process. But that's getting ahead of the story.

Sparked by the Nixon Doctrine, U.S. foreign arms sales jumped from $1.4 billion in 1971 to over $16 billion by 1975. In terms of sheer volume of sales, the monarchies of the Middle East and Persian Gulf were far and away the most important customers. Iran and Saudi Arabia alone accounted for more than two-thirds of the total growth in U.S. foreign military sales between 1971 and 1975. With more than $8 billion in purchases, the shah single-handedly made up a healthy share of this newfound bonanza for U.S. defense contractors, while Saudi Arabia's purchases of military goods and services jumped from a modest $15 million to an incredible $6 billion over the same five-year period. But the shah and the Saudi regime were not alone. U.S. arms sales to South Korea exploded to two hundred times their 1971 levels; nations as diverse as Brazil, Chile, Peru, Indonesia, Israel, Taiwan, and Zaire all received record levels of arms shipments from the United States during this period; and even the tiny desert sheikdom of Kuwait, which had purchased no weaponry at all from the United States in the year that the Nixon Doctrine was announced, got on the bandwagon, purchasing $353 million in U.S. weaponry in 1975.[47] Ultimately, however, it was the shah's—and Nixon's—arms trading follies that finally awakened Congress to the dangers of unrestrained arms trafficking.

3

Congress Steps In

In 1974, a full five years after Nixon's remarks in Guam ushered in a new era in U.S. arms sales policy, Congress finally took decisive steps to reform the U.S. role as the "arms supermarket" to the world, in Sen. Hubert Humphrey's memorable phrase. Spurred on by the revelations of presidential misconduct in the Watergate scandal and energized by the continuing battle to end the war in Vietnam, a handful of key members of the House and Senate made the arms sales issue part of a larger drive to reassert congressional authority in foreign and domestic affairs.

The U.S. Constitution clearly states that only the Congress has the power to declare war and that only the Congress can appropriate monies for any governmental purpose, domestic or foreign. The Nixon Doctrine threatened both of these constitutional principles by promoting weapons exports that indirectly involve the United States in dozens of overseas conflicts without any consultation with Congress or the public and providing most of the arms on a cash basis, thereby circumventing Congress's "power of the purse," which would have come into play if the equipment had been provided via military aid channels. Having fought so long for congressional input on questions relating to the war in Vietnam, Congress was not about to let the executive branch use uncontrolled arms sales to sow the seeds of a new generation of U.S. military adventures. Something had to be done.[1]

Exerting democratic control over the Nixon administration's far-flung arms sales initiatives became a top priority for an influential group of congressmen spearheaded by Senators Gaylord Nelson of Wisconsin and Dick Clark of Iowa, Congressman Jonathan Bingham of New York, and Sen. Hubert Humphrey of Minnesota, Nixon's opponent in the 1968 presidential election. As early as 1971, a "sense of Congress" resolution had urged Nixon to "use the power and prestige of his office to signify the intention of the United States to work actively with all nations to control the international sales and distribution of conventional weapons of death and destruction."[2] This plea for restraint fell on unsympathetic ears in the White House. As we have seen, Nixon was intent on using the "power and prestige of his office" to sell weapons, not control their sale.

By 1974, Congress was no longer satisfied with appeals to the president's sense of logic or morality. Arms sales had reached record levels for the second straight year, and Nixon and Kissinger showed no signs of slowing down. There was a movement afoot to legislate concrete limits on executive branch arms trafficking, to ensure that there would at least be some measure of public debate and congressional input into the new, multibillion-dollar U.S. arms sales program.

Nixon's resignation over Watergate in August 1974 left arms sales policy almost totally in the hands of his secretary of state, Henry Kissinger. Nixon's successor, Gerald Ford, had little foreign policy experience and was expected by many political insiders to defer to Kissinger on most major decisions, particularly those relating to sensitive arms sales arrangements. Kissinger's new ascendancy as *the* foreign policy decisionmaker of the Ford administration was a disturbing prospect to many members of Congress and a development that strengthened their resolve to move decisively to reform the process for reviewing and approving U.S. weapons exports. Bill Richardson, a congressman from New Mexico who served as Hubert Humphrey's staff aide on foreign policy issues in the mid-1970s, singled out Kissinger as a catalyst for congressional activism on arms sales: "The atmosphere was one of suspicion. . . . Henry Kissinger fueled a lot of that suspicion because he was making secret deals and not going through Congress."[3]

If anything, the congressional reformers may have waited too long to act. The Nixon Doctrine had transformed U.S. arms exports beyond recognition, and Congress was in danger of being totally left out of decisionmaking in this central area of foreign and military policy. By 1974, the sheer dollar value of weaponry exported by the United States had mushroomed under the Nixon/Kissinger policy to more than five times its 1970 levels, and the number of arms customers had grown as well, to the point where more than seventy nations were now on the receiving end of arms deals brokered by the U.S. government. It was a client list that would have been the envy of any private weapons dealer. But now the biggest deals were being made by government bureaucrats, not shadowy arms merchants.

Even more than the growth in the size and scope of U.S. transfers, Nixon's abrupt shift in emphasis from military aid to weapons sales had a devastating impact on the role of Congress in arms transfer policy. Under the terms of foreign assistance legislation passed shortly after World War II, all U.S. military aid funds had to be debated and approved by Congress. As long as military aid was the principal method of transferring U.S. weapons to other nations, the role of Congress in deciding whom the U.S. would arm—and for what purposes—was guaranteed. Indeed, Nixon and Kissinger's reluctant decision to pull U.S. troops out of Vietnam had been shaped by the success of Congress in restricting U.S. military assistance to Southeast Asia in response to the domestic antiwar movement. Slowly but surely, public opposition to Vietnam had moved Congress to act: voting down huge military aid requests and putting strict limits on how U.S. aid could be used had been important tools in reining in the imperial presidency and ending the war.

Kissinger complained bitterly in his self-serving memoir, *Years of Upheaval*, about the "cumulative constraints" Congress placed on U.S. military aid to Cambodia and South Vietnam, restrictions that he believed had "made inevitable the diplomatic impasse that served Hanoi's purposes." In Kissinger's Manichean worldview, it was these legislative restrictions, pushed by "antiwar critics," that "made the collapse of Indochina inevitable."[4] He refused to acknowledge that without limits on U.S. military assistance the war might have dragged on for years longer without a negotiated settlement, costing tens of thousands of additional lives and wreaking added destruction throughout Southeast Asia.

Restoring the president's freedom of action and cutting Congress out of the arms export decisionmaking process was a major consideration in Nixon and Kissinger's move toward stepped-up sales of U.S. equipment to key allies like the shah, Philippine dictator Ferdinand Marcos, and Korean strongman Park Chung Hee. Arms sales agreements could be quietly arranged by executive branch officials without "meddling" by the Congress, since members had no legislative authority to vote on cash sales of weaponry (as opposed to military aid). It was no accident that at the height of congressional assertiveness and input into the question of Vietnam, the Nixon administration was setting up a new mechanism for evading congressional scrutiny and control in military matters by making the sale of armaments a pillar of U.S. policy.

In a speech on the floor of the Senate on September 25, 1974, Gaylord Nelson, the populist Democrat from Wisconsin, summed up the frustration of many members of Congress over their increasing irrelevance in the arms sales decisionmaking process:

> Foreign military sales constitute major foreign policy decisions involving the United States in military activities without sufficient deliberation. This has gotten us into trouble in the past and could easily do so again.
>
> Despite the serious policy issues raised by this tremendous increase in Government arms sales, these transactions are made with little regard for Congressional or public opinion. The Department of Defense is consulted. The manufacturers of weapons and providers of military services are consulted. The foreign purchasers are involved. But Congress is hardly informed of these transactions, much less consulted as to their propriety.
>
> As it stands now, the Executive Branch of the Government simply presents Congress and the public with the accomplished facts.[5]

Nelson underscored his point by noting that Congress was so far out of the loop on arms export issues that members often learned of U.S. sales commitments not from the Pentagon or the State Department but from foreign press reports. Sales of F-4 Phantom jets to Saudi Arabia and a "giant arms deal" for Kuwait came to the attention of Congress only after the *Washington Post* picked up an Agence France-Press report on the subject. Negotiations to sell U.S. jets to Brazil came out in the Brazilian press long before Congress or the American public learned of the deal. And an administration plan to end a three-year ban on military aid to Ecuador was revealed only after a correspondent in the Ecuadorean capital of Quito wrote a story on it. As congressional analyst Richard Grimmett has observed, the nation's elected representatives were so poorly informed during these early years of the Nixon Doctrine that "once Congress learned of a prospective arms sale or transfer—usually through press accounts—it was generally too late to reverse the decision that had been made."[6]

Nelson, an early opponent of the Vietnam War and a longtime congressional gadfly, set out to remedy this sad state of affairs, which in essence had placed U.S.-government-sponsored arms trafficking beyond democratic control. The senator from Wisconsin was at a decided disadvantage in taking on this issue. His most passionate legislative concern was environmental protection, and he didn't even have a seat on the Senate Foreign Relations Committee, which would have to sign off on any significant reform in arms export decisionmaking. Nelson was an "outsider" to the Senate's normal processes of deliberating over foreign policy issues, and in normal times his chances of successfully pushing through a major reform in this area would have been virtually nil. But these were not normal times. The extreme public and congressional distrust of the executive branch fostered by Watergate and Vietnam gave Nelson the political opening he needed.

Nelson proposed an amendment to the Foreign Assistance Act requiring congressional notification of major U.S. weapons sales, in order to "give the Congress the opportunity to study the circumstances surrounding each major sale, and to assess the foreign policy impact of each such transaction."[7] The amendment provided a mechanism by which, for the first time, Congress could reject a proposed arms sale through passage of concurrent resolutions of disapproval in both the House and the Senate. Equally important, Congress would be routinely notified in advance of major arms sales rather than learning about them for the first time in the newspapers, if at all. The idea for the legislative veto and congressional notification was developed by Nelson staffer Paula Stern, who spent more than two years refining it in response to feedback from the Pentagon, the State Department, and members of Congress.

The Nelson amendment took a long and tortuous path through Congress, a path dictated by Nelson's outsider status, which deprived him of a direct role in any of the House–Senate conferences that were ironing out the final details of the Foreign Assistance Act. The amendment first passed the full Senate on June 25, 1973, but it didn't survive the conference committee on that year's foreign aid bill, so it was back to the drawing board. In the heated legislative environment of the fall of 1974, in the wake of Nixon's resignation, the amendment again passed the full Senate, although Stern recalls that "we were hanging by our fingernails that it might get reversed" under a standing procedure that allowed for a second vote on particularly close cases. The amendment was dropped by the foreign aid conference committee yet again, but Nelson wasn't going to give up this time. On December 3, 1974, he reintroduced the amendment with the support of a number of prominent fellow Democrats, including his colleague William Proxmire of Wisconsin, Walter Mondale of Minnesota, Alan Cranston and John Tunney of California, Edmund Muskie of Maine, and Edward Kennedy of Massachusetts.[8]

Nelson's final pitch for the amendment leaned heavily on the constitutional argument that Congress should be an equal partner with the president in major foreign policy matters. He believed that his amendment was "vital if we are to move this country closer to responsible public deliberation of one of the most vital areas of American foreign policy making. . . . Congress has come a long way in righting the imbalance whereby the executive branch of this Nation can and does involve the United States in military situations overseas without congressional and public debate, discussion, or deliberation. This is the reason for this amendment." Nelson received a vital assist from Hubert Humphrey, who explained to his colleagues on the Foreign Relations Committee that he had spoken with "the distinguished Senator from Wisconsin" and "this particular amendment, I think, does no injustice to the purposes of this bill . . . and I am prepared to accept the amendment." With Humphrey's endorsement, Nelson's proposal passed by a voice vote and was once again made part of the Foreign Assistance Act.[9]

Much to Kissinger's chagrin, Nelson's amendment survived the final negotiations on the foreign aid bill and was signed into law on December 31, 1974. Looking back on all the twists and turns the amendment took on the way to becoming law, Paula Stern says, "When I think about it, it was quite remarkable that we got the damned thing passed."

It remained to be seen whether this new tool of congressional oversight would cramp Kissinger's ability to wheel and deal in armaments to further his penchant for secretive diplomacy. The executive branch had lost the war over the congressional veto, but it had won one significant battle by whittling down the amount of advance notice Congress would receive on pending sales from Nelson's original proposal, from thirty days to twenty, a woefully inadequate amount of time for any member of Congress to study a major arms sale and build an effective coalition to stop it. And Congressman Bingham's proposal that the time period be twenty legislative days (days when Congress was in session) was changed in conference to twenty calendar days, leaving open the possibility that the president might announce major sales right before a recess in hopes that they would slip by unchallenged.[10]

This extremely brief notification period was even more troublesome because of the nature of the arms sales decisionmaking process itself, which stacks the odds against any effort to generate successful congressional opposition to a given deal. Major arms deals have what analyst Michael Klare has called a long "prehistory," lasting anywhere from several months to five years or more. This prehistory includes a series of informal discussions, exchanges of information with foreign governments, demonstrations of specific military equipment for representatives of the potential purchasing nation by the Pentagon and U.S. military contractors, and reviews within the State Department, the Pentagon, the National Security Council (NSC), and other relevant executive branch agencies. All of these activities generate powerful political momentum behind a sale, so that by the time a foreign government makes a formal request for a specific weapons system, "the ball game is over," according to an official of the Arms Control and Disarmament Agency (ACDA) familiar with the process. As Klare points out, not only are congressional opponents of a particular sale put in the awkward position of attempting to revoke a "de facto commitment to the nations involved" that may have been developed over a period of several years, but they are also deprived of information on any misgivings about the sale within the executive branch. Any hearings Congress might choose to hold on the deal invariably meet with a united front in support of the sale on the part of the relevant executive branch agencies, which have already had their debates and resolved their differences over the proposed export before notifying Congress about it.[11]

In the years after the Nelson amendment was signed into law, it became increasingly evident that twenty days' notice was a pathetically short period of time for even the most determined member of Congress to overcome the overwhelming bureaucratic momentum that tends to develop behind most significant arms sales in the months and years before Congress learns of their existence. Nelson had succeeded in his immediate objective of ensuring that Congress was informed of major sales before the fact, but it was still not clear whether members would get the information early enough to make a difference.

Taking Control: From Turkey to Angola

The passage of Nelson's amendment, over vigorous opposition from the Ford administration, was only one step in a growing campaign of congressional activism in arms export decisionmaking. In addition to drastically cutting U.S. aid to Vietnam, in 1974 Congress passed an embargo on U.S. arms transfers to Turkey in response to that nation's invasion and occupation of northern Cyprus. The use of Turkey's U.S.-equipped armed forces to invade Cyprus, and the prospect of war between Turkey and Greece, another major U.S. arms client, fueled critics' claims that U.S. policy on arms exports had spun completely out of control.

The standoff between Greece and Turkey marked the third time in three years that the United States was in the embarrassing position of supplying armaments to both sides of a conflict: U.S. weapons had been used by both India and Pakistan in their 1971 war, a conflict that had resulted in the breaking off of West Pakistan and its transformation into the independent nation of Bangladesh. Massive U.S. sales to Israel and several of its Arab adversaries in the immediate aftermath of the 1973 Middle East war raised the question of whether the next war in that region would be fought with U.S. armaments on both sides of the battlefield. And now Greece and Turkey, both favored recipients of U.S. military aid dating back to Truman's anticommunist commitment of the late 1940s, were poised to go to war over Cyprus.

In an op-ed article appropriately entitled "Uncle Sam, Arms Dealer," journalist and former Kissinger aide Andrew Hamilton cited the crisis over Cyprus as the latest evidence putting the lie to Pentagon claims that arms sales could be used to promote "cooperation and partnership" in the service of U.S. foreign policy objectives and ensure a "balance of power" that would prevent the outbreak of war in critical regions:

> On July 15th, spurred by a military government in Greece critically dependent on American military aid and political support, officers of the Greek Cypriot national guard deposed the President of Cyprus, Archbishop Makarios, and precipitated a continuing crisis. On July 20, Turkish troops in American uniforms and carrying American weapons invaded Cyprus from American-made aircraft, and helicopters and ships carrying American-made trucks and tanks. They were supported by a navy and air force equipped and armed by the United States.
>
> When, next day, Greece began marshalling its American-equipped army aboard American-built landing craft for a counter-invasion, there was imminent danger of war between two nations whose military establishments were largely made in the U.S.A. While Washington did at last persuade the Greeks not to attack, it had failed to restrain either the coup against Makarios or the Turkish invasion.[12]

In light of such obvious evidence to the contrary, Nelson and his colleagues in Congress were no longer inclined to accept Pentagon and State Department arguments about the "prudent" use of U.S. arms. An embargo on U.S. arms shipments to Turkey was passed after what one congressional analyst described as a "protracted and bitter battle."[13]

Congressional activism on arms sales was carried a step further in 1975, when Senator Clark won passage of an amendment bearing his name that cut off CIA covert arms assistance to South African–backed rebel movements in Angola. Secret arms sales had been a routine part of U.S. foreign policy throughout the post–World War II era, but until Clark's amendment, Congress had never attempted to stop a covert military aid program. Pres. Dwight Eisenhower had quietly funneled weapons into Iran in support of the coup that brought the shah back to power in 1953, and in 1954 Gen. Carlos Castillo Armas had received CIA arms and training for his successful effort to overthrow the democratically elected government of Jacobo Arbenz in Guatemala. Military coups in Brazil in 1964 and Chile in 1973 had been aided by CIA support with logistics and intelligence, as well as some U.S.-supplied weaponry.

In 1975, the CIA opened up a major new front in the covert arms supply business in the southern African nation of Angola, which was on the verge of gaining its independence from Portugal. At Kissinger's urging, the agency began supplying weapons to Holden Roberto's National Front for the Liberation of Angola (FNLA) and Jonas Savimbi's National Union for the Total Independence of Angola (UNITA) to strengthen their hands in a struggle for power with the Marxist-oriented Popular Movement for the Liberation of Angola (MPLA), which was receiving support from the Soviet Union. Portugal had set a date of November 11, 1975, for withdrawal from its longstanding colony, and Kissinger was desperate to shore up one or both of the anti-Soviet factions of the independence movement, which lagged far behind Dr. Agostinho Neto's MPLA in terms of popular support within Angola.

As had happened so often in its Cold War crusade against progressive movements in the Third World, the United States had chosen a sorry pair of allies in Angola. Roberto, the brother-in-law of Zaire's dictator, Joseph Mobutu, and a paid CIA intelligence "source" since the late 1960s, seemed more interested in lining his pockets than liberating Angola. Savimbi, a more ambitious and charismatic figure, was the ultimate opportunist, spouting Maoist rhetoric one year as he sought Chinese aid and cutting a deal with white minority regimes in South Africa and Rhodesia the next, after being offered more extensive military support. In the judgment of Nathaniel Davis, the U.S. ambassador to Angola, neither man was a likely candidate to outmaneuver the MPLA's Neto on either the political or the military front. The best that might be hoped for would be a political compromise in which UNITA and FNLA participated with Neto's organization in a coalition government. In typical fashion, Kissinger stubbornly ignored warnings from his own ambassador and analysts within the CIA that a major covert military aid program would only embroil the United States in a civil war that would be counterproductive militarily and embarrassing politically, given Savimbi's growing ties with the apartheid regime in South Africa.[14]

At the same time that Nelson's amendment to the Foreign Assistance Act was working its way into law, Congressman Leo Ryan of California and Sen. Harold Hughes of Iowa were successfully promoting another amendment that required the reporting of all significant CIA covert actions to eight relevant committees of Congress. It was through this reporting requirement, implemented in 1974, that Senator Clark, who served as the chair of the African Affairs Subcommittee of the Senate Foreign Relations Committee, first learned that the CIA was running a covert arms supply operation in southern Africa. At the time, CIA director William Colby had sworn to Clark that no U.S. weapons were going to any of the rebel factions in Angola, that they were being sent only to the Mobutu regime in Zaire to replace the arms it was channeling to Roberto and Savimbi. This may have seemed like a distinction without a difference, but to Clark it was an important point—if no U.S. arms or CIA trainers were going into Angola, it would be much less likely that the United States would get directly involved in the conflict.

Colby's cover story didn't hold up for long. Clark returned from an August 1975 fact-finding tour of the area convinced that the CIA was directly aiding South Africa and Savimbi's UNITA forces in the Angolan conflict. The former head of CIA operations in Angola, John Stockwell, has since reported that the agency went out of its way to "coach" its Angolan contacts to give Clark a slanted picture of U.S. involvement that would throw him off the trail. But Clark wasn't fooled by the CIA's public relations line, according to Stockwell:

> Senator Clark returned from his trip skeptical of his CIA briefings and of the Angola program. He was concerned that we were secretly dragging the United States into a broad conflict with dangerous, global implications. Specifically, he was concerned (a) that we were in fact sending arms directly to Angola; (b) that Americans were involved in the conflict; and (c) that the CIA was illegally collaborating with South Africa.[15]

Clark's ability to take action against the CIA's arms shipments to Angola was drastically restricted by the nature of the new law. Members of Congress were sworn to secrecy on any CIA briefings pertaining to covert actions, a restriction that severely undercut their ability to open a public debate over activities they deemed unwise or contrary to U.S. interests. But once reports of U.S. arms supplies to Angola were leaked to the press in September 1975, Senator Clark had the hook he needed to hold hearings on the whole issue of U.S. involvement there. The situation was even worse than Clark had suspected, although he was finally informed of its true dimensions almost by accident.

At a December 5 hearing of Clark's subcommittee, State Department representative Edward Mulcahy showed up late for his scheduled testimony. In the meantime, unbeknownst to Mulcahy, CIA witness William Nelson had gone on at some length about the precise nature and extent of CIA activities in arming and supporting the South African/Savimbi alliance in Angola. Nelson was a close associate of William Colby, and he apparently felt he had nothing to lose by telling the truth about U.S. operations in Angola now that his mentor had been asked to resign as director of the CIA. As a result of Nelson's unexpected openness, when Mulcahy arrived and launched into the Ford administration's party line on the issue, describing a minimal U.S. role in the Angolan civil war, Clark was able to "confront Mulcahy with . . . Nelson's testimony, trapping the Administration in a lie."[16]

Within two weeks of the hearing, Clark had drafted an amendment barring any CIA or Pentagon involvement in military support, training, or shipment of armaments to Angola. He obtained passage in the Senate by a margin of 54 to 22. The House followed suit in late January, and on February 9, 1976, the amendment was signed into law. President Ford approved the Clark amendment under protest, firing off a letter to Congress stating that he was "deeply disappointed" over the cutoff of covert aid to Angola and saw it as "an extremely undesirable precedent that could limit severely our ability to play a positive and effective role in international affairs." As intelligence expert John Prados has observed, the Clark amendment marked "the first time a covert action had been halted by congressional order," and it held out hope that Congress might be able to control the secret as well as the overt side of the U.S. government's arms trafficking activities. But, after the legislation had become law, in an intriguing final twist that should have set off alarm bells in Congress at the time, President Ford's newly installed director of central intelligence, George Bush, "refused to say whether United States aid to Angola had halted," as Prados reports.[17]

The events of the next decade and a half were to provide repeated lessons that passing legislation prohibiting covert military aid to a particular nation or political movement was in and of itself no guarantee that the president and the intelligence community would refrain from the prohibited activities. But from the perspective of 1975, Clark's amendment looked like a major turning point in the battle to gain effective congressional control over the executive branch arms sales juggernaut. From military aid to large foreign sales to covert weapons shipments, Congress had reasserted its prerogative to play a role in deciding whom the United States would arm.

Comprehensive Reform: The Arms Export Control Act of 1976

While the introduction of the legislative veto and the passage of embargoes on Turkey and the Angolan rebels had shifted the balance of arms sales decisionmaking back toward Congress, many senior members still felt that the executive branch had too many cards in this dynamic and dangerous area of U.S. policy. Not least among them was old Nixon rival and Senate elder Hubert Humphrey, who decided to lead the legislative charge to undo the worst aspects of the Nixon Doctrine.

After the grueling experience of four years as Lyndon B. Johnson's vice president and his narrow loss to Richard Nixon in the 1968 presidential election, Humphrey had returned to the Senate in 1970 determined to make his mark as a legislator. Humphrey was a consummate legislative insider who knew how to cut deals to get a bill through Congress. A 1975 *Los Angeles Times* profile described him as "a mixture of competence, vigor, and undisciplined enthusiasm." The article went on in tones of unstinting praise, asserting that "not many persons in Washington know as much about government as he does. And not many are as pragmatic."[18]

It would take all of Humphrey's legislative skills and considerable prestige among his fellow members of the Senate to steer his latest bill, the Arms Export Control Act, through Congress and into the statute books, but he was clearly committed to the task. Former Humphrey aide Bill Richardson recalled that it was the senator's "passion to bring some . . . accountability to the arms transfer process." Humphrey was spurred in part by a desire to undo the dangerous legacy of his longtime rival Richard Nixon, Richardson implied: "There was a feeling that the Nixon/Kissinger policy was just out of control and we had no handle on it." This feeling was particularly strong with respect to massive sales to Iran, which in Richardson's view were "obviously to prop up the Shah," not for any larger strategic purpose. In addition, Humphrey must have known that his days as a senator were drawing to a close. He was already ill with the cancer that ultimately claimed his life, and he viewed the Arms Export Control Act as "one of his crowning final achievements," according to Richardson.

In his first hearings on the bill, Humphrey set a lofty moral tone, arguing that on the eve of "the Bicentennial of our nation's birth . . . it is important for Congress to reflect on what we, as a people, want America to stand for. The United States, as the leading actor, has a great capacity for leadership in the control of trade in conventional arms." He dismissed the usual argument against controlling the arms trade:

> It's not enough to say that everyone else is selling arms. That is the excuse for every kind of misdeed, everyone else is doing it, why not me.[19]

Humphrey's prestige among his peers and his sophisticated understanding of the legislative process were complemented by a rising level of indignation among many of his younger Senate colleagues over runaway executive branch arms trading. The result was a kind of "good cop, bad cop" approach to Ford administration witnesses who appeared before Humphrey's Foreign Relations Committee panel to discuss the new export control initiative. During a November 1975 session, Sen. John Culver of Iowa challenged Secretary of State Kissinger to follow through on a proposal by 102 members of Congress to "call an international conference of major arms producers to bring this pathological competition in foreign military sales under some form of rational control." Then Culver lashed out at Kissinger for his constant references to how "complex" arms sales decisions were, the not so veiled implication being that they were too complicated for Congress to comprehend or play a meaningful role in.

> SENATOR CULVER: Mr. Secretary, I am under no illusions whatsoever about the degree of complexity involved in this problem, nor, I am afraid, the degree of danger if we continue on our current course. The real question I have for you, sir, is whether or not you believe that it is an appropriate responsibility of this Government in view of the fact that we sell one-half of the world's arms today, with no apparent coherent policy but rather a form of checkbook diplomacy, whether or not you feel we have a responsibility to assume a role other than just merchant of death, and whether or not we are going to take the initiative of seeking some sort of rational control

of this problem, because without the U.S. leadership in this area, I see very little hope that it can be.

SECRETARY KISSINGER: Senator, without accepting either your adjectives, or most of your nouns, I accept the proposition that the United States has the responsibility to see what it can do to limit the arms race in the Middle East.

CULVER: And we are going to exercise that?

KISSINGER: We will attempt to exercise it, yes.[20]

In contrast to Culver's aggressive questioning, Humphrey was congenial and matter-of-fact, choosing not to attack Kissinger but rather to ask him straightforwardly if he clearly understood the intent of several major provisions of the bill. Kissinger, in a rare moment of apparent humility, acknowledged that he had not understood a key portion of the proposed legislation "until you explained it to me a little earlier." Kissinger went on to say on the Ford administration's behalf that "we would like to study your bill with sympathy and to put before you, for your consideration, any modifications we might have of specific provisions." Kissinger's cooperative attitude made it appear that Humphrey was well on the way to another substantial legislative accomplishment.[21]

Taken at face value, the proposed reform seemed to mark a radical departure from the secretive arms dealing of the Nixon/Kissinger era and a return to openness and democratic control in the field of weapons exports. The legislation included a $9 billion ceiling on total U.S. arms transfers, as a first stab at reining in the galloping growth of the previous six years. It provided for much more detailed reporting to Congress on the content of proposed foreign military sales. And, in perhaps its most controversial aspect, the bill included seven separate legislative vetoes over weapons transfers, among them provisions authorizing Congress to cut off U.S. arms sales to countries that discriminated against U.S. citizens, engaged in consistent patterns of gross violations of human rights, or offered sanctuary to international terrorists. Each of the vetoes was to be accomplished by a concurrent resolution of the House and Senate, which meant that a majority vote in both houses of Congress would be the last word on the subject.[22]

If the legislation had survived intact, it would appear that the days of reckless executive branch wheeling and dealing in armaments were about to come to an end. But the road to passage of the Arms Export Control Act was not as smooth as these early signs indicated.

By the beginning of 1976, Kissinger had delivered a letter to Humphrey registering the Ford administration's "strong objections" to the bill's human rights and antidiscrimination provisions. And that wasn't all. Kissinger also upped the ante by questioning the constitutionality of the existing congressional veto mechanism that had been established under Gaylord Nelson's successful amendment of 1974. At issue was whether Congress could block a foreign arms sale by a simple majority vote on a concurrent resolution of disapproval in the House and Senate. The net effect of this so-called legislative veto was that Congress could decide the issue without the president having a chance to exercise his veto, which would have forced his opponents to muster a two-thirds majority in both the House and the Senate. The letter was the first clear sign that the Ford administration was philosophically opposed to sharing decisionmaking power over arms sales with Congress, contrary to Kissinger's reassuring testimony of the previous November.

Meanwhile, the major firms in the defense industry had also begun to rally their troops in opposition to Humphrey's bill, arguing that its immediate effect would be to slash U.S. weapons exports by one-half to three-quarters. A congressional aide interviewed by the *Washington Post* described a "quiet but pervasive" industry campaign to gut the bill, focused on "members with large defense industry constituencies as well as senior Armed Services Committee types on the Hill."[23]

The industry argument boiled down to a simple assertion that if U.S. arms makers could no longer sell to Arab regimes that discriminated against American Jews or to Third World dictators who routinely violated the human rights of their citizens, they would be losing out on the fastest-growing segments of the arms market. Industry lobbyist Mitchell Garrett even put in a plaintive pitch for the necessity of bribes, arguing that a provision of the new law requiring U.S. companies to report the commissions paid to obtain foreign contracts was a case of "Congress . . . trying to legislate a morality of the Middle East, the Far East, and Latin America." Since "commissions are a way of life in the rest of the world," why should U.S. firms be expected to be any more responsible than their competitors?[24]

The arms industry's lax view of foreign payoffs was not its strongest suit in fighting the Arms Export Control Act. In fact, Humphrey's initiative had been given added impetus by the Church committee's ongoing revelations of rampant bribery in the overseas sales efforts of Northrop, Lockheed, and other major defense and aerospace firms. Hundreds of millions of dollars in questionable "agents' fees" and outright bribes had been passed to foreign military and government leaders in Iran, Turkey, Japan, the Netherlands, and elsewhere by U.S. aerospace firms racing to cash in on the Nixon

Doctrine and growing OPEC oil revenues in their search for post-Vietnam sales outlets.

There was evidence that these corrupt practices had found their way into the U.S. political process as well. Northrop chairman Tom Jones had pleaded guilty to making an illegal $250,000 contribution to Nixon operatives for use in defending Watergate conspirators, and it was the subsequent probe into the company's finances that uncovered the existence of routine payoffs in the international marketing of military aircraft.

There was even some evidence that Nixon officials were not only aware of these overseas misdeeds but that they had tried to get in on the action. A Grumman sales representative alleged before Church's subcommittee that Nixon White House aide Richard Allen had solicited a $1 million payment to the Committee to Re-elect the President (CREEP) in return for efforts to get Nixon to push the sale of Grumman's E-2C radar plane in an upcoming visit to Japan, a charge Allen categorically denied. While it was never conclusively established whether this particular incident occurred, the growing list of allegations of bribery and influence peddling in U.S. foreign military sales made it clear to most members of Congress that money and corruption were driving U.S. arms policy at least as strongly as considerations of strategy and foreign policy.[25]

With this evidence of unbridled U.S. government-assisted arms trafficking looming in the background, Humphrey was able to overcome industry opposition and win majority support in both houses of Congress. In addition to the detailed provisions described above, the preamble to the legislation announced a clear change in direction from the Nixon/Kissinger years, asserting straightforwardly that it was the policy of the United States "to exert leadership in the world community to bring about arrangements for reducing the international trade in implements of war."[26]

But winning a majority in Congress was only half the battle. Stinging from criticism that he was an "accidental president" who didn't know how to take charge, Ford had spent a good part of 1976 sending legislation back to Congress for rewrites, in what was later described as the "war of the vetoes." While each individual veto was justified in terms of the merits of the legislation in question, some observers detected an additional motive—an effort to make Ford look "tough" and presidential in an election year. In line with this strategy and Kissinger's continuing desire to keep Congress out of arms sales decisions, Ford vetoed the Arms Export Control Act on May 7, 1976. He claimed that the bill would "seriously obstruct the President's constitutional responsibilities for the conduct of foreign affairs." He termed the legislative vetoes on sales to countries involved in blatant discrimination and human rights violations "misguided." He saw the arms sales ceiling—which would have frozen U.S. arms sales at levels that were nearly the highest that had ever been attained—as an "arbitrary" imposition that "limits our ability to respond to the legitimate defense needs of our friends and obstructs U.S. industry from competing fairly with foreign suppliers."[27]

A watered-down version of the bill was passed in June, but Humphrey and his colleagues had to give up a great deal to win Ford's approval. Among the provisions eliminated from the legislation was the $9 billion ceiling on U.S. arms transfers, which was transformed into a nonbinding "sense of Congress" that U.S. sales should not exceed then-current levels. Legislative vetoes based on considerations of human rights, violations of arms sales agreements by the recipient nation, unauthorized third-country transfers, and prohibitions on arms sales to nations harboring terrorists were all knocked down by Ford as well. That left only the original legislative veto power established under the Nelson amendment, with a notification period that had been increased to thirty calendar days from twenty. Even with all these concessions, Ford was leaning toward vetoing the legislation again, according to Bill Richardson, until Humphrey personally went to talk to him and persuaded him to sign it.

During the final congressional debates on the Arms Export Control Act, Sen. Edward Kennedy expressed his disappointment that "the President chose to veto the far stronger bill which we passed earlier this year." He pointed out that the new version of the bill was "only a modest extension of existing authority" but that "the key will be how we use that authority." He could not have imagined at the time that in the ensuing eighteen years, Congress would never successfully veto even one of the hundreds of arms deals presented to it by the executive branch. The threat of a veto has occasionally forced the president to scale down a particular package or hold off on a particular sale, but Congress has never actually voted down a sale once it has been formally notified of it.[28]

Despite this apparent congressional rubber stamp for arms deals, key figures involved in creating the legislative veto remain satisfied that it has served its purpose. Confronted with the fact that the legislative veto has never been used, former Gaylord Nelson staffer Paula Stern replied without hesitation, "That's the way it should be. . . . The idea was not to create confrontation, the idea was to create a consensus between the executive branch and Congress." She also said that officials on the NSC staff have indicated that the mere existence of a congressional veto has allowed them to "sort out the dogs [sales that never should have been proposed in the first place]," by arguing that "this will never fly with Congress." Bill Richardson seconded this point, maintaining that the legislative veto is "a source of deterrence in that the executive branch thinks twice before submitting a big package. . . . It's a source of restraint on what could [otherwise] in the long run be unlimited sales by the executive branch." And he added that in cases of big packages to Arab regimes like Saudi Arabia the threat of congressional action has been used "to at least temper the package, reduce the package. . . . But it's still a big package."

The role of Congress in reviewing arms sales under Humphrey's act is a far cry from the shared decisionmaking over major issues of war and peace that was envisioned in the Constitution. It appears that the Arms Export Control Act has over time had a more modest impact, ensuring that Congress is at least informed of most major arms sales and has a chance to chip away at the margins of the largest, most controversial deals. The evidence suggests that Humphrey, who included a chapter in his autobiography entitled "Compromise Is Not a Dirty Word," may have given up too much in his eagerness to get his pet legislation on the books.[29] And the majority of members of Congress since Humphrey's time have either been bought off by pork barrel lobbying on the part of defense contractors or have been too scared off by the popularity of chief executives like Ronald Reagan to use the Arms Export Control Act to curb the arms trade.

The inability of Congress to put an enforceable lid on runaway U.S. arms sales allowed a series of presidents to maintain the upper hand in arms sales decisions and limit congressional input to a handful of high-profile cases. But in 1976, it appeared that Congress had taken Humphrey's lead and reasserted its rightful authority on this life-and-death issue.

4

The Carter Policy: Why Not Restraint?

Jimmy Carter's long-shot bid for the presidency in 1976 often took on the appearance of a moral crusade rather than a traditional political campaign. Running as a Washington outsider and a born-again Christian, the relatively unknown governor of Georgia was staking his chances on his ability to convince voters that he was uniquely suited to the task of restoring morality to U.S. foreign policy and personal integrity to the White House in the wake of Vietnam and Watergate.

While Carter's most visible campaign theme was his pledge to place human rights at the center of U.S. foreign policy, the issue of curbing arms transfers was an important secondary theme. At a luncheon address to the Foreign Policy Association in New York on June 23, 1976, candidate Carter raised the issue of arms exports for the first time in a U.S. presidential campaign. He told his audience, an impressive collection of New York's business and political elite, that he was "particularly concerned by our nation's role as the world's leading arms salesman." He pulled no punches in his criticism of the Nixon/Ford policy of unrestrained arms dealing, attacking it as hypocritical: "The fact is that we cannot have it both ways. We cannot be both the world's leading champion of peace and the world's leading supplier of the weapons of war." No longer, implied Carter, could the president of the United States "justify this unsavory business on the cynical ground that by rationing out the means of violence we can somehow control the world's violence." Sounding like a committed disarmament campaigner, Carter promised, if elected, to "increase the emphasis on peace and reduce the commerce in arms."[1]

Carter's commitment to arms sales restraint was more than just a useful talking point to be trotted out before an audience of New York liberals. He made it a major theme of his fall election campaign against Gerald Ford, most notably during a nationally televised debate held in San Francisco on October 6, 1976. He vigorously criticized U.S. arms sales policy at four different points during the debate, calling the approach adopted during the early and mid-1970s "contrary to our longstanding beliefs and principles" as a nation. Carter made sure to lay the blame for runaway arms trading squarely on Nixon and Ford, noting that "when this Republican administration came into office we were shipping about $1 billion worth of arms overseas, [but] now we're shipping $10–12 billion overseas to countries that quite often use these weapons to fight each other." In his closing statement, Carter highlighted the issue one more time, arguing for an abrupt change of course in U.S. policy: "Can we become the breadbasket of the world instead of the arms merchant to the world? I believe we can and we ought to."[2]

While some observers dismissed Carter's high-minded rhetoric as grist for the campaign mill, arms industry executives sat up and took notice. They were horrified at Carter's anti-arms-sales stance. An influential lobbyist recalls that during the 1976 election, weapons-exporting firms felt the Democratic candidate was "getting a bit shrill on the subject of arms sales," leading to charges from the industry that "Jimmy Carter was interested in exporting morality and nothing else." In fact, he asserts that "the rhetoric of the election so scared the industry that they got themselves organized even before Carter was elected." These efforts led to the founding of the American League for Exports and Security Assistance (ALESA), an alliance of several dozen of the heaviest hitters in the defense industry, specifically devoted to promoting U.S. arms sales and preventing the implementation of the kinds of restrictions envisioned by Jimmy Carter. The first head of the organization was Richard DeLauer, a top executive at the TRW Corporation who later went on to become a high-ranking Pentagon official in the Reagan administration. ALESA members included the giants of the industry—General Dynamics, Lockheed, McDonnell Douglas, Raytheon, Rockwell International—along with lesser known suppliers like the Pneumo Abex Corporation and Bromon Aircraft Company. Even a few unions, most notably the International Brotherhood of Teamsters, signed onto the new lobbying organization. The arms industry's efforts were initiated too late to head off Carter's election in November 1976, but

ALESA itself was to outlast the Carter administration and play a significant role in subsequent battles over U.S. arms transfer policy.[3]

Upon taking office in January 1977, President Carter moved quickly to implement his campaign promise to exert U.S. leadership in putting the brakes on the "burgeoning traffic" in weapons of war. His prompt action on arms sales restraint was in sharp contrast to his later image as a wavering, indecisive leader. On this issue at least, Jimmy Carter was determined to make his mark, and without delay. By the end of January, less than two weeks after Carter's inauguration, Vice Pres. Walter Mondale had already been sent to Europe to make initial contact with key U.S. allies to assess their interest in participating in a multilateral initiative to curb the arms trade. And Secretary of State Cyrus Vance was put to work immediately on the development of new guidelines for U.S. arms exports.[4]

Vance's guidelines would take several months to draft, but Carter was not content to wait for their release. Both President Carter and Secretary of State Vance continued to stress the importance of arms transfer controls in public statements and discussions with foreign governments while the policy review was under way. This was not an issue that Carter intended to "study to death." It was not an item he planned to drop from his agenda after a decent interval once its "complexities" came into focus, as all too often happens as arms control proposals wend their way through the government's defense and foreign policy bureaucracies. Jimmy Carter fully intended to make good on his campaign rhetoric on arms sales, even if he had to take control of policy in this area personally.

At a March 5 press conference, just six weeks after taking his oath of office, Carter reaffirmed what one aide has described as his "deep personal commitment" to reining in American arms exports. He told reporters that he planned to take "a hard look" at the $12 billion a year in U.S. arms sales, because "I think that if there is one person in the government that ultimately has the responsibility to take a position and then explain the consequences of that decision to the American people, it's the President." He went on to report the he had "been in touch with the Soviet leaders, with the French leaders, and with the British to join with us in an effort to cut down on the quantity of arms sold throughout the world. And they've responded favorably so far." Carter concluded by underscoring his vision of arms sales reductions as part of a larger project of demilitarizing the U.S. economy and U.S. foreign relations: "I feel very strongly about this. And I believe that in the long run, our own economy and the world peace will be enhanced by shifting the production and expenditure of funds to other services or goods." This was Carter's way of letting it be known that he did not intend to be swayed from his course by the pork barrel arguments of the Pentagon and the defense contractors, who were experts at using the specter of lost jobs in key districts to scare members of Congress into voting for questionable weapons programs. Arms sales posed a similar problem, since in the era of post-Vietnam cuts in the Department of Defense budget it was often foreign sales that kept key weapons production lines in business. Carter had taken the rhetorical initiative by pointing to the long-term benefits of weaning the U.S. economy from its weapons fix, but he was not going to have the last word on this subject, as the industry and its allies in the Pentagon poised themselves for a political counterattack.[5]

Vance was no less committed to this new initiative than the president himself. He raised the issue of limiting regional arms purchases in a March 1977 tour of all the nations of the Middle East. Even more important, arms transfer restraint was one of the issues on the agenda when the new secretary of state held his first meeting with Soviet foreign minister Andrei Gromyko in Moscow later that month.

All this early activity put tremendous pressure on the Carter administration to deliver on its new policy direction. Two former administration officials who were directly involved in putting the arms transfer restraint policy into practice were only slightly overstating the case when they asserted that "by March 1977, the administration had staked its domestic and international reputation as a superpower on gaining concrete results on arms sales."[6]

This high-stakes commitment to making a difference on the arms sales issue was apparent in the tone of the final text of Carter's arms transfer policy statement, Presidential Directive 13 (P.D. 13), which was publicly released on May 19, 1977. The opening passages of the new pronouncement were if anything even more forthright and uncompromising than Carter's earlier statements on the subject.

> The virtually unrestrained spread of conventional weaponry threatens stability in every region of the world. . . . Each year the weapons transferred are not only more numerous but also more sophisticated and deadly. Because of the threat to world peace embodied in this spiralling arms traffic and because of the special responsibilities we bear as the largest arms seller, I believe that the United States must take steps to restrain its arms transfers.[7]

The statement went on to proclaim an outright reversal of the Nixon/Ford approach, whereby the president and his key foreign policy advisers were pushing arms exports at a rate that made even some officials in the Pentagon uncomfortable.

> I have concluded that the United States will henceforth view arms transfers as an exceptional foreign policy implement, to be used only in instances where it can be clearly demonstrated that the transfer contributes to our national security interests. . . . In the future the burden of persuasion will be on those who favor a particular arms sale, rather than those who oppose it.[8]

Presidential Directive 13 backed up this tough talk by introducing six new categories of controls over U.S. arms exports that were meant to guide all future executive branch decisionmaking on arms transfers. Through this vehicle, Carter was attempting to institutionalize his policy departure by means of what was in effect a sweeping executive order.

First, picking up on the legislative proposal that had been vetoed by Gerald Ford, Carter proposed a dollar ceiling on new orders of U.S. weaponry under the Pentagon's Military Assistance and Foreign Military Sales Programs. Sales of "weapons and weapons-related items" for 1978 would be targeted at a level below those attained for 1977. The aim of U.S. policy would be to continue to impose reductions on new U.S. weapons exports every year until the multibillion-dollar arms trading binge of the Nixon/Ford era was finally brought to a halt.

Second, in a move to stem regional arms races, Carter pledged that the United States would not be the first supplier to introduce advanced weapons systems that went beyond existing levels of military technology already present in a given region. In addition, no weapon would be sold to foreign buyers until it had "been operationally deployed with U.S. forces." This requirement was a direct response to the situation that had emerged under the Nixon blank check policy toward Iran, in which the military services and major contractors were falling all over each other in an effort to sell Iran systems like the F-14 and F-15 fighter planes before they were in service with U.S. forces. From the military's point of view, selling items so early was a convenient way to lower the unit costs of advanced systems by increasing the number of orders up front, but it also raised security concerns about the danger of these advanced systems falling into the hands of a hostile power. Carter was now sending a strong signal to the bureaucracy that foreign sales should no longer be viewed as a means of subsidizing development of expensive new weapons systems for U.S. forces.

Third, under Carter policy, the "development or significant modification of *advanced* weapons systems *solely for export*" would no longer be allowed, another indication that arms sales were to be the exception, not the rule.

Fourth, coproduction agreements, under which foreign recipients manufactured all or part of a U.S.-supplied system, would be eliminated for "significant weapons, equipment, and major components." One of the underlying dangers of the Nixon Doctrine had been the ease with which nations like Taiwan, South Korea, and Iran could get access to U.S. production technology, which threatened to make them arms suppliers in their own right, further fueling the international arms race. President Carter wanted to put a stop to this aspect of the trade, with the exception of some minor parts production and final assembly of U.S. systems overseas.

Fifth, in a further move to control the proliferation of U.S. arms technology, the United States would make it clear from the outset that for certain weapons systems, it would not "entertain any requests" for the later retransfer of that equipment to third countries. Controlling the ultimate destination of U.S.-supplied arms had always been a difficult task, and this provision was aimed to make it a viable option by putting U.S. concerns on the table when the initial sale was made.

Sixth and finally, regulations would be implemented "requiring policy level authorization by the Department of State for actions by agents of the United States or private manufacturers which might promote the sale of arms abroad." It would now be U.S. government policy that "embassies and military representatives abroad will not promote the sale of arms." This provision came to be known by critics in the industry and the arms sales bureaucracy as the "leprosy letter," as if Carter were instructing government personnel to avoid U.S. arms merchants like the plague. This flight of hyperbole was a measure of the industry's dismay at the prospect of losing the aggressive government support for its marketing efforts that it had come to expect during the golden years of the Nixon Doctrine.[9]

Taken as a whole, the Carter guidelines represented a remarkably comprehensive initiative to root out the arms sales addiction that had grown to dominate U.S. foreign policy during the Nixon/Ford period. By speaking both to large issues of policy, like what volume of arms the United States should sell in a given year, and to smaller but equally critical issues of day-to-day implementation, like how U.S. government personnel should interact with arms manufacturers seeking to sell weapons abroad, Carter's approach seemed to be setting the stage for an effective reversal of Nixon's pro-sales policy.

But the most important emphasis of the Carter policy directive was its commitment to exerting U.S. leadership toward a multilateral system of arms transfer restraints that would draw in the other major arms supplying nations. The changes in the way the United States planned to do business in the field of arms exports were carefully crafted with an eye toward encouraging other nations to adopt similar controls. Far from being a naive exercise in "unilateral restraint," as it was portrayed by industry and Pentagon critics, the Carter policy offered a way for the United States to lead by example, curbing its own exports while simultaneously discussing multilateral limits with other major supplier nations. Administration estimates put the U.S. share of the world arms market at roughly 50 percent, leading Jimmy Carter to observe that "because we dominate the market to such a degree, I believe that the United States can and should take the first step."

In four months of concentrated effort, the Carter administration had made an impressive start toward reining in the arms trade by completing a comprehensive review of policy, issuing detailed policy guidelines, and engaging in preliminary discussions on the issue with major arms suppliers and recipients.

Carter capped this first phase of his drive for export controls by making his arms transfer policy statement the centerpiece of his commencement address at Notre Dame on May 22, just a few days after the guidelines were formally released. Carter was relaxed and hopeful, stopping at the beginning to crack a few jokes before launching into his vision of a new U.S. leadership role in a rapidly changing world. On the arms trade in particular, Carter stated flatly that "competition in arms sales is inimical to peace and destructive of the economic development of poorer countries." He then went on to proudly tick off the six points of his new restraint policy.[10]

Unfortunately for arms control advocates, the release of P.D. 13 and its public unveiling at Notre Dame may well have marked the high point of Jimmy Carter's effort to slow down the trade in advanced instruments of war.

The Bureaucracy Fights Back

While Carter's personal commitment to arms transfer control appeared unshakable, elements of the national security and foreign policy bureaucracies were already quietly but effectively working to undermine the new policy even before its formal announcement. In anticipation of a decision to place a ceiling on future U.S. arms sales based on fiscal year 1977 levels, officials in the Pentagon and State Department hastily pushed through $4 billion in pending sales between January and March 1977, while the arms sales review was still under way. According to one State Department official who was directly involved in implementing the arms transfer control policy, "the bureaucracy conspired" behind Carter's back to render his arms sales ceiling meaningless and ineffectual. As a result, total orders for U.S. arms, training, and military services for 1977 exceeded $12 billion, a level comparable to the volume of sales during the last year of the Ford administration. And in the categories of sales specifically covered by the proposed ceiling—which were limited to transfers of weapons to the Third World in deals brokered by the Pentagon—the gap between Carter and Ford totals would be virtually indistinguishable. This behind-the-scenes tactical maneuvering meant that any policy of freezing or modestly reducing sales for fiscal year 1978 could now be readily accommodated without departing significantly from the levels that were generated during the Nixon/Ford boom years.[11]

A State Department official involved in implementing the arms transfer control policy said that Carter was "very angry when he found out" about this bureaucratic sleight of hand. The president responded by demanding to see *every* arms sales proposal from that point on, so that he could personally review and approve it. The arms export establishment had won an early skirmish, but, at least for the moment, Carter was not about to sit back and let them win the war.

Gen. Ernest Graves, who ran the Defense Security Assistance Agency, confirmed the point that the bureaucracy had effectively taken the teeth out of Carter's arms sales ceiling: "We had the ceiling but it never really affected the amount of sales. . . . It was set at such a level that we were able to make all the sales we wanted." He could recall only one sale that was affected by the ceiling in his four years on the job, a request from the shah of Iran for four costly combat ships, cruisers outfitted with the high-tech Aegis missile defense system. "Other than that, everyone went ahead and sold what they wanted to," according to Graves.

The CAT Talks: The Beginning of the End

While one part of the bureaucracy was hard at work undercutting Carter's arms transfer reduction initiative, another part, made up of presidential appointees who agreed with the goals of the new policy, was busy on the diplomatic front, initially without much success. Vice

President Mondale's early appeals to European leaders had been "summarily rebuffed," according to one inside account, and Leslie Gelb, head of the State Department's Bureau of Politico-Military Affairs, recalls that when he visited European capitals later in the year to press for participation in arms transfer reduction talks, his requests were "greeted with laughter." The Europeans pointed to U.S. dominance of the market, in which it was outselling each of the major European suppliers by a four-to-one or greater margin, and suggested that the United States first try to reach agreement with the Soviets on limiting sales, and then get back to them.[12]

Somewhat to the surprise of U.S. officials, the Soviets not only agreed to talk but actually seemed ready to engage in serious negotiations. The resulting bilateral discussions came to be known as the Conventional Arms Transfer (CAT) talks.

After a getting-to-know-you meeting in December 1977 that U.S. chief negotiator Gelb described as "perfunctory," the pace began to pick up in 1978. At the next meeting, in May 1978, the two sides issued a joint communiqué declaring that "the problem of limiting international transfers of arms is urgent" and tying the talks to the commitments made during the 1972 Strategic Arms Limitation Treaty (SALT) negotiations to seek a "cessation of the arms race."[13]

By the third meeting, held in July 1978, the U.S. and Soviet negotiating teams had agreed that the framework of an arms transfer restraint regime should encompass the following elements: common political and legal criteria for deciding who should receive arms; common guidelines on what kinds of arms should be limited; and mutually agreed-upon mechanisms for implementing restraints within major regions. This consensus on how to proceed appeared to have set the stage for productive negotiations on specific control measures at the next session of the talks. Proposals had already been put on the table that would limit the transfer of weapons easily diverted for use by terrorists (such as shoulder-fired antiaircraft missiles) and curb the sale of weapons that could have indiscriminate effects on civilian populations (such as cluster bombs and napalm). As Barry Blechman, the deputy chairman of the U.S. delegation, described this stage of the talks, "We made progress because we'd make a proposal, and the Soviets would eventually agree to it." In his view, the Soviets were being so agreeable because they saw the CAT talks as an investment in a continued "warming" of U.S.–Soviet relations. Whatever the reason, the CAT talks were beginning to look like they might actually succeed.

One sticking point in the talks so far had been Soviet reluctance to engage in discussions about limiting sales to specific regions, an approach favored by U.S. chief negotiator Leslie Gelb. But in the wake of the July 1978 meeting, the Soviets reversed their position and agreed to regional discussions. The United States had been pushing for negotiations on limiting transfers to Latin America and sub-Saharan Africa, areas where the volume of U.S. sales was small but where the Soviets had important commitments to clients such as the socialist regimes in Cuba and Angola. The Soviets had a different idea about which regions warranted priority discussion—they were much more concerned about the arming of nations on or near their borders, and they proposed discussions of sales to the Persian Gulf and Asia. They were particularly concerned about closing the door to possible Western arms sales to their communist rival China, which had been gradually improving its ties with the United States since the Nixon/Kissinger "opening" in 1972. Talks about the Persian Gulf and Asia had the added advantage of dealing with the two areas that accounted for the vast bulk of arms sales to the Third World, over three-quarters of the total.

In a visit to Moscow in the fall of 1978, Gelb held to the U.S. position that regional talks should initially focus on Latin America and Africa, but he told his Soviet counterpart, Lev Mendelevich, that the United States would entertain discussion of other regions at the next round of talks scheduled for December 1978 in Mexico City. Both Gelb and Blechman felt that major strides had been achieved in just over a year of discussions, and Gelb told a congressional committee that there was now a "realistic possibility" that Americans and Soviets could agree on common guidelines for restraining their arms sales to the Third World, guidelines that could then be used as the basis for recruiting major European suppliers as well.

Gelb's optimism did not take into account the intervention of Zbigniew Brzezinski, President Carter's hard-line national security adviser. Brzezinski had stayed out of the CAT talks, but now that there was the prospect of real progress he forcibly inserted himself into the debates over how to proceed. He was adamantly opposed to regional talks. First, he felt that even the discussion of limits on sales to the Persian Gulf would be perceived as a sign that the United States was distancing itself from the shah of Iran, who was facing a growing challenge to his rule from internal opponents. Second, unbeknownst to the U.S. negotiating team, Brzezinski was in the final stages of a secret effort to normalize American relations with China, and he wanted to have a free hand to offer them military technology in exchange for increased cooperation in countering Soviet global policies. And last but certainly not least, Brzezinski involved himself in the CAT process as a way to "get at Vance," as one former State Department official put it.

The talks were caught up in the larger battle between Brzezinski and Vance for control of U.S. foreign policy, which centered on their contrasting views of U.S.–Soviet relations. Vance favored continuing diplomatic initiatives and negotiations with the Soviet leadership on issues such as strategic arms and regional conflicts, while Brzezinski was pressing an increasingly confrontational, Cold War strategy. The issue of regional discussions was Brzezinski's handle for trying to overturn the whole Carter arms transfer restraint policy. As one Carter staffer put it, "Brzezinski hated the policy, so he used this issue to kill the talks." On the CAT talks, as in so many other areas of Carter's foreign policy, the hard-line views of the president's national security adviser would ultimately win out.[14]

Brzezinski's ability to derail the arms sales limitation talks was enhanced because Cyrus Vance was not paying much attention to the negotiations. Leslie Gelb, the assistant secretary of state for politico-military affairs, was running the talks. Gelb later remarked that to put someone at his level in the bureaucratic hierarchy in charge of the initiative was in itself a telling indication that the talks were not a high priority for the Carter foreign policy team. Even Gelb delegated most of the detail work on the CAT negotiations to a group of fairly low-level staffers at the Arms Control and Disarmament Agency. As one former ACDA staffer who worked on the talks put it, "We did the scut work. . . . It was stuff no self-respecting GS-15 would commit themselves to doing." Because the principal background work on the arms transfer control initiative had fallen to this group of relatively young junior staffers, some administration insiders referred to them as "the Mod Squad."

While Vance was preoccupied with other issues, such as the ongoing SALT II nuclear arms limitation negotiations with the Soviet Union, Brzezinski made his move. He had recruited Secretary of Defense Harold Brown to his side of the argument, and Brown soon began echoing Brzezinski's position that even the most preliminary, theoretical talks about the possibility of eventual limitations on arms transfers to China or the Persian Gulf would jeopardize U.S. interests in those areas. Winning Brown's support was no small matter, for as one former Carter official noted, once his secretary of defense sided with his national security adviser, the president generally went with their position.

The issue came to a head at a series of meetings of the Special Coordination Committee (SCC) of the NSC, the interagency group responsible for U.S. negotiating strategy for the Mexico meetings. The debate was heated, to put it mildly. For example, at one meeting, as Brown warmed to the theme of why discussions about reining in Persian Gulf arms sales might undermine the shah of Iran, ACDA deputy director Barry Blechman shouted from the back of the room, "Harold, you don't really believe that!" But unfortunately, as Blechman later acknowledged, Jimmy Carter himself had accepted Brzezinski's dubious thesis that "somehow even discussing Soviet proposals to limit sales to the Persian Gulf would undermine the Shah and cause further instability." The president's headstrong national security adviser had clearly gained the upper hand in his latest bureaucratic battle.

Finally, at the SCC meeting on November 27, just a few weeks before the Mexico round of talks was set to begin, Brzezinski pulled out all the stops, arguing that the U.S. delegation should be instructed to break off negotiations if the Soviets so much as mentioned controlling the arms flow to the Persian Gulf or East Asia. Gelb countered that the U.S. side was obliged at least to listen to Soviet proposals on these regions, even if they went on to reject them. To do otherwise would contradict the promise made by the United States to the Soviets in the previous round of the talks.

Brzezinski's view prevailed. Gelb and the members of his team left for Mexico with explicit instructions to "leave the table and walk out if the words 'Persian Gulf' were even mentioned," as one member of the delegation put it. According to another participant in the talks, these instructions were "unprecedented in negotiating history" because of the way they tied the hands of the U.S. delegation in advance. To avoid any misunderstanding (and to thwart any possibility of making progress), Gelb was told to inform the lead Soviet negotiator, Mendelevich, of the change in U.S. position before sitting down for the formal talks. When Gelb took Mendelevich aside to explain this 180-degree turn, the Soviet negotiator laughed out loud and said, "You're joking." But once it was clear that this was in fact the new U.S. stance, an angry Mendelevich put in a call to Soviet ambassador to the United States Anatoly Dobrynin asking whether they could proceed with discussions dealing only with sales to Latin America and Africa. He later informed Gelb that Dobrynin had been willing to proceed even on these terms, but in the meantime Vance had suggested to his Soviet counterpart that they table *all* regional discussions. The secretary of state apparently felt that the issue could cause an "explosion" that would harm the overall pattern of U.S.–Soviet ties, and he was willing to let the CAT talks stall rather than risk their degenerating into a sore spot between the two superpowers. According to Gelb, even under the onus of Brzezinski's efforts to scuttle the talks, "we could have gotten somewhere" if Vance hadn't given up on the negotiations.[15]

The remaining time in Mexico was rather strained as the two delegations alternated between cooling their heels at the pool and trying to make some headway on technical military and arms control issues raised by the talks. As one U.S. participant described it, "We sat around in Mexico for a week doing nothing." Gelb sent a series of cables to Brzezinski seeking some flexibility in the U.S. position, but to no avail. Even this lower level of activity was too much for Brzezinski, who sent an imperious cable to Gelb threatening to remove him as head of the U.S. delegation because of his "inability to follow the President's instructions." The appropriate person to deliver such a message would have been Warren Christopher, Gelb's superior in the State Department chain of command, not the president's national security adviser, but this was a classic example of Brzezinski's one-man, cowboy style of bureaucratic infighting, so similar to that of his Republican rival and predecessor, Henry Kissinger. Gelb replied that he would come back to Washington and leave Blechman in charge of the talks. Since Blechman was as committed an arms controller as Gelb, Brzezinski opted not to recall Gelb, but the negotiating team's rigid, self-defeating instructions did not change.

On the last day of the Mexico meetings, the members of the U.S. delegation were presented with a bracing reminder of just how far out of the bureaucratic loop their efforts had fallen. Over breakfast they were shocked to read the headlines announcing "U.S. Recognizes People's Republic of China." Brzezinski's secret talks had borne fruit, and his second major reason for intervening to thwart the CAT talks—along with the publicly acknowledged motive of bolstering the shah of Iran—now became clear. He wanted to be free to offer future arms and military technology sales to China as an inducement to closer U.S.-Chinese relations, unencumbered by any agreements struck with the Soviets by those pesky arms controllers at the State Department. As one ACDA staffer later summed it up, "There was no way that Brzezinski was going to let what he perceived as a bunch of mid-level, preoccupied flakes . . . impinge on one of his most central foreign policy initiatives."

Within a few months of the Mexico meeting, the CAT talks were a dead issue, for all practical purposes. Despite his bitter battles with Brzezinski, chief U.S. negotiator Leslie Gelb laid the blame for the failure of the talks elsewhere: on the president himself. In an interview in the spring of 1991, Gelb noted it was Carter that "started them in motion, then abandoned them." Bureaucratically, the talks "became an orphan," said Gelb. "I only wish that President Carter hadn't let Zbig destroy what could have been a useful, long-term enterprise . . . that could have headed off a lot of the problems we now face in areas such as missile proliferation."[16]

Carter's Contradictions: Trading Arms for Influence

The demise of the CAT talks marked the beginning of the end of the Carter arms transfer restraint policy, but the warning signs were evident much earlier. And while there was no question that part of the problem was that hard-liners like Brzezinski and midlevel bureaucrats in the Pentagon and State Department were working diligently to sidetrack this historic initiative, the president's own contradictory views on the issue were equally part of the problem. While no one close to Carter questioned his depth of commitment to promoting human rights and controlling runaway arms sales, his rather traditional views of what constituted U.S. national security interests and his willingness to use arms transfers in pursuit of other military and foreign policy objectives soon overwhelmed his personal convictions about the need for arms sales restraint. He supported the notion of curbing U.S. arms exports, but not if it undermined relations with influential regional allies like the shah of Iran, not if it jeopardized U.S. access to military bases in critical areas like the Persian Gulf, and not if it stood in the way of promoting long-standing goals like the Israeli–Egyptian peace accords. The result was that Carter would agonize over arms sales decisions, but more often than not he would end up approving sales to traditional U.S. allies.

The process itself was revealing. Woolf Gross, who worked as a politico-military adviser to the assistant secretary of state for the Near East and South Asia throughout the Carter administration, was involved in preparing memos on potential sales for the president's review and approval. As Gross describes it, the memos would come to the White House on "long sheets, like toilet paper," with rationales for "each reportable arms sale." Gross says that the memos would generally come back marked with the president's approval, but also "with the philosophy of Jimmy Carter with respect to a particular sale scribbled in the margins." Leslie Gelb confirms this point, noting that "there was a box at the bottom of each [arms sales offer] for him to check—approve or disapprove—and he'd write over the box and in the margins until he ran out of space." Gelb felt strongly that "this was no way for the president to spend his time." Gross, who later went on to become a vice president for international marketing at the Northrop Corporation, attributed the practice to Carter's "good Baptist, better every day in every way" outlook, combined with a conviction that the U.S. policymakers should "wear our very own hairshirt and protect our exporters from exporting." Philosophical scribblings aside, Gross maintains that arms sales were on the whole cleared more quickly and in larger quantities under Carter's hands-on approach than even in the heyday of the subsequent Reagan administration's aggressive arms sales promotion policy.

Ultimately, the reason Carter was able to swallow his moral qualms and keep U.S. arms flowing overseas at rates comparable to those reached at the height of the Nixon/Ford era was that for all his protestations, he still seemed to believe that arms sales were an appropriate tool for shoring up allies like the beleaguered shah of Iran, maintaining a "balance of power" in volatile regions like the Middle East, and paving the way for U.S. military intervention by maintaining influence with nations that could supply military facilities and support to U.S. forces in a crisis. In most cases these seemingly pragmatic short-term objectives—the comfortable, pat formulations of the foreign policy bureaucracy—took precedence over Carter's concerns about the role of weapons transfers in fueling regional arms races, supporting human rights abuses, and fostering unnecessary military buildups in impoverished developing nations. Carter might grumble that the United States was selling too many arms, but when push came to shove he almost always said yes.[17]

The first test case of the Carter policy came barely a month after it had been announced, when a request from the shah of Iran to purchase ten advanced Boeing Airborne Warning and Control System (AWACS) aircraft landed on his desk. In the words of Gary Sick, an Iran specialist who served on Carter's NSC, the administration's "overriding consideration" with respect to relations with Iran was to "ensure that the cooperative relationship that had been developed over nearly four decades would be preserved and that Iran would remain a strong, reliable and friendly ally in the vital region in the Persian Gulf." Furthermore, he stressed, "the importance of the security relationship was paramount—even if that relationship should require some accommodation in the areas of human rights or arms limitations."[18] Carter administration officials were willing to wink at the shah's human rights abuses and indulge his overdeveloped appetite for armaments as long as he kept playing his part as "guardian of the oil lanes" and protector of the conservative, pro-U.S. monarchies of the Persian Gulf region.

Carter received a memo from the NSC urging him to approve the sale on the grounds that the shah needed an air defense system and that the AWACS would ultimately be cheaper to maintain and staff than a more cumbersome, land-based air defense system requiring major construction throughout the country. The memo also took note of opposition to the sale, particularly within the State Department, where a number of analysts felt that it would undercut the new arms transfer directive before it had a chance to get off the ground. Carter turned the memo around in less than twenty-four hours, approving the sale but crossing out the number "ten" and writing in "seven" instead. This "70 percent solution" was seen by Gary Sick and some others in the national security bureaucracy as a clear signal that "the days of the blank checks were over: the United States would exercise its own judgment in reviewing Iran's requests, even if that meant occasional disagreements with the Shah."[19]

This nuanced and perhaps somewhat self-serving view of Carter's decision to make a multibillion-dollar sale of the most advanced radar aircraft in the world to the Iranian dictator was lost on key members of Congress and arms control supporters within the executive branch, who rightly saw it as a glaring contravention of the policy Carter had just finished enunciating so eloquently and passionately. Barry Blechman felt that the AWACS sale "so blatantly contradicted the policy that it sent the wrong signal to the bureaucracy—wait it out, and there will be an exception made." Congress commissioned a study of the proposed sale by the General Accounting Office (GAO), which found that the AWACS, a radar plane that provides surveillance and targeting data to other aircraft, could just as easily be employed by the shah in an offensive air strike as it could in a defensive mode. In addition, word leaked out to the press that CIA director Stansfield Turner had expressed concern about the possibility of the Iranian AWACS falling into Soviet hands.

The depth of potential congressional opposition to the sale became clear on July 22, when Senate majority leader Robert Byrd sent a letter to President Carter urging him to withdraw the AWACS offer, citing his security concerns about how the shah might use such an advanced system and what would happen if it fell into the "wrong hands" (by which he meant either the Soviets or a radical group inside Iran). Carter was undeterred, and he swiftly sent back a letter to his fellow Democrat making it clear that he had no intention of withdrawing the Iranian sale.[20]

But Carter soon had a change of heart. Six days later, the House International Relations Committee passed a resolution of disapproval on the Iranian AWACS sale—an extremely unusual occurrence—by a vote of 19 to 17. In the meantime, several influential members of the Senate Foreign Relations Committee sent the president a letter urging, as Robert Byrd had done, that he withdraw the offer to sell sophisticated radar planes to the shah. The senators also suggested a number of restrictions that should be placed on the program if the sale were to go ahead, including the following:

> [T]hat the planes would not include certain sensitive encipherment equipment; that security arrangements be developed to insure adequate protection of the Iranian AWACS; that the AWACS only be used for defensive purposes; that the "multiplier" effect of the AWACS be taken into account in considering future sales to Iran; that cadre training of Iranian crews take place entirely in the United States, and that no U.S. personnel would be on AWACS operational flights; and that a study be conducted on Iran's capacity to absorb high technology defense items.[21]

Sensing a possible defeat in both the House and Senate, Carter decided to withdraw the Iranian AWACS from consideration until after the summer recess, to give the administration time to regroup and find a strategy for winning congressional support.

On September 7 the sale was reintroduced, and in Senate hearings two weeks later Carter administration witnesses assured a Foreign Relations Committee panel that the shah had agreed to all of the conditions set out in the senators' July letter. By thus bowing to congressional sensitivities, Carter enlisted senators Clifford Case and Hubert Humphrey, who sent letters to each of their colleagues urging them to support the AWACS sale now that "the assurances we have requested have been agreed to." They were able to win over their colleagues, and Congress took no further action in opposition to the sale.

Given the complete lack of congressional participation in arms sales decisionmaking during the Nixon era, many Capitol Hill insiders considered this diplomatic dance between the Carter administration and the Senate a sort of victory for the Congress; in the words of one analyst, it resulted in "Congress having an input" on the "scope" of the Iranian AWACS sale.[22] But from a broader perspective, what had Congress really accomplished? The shah was getting his AWACS, and the promises about how they would be used were by and large beyond the ability of Congress to verify or monitor. Humphrey and his colleagues had traded the illusion of "input" and "consultation" for the real exercise of power that would have come from vetoing the sale.

The fight over the Iranian AWACS deal foreshadowed a depressingly familiar pattern in which Congress routinely gave in to the president on even the most ill-advised weapons sales, in return for a few paper conditions and the illusion that Congress was being meaningfully consulted.

For those in the Carter White House, the lesson learned from the AWACS fight was that they had to cultivate Congress and control the terms of debate from the outset if they wanted a smoother ride for controversial arms sales offers in the future. They were going to need all the tactical skill they could muster for the next big sale, the Saudi–Israeli–Egyptian "jet package" of 1978. The deal was a spillover from the Nixon/Ford years, when Secretary of State Kissinger pushed Gerald Ford to support the sale of McDonnell Douglas F-15 fighter aircraft to Saudi Arabia. Ford had agreed in principle to make the sale before going down to defeat in the 1976 presidential elections. In a pattern that was to repeat itself time and again in the post–Nixon Doctrine era of U.S. arms sales policy, an incoming president had inherited significant arms sales commitments that he felt hard-pressed to reverse for fear of rupturing relations with a long-standing ally.

Upon taking office, Carter agonized briefly over the F-15 sale, but his doubts were overcome by advice from the Pentagon, State Department, and NSC to the effect that "the U.S.–Saudi relationship could not stand a policy reversal on the F-15 sale," in the words of one congressional study on the deal. In a variation on the themes that had been used to sustain virtually unregulated sales to the shah of Iran, the Saudis' control of critical oil resources, their support of conservative forces in the Middle East, and their use of their growing financial clout on behalf of U.S. interests were all considered more important than stopping the Middle East arms race. When Crown Prince Fahd visited Washington in May 1977, Carter personally informed him that he would honor Ford's pledge to sell F-15s to Saudi Arabia. This behind-the-scenes commitment came just weeks before Carter's arms transfer control policy was to be formally announced.[23]

With the fight with Congress over the Iranian AWACS fresh in their minds, Carter strategists decided to wait for the right political moment to introduce the Saudi F-15 sale. And in an attempt to blunt potential criticism that the sale would be detrimental to Israel, with which the Saudis were still technically in a state of war, it was decided that the sale would be presented to Congress as part of a package including seventy F-16 and F-15 fighters for Israel, sixty F-15s for the Saudis, and fifty Northrop F-5Es for Egypt. On February 14, 1978, the three-part deal was announced to the public and the Congress, and a week later Secretary of State Vance made it clear that the administration would treat the deal as a package: if one part was turned down, they would withdraw the other two parts as well. In this way it was hoped that supporters of Israel in the Congress would be able to swallow the sale to Saudi Arabia knowing that Israel would be receiving a larger number of aircraft in its part of the package.

At first blush, the gambit of giving Congress the three separate plane sales in an all-or-nothing package seemed like it might backfire. Key members were highly critical of a move they viewed as a manipulative, strong-arm tactic. A flurry of resolutions was introduced in both the House and Senate against all three of the sales. By early May it appeared that the administration's chances of heading off defeat in the House were extremely poor, and the White House lobbying effort shifted to the Senate. Since the Arms Export Control Act required a majority of both houses of Congress to reverse an arms sale, a victory for Carter's position in the Senate would be enough to keep the deal on track.

Sources in the Senate indicated that "the critical factor in altering the outcome of the debate" was a May 9 letter from Secretary of Defense Harold Brown to Senate Foreign Relations Committee chairman John Sparkman of Alabama. In the letter, Brown promised that the Saudis would not base their new F-15s within striking distance of Israel and that the United States would not supply the Saudis with bomb racks, advanced air-to-air missiles, or aerial refueling equipment "that would increase the range or enhance the ground attack capability of the F-15."[24] Brown's assurances won over Sen. Abraham Ribicoff of Connecticut, a strong supporter of Israel. Ribicoff's lobbying efforts, along with those of Republican minority leader Howard Baker of Tennessee, were enough to defeat the main resolution against the plane package by a 54-to-44 margin. A senior Carter aide cited "timing and format" as the keys to winning congressional acceptance of the sale, indicating that administration insiders had known from the outset "that it would be a bloody battle."[25] So, in an attempt to buy political loyalty and leverage in the Middle East via arms sales, Jimmy Carter took another giant step toward abandoning his policy of restraint.

The fall of the shah of Iran in December 1978 at the hands of his own people should have punctured a huge hole in the notion that supplying arms to U.S. friends was the key to stability and a balance of power, but Carter administration policymakers, increasingly dominated by Zbigniew Brzezinski, were blind to these lessons of the Iranian revolution. The shah could not have been more heavily armed, but his ability to serve as a pro-U.S. policeman of the Gulf and a firebreak against Soviet intervention (an unlikely prospect in any event) was swept aside by a popular rebellion fueled by his repressive policies, rampant corruption in his inner circle, and vast inequalities of wealth and income that were being accelerated by his grandiose military industrialization strategy. The end result of nearly a decade of giving the shah almost any weapons system he could pay for was not the stability advertised by the Nixon/Ford and Carter administrations but rather the ushering in of an Islamic fundamentalist, profoundly anti-U.S. regime headed by the Ayatollah Khomeini, who had been campaigning against unfair U.S. influence and privileges in Iran for over two decades. This regime now controlled billions of dollars' worth of U.S.-supplied ships, fighter aircraft, helicopters, and artillery—an object lesson regarding the folly of relying on arms sales as a central pillar of U.S. foreign policy.

The fall of the shah yielded quite a different lesson for Carter's foreign policy advisers. With the exception of Cyrus Vance, who held firm on the need for diplomacy as the leading edge of U.S. policy, there was a headlong rush toward military solutions that soon became a stampede when the Soviets invaded Afghanistan in December 1979. The president who had once spoken of curbing arms sales and promoting world peace now reverted to a classic Cold War stance. A new "Carter Doctrine" was proclaimed, announcing to the world that the U.S. would counter any attempt to wrest control of the Persian Gulf oil fields from its chosen allies in the region "with military force, if necessary." To carry out this threat, the Pentagon was fast at work assembling a "rapid deployment force" with the capability of putting two hundred thousand U.S. troops anywhere in the world on short notice. And to support this new interventionary force, Carter policymakers made ample use of arms transfers to the Middle East, offering increased military assistance to countries like Kenya, Oman, and Somalia in exchange for their willingness to give U.S. forces access to their military facilities in the event of a U.S. invasion of the Middle East. Far from replacing direct intervention, as had been promised under the Nixon Doctrine, arms transfers were now being used to facilitate U.S. intervention—a worst-of-both-worlds scenario in which the United States would not only intervene in regions like the Middle East but would continue to fuel arms races that would put any U.S. interventionary force at grave risk.[26]

In the end, Carter succumbed to the host of strategic and political rationales for arms exports underlying the Nixon Doctrine. And, in an Orwellian twist, he even used arms exports to win support for what many observers see as his principal contribution to peace, the Camp

David accords. Amidst all the euphoria over the historic effort to bring Egypt and Israel together in negotiations, and the successful conclusion of a bilateral peace treaty, there was very little questioning of the underpinnings of the deal. The Camp David accords were sealed with $4.5 billion in arms credits for Israel and Egypt, paving the way for Egypt to become a new, post-shah surrogate in the Middle East even as Israel was kept one step ahead with its own yearly infusion of U.S. arms and technology. General Graves, who helped draw up the list of U.S. military equipment that Egypt would receive in return for signing onto the peace agreement, argued persuasively that it was Camp David that marked the end of efforts to cut back on weapons exports: "That was when the Carter policy was trashed. . . . All of this kind of put an end to the notion that arms transfers aren't the way to pursue international goals, because they were at the heart of this."[27]

The transformation of the Camp David peace accords into yet another opportunity to push U.S. arms overseas was the final nail in the coffin of Carter's arms sales restraint program, the tragic flaw in his quest for a negotiated peace in the region. For while the accords brought peace between Egypt and Israel, they also kept alive a Middle East arms race that would continue to break out in a series of civil wars and intercountry conflicts over the next dozen years, from Lebanon to the Iran–Iraq war to the Gulf War of 1990–91.

Jimmy Carter, a president as morally and philosophically opposed to trafficking in advanced armaments as any chief executive in U.S. history, was ultimately no match for the twisted strategic logic and inbred economic and political rationales that made selling arms a seemingly natural tool of U.S. foreign policy. It remained for Ronald Reagan to take Carter's disappointing turn toward trading arms for influence and transform it from an embarrassing contradiction of stated U.S. policy into an unabashedly celebrated instrument of U.S. relations with the rest of the world.

5

Reagan's Supply Side Foreign Policy

After a campaign built on the twin themes of cutting taxes and ensuring that the United States would once again "stand tall" and play a decisive role on the world stage, Ronald Reagan took office with a straightforward policy agenda. He was going to erase the sense of "malaise," "weakness," and "vacillation" that popular mythology had ascribed to the Carter presidency, and he was going to do so using a few simple tools.

On the domestic front, Reagan was going to apply the theory of supply side economics to cure inflation and stimulate growth. This approach, suggested by the work of a little-known economist named Arthur Laffer, involved at best a tremendous leap of faith, at worst a massive case of false advertising. The core of supply side theory was the notion that the government could increase its overall revenues by cutting tax rates. The removal of the heavy hand of government, it was said, would liberate the forces of enterprise and enthusiasm among workers and business owners alike to such a degree that there would be an unprecedented spurt of economic growth. This in turn would allow the government to collect more revenues, even with its new, lower tax rates, because the economy as a whole would be growing so much faster. The budget would be balanced, businesses would keep more of their profits, workers would keep more of their wages, and everyone would prosper happily ever after, or so the story went.

Despite its serious flaws as an economic policy, supply side theory meshed perfectly with Reagan's upbeat, simplistic worldview. By seeming to offer abundant benefits with little or no sacrifice, it met the requirements of the new president's policy of conservatism with a human face. Never mind that the nation was soon plunged into the deepest recession since the 1930s, or that the federal government ran up more debt under Reagan than under all prior U.S. administrations combined, or that the ranks of the poor swelled to their highest levels since the late 1950s and early 1960s, before the advent of major federal antipoverty programs. In Reagan's narrow field of political vision, supply side economics was bound to work, and he wasn't going to abandon it just because of evidence to the contrary, no matter how glaring. Any unpleasant news that didn't fit the predictions of supply side theory was the fault either of his predecessor, Jimmy Carter, or of the news media, which Reaganites accused of constantly harping on the negative. At the height of the 1982 recession, the mean-spirited side of Reagan's outlook was briefly glimpsed when he berated the major television networks for treating it like national news every time "some fellow out in South Succotash someplace has just been laid off."[1]

This willfully unrealistic approach to domestic economic policy had a counterpart in the Reagan foreign policy, where the administration turned to arms sales as an all-purpose solution to even the most complex strategic and political problems. To the Reagan foreign policy team, selling weapons to "friendly" nations was a quick, convenient way to get tough with the Soviets and their purported allies in the Third World without having to risk U.S. lives or taxpayer dollars that direct military intervention would entail. By appearing to offer all gain with no pain—exerting military influence without resorting to full-scale war—weapons exports were the foreign policy equivalent of Reagan's rosy "supply side economics" scenario for domestic policy.

Like his economic strategy, the Reagan "supply side foreign policy" concealed serious long-term risks beneath its upbeat rhetoric: the risk of an unending string of military entanglements abroad, and the risk of permanently undermining the democratic process at home.

El Salvador: The "Textbook Case"

It fell to Secretary of State Alexander Haig, a former Kissinger protégé and commander of NATO with an ego large enough to fill the White House, to fire the first shot in the administration's drive to use arms shipments as the centerpiece of its new, "get tough" foreign policy. Haig was in charge of the release of "Communist Interference in

El Salvador," a State Department White Paper made public in February 1981, barely a month after Reagan took office. It provided a capsule view of the administration's mind-set on the subject of arms transfers and revealed the willingness of Reagan policymakers to resort to distortion, manipulation, and outright lies in promoting weapons exports to their chosen allies.

The State Department report made stunning charges of an international conspiracy to supply insurgents fighting against the U.S.-backed regime in El Salvador with "nearly 800 tons of the most modern weapons and equipment," of which "nearly 200 tons" were allegedly delivered through Cuba and Nicaragua in time for the Salvadoran guerrillas' highly touted "final offensive" against the government in January 1981. Hearkening back to the harshest anticommunist rhetoric of the Cold War, Haig described the Soviet–Cuban–Nicaraguan arms shipments alleged in the White Paper as a "textbook case of indirect armed aggression by Communist powers through Cuba." The Reagan administration's proposed solution was to send $20 million in emergency arms aid to the Salvadoran regime, a sum greater than all U.S. military assistance to that nation for the previous twenty years combined. And in his typical dramatic style, Haig went further, darkly hinting at a press conference that it might ultimately be necessary to "go to the source" to stop the arms flow to El Salvador, a veiled reference to possible military action against Cuba.[2]

The press and the Congress were by and large taken in by the White Paper and the accompanying briefings. Pentagon officials displayed hazy photographs of trucks alleged to have carried weapons into El Salvador and brandished captured documents purported to represent the Salvadoran guerrillas' weapons shopping list. Every conceivable U.S. "enemy" of the past four decades, from Vietnam to the Soviet Union to Czechoslovakia to the Palestine Liberation Organization, was portrayed as part of a worldwide arms supply network for the "communist insurgency" in El Salvador. One of the few areas in which the Carter human rights policy had actually slowed the flow of U.S. weaponry was now being transformed into a test of the Reagan foreign policy team's resolve in combating global communism.

But somehow, the administration's case seemed almost too neat, too convenient. If the arms supply scheme was truly so massive, why hadn't it been noticed before? And if sophisticated weapons had already been delivered to the Salvadoran guerrillas, why did reporters like Ray Bonner of the *New York Times*, who traveled with the rebels, report that in large parts of the country the rebel forces were still armed with World War II–era rifles?[3] Last but not least, there were questions about the "captured documents" that formed such a compelling part of the Pentagon and State Department briefings on the arms flow to El Salvador. Would a guerrilla army in the field really keep such a detailed ledger of its arms purchases and carry it around where it could be lost or captured in battle?

Jonathan Kwitny of the *Wall Street Journal* was one of the first journalists to ask these and other potentially embarrassing questions. After several months of digging, he managed to set up an interview with Jon D. Glassman, the State Department analyst who had actually written the White Paper. Amazingly, given the credibility the document had received in the media up to that point, Glassman openly acknowledged that important parts of it were "misleading" and "overembellished." In a front-page piece that ran on June 9, 1981, nearly four months after the White Paper release, Kwitny provided a damning critique of the main piece of "evidence" used to justify the U.S. rush to arm the military-dominated junta in El Salvador.

First, how did Glassman come up with the estimate of two hundred tons of arms shipped to the Salvadoran guerrillas via Nicaragua? The initial impression given by the Reagan administration had been that these numbers had come directly from documents captured from Salvadoran guerrilla forces. In fact, Glassman admitted, none of the documents mentioned receiving the massive amounts of armaments cited so authoritatively in the White Paper—these figures were "extrapolated" from intelligence data. How had this been done? Well, Glassman explained, there were indications of increased air traffic between Cuba and Nicaragua in the year leading up to the Salvadoran guerrillas' January 1981 offensive, so it was assumed that all this activity represented the shipment of weapons destined for El Salvador. In addition, one of the alleged guerrilla documents made reference to four cargo-carrying trucks, so an estimate was made of how much weaponry one of these trucks could hold. It was then assumed that these trucks were in fact carrying weapons, and their estimated capacity was multiplied by how many trips might have been made. The result of this totally speculative exercise was the State Department's "definitive" estimate of two hundred tons of weaponry shipped to the Salvadoran guerrilla forces.

In short, there was no hard evidence of huge arms shipments. It had been concocted by Glassman and his colleagues to fit the urgent need of the new Reagan administration to justify a major increase in U.S. military aid to the government of El Salvador.

Finally, what about the famous captured documents? For starters, widespread attributions of specific passages from the documents to

Salvadoran Communist Party leader Shafik Handal and a guerrilla leader named Ana Guadalupe Martinez were simply false. The State Department had no idea who had written the documents in question. "We completely screwed it up," Glassman admitted. On the more basic question of the legitimacy of the documents, Kwitny wondered if Glassman had checked to make sure they weren't forgeries produced by either the CIA or Salvadoran intelligence as a way of justifying an influx of U.S. military aid. Glassman responded that he had asked the CIA just that, and "their answer to each of those questions was no." Given the agency's history of relying on false documents and chronologies to get its way, Glassman's approach demonstrated either an incredible naïveté or a willingness to collaborate in creating a distorted view of the arms flow into El Salvador.[4]

However questionable the underlying evidence, Glassman's paper clearly fulfilled the Reagan administration's political need to paint the war in El Salvador as a battle in the larger struggle against world communism.

The effect of Kwitny's revelations—that the main evidence of an international communist conspiracy to arm the Salvadoran rebels was heavily doctored, if not completely fabricated—should have been devastating. But as the Reagan administration's policymakers and spin doctors were soon to learn, as long as they could keep the charges flying and the president sounding convinced and unflappable, a little thing like evidence would not necessarily slow down the policy juggernaut.

Portraying the Salvadoran guerrilla forces as a surrogate of the Soviets' "evil empire," as Reagan later described it, was only half the battle. Administration representatives also took great pains to downplay reports from independent monitoring organizations about the Salvadoran government's long history of human rights abuses. Military and police forces, often in cooperation with right-wing death squads that had overlapping memberships with the regular armed forces, were responsible for tens of thousands of civilian deaths in the first few years of the Reagan policy of stepped-up military aid to El Salvador. In one particularly infamous incident that occurred in December 1981, U.S.-trained forces massacred more than 790 civilians in the hamlet of El Mozote. By 1983, over 40,000 civilians had been murdered in El Salvador's civil war—nearly 1 percent of the country's population—and the vast majority of the deaths had come at the hands of U.S.-armed and -trained military forces and the right-wing death squads that were closely allied with them.[5]

No one was exempt from the surging violence in El Salvador,

which had begun in 1979 and gained worldwide attention in 1980, the year before Ronald Reagan took office. On March 24, 1980, in one of the most shocking incidents, Archbishop Oscar Romero was assassinated by a member of a right-wing death squad while celebrating mass in San Salvador's main cathedral. His "crime" had been giving a sermon the day before in which he had denounced human rights abuses by the military and called upon military personnel to disobey their commanders rather than participate in the government's promotion of "reforms bathed in blood." In December 1980, four U.S. churchwomen, nuns from the Maryknoll order who had been working with El Salvador's poor, were murdered by members of the Salvadoran National Guard. And on January 5, 1981, two U.S. advisers who had worked on El Salvador's extremely modest land reform program were gunned down at a restaurant by right-wing assassins.

In what had become its typical practice, the Carter administration's response to this wave of violence was erratic and equivocal. To its credit, the administration suspended all U.S. military and economic aid to El Salvador the day after the four nuns were killed. But just five weeks later, responding to a major antigovernment offensive by Salvadoran guerrilla forces, Carter reversed himself, releasing over $5 million in arms and sending a half dozen military advisers to help direct the government's war effort. On January 17, just a few days before leaving office, Carter approved an additional $5 million in emergency military aid to the Salvadoran junta. In two weeks the human rights president had signed off on sending more arms to the repressive government in El Salvador than it had received from the United States in the previous decade. The message was clear: bolstering this corrupt military regime against its leftist opponents was going to take precedence over human rights concerns.[6]

The Reagan administration picked up where the Carter policy left off, but rather than downplaying human rights concerns, Reagan officials virtually abandoned them. The routine response of Reagan policymakers to the growing tide of violence and death in El Salvador, much of it fueled by U.S. arms and training, was to blame it on the guerrillas, despite strong evidence that it was not the rebels who caused the bloodshed. The administration's second line of defense was to argue, as Ronald Reagan did in January 1982, that "the Salvadoran Government is achieving substantial control over all elements of its own armed forces, so as to bring an end to the indiscriminate torture and murder of Salvadoran citizens." If we kept sending them arms and advisers, Reagan implied, the Salvadoran military would eventually clean up its act. But even his promise of human rights improvements had a hollow ring to it, pledging only that "indiscriminate" government violence against its own citizens would be brought to an end, implying that "selective" or "justified" torture and murder might continue. By the end of 1983, a secret State Department report unearthed by journalist Bonner had revealed that contrary to Reagan's assurances, Salvadoran government forces had no intention of reforming: "The military exerts a pervasive influence over the nation . . . and has sought to shield from justice even those who commit the most atrocious crimes."[7] Human rights abuses by U.S.-backed government forces in El Salvador continued to be overlooked by Reagan policymakers, taking a back seat to hyped charges of "communist interference" in arming left-wing guerrilla movements. The Reagan administration was to rely on similar arguments to justify accelerated weapons exports to regimes in Guatemala, Argentina, Pakistan, and a host of other right-wing dictatorships. El Salvador was a "textbook case" all right, just as Alexander Haig said it would be in the early months of the first Reagan term. But the lesson to be learned was not about communist aggression—it was about the Reagan arms sales policy, which seemed to be stuck on an ideologically driven automatic pilot, so that no amount of evidence regarding the atrocities committed by U.S.-supplied forces was likely to stem the flow of U.S. weaponry to any ally that raised the banner of anticommunism.

Reagan's New Policy: Preaching to the Converted

Arming right-wing regimes like the Salvadoran government satisfied the political objectives of the Reagan policy, but it did little for the president's friends in the arms industry who were looking for new foreign markets in the wake of Carter's defeat. Even in a "good year," the value of equipment shipped to Central America—consisting primarily of guns, ammunition, and perhaps a few helicopters or light aircraft—was not going to offer much in the way of business to the Lockheeds and McDonnell Douglases of the world. These giants of the industry were waiting to hear what Ronald Reagan planned to do for them.

They didn't have to wait long. Reagan chose to preview his new arms transfer policy to the industry even before an official policy directive was made public. He delegated the task to James Buckley, his newly appointed undersecretary of state for security assistance, science, and technology, who unveiled the new Reagan policy in a keynote speech at the May 1981 convention of the Aerospace Industries Association. Buckley, a longtime conservative activist, brother of conservative pundit William F. Buckley, and a former senator from New York State, was the perfect man for the job. He relished the task of launching a partisan rhetorical attack on Carter's arms transfer restraint policy and introducing the new, conservative vision of the role of weapons exports in U.S. foreign policy.

Buckley observed at the outset of his remarks that the setting was "superb" for the message he had come to deliver. He was speaking at colonial Williamsburg, upon whose streets the founding fathers of the Republic had wrestled with the issues of how best to preserve freedom and democracy. Without a trace of irony, Buckley implied that the new Reagan foreign policy was a straightforward continuation and vindication of the original commitment to democracy upon which the United States had been founded nearly two hundred years ago. It would be several years before the administration's secret wheeling and dealing in the Iran/contra scandal revealed in startling detail how diametrically opposed the Reagan policy was to the basic principles of democracy.

Buckley was speaking before a particularly receptive audience, whose livelihoods would be dramatically affected by Reagan's arms export policy. Their economic interest in the topic was so obvious that Buckley did not even need to mention it. He came out swinging, ridiculing American policies of the 1970s as a futile attempt to deny the reality of the U.S. role as an "imperial power." He blamed Congress and the Carter administration for presiding over "an American withdrawal from world responsibilities that contributed to a dramatic shift in global power relationships." In contrast, Buckley painted a vivid picture of the rival Soviet empire on the march. The results had been disastrous, in his view. The combination of Soviet aggression and U.S. vacillation had led to a situation in which the nation had lost "our nuclear superiority," "our naval forces had been reduced by half," and the "Soviets [had] established strategic beachheads in Africa and the Middle East."

But the crowning blow to U.S. power, prestige, and influence had come, in Buckley's view, when "the Carter Administration adopted policies toward the transfer of arms to our friends and allies which substituted theology for a healthy sense of self-preservation." According to Buckley, "It was the Carter view that such transfers were inherently evil or morally reprehensible, or both."

The Reagan administration would have no such moral qualms about selling weapons. Buckley made it clear that President Reagan would work to eliminate congressional restrictions on sales to nations with records of human rights abuses or programs aimed at developing their own nuclear weapons. Far more important than punishing dictators or trying to stem nuclear proliferation, in the Reagan worldview, was avoiding the "awkward result of undercutting the capabilities of strategically located nations in whose ability to defend themselves we have the most immediate and urgent self-interest." Other goals and values would have to take a back seat to the priority of winning a global war for position and influence with the Soviet Union and its allies.

In fact, Buckley argued, selling weapons in exchange for allegiance to U.S. political or military objectives was not only pragmatic, it was in keeping with the highest moral ideals of the nation. The challenge facing America "was not to strip ourselves of power but to focus that power for the common good. . . . This is the stated objective of the Reagan Administration, and it is one based on the long overdue reaffirmation of our confidence in ourselves and the rightness of our cause. We are the last best hope on earth; and we have no responsible choice but to act accordingly." In the Reagan era, no lever of international influence would go unused, certainly not one as powerful, lucrative, and seemingly risk free as foreign military sales.

Buckley's final flourish encapsulated the new foreign policy vision in the clearest possible terms:

> I know that conservatives are often accused of being simplistic; and as a self-confessed, card-carrying member of that fraternity, I might as well confess that I harbor the simplistic notion that on the world's stage today it is possible to divide the actors between the good guys and the bad guys; and we might as well understand that the bad guys are playing for keeps.
>
> A few years ago that great American philosopher, Leo Durocher, made the observation that good guys finish last. It is the intention of this Administration to prove him wrong.[8]

Buckley's speech was an unqualified success. The new approach sounded almost too good to be true, but no one among the assembled representatives of the aerospace industry was inclined to analyze it too carefully. They had heard what they came to hear: that the Reagan administration would be an unapologetic salesman of U.S. weapons, making arms transfers a central tool in a stepped-up battle against the Soviet Union and its alleged allies from El Salvador to Angola.

Buckley's rhetoric was followed up with a July 1981 policy directive on conventional arms transfers that officially overturned the Carter policy in almost every significant detail. Rather than serving as "an exceptional instrument," as Carter had pledged, arms transfers would now be seen as "an essential element of our global policy." This philosophical shift was matched at the bureaucratic level as well, as each of the six major controls imposed by Carter were repealed. In their place, a government policy of arms sales facilitation was implemented.[9]

Reagan administration officials quickly rushed through a series of reforms to streamline the U.S. government's arms supply system. First, they sought to provide quicker delivery of U.S. armaments to potential client states. Major Foreign Military Sales (FMS) cases could take six years or more from the time an order was placed by a foreign government until the first weapon was actually delivered. Picking up on an idea that had been promoted by Texas senator John Tower, a loyal friend of the defense industry, the Pentagon set up a Special Defense Acquisition Fund to speed the delivery of arms to U.S. allies. The fund would purchase and stockpile "frequently ordered pieces of U.S. equipment," from machine guns to military trucks to helicopters, so that they could be shipped out as soon as a foreign government ordered them. It would be supported to the tune of a billion dollars a year.

In addition to shortening delivery times, the Reagan policy provided easy financing for foreign dictators shopping for fighter planes or other U.S. military hardware. In the first Reagan term alone, grants and subsidized loans for the purchase of U.S. weapons were increased from $3.2 billion to over $6.4 billion, growing to encompass more than half of all direct U.S. foreign aid and pushing economic development aid to poorer nations out of the picture. This militarization of the foreign aid process was in keeping with the Reagan administration's assumption that the Cold War policy of using arms sales to cement a network of anticommunist alliances around the globe would continue to be the most important method of exercising power in world affairs for the foreseeable future.

Third, in a move that captured more than any other the spirit of the new administration's stance, the Reagan State Department rescinded Carter's so-called leprosy letter, urging embassy personnel instead to provide U.S. arms manufacturers with "all the courtesies which would be provided to any other U.S. business."[10]

Reagan's Resolve: The AWACS Controversy

Ironically, Ronald Reagan's first major foreign policy clash with Congress came over a proposed arms deal with Saudi Arabia that had been struck under the "restrictive" policy of the Carter administration. The sale was bound to be controversial because it included five Boeing AWACS radar planes, a sophisticated system that had been offered to only one other developing nation, Iran, and had certainly never been offered to an adversary of Israel like the Saudi regime. On top of that, at a price tag of $8.5 billion, the Saudi sale would be the largest single arms export in U.S. history. Aware of the opposition it was sure to generate, Carter officials had even offered to present the sale to Congress during the lame-duck period between Carter's defeat and Reagan's January 1981 inauguration, as a way of taking the heat off the incoming Reagan foreign policy team. But Reagan's advisers declined, preferring to handle the job of steering this sale through Congress themselves.

The Saudi deal was further confirmation, if any were needed, of how far the Carter policy had strayed from its original principles. Apart from denying advanced fighter planes to South Korea and several Latin American nations, and temporarily putting the brakes on military aid to repressive regimes like that of Anastasio Somoza in Nicaragua or the military junta in El Salvador, Jimmy Carter's policy was rooted in the same basic "arms for influence" calculation that had sparked the U.S. arms sales boom in the first place. In fact, according to a DSAA official who has served in the Ford, Carter, Reagan, Bush, and Clinton administrations, the Carter policy *as actually carried out* served as a guide in designing the Reagan approach: "The Reagan arms transfer policy that was announced in 1981 was basically just a description of how the Carter policy was implemented." The Reaganites were simply closing the gap between rhetoric and reality by abandoning any pretense of restraint.

In pushing the AWACS sale to Saudi Arabia as its first major arms sales proposal, the Reagan administration was putting itself to a test of political muscle with the pro-Israel lobby, spearheaded by the American Israel Public Affairs Committee (AIPAC). AIPAC and its network was practically the only organized political force with the clout needed to derail an arms sale. Indeed, in the few cases during the 1970s when arms deals had been scaled down or delayed because of congressional opposition, they had invariably involved exports to Saudi Arabia opposed by Israel, AIPAC, and major American Jewish organizations.

But the AWACS deal was no run-of-the-mill arms sale. Not only was the tremendous cost and sophistication of the radar planes themselves a significant issue, but the $8.5 billion deal also included extra fuel tanks, bomb racks, and air-to-air missiles that could extend the range and combat capability of the Saudi fighters. This was precisely the kind of equipment that the Carter administration had promised *not* to sell to the Saudis when Congress had reluctantly signed off on the F-15 deal in 1978. In addition to the ever-present issue of what the AWACS/F-15 upgrade might mean for Israel's security, there was also a question of congressional pride: could Congress let the executive branch ride roughshod over an explicit pledge that had been made three years earlier, albeit under a different administration? Wouldn't acquiescing on this aspect of the sale merely concede the inability of Congress to have even marginal input into arms sales decisions?

Congressman Jonathan Bingham of New York, a staunch supporter of Israel, drew first blood in the congressional debates over AWACS when he debunked the myth that the plane was only a defensive system. While it was true that the aircraft could be extremely useful in an air defense role, tracking incoming planes and providing information and coordination to the aircraft charged with shooting them down, this same capability could be used in an offensive mode. In support of his point, Bingham cited Boeing's own description of what its aircraft could do:

> The primary advantage of the E-3A [AWACS] is that . . . it can command and control the total air effort: strike, air superiority, support, airlift, reconnaissance, and interdiction. . . . The E-3A can monitor the marshalling of airplanes at bases behind enemy lines and command friendly aircraft to attack while enemy forces are still on the ground. The E-3A can interoperate and inform friendly ground and naval forces.[11]

In short, the AWACS could prove as useful in a preemptive, offensive strike as it could in a reactive, defensive role. While it was not clear that the AWACS alone would erode Israel's significant technological edge, the notion that the plane would make no real contribution to the Saudis' offensive military options was simply wrong.

While congressional opponents of the sale focused on the potential threat to Israel, administration officials tried to turn the argument into yet another debate about the need to combat the "Soviet threat." Citing the 1979 invasion of Afghanistan and the relatively recent fall of the shah of Iran, Undersecretary of State Buckley argued that the whole Persian Gulf area, "once a secure source of the petroleum essential to Western economies . . . has become an area which is extremely vulnerable to attack by regional forces, while exposed to a potential offensive by the Soviet Union." Buckley's boss, Secretary of State Haig, took this scare-mongering a step further by painting a domino scenario in which the whole Middle East might well be dominated by communists and terrorists if the AWACS sale didn't go through:

> Our enemies and the enemies of peace have not been idle. Just last week, Iranian planes bombed oil facilities in Kuwait, and the turmoil in Iran itself poses even larger dangers to U.S. interests and to world peace. Libya, Ethiopia, and South Yemen have recently joined together in an unholy alliance aimed through the Sudan at Egypt and through North Yemen at Saudi Arabia. Qaddafi has threatened to destroy the oil facilities of Saudi Arabia, and his planes have bombed the Sudan.[12]

Haig neglected to explain how the sale of five radar planes alone could be expected to stem this greatly exaggerated tide of aggression and subversion, but his tirade was typical of the sort of ideological overkill that was beginning to characterize the Reagan administration's rationales for major arms transfers.

It fell to Fred Ikle, undersecretary of defense for policy, to offer the *real* military motivation for the AWACS sale in his testimony to Congress in late September 1981. Fourth on his list of arguments for the AWACS sale was a sobering revelation—the planes were envisioned as a tool for facilitating future U.S. military intervention in the Middle East:

> [The AWACS sale] will increase the effectiveness of our own military capabilities should we be called upon to deploy U.S. forces in the area. The extensive logistics base and infrastructure that will be necessary as part of this equipment will be fully compatible with U.S. systems. If the Saudis, instead, buy European equipment, this compatibility will be lost, and we could not move in as rapidly and effectively to protect our interests.[13]

Unfortunately, Ikle's forthright presentation of the only logical military rationale for the AWACS sale was largely ignored by Congress at the time of the debate, which centered instead on a test of influence between pro-Israel and pro-Saudi lobbies and on the question of whether the Saudi political and economic support for U.S. foreign policy objectives would dry up if the sale were canceled.

Ikle's assertion that arms sales to the region were now to be considered openly as part of an interventionary strategy—not a substitute for it, as in the Nixon Doctrine's formulation—remained in the background until ten years later, when George Bush sent more than five hundred thousand U.S. troops to Saudi Arabia as part of Operation Desert Storm. Unbeknownst to Congress or the public, the 1981 AWACS deal had helped set the stage, politically and militarily, for the 1991 U.S. intervention to reverse Saddam Hussein's invasion of Kuwait. (The role of U.S. arms sales in fueling military intervention in the Persian Gulf region will be discussed in more detail in chapter 10.)

Policy issues aside, the AWACS vote came down to a battle of lobbyists. As with the 1978 F-15 package, the chances of avoiding a vote of disapproval in the House had already been given up for lost, so the battle moved to the Senate. The most influential lobbyist of all was Ronald Reagan, who made scores of phone calls to wavering senators asking them to support the sale, promising a variety of budgetary and legislative favors in return for their votes.

The president had also mobilized a small army of officials, from the secretaries of state and defense on down the line, to make the administration's case to Congress in formal hearings, informal briefings, and any other available forum. Among the administration's lobbyists for the sale was an air force general named Richard Secord, who had helped negotiate the terms of the deal with the Saudis, and an energetic marine colonel named Oliver North, who was involved in scheduling interagency strategy sessions to coordinate administration positions on the AWACS.

Perhaps most important of all, in his efforts to promote the AWACS sale Reagan was able to count on "the aggressive involvement of the entire spectrum of the American business community," an effort that journalist Steven Emerson has described as "the most extensive business lobbying goal ever pursued by American business on a foreign policy issue." Headed up by lawyer-lobbyist Fred Dutton and Prince Bandar bin Sultan, the charismatic Saudi military attaché in Washington who later became his nation's ambassador to the United States, the effort ultimately encompassed hundreds of companies involved in selling the Saudis everything from arms and oil to flowers and rice. Boeing was a key player, as was United Technologies, the manufacturer of the AWACS engine, and Mobil Oil, a partner in the Saudi oil-producing firm Aramco. Boeing and United Technologies alone sent out over sixty-five hundred telegrams to subsidiaries, subcontractors, and suppliers throughout the country, urging them to let Congress know that they supported the sale. While strategic arguments were used to dress up the case, the basic appeal was to naked economic self-interest. United Technologies chairman Harry Gray asserted that "a Senate veto of the air defense package would cost our nation dearly in a weakened relationship with a staunch friend in the

Arab world, diminished presidential influence for world peace and stability, lower U.S. credibility in the world's capitals, and lost U.S. exports and jobs." Boeing president E. H. Boullion argued in his telegram that "without this sale . . . the AWACS production line will be ended," a familiar refrain that surfaced time and again in debates over arms sales in the years to follow.

These requests for lobbying assistance, made to firms that depended on Boeing and United Technologies for significant business, could hardly be turned down. One small businessman who had contracts with United Technologies described Gray's approach as "raw economic blackmail. . . . When Harry Gray asks vendors to lobby on the AWACS what choice do we have? How do we know that our refusal to support the AWACS won't be used against us later?" Whatever you choose to call it, Gray's hardball tactics worked. Steven Emerson estimates that up to 70 percent of the thousands of corporate letters and telegrams sent to Congress in favor of the AWACS sale were generated as a result of appeals by Boeing and United Technologies to their suppliers.

The most impressive corporate outreach effort of all came from Saudi Arabia on the day of the AWACS vote. Twenty-three influential executives, ranging from the CEOs of Rockwell International, IBM, and H. J. Heinz Company to Henry Luce of *Time* magazine and Pres. Matina Horner of Radcliffe College, were in Saudi Arabia on a "fact-finding mission" sponsored by *Time*. At the urging of Fred Brophy, the CEO of General Telephone and Electronics (GTE), they sent a confidential telegram to twenty key senators stressing the damage a veto of the AWACS sale would do to "U.S. credibility in the Arab world" and "U.S. ability to protect its legitimate interests in the Middle East." Henry Heinz reportedly told the group that his son John, then a senator from Pennsylvania, could be counted on to vote for the AWACS sale if his vote was needed to stave off defeat.[14]

This economic campaign on behalf of the AWACS sale was motivated almost entirely by a desire to curry favor with the Saudi leadership and ensure a large Saudi market for U.S. military and civilian products. The Saudis encouraged the corporate stampede to line up behind the AWACS sale by putting out the word that they would take into account companies' actions, or lack thereof, in deciding on future business contracts. And there is no question that this pork barrel lobbying played a critical part in getting the sale through Congress, both through the pressure exerted on individual members and in the ensuing debates. Steven Emerson reports that one midwestern senator heard from every major CEO in his state on behalf of the AWACS deal. And Sen. Charles Percy of Illinois hit hard on the economic issue in his defense of the deal:

> We do have $35 billion of contracts with Saudi Arabia. The Saudis have always tried to favor American corporations. Over 700 of them have these contracts. Hundreds of thousands of American jobs depend on Saudi Arabia. Now, it's not that you would ever put the security of Israel against dollars, but I think we have resolved the question of the security of Israel. The President would never have done this if he ever felt it would endanger the security of Israel.[15]

(Neither Percy nor his colleagues seriously questioned what the AWACS sale might mean for the future security of the United States, implying a tacit commitment to defend the corrupt Saudi monarchy come hell or high water. This issue will be discussed in chapter 10, in the context of the overall U.S.–Saudi arms sales relationship.)

When push came to shove, the combination of Ronald Reagan's personal lobbying effort and an intense campaign of industry pressure was enough to overcome the considerable political clout of supporters of Israel in the Congress, and the package cleared the Senate when fifty-two members voted against killing the AWACS sale, versus forty-eight in favor.

The Reagan Results: Record Sales

By the end of Reagan's second full year in office, the new arms export promotion policy was taking full effect. Spurred in part by the success of the administration's impressive lobbying effort on behalf of the AWACS, foreign orders for U.S. arms during fiscal year 1982 topped $20 billion for the first time ever, outpacing even the peak years of the Nixon/Kissinger arms boom. This "achievement" was the result of a four-pronged assault on the few restraints that had survived the rightward drift of the Carter administration during 1979 and 1980.

The first limitation to fall was the sophistication barrier.[16] Besides the major exceptions made for the shah of Iran and other sales to the Middle East, the Carter administration had selectively adhered to its policy of not being the first nation to introduce a new, more advanced level of military technology into a region. In practice, this primarily meant denying top-of-the-line fighter aircraft to developing nations in Asia and Latin America. A long-standing request for F-16s by South Korean strongman Park Chung Hee had been turned down despite

Secretary of Defense Harold Brown's personal support for the sale. And, in a move that irked Israeli government officials, an export to Ecuador of the Kfir fighter, an Israeli copy of the French Mirage powered by U.S.-made General Electric engines, was vetoed by Carter officials under provisions allowing the United States to control third-country transfers of weaponry that incorporates U.S. technology. Reagan policymakers swept aside this informal prohibition on the sale of advanced fighters almost immediately, quickly offering F-16s to Venezuela, South Korea, and Pakistan, much to the delight of the plane's manufacturer, General Dynamics.

The next major casualty of the Reagan policy was the proliferation barrier. Reagan's proposed sale of F-16 fighters to Pakistan raised the issue of that country's ongoing violation of section 669 of the Foreign Assistance Act, the Symington amendment, which prohibited U.S. military aid to developing nations with active nuclear weapons programs until such time as they pledged to halt those programs. The Reagan administration sought and won an exemption for Pakistan and proceeded to negotiate a six-year, $4 billion military and economic aid package with Mohammad Zia ul-Haq's regime. The principal rationale for this infusion of aid was the effort to win Zia's support in the CIA's covert battle to dislodge Soviet troops from Afghanistan by funneling arms through Pakistan to anti-Soviet Afghan rebel organizations. It later emerged that the Afghan arms pipeline was rife with corruption and intrigue, with as many arms being diverted for sale to drug runners and local thugs inside Pakistan as made it to the Afghan fighters. But at the time, Reagan officials like James Buckley and Alexander Haig sold the Afghan program as a new bulwark against the Soviets, with Zia cast as a sort of junior shah of Iran.

Like the shah, Zia had his own ideas and his own obsessive ambitions. He had dismissed an aid package of several hundred million dollars offered late in the Carter administration as "peanuts." Even as he benefited from his newfound friend in Washington, the Pakistani dictator continued to nurture his nuclear ambitions. In the mid-1980s, Zia openly mocked international concerns regarding his quest to develop nuclear weapons, bragging that "Pakistan can build the Bomb any time it wishes."[17] But even this threat to break into the nuclear club was ignored in the rush to build up an anti-Soviet client on the borders of Afghanistan.

Human rights barriers to U.S. arms sales were also rapidly cast aside under the Reagan arms sales policy. Legislative and administrative restrictions on supplying weapons to repressive regimes were systematically dismantled at Reagan's behest. The impact was most noticeable in Latin America, where Reagan policymakers quickly went after the vestiges of Carter's human rights policy, stepping up aid to the Salvadoran junta, beating back a four-year effort by Congress to maintain military aid prohibitions on Guatemala, and overturning legal restrictions on arms sales to the notorious military regime in Argentina, which had specialized in the kidnapping and torture of its own citizens. Sales to Central and Latin America increased threefold in Reagan's first four years in office, providing a useful outlet for makers of guns and ammunition, helicopters, and other light armaments used in antiguerrilla warfare.

Last but not least, the Reagan team expanded their early policy of easing the financial barriers to the acquisition of U.S. weapons through low-interest loans and direct grants to Third World regimes seeking U.S. military hardware. These funds more than doubled from 1981 to 1985, making possible increased arms purchases by Morocco, the Sudan, and other impoverished Third World nations whose needs would have been better served by targeted programs of economic aid.[18] At the same time that it was getting easier for Third World dictators to get subsidies to buy U.S. fighter planes, average citizens in the United States saw drastic cutbacks in federal loans for housing, education, and other essential services.

The flood of new arms orders stimulated by the Reagan policy certainly represented a good business opportunity for U.S. defense contractors, but these deals came at a high price in terms of international security. More and more frequently, U.S. weapons were being used by U.S. allies to escalate local and regional conflicts.

The renewed aggressiveness of Israel was a prime example. Israel's June 1981 use of U.S.-supplied F-15 and F-16 fighter aircraft to attack Iraq's Osirak nuclear reactor prompted a brief slap on the wrist from Reagan administration policymakers, but nothing more. Secretary of State Haig imposed a ten-week suspension on deliveries of new fighter aircraft until the State Department could determine whether Israel had violated its pledge to employ U.S. arms for "defensive purposes" only. Haig then lifted the suspension in August 1981 without ruling on whether U.S. law had been violated, musing that "I think one in a subjective way can argue to eternity as to whether or not a military action may be defensive or offensive in character." He went on to indicate that Israel had not provided any new assurances about how it would employ U.S. arms in the future.[19]

This tepid response to the Israeli raids left the Reagan administration unprepared to deal with the clearly aggressive use of U.S.-supplied airplanes and cluster bombs in the subsequent Israeli invasion of

Lebanon in June 1982, an attack that leveled large parts of Beirut and killed thousands of civilians. Despite some public hand wringing about Israeli tactics by a few Reagan administration officials, Israel essentially prosecuted the war with the acquiescence of the United States. The administration's failure to rein in its ally and arms client set the stage for the ill-fated U.S. peacekeeping presence in Lebanon, which in turn led to the 1983 bombing that cost the lives of 241 U.S. Marines. Reagan's "risk free" arms transfer policy had claimed more U.S. victims in one incident than had died in combat in the previous eight years.

The whole experience of the war in Lebanon gave the lie to the notion that U.S. arms supplies could be carefully calibrated to create a "balance of power" in a volatile region like the Middle East, much less provide the United States with leverage over how the arms it provided were used by its allies.

Israel wasn't the only U.S. ally to take advantage of the new Reagan philosophy on arms sales to carry forward its own aggressive designs. Morocco's King Hassan turned to the Reagan administration for aid in his war of annexation in the Western Sahara, a former Spanish colony that had been fighting for its independence since 1975 under the leadership of the Polisario liberation movement. Hassan had other ideas for the territory—he wanted to make it a new province of Morocco, in large part so he could control the revenues generated by the phosphate mines in the northwest corner of the Sahara. The Carter administration had initially attempted to strike a neutral posture, adhering for a time to its stated policy of refusing to supply any arms to Morocco that could be used outside Moroccan territory. By 1979, Carter policy had undergone a pronounced tilt toward Morocco, symbolized most clearly by a sale of Rockwell OV-10 counterinsurgency aircraft for use in Hassan's war against the Polisario guerrillas. But even at that point, the Carter policy had at least tried to link further arms sales to Morocco to the pursuit of a negotiated settlement of the Sahara war.

The Reagan administration, in contrast, abandoned any pretext of neutrality by removing the link between arms supplies to Morocco and a negotiated solution to the conflict. Instead, the Reagan policy sought to promote Morocco's pursuit of military victory in the Sahara by tripling U.S. military assistance to Hassan's regime, selling Morocco cluster bombs and M-60 tanks, and providing intelligence information and aerial reconnaissance aid to the Moroccan army in its quest to locate Polisario forces in the desert. U.S.-supplied radar was also used to monitor a four-hundred-mile-long "wall of sand" that had been built by Morocco to keep Polisario forces out of the phosphate-rich northwestern corner of the Sahara that had been occupied by Moroccan forces.

This extensive U.S. military support served to prolong Morocco's war of occupation and embolden King Hassan in his effort to override Polisario's legitimate claim to the Western Sahara, a claim that has been recognized by the United Nations, the Organization of African Unity, and more than sixty nations around the world. The result of Hassan's U.S.-inspired intransigence was eight years of war, thousands of casualties on both sides, and billions of dollars drained from Morocco's already impoverished economy. As of mid-1994, plans for a UN referendum to determine whether the former residents of the Western Sahara would prefer independence or union with Morocco were mired in political and bureaucratic squabbles between the Moroccan government and a woefully understaffed UN peacekeeping force. The eminently sensible solution of holding an election to determine the area's future could have been implemented ten years earlier if the Reagan administration's arms sales policy had not encouraged Hassan to fight on in the face of nearly universal international opposition to his war of occupation.[20]

The behavior of U.S. arms clients like Israel and Morocco underscored the fact that far from merely providing the means for allies to "defend themselves," as James Buckley and other Reagan administration officials had persistently asserted, the Reagan policy of unrestrained arms transfers had given a green light to key U.S. allies to engage in aggressive actions that were sowing the seeds of further war and instability. But these messy details were of little interest to the president's supporters in the military industry, who were too busy raking in the profits from Reagan's new policy to worry about the loss of a few thousand lives or the escalation of a war here or there. The elements of Reagan's arms sales program—offering easy financing for arms exporters and lifting barriers on sales of advanced weaponry based on considerations of human rights, nuclear nonproliferation, or the dangers of fostering regional arms races—were remarkably similar to the program put forward by the American League for Exports and Security Assistance, the industry lobbying group that had been formed in response to Jimmy Carter's anti-arms-sales rhetoric in the 1976 presidential campaign.[21] This was no accident. Scores of major military contractors worked actively for Ronald Reagan's election in 1980, pouring hundreds of thousands of dollars into the coffers of the Republican Party, specific Republican congressional candidates, and the Reagan/Bush campaign.

The arms industry's investment in a Reagan presidency paid off handsomely. McDonnell Douglas's annual foreign military sales contracts topped $1 billion three separate times during the early 1980s on the strength of the Reagan arms export policy, primarily as a result of increased overseas sales of its F/A-18 aircraft and its Harpoon antiship missiles. General Dynamics and General Electric both tripled their weapons exports between 1981 and 1985, while Lockheed's arms sales more than doubled over the same period. By the mid-1980s, arms exports had increased to more than 5 percent of total U.S. exports, and the dependency of individual companies on foreign sales was creeping back up toward levels not seen since the height of the Nixon/Kissinger boom of the mid-1970s.[22] The major weapons-exporting firms could not have been happier with the Reagan policy if they had been allowed to write it themselves.

Major public sales of fighters, tanks, and missiles were only the most visible facet of the Reagan administration's arms export policy. It wasn't until his second term that the other, parallel track of Ronald Reagan's policy—his penchant for covert arms sales—was fully brought into the light of day. Reagan's unprecedented reliance on secret arms deals represented his most notable—and most pernicious—contribution to the checkered history of executive branch arms trafficking.

6

The Reagan Doctrine: Arming Anticommunist Rebels

Fresh from his landslide victory over Walter Mondale in the 1984 elections, Ronald Reagan chose the occasion of his 1985 State of the Union address to up the ante in his use of arms exports as the linchpin of his administration's global anticommunist crusade. Before a national television audience and a chastened and respectful gathering of members of the House and Senate, the president asserted that "we must not break faith with those who are risking their lives—on every continent, from Afghanistan to Nicaragua—to defy Soviet-supported aggression and secure rights which have been ours from birth."[1]

To Reagan, the ultimate expression of faith in freedom did not involve moral appeals or diplomatic support—it meant supplying arms. The recipients of these weapons shipments were a widespread collection of anticommunist rebel movements attempting to overthrow leftist regimes on four continents, in Angola, Afghanistan, Nicaragua, and Cambodia. Some conservatives in the Reagan camp wanted to extend this strategy of war by proxy even further, to Ethiopia, Mozambique, Eastern Europe, and perhaps the Soviet Union itself.

Reagan's pledge to support anticommunist "freedom fighters" was quickly labeled the "Reagan Doctrine" by neoconservative pundit Charles Krauthammer, and the term stuck. Supporters of the doctrine saw it as a long-overdue attempt to go beyond the strategy of containment of communism that had dominated U.S. foreign and military policies in Republican and Democratic administrations alike throughout the post–World War II era, to an aggressive policy of rolling back communism in areas of the Third World where nominally socialist governments had come to power with assistance from the Soviet Union.

Far from representing a radical shift in Reagan's thinking, the idea of arming right-wing rebel movements had firm political roots in his Cold War mind-set. In the early 1960s, while he was serving as a paid spokesperson for the General Electric Corporation, Reagan frequently warned his listeners about the "war" against the United States and its values that "was declared a hundred years ago by Karl Marx and reaffirmed fifty years later by Nikolai [*sic*] Lenin." He added ominously that "we are losing that war because we don't know we are in it." In 1967, while he was governor of California, he foreshadowed the Reagan Doctrine when he gave a speech suggesting that "the United States might consider promoting wars of its own on Communist territory." Reagan amplified this point in a mid-1970s interview with *U.S. News and World Report* when he asserted that "this nation should have a master plan, if you want to call it that, based on what we believe is the enemy's master plan. . . . Maybe part of the answer in a hot spot such as Vietnam is to give the enemy something else to worry about in another corner of the world. . . . Maybe [the enemy] ought to have some unrest in some corner of his realm to worry about." And Reagan reaffirmed his anticommunist worldview during the 1980 presidential campaign when he told a *Wall Street Journal* reporter, "The Soviet Union underlies all the unrest that is going on. . . . If they weren't engaged in this game of dominos, there wouldn't be any hot spots in the world."[2]

Given this black-and-white view that every significant conflict was part of a worldwide struggle between communist bad guys and anticommunist good guys, it came as no great surprise that Reagan was willing to arm virtually any movement, no matter how extreme or undemocratic, that called itself anticommunist or aligned itself against an alleged Soviet ally.

Reagan's hard-line approach to leftist forces and regimes in the Third World was given a veneer of intellectual respectability by the writings of neoconservative political scientist Jeane Kirkpatrick, who so impressed the president that he chose her as his representative to the United Nations. In an infamous 1979 article entitled "Dictatorships and Double Standards," Kirkpatrick made a specious distinction between "totalitarian" communist regimes like East Germany, Cuba, and the Sandinista government in Nicaragua and right-wing dictatorships allied with the United States, like those in Haiti, Argentina, and Chile, which were "merely authoritarian." In Kirkpatrick's view, leftist regimes were more repressive, more violent, and more impervious to democratic reform, whereas U.S.-supported dictatorships like those that had ruled large parts of Latin America, Asia, and Africa were corrupt and conservative but amenable to democratic reforms, if implemented slowly and nonviolently. In short, "our" dictatorships were okay, while those supported, installed, or even recognized by the Soviets were to be vigorously opposed. Kirkpatrick's theory bore no resemblance to the actual behavior of right-wing regimes that received U.S. military and economic assistance, many of which were more violently repressive and less open to reform than her so-called totalitarian examples, but that was almost beside the point. Her perspective provided a neat ideological package for the policy direction that Reagan was already inclined to pursue.[3]

The new approach was quintessential Reagan. He was projecting an image of "getting tough" with the Soviets, but it was all couched in the comforting rhetoric of helping the underdog, as represented by groups like the Nicaraguan contras, whose leadership Reagan once described as the "moral equivalent of our founding fathers." And there was a sort of "self-help" ethos attached to the initiative, with the U.S. supplying the materials rebel forces needed to liberate themselves. Reagan gave no indication of understanding the complexities or dangers involved in committing the United States as the arsenal and political guarantor to right-wing movements dedicated to the overthrow of established governments in every corner of the globe.

Perhaps the most Reaganesque touch of all was the need to go public with all of this. The CIA had long been involved in covert arms supplies, but in the past some attempt had been made to disguise U.S. involvement, at least until after the outcome had been determined, and to downplay the importance of U.S. covert intervention if it came to light. But Ronald Reagan was different: he wanted to take credit for the overthrow of established governments with U.S. arms, even as the battles were still going on. This open contempt for international law could easily have been interpreted as a vicious, venal policy in the hands of a less sympathetic political front man. But presented in the context of Reagan's syrupy, sweet, and ultimately naive view of the world, many Americans found it to be a benign approach to world affairs, a sort of "father knows best" foreign policy.

As appealing as it may have sounded on paper, Reagan's policy of arming right-wing rebels posed severe political and military risks in practice. The reality of the Reagan Doctrine was a far cry from the president's rosy scenarios and soothing rhetoric.

Origins of the Doctrine: Reagan's Anti-Sandinista Obsession

Perhaps no one episode would more clearly confirm the inherent dangers of the Reagan Doctrine than the obsession with overthrowing the Sandinista government in Nicaragua, a small, impoverished nation with a population roughly the size of Brooklyn's. Reagan and his advisers were willing to go to any extreme to provide arms and training to the Nicaraguan opposition, even if it meant violating the democratic principles that are supposed to govern foreign policy decisionmaking in the United States.

The notion of driving the Sandinistas from power was already on the agenda even before Reagan took office, thanks to a plank that had been placed in the 1980 Republican platform by James Carbaugh, an aide to ultra-right-wing North Carolina senator Jesse Helms. The plank not only declared that Reagan's party "deplored" the "Marxist takeover of Nicaragua and Marxist attempts to destabilize El Salvador and Guatemala," but it went further to pledge support for "the efforts of the Nicaraguan people to establish a free and independent government." Carbaugh acknowledged that the latter phrase was code for "overthrowing the Nicaraguan government."[4]

The platform language was a classic example of the tendency of Reaganite Republicans to ignore complex political realities when they conflicted with their distorted political belief system. The new government in Nicaragua was hardly the group of communist "demons" that Reagan conservatives held them to be. The Sandinistas were a diverse coalition that included Marxists, social democrats, progressive religious activists, and members of the business classes who had been united by their desire to rid Nicaragua of the legacy of half a century of dictatorial rule by the U.S.-backed Somoza dynasty. Far from representing a victory for "communism in this hemisphere," as Reagan administration ideologues were fond of saying, the ascension of the Sandinistas to power appeared to hold out hope for the development of a progressive democratic government in Nicaragua. They had only been in power for a year when the Republican Party targeted them for extinction, but the early signs were that the Sandinistas would pursue a mixed economy with considerable scope for private ownership, opposition newspapers would be permitted to operate with relative freedom, and freedom of religion would be respected. One of the government's priority projects was a nationwide literacy campaign, hardly the kind of initiative one would expect from a "totalitarian" regime intent on oppressing its own people and threatening its neighbors. In fact, the Carter administration had appeared ready to pursue normal relations with the Sandinistas and had offered an economic aid package, albeit with political strings attached. There appeared to be no reason why U.S. relations with Nicaragua should deteriorate into the combative, counterproductive pattern that had marked U.S. policy toward the Cuban revolution.

But to the clique of conservative advisers who had the ear of the new president, these nuances weren't even worth mentioning. Nicaragua offered a perfect scapegoat for their approach of blaming rebellions against pro-U.S. regimes in Central America on an international communist conspiracy rather than on legitimate opposition to the unjust policies of the military juntas that dominated El Salvador, Guatemala, and other states of the region. Within three months of taking office, Reagan had suspended U.S. economic assistance to the Sandinista government. By the end of 1981, he had signed off on a $19 million covert action plan aimed at destabilizing the new regime by arming and training a loose band of opposition forces.[5]

The point of Reagan's aggressive anti-Sandinista policy was never to encourage democracy—that was a convenient cover story. The real goal of the Reagan Doctrine in Nicaragua was to install a regime that the U.S. government could control, one that would favor private property and foreign investment over the needs of the majority of its own people. The means for achieving this end would be a steady supply of U.S. arms and training to anti-Sandinista forces. But it wasn't that simple. It wasn't merely a question of providing military support for a well-established, well-organized opposition movement fighting Sandinista rule. There was no such force. Before it could send the weapons, the Reagan administration had to come up with suitable recipients. Reagan's policy of "arming freedom fighters" would entail a direct, ongoing intervention in the internal political affairs of Nicaragua and growing involvement by U.S. personnel in acts of war.

From the outset, Reagan's administration took an active role not only in supporting the contra movement but in creating it, a salient fact that was largely ignored in the thousands of mainstream media stories about Nicaragua that grabbed headlines and topped off newscasts throughout the 1980s. State Department envoy and ambassador-at-large Vernon Walters, a retired army general and former deputy director of the CIA, worked through the early months of 1981 to pressure the various anti-Sandinista factions to form a united front. The resulting organization included groups ranging from the September 15th legion, a paramilitary band headed by Somoza's former chief of intelligence Ricardo Lau, to Jose Francisco Cardenal's Nicaraguan Democratic Union, the only major anti-Sandinista force that had not been founded by former National Guardsmen. Former contra leader and Cardenal associate Edgar Chamorro exposed the U.S. hand in the formation of the contras in testimony before the World Court in 1985:

> [The Nicaraguan Democratic Union] initially opposed any linkage with the Guardsmen . . . [but] the CIA and high ranking United States government officials insisted that we merge with the Guardsmen. Lt. Gen. Vernon Walters . . . met with Cardenal to encourage him to accept the CIA's proposal. We were well aware of the crimes the Guardsmen had committed against the Nicaraguan people while in the service of President Somoza, and we wanted nothing to do with them. However, we recognized that without help from the United States we had no chance of removing the Sandinistas from power, so we eventually acceded to the CIA's and General Walters' insistence that we join forces with the Guardsmen.[6]

On August 10, 1981, at a meeting in Guatemala City, Guatemala, the CIA's plan came to fruition, and a new, umbrella resistance movement called the Nicaraguan Democratic Force (FDN) was formed. For all intents and purposes, the FDN *was* the contra movement, until it was supplanted in 1985 by the supposedly broader United Nicaraguan Opposition, again at the behest of the United States. From the beginning, the leadership, tactics, and political statements of the contra movement were to be made in the U.S.A. Despite Reagan's rhetoric, this was no group of nascent democrats—they were essentially a CIA front group drawn from those who had lost privilege, rank, or both when the Sandinista revolution overthrew Somoza in July 1979. According to Chamorro, after Cardenal's group united with the former Somoza military men, the CIA delivered on its end of the bargain: "Soon after the merger, the FDN began to receive a steady flow of financial, military, and other assistance from the CIA."[7]

At first, the U.S. military role was conducted by proxy, at base camps in Honduras where CIA-funded Argentinian military advisers trained the anti-Sandinista army. Contra military leader Enrique Bermudez described the arrangement succinctly: "The Hondurans will provide the territory, the Americans the money, and the Argentines the front."[8]

As reports of this covert action filtered back to Congress, key members began to question whether Reagan's policy had gone beyond shipping arms to providing full-scale support for a secret war to topple the Sandinista government. Reagan administration officials vehemently denied this, claiming that the sole purpose of U.S. arms and training was to give the anti-Sandinista forces the wherewithal to intercept arms shipments that were allegedly making their way from Nicaragua to the Farabundo Marti National Liberation front in neighboring El Salvador, as "documented" in the February 1981 White Paper. This "interdiction" policy was a convenient fiction from the outset, designed to allow the Reagan administration to sponsor a war against the Nicaraguan government without acknowledging it, thereby getting around their obligation to inform Congress of the scope of the president's secret war.

To quell these doubts, House Intelligence Committee chairman Edward Boland of Massachusetts sponsored an amendment in 1982 that explicitly prohibited the contras from using any of their U.S. arms aid "for the purpose of overthrowing the government of Nicaragua or provoking a military exchange between Nicaragua and Honduras." The Reagan administration reluctantly supported the Boland amendment rather than a proposal by Congressman Tom Harkin of Iowa that would have cut off all covert aid to the contras. With administration support in hand, the first Boland amendment passed the House of Representatives by a unanimous vote of 411 to 0. It was reinforced in late 1983 with the passage of a $24 million cap on aid to the contras for the year to come, coupled with a continuing prohibition on the use of contra aid to overthrow the Sandinistas. Both initiatives were based on the naive assumption that a bunch of former National Guardsmen and disgruntled former property owners were going to risk their lives for the altruistic purpose of preventing the alleged flow of arms from Nicaragua into neighboring El Salvador, all the while putting aside their primary objective, which had always been to bring down the Sandinista government.

On the eve of the public debate on the first Boland amendment, contra military chief Bermudez underscored this point, asserting flatly that "it is unacceptable to us to carry out missions to interdict Cuban and Russian supply lines to El Salvador. We are Nicaraguans and our objective is to overthrow the Communists and install a democratic government in our country." Another contra official seconded Bermudez's point, expressing surprise at the notion that they were to use their U.S. aid solely to track down arms destined for El Salvador: "If that's what the CIA told Congress, they forgot to tell us."[9]

In part out of an awareness that the "arms interdiction" rationale could not hold up in the face of such obvious evidence to the contrary, in September 1983 Reagan signed a new intelligence finding that justified support for the rebels as a way to "pressure" the Nicaraguan government to stop their alleged "subversion" of neighboring countries. A bone was thrown to congressional critics, in the form of a pledge that no U.S. personnel would be directly involved in military action inside Nicaragua. But despite these reassurances that the United States was not going to play an active operational role in the conflict, CIA involvement in the secret war intensified. It was revealed in April 1984 that CIA teams had carried out the mining of Nicaragua's harbors. The normally mild-mannered Boland was outraged, and he took to the House floor to vent his anger: "The first announcement—the first announcement—of the mining was made by the contras—the contras—not by the Intelligence Committee, not by the CIA, not from briefings we heard, but made by the contras. . . . Acts of war by the United States against Nicaragua are wrong, absolutely wrong."[10]

This incident was followed by revelations later in the year of a CIA "training manual" for the contras that suggested selected assassinations of local Sandinista officials as a way to foster psychological insecurity among the populace and undermine the authority of the regime. In a way that even the most docile member of Congress could not ignore, these activities decisively contradicted the Reagan administration's questionable assertions that it was merely providing support to the contras to help them "pressure" the Nicaraguan government. The line between supplying "only" arms and training and waging a U.S.-directed war against the Sandinistas had clearly been crossed by Reagan policymakers, and no one had even bothered to inform the Congress, much less the public.

These methods proved too much for even hard-line conservatives like Sen. Barry Goldwater, the cochair of the Senate Intelligence Committee. Goldwater dashed off a message to CIA director William Casey to let him know that he was "pissed off" that the mining of Nicaragua's harbors had been hidden from him. This mood in Congress fueled a total cutoff of aid to the contras in October 1984, under the second version of the Boland amendment. In language that was later to be a matter of heated dispute in the congressional Iran/contra investigations, the new Boland amendment flatly prohibited the use of "funds available to the CIA, DOD [Department of Defense], or any other agency or entity of the United States government involved in intelligence activities" for "supporting, directly or indirectly, military or paramilitary operations in Nicaragua." Boland and his colleagues were clear that this new law would put an end to U.S. government involvement in the secret war against the Sandinistas. Boland asserted that "the compromise provision clearly ends U.S. support for the war in Nicaragua." Even Republican stalwart Congressman Dick Cheney of Wyoming grudgingly acknowledged that it was a "killer amendment" that was intended to force the contras "to lay down their arms."[11]

But even before the second Boland amendment had passed, Oliver North had already been put to work raising funds that the contras could use to "keep body and soul together" in the event of a total congressional aid cutoff. At a June 1984 meeting of Reagan's National Security Planning Group, a decision was made to evade congressional limitations on contra funding by seeking contributions from allied nations. The notes from the meeting make it painfully evident that far from being out of the loop in the Iran/contra scandal, both President Reagan and Vice President Bush were at the center of the decision to defy Congress and the Constitution to finance the covert contra arms supply network:

> NATIONAL SECURITY ADVISER ROBERT MCFARLANE: There seems to be no prospect that the Democratic leadership will provide for any vote on the Nicaraguan program.
>
> PRESIDENT REAGAN: It all hangs on support for the anti-Sandinistas. How can we get that support in Congress? We need to be more active.
>
> UN AMBASSADOR JEANE KIRKPATRICK: If we can't get the money for the anti-Sandinistas, then we should make the maximum effort to find the money elsewhere.
>
> SECRETARY OF STATE GEORGE SHULTZ: I would like to get the money for the contras also, but Jim Baker said that if we go out and try to get money from third countries, it is an impeachable offense.
>
> CIA DIRECTOR WILLIAM CASEY: Jim Baker said that if we tried to get money from third countries without notifying the oversight committees it could be a problem.
>
> SECRETARY SHULTZ: Baker's argument is that the U.S. government may raise and spend funds only through an appropriation of Congress.
>
> PRESIDENT REAGAN: We must obtain the funds to help these freedom fighters.
>
> VICE PRESIDENT BUSH: The only problem that might come up is if the United States were to promise to give these third countries

something in return, so that some people could interpret this as some kind of exchange.

McFARLANE: I certainly hope none of this discussion will be made public in any way.

PRESIDENT REAGAN: If such a story gets out, we'll all be hanging by our thumbs out in front of the White House until we find out who did it.[12]

So, in the midst of his 1984 reelection campaign, with Congress and 70 percent of the public opposed to his contra aid policy, Reagan made it clear to his staff that he was determined to come up with the money somehow, Congress and the Constitution be damned. Even after his top foreign policy aide raised the specter of impeachment in connection with soliciting funds from other countries to evade the will of Congress, Reagan made it clear that he wanted to go ahead with the plan. His main concern was that no one leak the details to the American people, not whether he was about to break the law.

However problematic it was legally, pursuing third-country contributions worked extremely well as a way of obtaining funds for the contras. Saudi Arabia alone kicked in $32 million, starting at a rate of $1 million per month in mid-1984 and upping that figure to $2 million per month in 1985.[13]

President Reagan was well aware of this arrangement with the Saudis; he even discussed it with the Saudi leader at the White House. Although Reagan has denied making a direct appeal to King Fahd, he admits talking to him about the money for the contras during the king's February 1985 visit to Washington. Whether or not Reagan made the funding pitch, his discussions with Fahd indicate that he knew that his administration was following through on this plan.[14]

Congress did not learn of these extraordinary efforts to evade the legal prohibition on U.S. support for the contras until almost three years later, when the Iran/contra scandal broke. This stunning defiance of the right of Congress to have information and input regarding whom the United States ships arms to was worse than the worst days of the Nixon Doctrine. At least in the mid-1970s, members of Congress might learn of major public deals within a few weeks or months by reading about them in the paper, and covert deals would be reported to key congressional committees under the provisions of the Hughes/Ryan amendment. Reagan's policymakers had simply ignored these laws and rendered Congress irrelevant to the arms transfer decisionmaking process.

In addition to the president himself, another Reagan administration official who played a direct role in discussions with third-party governments over support for the contras was Vice President Bush. In February 1985, shortly after Reagan's reelection, Bush went to Honduras as an "emissary" of Oliver North's contra support effort to inform Honduran president Suazo that he would receive $100 million in expedited military, economic, and CIA aid *if* his country agreed to expand its role as a base for the contras in their war against the Sandinistas. Up to this day, Bush has vehemently denied that there was any deal cut with the Hondurans, as he indicated at a 1990 presidential press conference:

> Honduras—there was no quid pro quo. And for those who suggest there was, the onus is on them. The word of the President of the United States, George Bush, is there was no quid pro quo.[15]

But Bush's feverish assurances were contradicted by another president—Ronald Reagan—during his testimony under oath at the criminal trial of former NSC director John Poindexter:

> MR. BECKLER [ATTORNEY FOR THE SPECIAL PROSECUTOR'S OFFICE]: So, in other words, [if] some aid and assistance was given to them [the Honduran government], you would expect some aid and assistance back from them in combatting the spread of the Sandinistas?
>
> PRESIDENT REAGAN: Yeah.[16]

Oliver North has weighed in as well, indicating in his book, *Under Fire*, that it was well understood within the Reagan camp that of course there was a quid pro quo of U.S. aid to Honduras for Honduran support for the contras. North quotes from an NSC briefing memo prepared for President Reagan prior to one of his meetings with President Suazo of Honduras:

> In your meeting it will be important to reiterate to Suazo the importance we attach to his continued cooperation in enabling the FDN [the contras] to remain a viable element of pressure on the Sandinistas. Without making it too explicit, it would be useful to remind Suazo that in return for our help—in the form of security assurances as well as aid—we do expect cooperation in support of our mutual objectives. In this regard, you could underline the seriousness of our security commitment, *which the Hondurans seem to regard as the main quid pro quo for cooperating with the FDN* [emphasis added].[17]

The Honduras affair wasn't the only example of George Bush's implausible efforts to deny involvement in the Iran/contra affair. One of the more comical episodes of Bush's attempt to cover up his role in the secret arms scheme involved a series of meetings he had as vice president with Felix Rodriguez, a former CIA operative who was running the logistics end of Oliver North's contra arms supply network out of Ilopango air base in El Salvador. Bush had known Rodriguez, who also worked under the pseudonym "Max Gomez," since the mid-1970s. In fact, Rodriguez had received the CIA's Intelligence Star of Valor in 1976, the same year that Bush was director of the agency. Donald Gregg, another former CIA man who was serving as Vice President Bush's national security adviser, set up three meetings between Bush and Rodriguez at the White House during 1985 and 1986, supposedly to discuss Rodriguez's activities in Central America. Both Bush and Gregg have claimed that these meetings stuck strictly to discussions involving support for the government of El Salvador, with no mention of Rodriguez's central role in funneling arms to the contras. Gregg even sent Bush a memo in preparation for one of the meetings in which he cited the topics to be discussed as "the status of the war in El Salvador and the resupply of the contras." In his confirmation hearings for the post of Bush administration ambassador to South Korea, Gregg tried to explain away the reference to "resupply of the contras" as a secretarial error, arguing that it should have said "resupply of the *copters*," shorthand for helicopters being shipped to the Salvadoran military. Senate majority leader George Mitchell slammed Gregg's explanation as "pathetic" and "implausible." Sen. Al Gore wondered aloud "whether Mr. Gregg takes the U.S. Senate to be filled with gullible people. It's absurd on its face."[18]

Absurd or not, the Senate ultimately accepted Gregg's explanation, and they confirmed him as the Bush administration's ambassador to South Korea in September 1989. Neither Gregg nor Bush were ever held accountable for their role in concealing the illegal Iran/contra arms deals from Congress.

The Iranian Initiative

As troubling as the undemocratic methods of arming the contras were, there might never have been a full-blown public scandal at all if the Reagan/Bush secret arms sales policy had been limited to defying the Boland amendment. It was the second prong of Oliver North's covert enterprise, trading arms with Iran in exchange for assistance in freeing

U.S. hostages in Lebanon, that was so far out of line with stated administration policies that it set off alarm bells that could not be muted even by the master spin doctors in the Reagan White House. The "no deals with terrorists" line had been repeated by President Reagan, Vice President Bush, and Secretary of State Shultz since U.S. hostages were first taken in Lebanon in 1984 in retaliation for the U.S. support of Israel's invasion of Lebanon; even the most confirmed antiadministration cynic would have a hard time imagining that the Reagan team was trading arms with Iranian factions close to the hostage takers in exchange for their release. But they were. The fact that Reagan and important players in his administration accepted the notion that the United States could trade arms for hostages with a motley crew of Iranian "moderates" and middlemen was a measure of how deeply entrenched the U.S. government's arms sales addiction had become. Reagan and his men had reached the point where they believed that literally any foreign policy problem could be solved by throwing weapons at it.

The concept of swapping arms for hostages was approved by Reagan in a discussion with his national security adviser, Robert McFarlane, in July 1985, while the president was in the hospital recuperating from surgery. A plan was broached in which Israel would ship some of its U.S.-origin missiles to Iran in exchange for the release of U.S. hostages held by pro-Iranian factions in Lebanon. The United States would replace all the weapons that Israel transferred to Iran. Through the summer and fall of 1985, Israel shipped 504 TOW antitank missiles and 80 Hawk antiaircraft missiles to Iran at the behest of the United States, in exchange for which one U.S. hostage, Rev. Benjamin Weir, was released by his Lebanese captors.

In early 1986, over the protests of key advisers, including Secretary of State Shultz and Secretary of Defense Caspar Weinberger, Reagan approved an expansion of the arms-for-hostages deals in which Israel's intermediary role would be eliminated and arms would be sold to Iran directly out of U.S. stocks instead. These deals proceeded apace throughout 1986, until the Iran/contra operation was exposed to full public view in November of that year. Before it was over, North and his men had provided Iran with over two thousand TOW antitank missiles, eighty Hawk antiaircraft missiles, and significant spare parts for Iran's F-14 aircraft fleet. In the process, three U.S. hostages were freed, three more were taken, and the U.S. government sent out a message to terrorist organizations worldwide that a U.S. hostage could be worth more than his or her weight in weapons, if you played your cards right. As George Shultz noted in his memoirs, the arms-for-hostages swap was fatally flawed because "if hostage takers find out that they can 'sell' their hostages, their crimes will never cease."[19]

The Iran initiative was facilitated by "the enterprise," a complex web of secret bank accounts and front companies that was being run for North by Richard Secord and his business partner, Iranian arms broker Albert Hakim. Secord retired from the Pentagon in 1983 following allegations that he had been involved in a shady business deal with former CIA operative Ed Wilson, who was convicted of illegally shipping plastique explosives to Libya's Muammar Qaddafi. Secord was never charged with any wrongdoing in connection with his alleged dealings with Wilson. He then joined Hakim at the Stanford Technology Group, a business involved in brokering high-tech equipment sales. William Casey recommended Secord to Oliver North as the man he needed to help him run his shadow foreign policy out of the White House (see chapter 9).[20]

At first, Secord helped with fund-raising and advised contra leader Adolfo Calero on where to buy the weapons he needed. But his role soon expanded into logistics—buying planes and setting up airstrips and warehouses in El Salvador, Honduras, and Costa Rica for delivering weapons to contra forces inside Nicaragua.

Secord's secret network came into play in the direct U.S. deals with Iran, and it served as the link between the "Iran" and "contra" aspects of the Iran/contra scandal. North realized after earning $800,000 profit on a November 1985 shipment of Hawk antiaircraft missiles that selling arms to Iran could become a cash cow that could be used both to finance the contras and to support other covert actions in the future. During his Iran/contra testimony, North claimed that the notion of skimming profits off the Iranian arms sales to fund the contras was a "neat idea" that Iranian middleman Manucher Ghorbanifar suggested to him in the men's room at a 1985 meeting in London. This apocryphal story may tell as much about North's penchant for embellishment as it does about how the diversion scheme was actually hatched. Tapes uncovered by congressional investigators demonstrate that the idea was actually brought up in an open meeting with a number of other people present. But the spirit of North's version does ring true in at least one respect: the decision to compound the inherent illegality of the Iran and contra arms dealings by connecting the two initiatives was arrived at almost casually, with the input of an arms dealer of questionable integrity weighing more heavily than the views of any member of Congress or anyone in the president's own cabinet. In farming out the contra supply operation to North and Secord's network, Reagan had in effect privatized the conduct of U.S. foreign policy as well.[21]

Ghorbanifar's role in thinking up the diversion idea was not the only example of free-lance arms dealers taking control of critical strategy decisions to the exclusion of key elected or appointed U.S. government officials. Hakim, Secord's business partner and the financial mastermind of the enterprise, was delegated by North to handle sensitive, point-by-point negotiations with Iranian government contacts regarding the next steps in the arms-for-hostages exchange. Hakim's role prompted the following exchange with the counsel for the congressional Iran/contra investigating committee:

COUNSEL: Did you feel like you had been Secretary of State for a day?

HAKIM: I would not accept that position for any money in the world, sir.

COUNSEL: Well, you had it better than the Secretary of State in some sense. You didn't have to get confirmed, correct?

HAKIM: I still believe that I have it better than the Secretary. . . . I can achieve more.

Hakim went on to note that he would be "honored" if the secret deal he struck with the Iranians on behalf of North's network came to be known as the "Hakim accords."[22]

As startling as Hakim's role as a shadow secretary of state was, it was Ghorbanifar's diversion strategy that kept the Iran/contra scheme alive and drove the conspirators to further extremes of lawlessness. The prospect of running the contra supply operation from the profits on the arms sales to Iran also provided the main rationale for cutting Israel out as the middleman in the deal. Using the Secord/Hakim enterprise to sell U.S. weapons directly to Iran would provide more control over pricing—and profits. The weapons were technically "sold" by the army to the CIA, which then handed them over to Secord and Hakim for sale to Iran. The enterprise raised over $16 million by overcharging Iran for an impressive array of U.S. missiles and spare parts, but only a few million of those dollars ever made it to the contras. The bulk of the money—over $8 million—remained in a private Swiss bank account controlled by Hakim, and he had no intention of giving it back.[23]

The Investigation: Congress Drops the Ball

When Iran/contra finally hit the headlines in the fall of 1986, it was the so-called diversion—the transfer of profits from the arms sales to Iran to Secord and Hakim's pro-contra enterprise—that was the focus of media attention and congressional investigation. Never mind that the Reagan administration had violated the Boland amendment by arming the contras when Congress had prohibited it, undermined the Constitution by running a secret war using a shadow government that was accountable neither to Congress nor to the public, repeatedly lied to Congress and the public about these endeavors, and then shredded documents to cover up these crimes. All of this was viewed as secondary to the narrower question of what Ronald Reagan knew about the diversion and when he knew it.

The congressional hearings seemed as if they had been designed to fail from the start. Iran/contra committee chairman Lee Hamilton, who had already been duped by McFarlane's bald-faced lies about the existence of a secret contra supply network two years earlier, agreed to limit the inquiry to just three months. As Iran/contra investigator Pamela Naughton has noted, "The minute you tell the subject of an investigation, 'Don't worry. We're all going to go away in another few months,' there is every incentive, then, to simply stall and stonewall and wait until we indeed go away. And that's unfortunately what happened."[24]

Hamilton acknowledged that the limits on the investigation were not set by how long it might take to determine if President Reagan had committed an impeachable offense, but that it was a "political decision." In Hamilton's view, "A President was in danger of being crippled by these events and we did not think it was in the country's benefit to extend this out for a long period of time."[25] But what of the benefit to be had by punishing official lawlessness and making sure that the president never again wages war through covert arms sales in violation of the will of Congress and the Constitution?

The performance of Congress since the Iran/contra hearings has been even less encouraging to observers who had hoped the scandal might prompt the legislative branch to reassert some control over both the covert and public sides of the arms trade. Only a handful of the congressional investigating committee's more than two dozen recommended reforms to prevent a repeat of Iran/contra were even taken up for consideration. One of the most important proposals, a bill that would have required that Congress be notified of all secret arms sales and other covert actions within forty-eight hours, was so watered down by the time President Bush finally signed it into law in 1991 that it essentially left it in the president's hands to decide when and how to notify Congress of secret weapons shipments. The law calls for prior notification of most covert actions, but it preserves language dating back to the 1974 Hughes/Ryan amendment that allows the executive branch to provide notice in "a timely fashion" in cases in which advance notice is not provided to Congress. The spirit of this provision had been totally violated during Iran/contra, and the members of the investigating committee decided that a specific amount of time should be written into law to prevent similar abuses in the future. Ronald Reagan's idea of timely notice to Congress for his secret arms deals with Iran had been whenever it was convenient to do so without impeding the progress of an ongoing covert initiative. The Iran/contra operation had proceeded for nearly three years before Congress learned of its existence, not through any formal notification by the Reagan administration but as a result of a newspaper article that was published in a Beirut magazine. During the debate on revising the law, the members of the congressional intelligence committee expressed their view that timely notice should mean "within a few days," but President Bush held out for the right to wait longer in some cases. As Congressman Ted Weiss of New York noted in the floor debate on the bill, the new, allegedly improved law "allows the president still to claim that he can withhold whatever information that he wants." This left a potential opening for Bush or some future president to repeat Ronald Reagan's performance in the Iran/contra affair.[26]

On the subject of overt, public sales involving major systems like the AWACS or the F-15, congressional action in the wake of Iran/contra was equally uninspiring. Congress did hold a few hearings on a bill authored by three Democrats (senators Joseph Biden of Delaware and Claiborne Pell of Rhode Island and Congressman Mel Levine of California) that would have required Congress to vote on all sales of major combat equipment to Third World nations. This would have forced members of Congress to study prospective sales and go on record for or against, providing a vital element of accountability that is completely lacking in current arms sales procedures. But the bill disappeared without even a vote, due in large part to a highly effective industry lobbying campaign (this will be discussed in more detail in chapter 9).

Not only did Iran/contra expose the weaknesses in our own democracy when it comes to controlling runaway arms trafficking, it called the morality and legality of U.S. foreign policy into question on the international stage as well. Even before it became public knowledge that the Boland amendment had merely spurred an even larger, more devious covert operation headed up by an obscure lieutenant colonel, the Reagan administration had announced to the world that it was perfectly willing to flout international law in pursuit of its new military doctrine. When the government of Nicaragua took the issue of U.S. mining of Nicaraguan harbors to the World Court in The

Hague, the Reagan administration refused to recognize the court's jurisdiction, the first time a U.S. administration had done so in over forty years. In pursuit of its covert arms policy, the Reagan team was willing to do damage to an invaluable international forum for the peaceful resolution of disputes.[27]

Arming Freedom Fighters?

The first casualty of the Reagan Doctrine was the standing of the United States in the eyes of world public opinion. The most obvious contradiction in the president's proudly proclaimed new policy was its founding assumption that U.S. arms were in fact being used to empower "freedom fighters," latter-day democrats committed to replacing tyranny with governments of, by, and for the people. As has been noted above, Reagan's beloved Nicaraguan contras were led into battle by an officer corps overwhelmingly dominated by members of the hated national guard that helped keep the Somoza family dictatorship in power for nearly five decades.[28] And despite protestations that they had somehow turned over a new leaf, their prosecution of the war belied that assertion. As described by the human rights monitoring group Americas Watch, the behavior of the contras gave little indication of any democratic potential. A March 1986 report described routine contra murders of noncombatants:

> The testimony we obtained frequently showed gratuitous brutality: the contras not only murdered their victims; they also tortured and mutilated them. In some cases, they also killed members of the families of their targets.[29]

Some freedom fighters.

Even in Afghanistan, where at least the rebels were fighting a genuine case of Soviet aggression, the probability that a rebel victory would usher in a new era of democracy and freedom was hovering somewhere between slim and none. The seven rebel factions ranged from left-wing mujahadeen to conservative, Islamic, tribal movements that were more inclined to turn Afghanistan into a harsher version of the Ayatollah Khomeini's Iran than they were to pursue anything even remotely resembling democracy.[30]

In addition to the high uncertainty of a democratic outcome within Afghanistan, the implementation of the Reagan Doctrine has considerably weakened the prospects for establishing an enduring democracy in neighboring Pakistan, which served as the principal conduit for U.S. military aid to the Afghan rebel movements throughout the 1980s. Reagan's $4 billion plus military and economic aid package to Pakistan—offered in exchange for Pakistan's support of the Afghan rebels—encouraged the regime to devote over 60 percent of its scarce government funds to military purposes to the exclusion of the country's extensive social and educational needs.[31] As the Afghan war wound down in the early 1990s, Pakistan was mired in what one *Wall Street Journal* article described as "the worst outbreak of lawlessness in its history," and "the U.S., it turns out, inadvertently helped supply the firepower." The article went on to describe gangs of criminals and terrorists roaming the streets of major Pakistani cities virtually unchecked, fending off police with machine guns, grenade launchers, and other sophisticated armaments procured in the nation's scores of weapons markets. Much of this weaponry was siphoned off from U.S. aid supplies to the Afghan rebel forces, rerouted into what many Pakistanis have come to call their "Kalashnikov culture" of armed street violence. In tones that offer a slightly more down-to-earth echo of the rationales offered by U.S. government bureaucrats and corporate officials involved in the arms trade, a Pakistani arms dealer proudly displayed his wares: "This is a market, we buy and sell. We don't care who comes as long as he has money. . . . We're experts in weapons."[32]

The outbreak of violence and corruption in Pakistan was an unintended byproduct of the Reagan Doctrine, but its effects on Pakistani society may be a more accurate measure of the true impacts of relying on arms as the ultimate foreign policy tool than any of Reagan or Bush's unfulfilled promises about helping "freedom fighters" to foster "democracy."

In Angola, the administration's ally, Jonas Savimbi of UNITA, has continued to hold fast to the one constant in his career as a pseudorevolutionary: an opportunistic drive for power. As described by former CIA agent John Stockwell, Savimbi was a "charismatic megalomaniac," an unlikely candidate for sharing power even with other elites and organizations within Angola, much less the masses.[33] But in the increasingly conservative, self-deluding world of Reagan's Washington, a right-wing public relations campaign had succeeded in painting this ruthless military leader as a nascent democrat. In 1984, Congress succumbed to administration pressure and lifted the nine-year-old Clark amendment, which had banned covert arms aid to Savimbi and other anticommunist rebel forces inside Angola. Ten years later, Savimbi was still using his spoils from the Reagan Doctrine to thwart genuine democratic development in Angola, ignoring the results of a 1992 UN-sponsored election and attempting to gain power through force of arms instead. As of November 1994, the Savimbi forces had entered into a tentative peace agreement with the government which promised to bring an end to over two decades of civil war in Angola.

In Asia, Reagan's roster of "freedom fighters" included the Khmer People's National Liberation Front, a noncommunist coalition that had affiliated itself with the hated communist Khmer Rouge. Under the leadership of Pol Pot, the Khmer Rouge had been responsible for the murder, torture, exile, and displacement of over a million of his countrymen in the late 1970s. While U.S. aid did not flow directly to Pol Pot's forces, the assistance provided to his coalition partners increased the possibility that the Khmer Rouge could return to power in Cambodia, which would hardly be seen by any reasonable observer as a victory for freedom or democracy. As of mid-1994, Khmer Rouge forces, after boycotting UN-supervised elections, were still carrying on a campaign of violence and intimidation against Cambodia's elected government.[34]

Once the initial rhetoric was peeled away, even a cursory look at Ronald Reagan's chosen allies for his new, U.S.-armed anticommunist crusade demonstrated that there was hardly a democrat in the bunch. The real rationale for supporting this collection of armed thugs, right-wing ideologues and religious fundamentalists was that they were all fighting in opposition to regimes that were receiving direct or indirect support from Moscow. Rather than a battle cry of freedom, the Reagan Doctrine was an extreme manifestation of Cold War gamesmanship, reinforced by the new penchant for arms trading that had taken root in the decade and a half since Richard Nixon's remarks in Guam. In the Soviet Union and even among key U.S. allies in Europe, the Reagan Doctrine was seen not as a way to promote democracy but as a cynical power play by an insecure superpower trying to make one last grab for uncontested dominance on the world stage.

A Doctrine Run Amok: Arming Potential Adversaries

As if this damage to U.S. prestige were not serious enough, the Reagan Doctrine's fast-and-loose approach to doling out weaponry posed a direct security risk to U.S. citizens and military personnel alike. The covert network set up by Oliver North and his cohorts in the Iran/contra affair supplied the Khomeini regime with hundreds of millions of dollars' worth of missiles and valuable spare parts for U.S.

systems that had been transferred to Iran during the heyday of the shah's buying spree. Despite repeated assertions by high-level Reagan administration officials that the arms supplied to Iran were of limited military significance, an administration expert on Middle Eastern affairs told *Aviation Week and Space Technology* that "at U.S. instigation, the Iranians bought critical radar and landing gear components that at times . . . enabled Iran to double the number of sorties flown by its McDonnell Douglas F-4 aircraft against Iraq."[35]

Not only did U.S. weaponry supplied as part of the Iran/contra scheme improve Iran's ability to wage its war with Iraq, which dragged on from late 1980 through the middle of 1988, but earlier purchases made during the Nixon, Ford, and Carter administrations made the Iranian military a more dangerous opponent for U.S. naval forces stationed in the Persian Gulf to protect Kuwaiti oil tankers from 1987 onward. A *Washington Post* report filed in the summer of 1987, at the height of U.S. involvement in the Gulf "tanker wars" between Iran and Iraq, underscored this point:

> The American-made helicopters dragged mine-hunting sonar devices through the choppy waters of the Persian Gulf as their spinning rotors slashed the muggy air.
>
> Pilots and crewmen, trained in Florida, Texas, and Virginia, conversed in English over U.S.-built radios, occasionally flashing the thumbs-up sign to make their approval clear over the deafening din of the motors.
>
> To all appearances, the mine-sweeping action seemed to be part of the American naval mission to make the Gulf's treacherous waters safe for the transport of Kuwaiti oil. But in reality, the operation was being conducted by Iranian sailors employing U.S. equipment purchased during the era of the shah, and tactics learned when Iran and the United States were close military allies.[36]

Fear of U.S. arms in Iran being turned against U.S. forces in the Gulf figured in one of the most tragic incidents in the so-called tanker wars, when a U.S. cruiser armed with the advanced Aegis radar system shot down an Iranian passenger airliner, mistaking it for an F-14 fighter plane. The F-14 had been the shah's pride and joy, a state-of-the-art combat plane that had the capability of tracking and firing at up to eighty targets simultaneously, but there had been no indication that the Khomeini regime had the technical expertise or the spare parts to keep significant numbers of these sophisticated planes up and running. Nevertheless, in the heat of battle, the notion that Iran might have put one of the aircraft into service against U.S. naval forces was enough to spark a tragic error, for which the U.S. was forced to apologize, and even to offer modest compensation to the families of the innocent victims. But the Iranian government and its terrorist allies apparently had a different form of compensation in mind, in the form of an eye for an eye. When a U.S.-bound jet was blown up over Lockerbie, Scotland, a year later, the terrorist group taking responsibility for the bombing indicated that it was done in retaliation for the U.S. downing of the Iranian airliner in the Gulf. The U.S. investigation of the Lockerbie bombing has taken numerous twists and turns since then, with the indictment of two Libyan nationals in 1991; but families of the victims and expert analysts of the events leading up to the Lockerbie bombing remain convinced that Iran and Syria were also involved.[37]

The potential for U.S.-supplied arms to boomerang on U.S. forces and U.S. citizens was lost on Ronald Reagan and most of his foreign policy team, who saw only the benefits of trading arms for influence, not the strange and unpredictable ways that these weapons could come back to haunt the United States down the road.

Even the most successful application of the Reagan Doctrine, involving the supply of Stinger antiaircraft missiles to the Afghan rebels, had unintended, dangerous consequences for U.S. security. While these shoulder-fired missiles were credited with enabling rebel forces to shoot down an average of more than one Soviet aircraft or helicopter per day, shifting the balance of forces in the war in the process, not all of the missiles found their mark—or even made their way to the battlefront in Afghanistan.

A series of reports in mid-1987 indicated that a significant number of U.S.-supplied Stingers had been diverted from Afghanistan by Islamic fundamentalist factions within the rebel coalition and supplied to Iran, where they could have been put to use against U.S. forces. And at least one Stinger attack shot down a civilian Afghan airliner, sowing hatred of the rebels and distrust of the United States among many Afghanis. In belated recognition of the danger posed by the Stingers falling "into the hands of terrorist groups or unfriendly . . . governments," in early 1992 the Bush administration quietly launched an effort to buy back the remaining missiles that the Afghan rebel fighters had left over from their twelve-year civil war. This was extremely ironic given that the Reagan administration had staunchly resisted congressional efforts to impose any controls on the transfer or storage of Stingers in the Middle East and South Asia. Now Reagan's successor, George Bush, was being forced to beg and bribe the Afghan rebel factions to send back hundreds of U.S. missiles that they had received free of charge in the first place![38]

And of course, the most dangerous and costly example of back-door wheeling and dealing in arms coming back to threaten the United States directly was the U.S. role in building up Saddam Hussein's war machine in the five years leading up to his August 1990 invasion of Kuwait (the arming of Iraq will be dealt with in detail in chapter 11). But the absurd notion that the United States could arm both sides of the Iran–Iraq war—to free hostages, gain influence with "moderates" in Iran, *and* keep Saddam Hussein strong enough to prolong the war and create a stalemate—was a direct consequence of the ethos spawned by the Reagan Doctrine, in which supplying arms was seen as an all-purpose solution to even the thorniest foreign policy problem.

As destructive as the ultimate outcome of arms sales to Iran and Iraq was, there was very nearly an even more devastating result in Afghanistan. As the hundreds of millions of dollars of annual U.S. arms aid to Afghan rebels began to take their toll on Soviet forces, sparking cross-border raids by the Soviets against Afghan rebel camps in Pakistan, the possibility of a dramatic escalation of U.S. involvement was seriously contemplated in military and intelligence circles. If Soviet hard-liners had prevailed and "stayed the course" in Afghanistan, there was a possibility that the U.S. involvement that had begun as a modest arms supply operation late in the Carter administration could have escalated into a direct superpower confrontation. One prominent U.S. military analyst even suggested the possibility of using tactical nuclear weapons in Afghanistan. So much for the "risk free" Reagan Doctrine.[39]

Undermining Democracy at Home

Perhaps the greatest long-term danger inherent in the Reagan Doctrine and its supporting philosophy is the threat it poses to democracy in the United States. The code of ethics of the covert arms trader was clearly laid out by Oliver North in his testimony before the congressional Iran/contra investigating committees in the summer of 1987: in fighting a perpetual global "war" against communism, terrorism, and Third World radicalism, the ends justify the means, and misleading Congress and the public is just another tactic in the struggle. As North put it to the committees, "It is very important for the American people to know that this is a dangerous world; that we live at risk and that this nation is at risk in a dangerous world." But other than this generalized sense of "danger," fed by government propaganda of the sort that was used routinely by the Reagan administration in promoting its crusade on behalf of the contras, there was not much else that North and his cohorts felt that Congress or the public had a right to know. In fact, North went on to explain, "by their very nature covert operations or special activities are a lie. There is great deceit, deception practiced in the conduct of covert operations."

And while North assured the committees that the conduct of the Iran/contra schemes had not "intentionally deceived the American people," the public and Congress were being systematically kept in the dark about activities and practices that went to the heart of how the United States conducts its foreign relations. In fact, North revealed that CIA director William Casey had an even more ambitious plan for using the network of front companies, secret bank accounts, and contract employees that were running the Iran/contra arms supply enterprise:

> Director Casey had in mind, as I understood it, an overseas entity that was capable of conducting operations or activities of assistance to the U.S. foreign policy goals that was a "stand alone," it was self-financing, independent of appropriated monies and capable of conducting activities similar to the ones that we had conducted here.

Apparently, only Casey's death and the disclosure of the Iran/contra operation kept this plan from going into effect.[40]

As New Hampshire Republican senator Warren Rudman, the cochairman of the joint congressional Iran/contra investigating committee, commented a few days after North's revelations, "If you carry this to its logical extreme, you don't have a democracy anymore."[41]

Misleading Congress and the public about the details and goals of U.S. covert arms dealing and secret military support operations was the central aspect of the threat to democracy posed by the Reagan Doctrine. As veteran national correspondent Daniel Schorr aptly described the mind-set of Reagan administration operatives, "Under the sun of President Reagan's smile, the White House covert warriors seemed to function in a fantasy world where no harm could come to their crusades for democracy abroad as long as they could be kept secret from the democracy at home."[42] By pursuing the capability to support right-wing guerrillas from a revolving fund drawn from the profits of secret arms deals, the Casey/North enterprise held out the prospect of operating entirely outside the purview of Congress, free from the congressional "power of the purse" that the founders of the nation had seen as an essential check on overreaching by the executive branch. The offhand scheme of Iranian middleman Manucher Ghorbanifar, which Ollie North had described as a neat idea—secretly selling U.S. arms at inflated prices and using the profits to fund other covert operations—almost became a central tool of U.S. foreign policy. This outrageous effort to evade Congress was reminiscent of Nixon and Kissinger's earlier turn to arms sales in the mid-1970s in their effort to wrest total control of foreign policy back from a restive Congress. But this new twist on that old maneuver was far more sinister, implying a massive worldwide secret arms apparatus that would have more control over U.S. foreign policy than appointed members of the president's cabinet or elected members of Congress. The result would have been a total lack of accountability by the executive branch on foreign policy and essential issues of war and peace and, ultimately, a short-circuiting of democracy.

As for Congress, after abdicating its responsibility to call Ronald Reagan to task for hatching the unconstitutional scheme that was Iran/contra, congressional leaders have yet to enact one significant reform that would prevent another Iran/contra scandal from occurring. Far from showing that "the system worked," the conduct of the congressional Iran/contra investigation called into question whether the legislative branch has the political will to exercise its constitutional functions, or whether a band of military men, intelligence operatives, and free-lance arms dealers will continue to be entrusted with more responsibility for deciding the direction of U.S. foreign policy than our own representatives and senators.

7

Bush Policy: Institutionalizing Arms Sales Promotion

Arms sales policy was a footnote to the 1988 presidential campaign, in large part because George Bush and his handlers worked overtime to keep it that way. Bush's most notable references to the arms sales issue during the campaign were his repeated denials of any involvement in Iran/contra. During the Democratic primaries, Michael Dukakis had pointedly denounced the insanity of uncontrolled arms sales to the Persian Gulf, but by the time the general election rolled around he was so much on the defensive against Republican charges that he was a card-carrying liberal who was soft on crime and national defense that he was unable to make an effective issue of Bush's complicity in Reagan's runaway arms sales initiatives.

In fact, the strongest criticism of Bush on the arms sales issue came from within his own party, during the runup to the February 1988 Iowa presidential caucuses. Former Reagan administration secretary of state and rival presidential candidate Alexander Haig was the first to take Bush to task. At a candidates' forum in December 1987, Haig hit hard at Bush's contradictory assertion that he was both a trusted adviser to the president on foreign policy issues and a bit player who was totally "out of the loop" on the Iran/contra arms deals.

He's running for president now. The American people are entitled to know what position he took during this storm that imperiled our nation's vital interests. Where was George Bush during the storm? Was he the co-pilot in the cockpit, or was he back in economy class?[1]

Two front-page stories in the January 7, 1988, edition of the *Washington Post* appeared to dash any hopes that the Bush presidential campaign would be able to put the issue behind them in time for the Iowa caucuses: "Bush Regularly Attended Meetings on Iran Sales: Records Indicate Knowledge Understated" and "Questions Dog Vice President: Bush Yet to Provide Full Account on Iran." Rival candidates Jack Kemp and Robert Dole also called for Bush to "clear the air" on his role in the scandal, and it was widely expected to be a major point of contention in a critical Republican presidential debate sponsored by the Des Moines *Register* later that same week.

At this point Bush and his campaign team, led by media adviser Roger Ailes, decided that Bush's best defense on the Iran/contra charges was a good offense. Henceforth when this issue came up, candidate Bush would attack his critics rather than answering their questions. When Des Moines *Register* editor James Gannon asked Bush about Iran/contra at the debate, Bush lashed out at him, claiming that the paper had unfairly accused him of not answering questions about his role in the affair, and added, "I resent it, frankly." This aggressive strategy was amazingly effective, as a *Washington Post* reporter who covered the event noted: "Once Bush fired back at Gannon . . . the issue faded and did not dominate the debate, as many had expected." And when Haig pressed Bush again to reveal what advice, if any, he gave Ronald Reagan on the matter, Bush was ready with another counterattack. He asked Haig, who served as de facto chief of staff in the final days of the Nixon administration, "What did you tell Mr. Nixon in the days of Watergate?"[2]

The single event that did the most to relegate legitimate questions about Bush's role in Iran/contra to the sidelines was his televised confrontation with CBS News anchorman Dan Rather on the evening of January 25, 1988, just two weeks before the Iowa caucuses. After airing a six-minute taped story about the role of Bush and his advisers Donald Gregg and Samuel Watson in the Iran/contra affair, Rather opened the interview by questioning Bush's judgment:

Mr. Vice President . . . Donald Gregg still serves as your trusted adviser. He was deeply involved in running arms for the contras and he

> didn't inform you. Now, when President Reagan's trusted adviser, Admiral Poindexter, failed to inform him, the President fired him. Why is Mr. Gregg still inside the White House and still a trusted adviser?

In keeping with the strategy he had reportedly worked out in advance with Roger Ailes, Bush threw Rather's question right back in his face. He mumbled a few words about having "confidence" in Gregg and then launched into an extended complaint against CBS News, claiming that he had been misled into thinking that they would be doing a general "political profile" of him, not a rehash of his role in Iran/contra, which Bush claimed had already been "exhaustively looked into." Bush proceeded to stall for time, interrupting Rather's questions at every opportunity and openly changing the subject several times, telling Rather that "I want to get my share in here on something other than what you want to talk about."

If the interview had ended on that note, the story of the encounter would have been something like "Bush Again Evades Questions About His Role in Iran/Contra." But just as Rather was finally beginning to pin Bush down, the vice president pulled out his secret weapon, a direct personal attack on Rather:

> I don't think it's fair to judge a whole career, it's not fair to judge my whole career by a rehash on Iran. How would you like it if I judged your career by those seven minutes you walked off the set in New York? Would you like that?

Bush was referring to an incident in September 1987 when Rather, angered because the start of the evening news was being delayed by coverage of the U.S. Open tennis matches, walked off the set and was unavailable when the network switched back to the news. Rather was visibly upset by Bush's pointed reminder of one of the most embarrassing moments of his career. During the remainder of the interview, Rather lost his composure and crossed the line from persistent questioning to editorializing. He even started one question with the following statement: "Mr. Vice President, you've made us hypocrites in the face of the world. How could you, how could you sign on to such a policy?" Bush was then cut off by Rather in the middle of an answer about whether he would hold a news conference before the Iowa caucuses to resolve the lingering questions about his role in Iran/contra. While Bush was still talking, Rather said, "I gather the answer is no" and signed off before Bush could reply.[3]

Roger Ailes, the negative campaigner par excellence, had certainly earned his keep this time. In fact, there was strong circumstantial evidence that the Bush camp, far from being "surprised" that the topic of the CBS interview would be Iran/contra, had consciously sought out the opportunity for a live interview on Iran/contra to project Bush as a tough, combative fighter who wasn't going to take any more criticism on the subject, period. The ploy worked to near perfection. The most vocal public reaction to the interview was that Rather was out of line, and subsequent news media coverage focused more on Rather's alleged gaffe than Bush's continued evasiveness on Iran/contra. Bush played up the confrontation to counter his image as a "wimp," gloating to his aides afterward that "the bastard never laid a glove on me." The next day, in a series of campaign stops in Wyoming, Bush regaled supportive crowds with tales of how he had taken on the mighty Rather and won, asserting that "it was tension city in there" and arguing that he deserved "combat pay" for the encounter.[4]

The Bush/Rather confrontation was a critical turning point in the treatment of Iran/contra issues during the 1988 presidential campaign. Although Bush's role came up again from time to time, neither the media nor Bush's opponents raised the issue with the same forcefulness that Bush had encountered during the months prior to his staged confrontation with Dan Rather.

Although he had managed to shift the tone and depth of the coverage, Bush was still extremely nervous at the prospect that his inconsistent, indeed ludicrous, denials of any significant involvement in the Iran/contra schemes would come back to haunt him. His anxiety was evident in a June 1988 interview with ABC's Ted Koppel in which the "Nightline" anchor brought up some of the same points Rather had raised in January and even played a partial tape of Rather's interview with Bush. Bush, who was speaking from a remote hookup in Houston, repeatedly called Koppel "Dan," until his trusty media adviser Roger Ailes finally held up a sign with "TED" written on it. Bush later explained his slips of the tongue by saying, "I just kind of got all blurred in there. The question line, though pleasant, was pretty much the same [as in the earlier Rather interview]."

The next day, Bush was greeted at the Denver airport by a group of two dozen reporters wearing name tags that said "Dan." But Bush and the press were able to laugh it off, and the Iran/contra issue never resurfaced as a serious issue in the fall campaign.[5]

The Industry's Candidate of Choice

Although George Bush spent most of the campaign distancing himself from any connection with arms sales issues, his victory in the November election was viewed as good news by arms exporting firms. The industry's confidence in the newly elected president's commitment to their agenda was based as much on Bush's résumé and record as it was on anything he had actually said during the campaign. As the first former director of the CIA to be elected president, Bush was a good bet to support the kinds of covert arms sales that had been such a prominent feature of the Reagan foreign policy. And as Ronald Reagan's loyal vice president, Bush had helped to preside over one of the greatest conventional arms sales booms in U.S. history, rivaled only by the peak years of the Nixon/Kissinger policy in the mid-1970s. Of equal importance from the perspective of industry officials, Bush owed them a personal debt of gratitude for providing a direct boost to his 1988 election campaign.

While heavy political contributions from the arms industry to presidential candidates are common, George Bush may have been the first candidate to have his most loyal campaigner literally paid for by military firms. John Tower—a former chairman of the Senate Armed Services Committee who also headed the presidential review commission that had cleared Bush of any wrongdoing in the Iran/contra affair—was in effect on loan to the Bush presidential campaign from the arms industry, earning $500,000 in "consulting fees" from the nation's largest military contractors during 1988 even as he spent much of his time campaigning for the Bush/Quayle ticket.

A review of Tower's consulting arrangements by *Washington Post* reporters Charles Babcock and Bob Woodward concluded that it was "often hard to pinpoint what Tower and his associates did for their fees" but that it "translated practically . . . to Tower using his 24 years of Senate and defense experience both for general advice and getting his clients in the door to sell their goods." Among the tasks Tower performed for clients such as Rockwell International, LTV, and Martin Marietta was providing advice and exerting his considerable influence on future funding of systems such as the B-1 bomber and the Star Wars missile defense system. Tower also embarked on a trip to India and Pakistan to help drum up business for LTV's Multiple Launch Rocket System. Obviously, his ability to open doors for his industry clients would be greatly enhanced by a Republican victory in the fall presidential election, so most of them continued to pay him his consulting fees throughout 1988 even though it was well known that he was spending at least half of his time on the road campaigning for Bush. This blatant conflict of interest, while apparently legal, provided the arms industry with a strong stake in a Bush presidency, even as it obliged Bush to be particularly sensitive to the industry's needs once he took office.[6]

Tower was an old and loyal friend of the arms industry. In fact, it was Tower who had first proposed creating a government-financed stockpile of arms that could be shipped to overseas allies on short notice. The stockpile, budgeted at $1 billion and known as the Special Defense Acquisition Fund, had been adopted as an official government program during Ronald Reagan's first term in office, providing a hidden subsidy to the military industry and setting the stage for scores of lucrative foreign arms sales throughout the 1980s. Tower's presence as a surrogate member of the Bush/Quayle ticket was a clear signal to the arms industry that George Bush intended to continue the promilitary, pro-arms-sales policies of his predecessor. But for the reputation for drinking and womanizing that derailed his nomination, Tower would have been appointed as Bush's secretary of defense.

In a series of interviews I conducted in early 1989, it was clear that the corporate arms traders were confident that Bush would be firmly in their corner, even without Tower to plead their case. As one lobbyist put it, Bush was expected to continue the Reagan policy of aggressive arms sales, but "he won't make any big pronouncements about it. That's just not George." George Bush's policy would emerge from his actions, not from his rhetoric, and that was just fine with his allies in the arms industry.

Parallel Addictions: U.S. Arms for the Andean "Drug Wars"

The strongest indication that George Bush shared Ronald Reagan's penchant for using arms transfers as an all-purpose policy instrument came in conjunction with his plan for dealing with a largely domestic problem, the so-called war on drugs.

The first sign that George Bush planned to solve the drug problem by throwing weapons at it came in late August 1989, when he interrupted his vacation at the family complex in Kennebunkport, Maine, to announce an emergency shipment of $65 million in military aid to the government of Colombia for use in combating drug traffickers. The equipment and training would be paid for out of a discretionary fund available to the president under the Foreign Assistance Act. It represented the largest shipment of arms ever authorized under the emergency provisions of the act.

At a single stroke, George Bush had set the stage for sending more U.S. weaponry to Colombia than it had received in the entire decade of the 1980s. And this was not just police and law enforcement equipment—the package included twenty Huey helicopters, a workhorse of U.S. counterinsurgency missions in Vietnam; a Blackhawk medical evacuation helicopter; a collection of small planes and assault boats; and a wide array of firepower ranging from small arms and machine guns to mortars, grenade launchers, and antitank weapons.[7] The die had been cast: George Bush was going to offer accelerated shipments of U.S. arms and advisers to Latin America as a primary tool in his strategy for solving the drug problem—a strategy that ignored the complex social and economic roots of the demand for drugs within the United States. Ironically, Bush sought to counter the Andean nations' economic addiction to a particularly lucrative and destructive illegal export by deepening the U.S. dependency on an equally deadly, albeit legal, export of its own.

Bush's Colombian gambit was just the first stage of an open-ended U.S. military aid commitment to the Andean nations of Colombia, Peru, Bolivia, and Ecuador. In his first nationally televised address shortly after Labor Day, 1989, Bush sketched out his plan for substantial increases in federal antidrug funding, including a five-year, $2.2 billion plan to provide arms, training, and other assistance to the Andean drug-producing nations. Few analysts noticed at the time that the portion of the plan devoted to militarizing the battle against drugs in these four Latin American nations actually outstripped the amount of federal aid set aside for the fifty states and thousands of localities within the United States that had been crying out for additional federal assistance for antidrug law enforcement and drug treatment programs.[8]

It became clear within weeks of the emergency arms shipment to Colombia that the provision of U.S. military aid to further the "war on drugs" had more to do with the U.S. government's arms addiction than it did with any need for this weaponry on the part of Colombian authorities. When the first arms shipments reached Colombia, it was quickly determined that the equipment was virtually useless to the police agencies that were on the front lines of Colombia's battle against the drug cartels. The *Washington Post* reported that "Colombian and U.S. officials here criticized much of the emergency aid arriving from the United States as not well-suited to fighting drug trafficking." A U.S. official familiar with antidrug efforts in Colombia pointed out that although "90 to 95 percent" of the work was being done by the police, the Bush emergency aid package "did not have a lot of what the cops would like to have"—hand-held radios, sophisticated communications gear, and surveillance equipment for use in tracking down drug traffickers and locating their base areas. Instead, the package included items like A-37 fighter jets, which sources in Colombia asserted were "more suited for conventional warfare" than for fighting the drug cartels. If anything, the planes might make matters worse, because "the primary function of the A-37 is bombing, and specialists say the airplanes could not be used effectively or accurately against the often tiny, well hidden drug laboratories without destroying much of their surroundings."[9]

While the Andean arms plan served Bush's immediate political need to show "resolve" on the drug problem, critics in the United States and Latin America argued persuasively that this militarization of the antinarcotics effort would have little impact on the production and importation of drugs, even as it embroiled the United States in guerrilla wars in Peru and Colombia and fueled human rights abuses by the notorious military forces of the Andean region.

The critics' fears were justified. Within months of the transfer of the new U.S. equipment to the Colombian armed forces, human rights groups in Colombia reported that the village of Llana Fria in Santander province had been strafed by U.S.-supplied A-37s and Blackhawk helicopters, forcing over fourteen hundred peasants to flee to neighboring villages. Similar bombing was reported in three other provinces, aimed not at the drug cartels but at leftist guerrilla organizations. Moreover, according to a report by the Washington Office on Latin America (WOLA), "witnesses claim that the attacks were not aimed at guerrilla camps, as the military said, but at civilian settlements." In a troubling echo of Vietnam era "pacification" tactics, the Bush approach in practice seemed to mean destroying the peasantry in order to save it from drug cartels and leftist guerrilla organizations. WOLA executive director Alexander Wilde told a congressional hearing that a major danger of stepped-up U.S. military aid to the Colombian armed forces under the guise of fighting drugs was that it would just "fuel further the crisis of human rights abuse . . . and undermine political stability, by strengthening the Colombian armed forces." Wilde described an alliance among the military, the drug cartels, and large landowners that was responsible for a "human rights emergency" in Colombia, a nation of thirty-one million people in which over twenty thousand were being murdered each year, many for political reasons. Wilde and other human rights advocates rightly questioned whether it made sense to put more firepower in the hands of the Colombian armed forces when it was more likely to be used to repress unions, peasants, and other popular organizations than to fight the drug lords, who often had a cozy relationship with the nation's military commanders to begin with.[10]

While the principal effect of Bush's Andean drug war strategy in Colombia was to foster human rights abuses by U.S.-equipped armed forces, in Peru there was an even greater danger. According to Congressman Peter Kostmayer, Democrat of Pennsylvania, Bush's antidrug arms program risked "getting the United States involved through the back door in fighting guerrilla wars."[11] In Peru, antidrug efforts focused on the infamous upper Huallaga Valley, an area in which half of the world's supply of coca leaf is grown by a network of nearly two hundred thousand peasants. In a marriage of convenience, the peasants were protected by the Maoist Shining Path guerrilla movement, a puritanical left-wing sect that is vehemently opposed to drug use by its own members. In return for helping the peasants fend off attacks by the Peruvian police and military and their U.S. advisers, Shining Path collected up to 15 percent of the revenue generated by sales of coca leaves in the valley as a sort of "protection money." In a moment of candor, State Department official Melvyn Levitsky acknowledged that in arming Andean military forces for the "drug wars," the United States was in fact choosing to take on a much larger fight: "Drug trafficking and Shining Path activities are inextricably tied together. You can't fight one without fighting the other."[12]

Conscious of public and congressional concerns about whether the new antinarcotics arms and training would embroil the United States in protracted jungle warfare in the Andes, the Bush administration took precautions to downplay the U.S. advisory role. In an effort to maintain "deniability" of direct U.S. military involvement, the State Department, through its relatively unknown Bureau of International Narcotics Matters, contracted out air supply and bombing missions in the Andes to a company called Corporate Jets, Inc. According to a front-page investigative piece by *New York Times* reporter Jeff Gerth that ran in June 1990, the firm—run by veterans of Air America, the CIA front company that operated in Southeast Asia during the Vietnam War—was hired to "fly United States helicopter gunships, transport planes, and crop dusters used by American drug agents and foreign police officers in operations barred to U.S. military personnel, like raids on cocaine laboratories." While this evasive bureaucratic maneuver allowed U.S. officials to deny that the United States was playing a combat role in the Latin drug wars, it also opened the door to corruption and profiteering by blurring lines of accountability and control over these quasi-covert operations (this will be discussed in chapter 9).

In the most dangerous development of all, on several occasions these private contractors involved the United States in the guerrilla war between the Shining Path rebels and the Peruvian government. These incidents included one in which U.S.-hired pilots flew helicopter gunships in a battle aimed at defending the U.S.-built antidrug base at Santa Lucia from a guerrilla attack. By mid-1990, five of the private air force's fifty-three aircraft had been destroyed, with a loss of ten lives.[13] It was only after Peruvian president Alberto Fujimori suspended the constitution and formed a military government in the spring of 1992 that the bombing raids against jungle drug laboratories were suspended and the majority of U.S. military advisers were finally withdrawn from Peru.

This partial pullback of U.S. military efforts in Peru did not alter the larger pattern of militarization of U.S. antidrug efforts in the Andean region. Over two hundred Pentagon officials remained on the scene in Peru, Colombia, Bolivia, and Ecuador. Most of them were "on assignment" to other agencies, such as the Drug Enforcement Administration (DEA), obscuring what Scripps Howard reporters Andrew Schneider and Peter Copeland have described as "the biggest U.S. operation ever in Latin America."[14] Although the Clinton administration has talked of putting more emphasis on reducing the domestic demand for narcotics and less on military and law enforcement approaches to the problem, the United States continues to give ample arms aid to Bolivia, Colombia, Ecuador, Guatemala, and numerous other client states in the name of fighting drug trafficking.

As is always the case with arms exports, no matter what the political rationale, there was also an economic aspect to the militarization of the "drug wars." As the Soviet threat began to lose its force, military firms like Raytheon and General Dynamics began touting high-tech military gear such as radars that could track drug smugglers' planes and night vision devices that could be used in operations against drug laboratories. As one DEA official noted, "Once the Congress started saying 'money for drugs' we immediately started hearing vendors talk about high-technology."[15] At a conference in Washington, D.C., in the spring of 1990, over two hundred representatives of military and electronics firms got together to discuss how they could profit from the Bush administration's emphasis on arming client regimes to fight the drug war with U.S.-supplied equipment. An ad for the conference that appeared in the trade journal *Defense News* played to the industry's hopes that the drug war might provide a boost to their sagging post–Cold War profit margins: "The Arsenal of Democracy won the Cold War . . . Can it win the drug war?"[16]

Middle East Arms Sales: Paving the Path to the Gulf War

Arms sales also played a central role in the Bush administration's most widely trumpeted foreign policy achievement, Operation Desert Storm. President Bush, Secretary of State James Baker, and Secretary of Defense Dick Cheney used a flood of new arms offers to persuade nations in the Persian Gulf to join the hastily assembled anti-Iraq coalition. In addition to these new deals, the legacy of previous U.S. arms sales arrangements helped ensure access to military facilities in the region for U.S. forces.

The essential role of arms sales diplomacy in paving the path to U.S. intervention in the Gulf was not fully appreciated by the press or the public in the months leading up to the U.S. military confrontation with Iraq. At the time of the U.S. buildup in Saudi Arabia in the fall and winter of 1990, much attention was paid to Bush's political resolve and diplomatic skill in pulling together an unprecedented military coalition to take on Saddam Hussein's occupying army in Kuwait. The image of Bush as world leader par excellence, eagerly speed-dialing one head of state after another to persuade him or her to line up behind his anti-Iraq initiative, became a media cliché. The fact that these leaders would be expecting something in return was less frequently remarked upon.

The Bush administration's use of weapons as political tools did much more than prepare the way for the U.S.-led military intervention in Kuwait. The trading of advanced U.S. weaponry for military cooperation in the Gulf War dramatically underscored the extent to which the initial Nixon/Kissinger concept of using arms sales in lieu of direct U.S. military intervention had come full circle to a policy of using arms sales to facilitate U.S. intervention.

Even before Bush began doling out weapons to the major partners in his Gulf War coalition, the stage for U.S. intervention in the region had already been set by a network of secret understandings linked to arms deals dating back more than a decade. These arrangements were the product of behind-the-scenes arms sales diplomacy that had been carried out by both the Carter and Reagan administrations, most notably the 1981 AWACS sale to Saudi Arabia.

Secord, AWACS, and Arms for Access

In the summer and fall of 1981, while the rest of the Washington press corps was following the ins and outs of the congressional debate on the Saudi AWACS deal and its potential impact on Israel's defense requirements, *Washington Post* investigative reporter Scott Armstrong was uncovering a wholly different rationale for the sale—a secret plan to use the AWACS as the centerpiece of an advanced command, control, and communications system linked to a state-of-the-art military base network that could serve as a launchpad for the U.S. Rapid Deployment Force.[17] The connection between AWACS and U.S. interventionary strategy for the region had been initiated during the Carter administration, when Pentagon officials recognized that the facilities U.S. forces had access to in Oman, Somalia, Kenya, and Diego Garcia Island in the Indian Ocean were all hundreds or thousands of miles from the scene where a U.S. defense of the Saudi oil fields would have to be mounted. The right of U.S. forces to use these more remote facilities had also been obtained through swapping U.S. military assistance and arms transfers, but none of these deals was on the grand scale of the secret arrangements surrounding the Saudi AWACS sale.

A central player in the Saudi deal was Maj. Gen. Richard Secord. Secord negotiated with his Saudi counterparts on this delicate issue during his stint as Defense Secretary Caspar Weinberger's chief adviser on Middle East arms sales in 1981 and 1982. When George Bush sent 250,000 U.S. troops to Saudi Arabia in August and September 1990, Secord was quick to point out that this massive deployment would not have been possible without a series of secret deals he struck with the Saudis and other Gulf sheikdoms around the time of the 1981 AWACS sale.[18]

Pentagon spokespersons and Secord himself have repeatedly denied that the formal link alleged by Scott Armstrong between the AWACS sale and access to Saudi military bases ever existed. In a 1991 interview I held with him at his office in Tysons Corner, Virginia, Secord vented his spleen toward the "conspiracy theorists" of the liberal media. Secord's face reddened in anger at the mere mention of Armstrong's name, and he baldly asserted that "Scott Armstrong and people like him are not only wrong, they're dead wrong."

Barely pausing for breath, Secord went on to affirm an important part of Armstrong's thesis: that there was at the very least an implicit link between U.S. sales of high-tech arms to the Saudis and U.S. access to Saudi military bases. Secord began by explaining why he hadn't pushed for a formal written agreement:

> You have to understand that in working with Arabs, it's not written agreements that count, it's building up trust. It was my position that if

we established with them a basis for trust, the necessary infrastructural tasks would get done, and that's by and large what happened.

Secord went on to imply that the "necessary infrastructural tasks" were the construction of Saudi military bases tailored to the needs of United States forces, and that the "basis for trust" included ready access to U.S. arms and training for the Saudis.

Secord then zeroed in on the precise motivation for the Saudi "overbuild program"—the term used by Pentagon insiders for the U.S. strategy of building more extensive military bases and communications facilities in the desert sheikdom than could possibly be used by the Saudi armed forces on their own. Secord indicated that the program "was deliberately undertaken by both sides with the understanding that they [the Saudi bases] could be used [by U.S. forces] in an emergency."

When I asked Secord directly whether the United States cut a deal with the Saudis, he said, "There was no put and take, no this for that, no quid pro quo." But he added that if the AWACS sale had not gone through, the "trust, confidence, and warm feeling of support for the United States would not have been there. . . . It would have been a great setback to our military relationship with the Saudis." So, without acknowledging an explicit quid pro quo, Secord conceded that the United States had used arms sales to the Persian Gulf to develop "a network of relationships, formal and informal, sort of like a spider's web," that set the stage for U.S. interventions in the region.

Secord admitted that this undisclosed component of the AWACS deal—which appeared to be the equivalent of setting up a secret mutual defense pact without consulting the Congress or informing the public—might be frowned upon in some circles, but he brushed aside any constitutional concerns raised by his covert arms diplomacy: "The green-eyeshade types didn't like what we were doing. . . . A lawyer-like mind rejects that kind of approach . . . but it worked, and it worked well." In his last word on the subject, Secord once again sought a measure of credit for his role in providing the political building blocks for the Gulf War: "Bush was nothing short of dazzling in putting together this coalition [against Iraq]. . . but the main infrastructural tasks had already been done long before Mr. Bush had anything to do with the Persian Gulf."

Cementing the Anti-Iraq Coalition: Arms for Allies

As important as access to base facilities was to Bush's military intervention in the Persian Gulf, it was only half the battle. He desperately needed allies in his crusade against Saddam Hussein, not so much for their military assets as for a show of political support. Bush particularly needed Arab allies, to help counteract the impression that the Gulf War was simply another case of a great power using force to meddle in the affairs of the region. Bush's adept use of arms sales and military aid to buy allies in the fight against Saddam Hussein was enough to win the admiration of even a hardened arms dealer like Richard Secord.

First in line for a massive infusion of arms was the official host and main beneficiary of Operation Desert Storm, the Saudi monarchy. By the end of August 1990, less than a month after Iraq's invasion of Kuwait, Congress had already been notified of the Bush administration's intention to sell the Saudis 24 F-15 fighter planes, 150 M-60A3 battle tanks, and 15,000 rounds of antitank ammunition for the M-60s, at a total cost of over $2.2 billion. But this was just the tip of the iceberg.

In mid-September 1990, roughly a month after the United States had deployed the first of over half a million troops on Saudi soil, the Bush administration announced plans to sell $20 billion worth of U.S. arms to Saudi Arabia—by far the largest single arms sale ever proposed. The package reportedly included dozens of advanced McDonnell Douglas F-15 fighter aircraft and Apache attack helicopters, hundreds of top-of-the-line General Dynamics M-1A2 tanks and FMC Corporation M-2 armored personnel carriers, several batteries of Raytheon Patriot air defense missiles, up to eleven Boeing AWACS radar planes, thousands of military trucks, hundreds of antitank and air-to-air missiles, and nine LTV Corporation Multiple Launch Rocket Systems. An official familiar with the sale described it as "basically the Saudi's wish list." And a congressional analyst suggested that the deal should be called "the defense industry relief act of 1990" because of the billions in revenue it would provide for military contractors.[19]

In normal times, a sale a fraction of this size to Saudi Arabia could be expected to arouse a considerable outcry from supporters of Israel on Capitol Hill, and maybe even an outright vote of disapproval. But the Bush administration had apparently calculated that no one would dare oppose an arms sale to the Saudis while they were playing host to hundreds of thousands of U.S. troops and pledging to fight alongside U.S. forces if military action was in fact initiated against Iraq. Bush's political gamble was half right. A group of pro-Israel senators led by Daniel Patrick Moynihan of New York, Terry Sanford of North Carolina, Senate Foreign Relations Committee chairman Claiborne Pell of Rhode Island, and Republican Bob Packwood of Oregon wrote to their colleagues urging them to press President Bush to scale down the mammoth sale to only those systems that Saudi Arabia could "put to use immediately in its defense." They argued persuasively that "most of the weapons in the proposed sale would not actually be delivered to Saudi Arabia for several years" and concluded that "it is manifest that they have little to do with the immediate crisis in the Gulf region." The senators further noted the folly of pouring more arms into the region:

> Recent events have provided the United States, the Soviet Union, and other major suppliers with sobering lessons about providing massive amounts of sophisticated weapons to states in this unstable region. American troops are at risk from American weapons captured in Kuwait; French forces headed for Saudi Arabia will soon be within range of aircraft and missiles France sold to Saddam Hussein. . . . Might we not consider alternatives to continuing to feed the escalation spiral of arms and more arms?[20]

This "Dear Colleague" letter paved the way for a letter to Bush himself, sent on September 26, 1991, in which fourteen senators asked the president to cut the sale back considerably, sending equipment of immediate relevance to the Gulf conflict and postponing the rest of the sale for at least six months. Unwilling to battle Congress over this point during a period when he would be seeking support for the overall Gulf military effort, Bush decided to reduce the size of the package. The deal that was finally agreed on called for "only" $7.5 billion in U.S. arms exports to the Saudis. It was still one of the largest sales in history, but it was only about a third of the size of the megadeal that had been floated in early September. The most conspicuous omissions from the original $20 billion package were the F-15 fighters and the AWACS radar planes, by far the most controversial parts of the package from the perspective of supporters of Israel. Beyond that, the numbers of systems like the M-1 tank, the M-2 infantry fighting vehicle, the Apache helicopter, and the Multiple Launch Rocket System were scaled back to anywhere from one-third to one-seventh the numbers contemplated in the original deal. Over the subsequent two years, the pursuit of the second part of the Saudi package would become a top priority for the arms industry lobby (see chapter 8).[21]

The Saudis were only the first of many U.S. clients to receive weaponry in exchange for their cooperation with U.S. military plans in the Persian Gulf. The small Gulf sheikdom of Bahrain received $37 million worth of M-60 tanks and night vision goggle sets as an adjunct to the $7.5 billion Saudi package. Israeli leaders spoke out forcefully about the need to receive additional U.S. military aid to maintain their qualitative edge over the Saudis and other potential Arab adversaries, and the Bush administration pledged to address those concerns. As a down payment, the Israelis received fifteen F-15 fighters, two Patriot missile batteries, and ten military cargo helicopters in September and October of 1990 alone. Additional U.S. military assistance to Israel would be put off until after the conclusion of the Gulf War in the spring of 1991 (see chapter 10).[22]

Egypt, whose participation in the anti-Iraq coalition was considered critical in providing political cover for U.S. intervention, may have received the most significant payoff of all. The Bush administration canceled $7 billion in Egyptian military debt to the United States, a sum representing all the outstanding loans Egypt had on hand for U.S. arms going back to the early 1980s. Beyond that considerable financial windfall, Egypt was allowed to purchase over $2 billion in new U.S. armaments on credit from the fall of 1990 through the summer of 1991, including forty-six General Dynamics F-16 fighter aircraft with a full complement of bombs, ammunition, and missiles.[23]

Vying with Saudi Arabia and Egypt for the role of greatest financial beneficiary of the Gulf coalition was Turkey, whose president, Turgut Ozal, had backed the U.S. initiative early on by closing its oil pipeline to Iraq and allowing U.S. forces to operate from Turkish bases near Iraq's northern border. Turkey received more than a 20 percent increase in its usual allotment of roughly $500 million in U.S. military aid. In addition, the Bush administration pressured the Saudis and other Gulf allies to contribute to a special fund that would allow Turkey to build up its military forces after the Gulf conflict. The most notable U.S. sale to Turkey was a $2.8 billion deal for coproduction of F-16 fighters, which was concluded during the summer of 1991; in addition, the U.S. agreed to allow components of the U.S. F-16s going to Egypt to be produced in Turkey, offering a potential lift to Turkey's efforts to build its own military aerospace industry.[24]

So, from Israel to Bahrain, and from Egypt to Turkey, George Bush and James Baker's high-speed diplomacy in assembling a military coalition to drive Saddam Hussein's forces out of Kuwait was aided at every turn by promises of U.S. arms, in the form of either cash sales or U.S. aid. The irony of using arms sales as the principal diplomatic tool in a military crisis that was itself the product of unrestrained arms trafficking to the Middle East was lost on Bush policymakers.

Post—Gulf War Arms Sales Policy: Rhetoric Versus Reality

Occasionally, George Bush or James Baker would talk about the administration's intention to do something to stem the flow of U.S. arms to the region after the war, but they never seriously followed up on those pledges. In fact, the two years from the outbreak of the Gulf War through the summer of 1992 were marked by a perverse pattern in which virtually every public statement by the Bush administration in favor of curbing arms transfers was immediately and decisively contradicted in practice.

For example, in August 1990, just a few weeks after President Bush first deployed U.S. troops to Saudi Arabia, Secretary of State Baker acknowledged on national television that U.S. and allied policies of providing arms and military technology to Iraq up to the eve of Saddam Hussein's invasion of Kuwait had helped spur the Gulf War in the first place: "It's worth looking at, in the future, arms sales practices and policies. . . . We should have been more concerned about this, perhaps going further back." Baker went on to note that the confrontation with Iraq "may provide a good lesson in that regard."[25] Yet, within a month of Baker's mea culpa the Bush administration had cleared major sales to Saudi Arabia and Israel through the Congress, as well as announcing its record $20 billion arms deal with Saudi Arabia. Despite Congress's small tactical victory in reducing the size of the Saudi sale, the Bush administration's pattern of matching the rhetoric of restraint with the reality of increased arms trading had been firmly established.

On February 6, 1991, on the eve of the ground war in the Gulf, Baker told the House Foreign Affairs Committee that the time had come to take concrete steps to stem the flow of armaments into the Middle East, "an area that is already overmilitarized." Three weeks later, the Senate Foreign Relations Committee received a confidential listing of potential U.S. arms transfers for the year to come, containing a record $33 billion in proposed sales, with more than half of them slated for the Middle East. And on March 1, Congress was informed of the $1.6 billion sale of forty-six General Dynamics F-16 fighter aircraft to Egypt.[26]

President Bush joined the chorus of voices calling for arms trade restraint on March 6, 1991, in his triumphant address to a joint session of Congress after the Gulf War cease-fire. Citing arms transfer control as one of his four key postwar goals, Bush observed, "It would be tragic if the nations of the Middle East and Persian Gulf were now, in the wake of war, to embark on a new arms race." Within two weeks of

Bush's address to Congress, the administration began publicly promoting a new $1 billion plan to use the Export-Import Bank to subsidize foreign arms sales, a move that would put that institution back in the military financing business for the first time since the Vietnam War. On March 19, Secretary of Defense Cheney further undercut the thrust of Bush's remarks when he told Congress in no uncertain terms that the United States would most likely sell more weaponry to the Middle East in the aftermath of the Gulf War, not less.[27]

Finally, on May 29, 1991, Bush unveiled his long-awaited Middle East Arms Control Initiative in a speech to the graduating class of the U.S. Air Force Academy. Bush pledged to seek "supplier guidelines on conventional arms exports" and "barriers to exports that contribute to weapons of mass destruction," with the ultimate goal of "halting the proliferation of conventional and unconventional weapons in the Middle East while supporting the legitimate need of every state in the region to defend itself."[28] In briefings by State Department officials after the speech, reporters were informed that the administration was seriously committed to pursuing discussions on reining in nuclear and conventional weapons exports among the "Big Five" suppliers—the United States, the Soviet Union, France, the United Kingdom, and China—nations that together controlled over 85 percent of the world market for major combat equipment.

Twenty-four hours after Bush's speech, Defense Secretary Cheney again struck a contrary note, announcing a deal to transfer ten F-15s to Israel and stockpile $200 million worth of U.S. weapons there. Less than a week later, Congress was informed of a $760 million deal to sell McDonnell Douglas Apache helicopters to the United Arab Emirates. And the following week, the Pentagon made its most visible showing ever at the Paris Air Show, providing personnel and aircraft from the Gulf War at taxpayer expense to help U.S. arms manufacturers make their sales pitch.[29]

As a counterpoint to the frenetic U.S. marketing efforts of June, the first round of the much heralded Big Five talks on arms control in the Middle East was held on July 8–9 in Paris, with representatives from the United States, France, the Soviet Union, the United Kingdom, and China attending. The five powers agreed to seek "rules of restraint" for conventional arms transfers and to meet regularly until the mechanisms for implementing them could be agreed upon and put into practice. Yet the Bush administration made a mockery of this new commitment as well: in the month of July alone, the United States announced agreements for the sale of over $7 billion in weaponry to over a dozen nations, including a major sale of cluster bombs and other munitions to Saudi Arabia, a sale of armored vehicles to Oman, and the $2.8 billion F-16 deal with Turkey.

In all, during two years of talking about reining in the arms trade, from August 1990 through August 1992, the Bush administration concluded deals for the sale of over $23 billion in U.S. arms to the Middle East alone.[30]

As the actions of the Bush administration made clear, promoting arms sales had become part of the administrative machinery of government. There is a large and growing arms export infrastructure that drives the United States to sell arms to almost any nation that asks for them, not out of a sober assessment of U.S. interests but rather as a result of a combination of short-term economic rationales and outmoded strategic concepts. Far from moving to dismantle this arms export infrastructure in keeping with the new realities of the post–Cold War world, the Bush administration spent most of its time and energy expanding and refining it to levels that would have amazed even the most hard-line members of the Reagan administration. Just as his friends in industry had predicted, George Bush hadn't made any big statements about arms sales, but he had moved quietly and effectively to place them at the center of U.S. relations with the rest of the world.

Institutionalizing Arms Sales Promotion

Even without John Tower, there had been ample indication from the outset that members of the Bush policymaking team would lend a sympathetic ear to the arms industry's concerns. Commerce Secretary Robert Mosbacher, a wealthy businessman and crack campaign fundraiser, was an aggressive proponent of stronger government efforts to promote all kinds of exports, commercial or military. Bush national security adviser Brent Scowcroft was a protégé of Henry Kissinger and the former head of the Washington office of his high-powered corporate lobbying firm, Kissinger Associates; Scowcroft had been an avid advocate of arms sales throughout his tenure at the National Security Council during the Ford administration. Perhaps most important of all from the industry's perspective was the appointment of Lawrence Eagleburger as Jim Baker's second in command at the State Department. After leaving the Reagan State Department in 1984, Eagleburger had served for five years as head of Kissinger Associates, during which time he was a consultant to numerous military firms and a board member of ITT, a major defense contractor. As one arms industry lobbyist said, "Larry's the most sympathetic guy who's been up there [as Deputy Secretary of State] for years."[31]

One of Eagleburger's first projects was to chair a series of meetings among top State Department officials during the summer of 1989 with the aim of "reorganizing the Department's handling of commercial defense trade." The first item on the agenda was an overhaul of the State Department's Office of Munitions Control (OMC).[32]

OMC was the little-known State Department agency responsible for granting roughly forty thousand to fifty thousand licenses annually for the export of military goods and services produced in the United States. It was a dull, bureaucratic function, but it was also critically important, for reasons of both economics and foreign policy. Without an OMC license, U.S. contractors could not legally make an overseas arms sale. But without careful review of license applications, including consultation with foreign policy and nonproliferation experts in the Pentagon, the Department of Energy, and elsewhere in the Department of State, the United States could unwittingly build up the arsenals of potential adversaries or aggressive regional powers.

The OMC had come under fire from industry and Congress alike for being slow and disorganized. In 1988, a series of hearings held by Sen. David Pryor of Arkansas revealed that OMC had only four trained licensing officers to handle the tens of thousands of requests it received each year, rendering sound judgments on the foreign policy implications of each sale virtually impossible. A Senate staff investigator described the agency as "a rabbit warren, with licenses stacked everywhere." While Pryor's critique focused on foreign policy, industry representatives were critical of the OMC on economic grounds. Arms company lobbyists complained that the agency was painfully slow in processing license applications, thereby costing them time, money, and potential foreign sales. These two sets of concerns converged in a move by Congress to upgrade the staffing and equipment at OMC, most notably by funding an increase in the number of licensing officers from four to twenty-four.

This beefing up of OMC was already under way when Eagleburger took over as deputy secretary of state, but it was left to him to put a decisive proindustry tilt on the process. Working with Richard Clarke, the newly appointed chief of the department's Bureau of Politico-Military Affairs, Eagleburger promoted the idea of subsuming the Office of Munitions Control under a new, larger body, the Center for Defense Trade. The name change was far from coincidental. Industry lobbyists had long pressed the point that words like "arms" and "munitions" had too negative a connotation, whereas the term "defense trade" highlighted the economic benefits of arms exports while downplaying the question of how the weapons might actually be used once they were sold.

On January 8, 1990, less than a year after George Bush took office, the Center for Defense Trade was officially inaugurated. It consisted of two components—an expanded OMC, now known as the Office of Defense Trade Controls, and a new Office of Defense Trade Policy. As the *New York Times* noted in a June 1992 editorial, the new agency was supposed to "regulate and facilitate U.S. defense trade," but "in practice, the center has spent a lot more time 'facilitating' than 'regulating.'"[33] This emphasis is clearly on display in the Center's quarterly newsletter, *Defense Trade News,* which it sends out to all registered arms exporters in the United States. Typical articles extol the agency's "Fresh Start for the '90s," promise "faster, more responsive licensing," and provide detailed instructions on such helpful technical matters as how to apply to get an item removed from the munitions list and put on the less stringent "commodity control list" administered by the Department of Commerce. An article in the first issue proclaimed that "all of us in the management team at the new Center for Defense Trade are eager to serve U.S. industry."[34]

The next step in Eagleburger's proindustry campaign was to enlist overseas embassy personnel as partners in the Bush administration's new export push. In July 1990, just a month before the outbreak of the Gulf War, Eagleburger sent a cable to all overseas posts urging embassy personnel to "get on board" and "help open doors" for U.S. military firms trying to sell their products overseas. The memo, drafted by the Center for Defense Trade, was a far cry from the Carter policy of the late 1970s, and it even went further than the Reagan administration's instructions to embassies, which spoke rather neutrally of providing "the same courtesies and assistance to firms that have obtained licenses to market items on the U.S. Munitions List as they would to those marketing other American products."[35]

According to a State Department synopsis of the cable's main points, it "advised embassies to be well-informed about, and responsive to, U.S. defense industry sales interests in host countries." Embassy assistance to arms firms was to entail providing detailed information on the host country's defense budget and procurement plans, including estimates of specific weapons needs. Eagleburger also encouraged embassy personnel to play an active role in scheduling appointments for U.S. company representatives with host country officials. And to make sure that no one would take these new responsibilities lightly, Center for Defense Trade director Charles Duelfer let it be known that in future State Department evaluations of the performance of specific embassies, help in marketing U.S. defense products "is one of the things they'll be graded on." One overseas representative of a defense firm, Thomas Peterson of Raytheon, told the *Legal Times* that Eagleburger's instructions had been a boon to his company's efforts to sell Patriot missiles to Turkey: "The embassy is talking to the Turkish government. Just about everything we've asked them to do for us, they've done."[36]

Industry had good reason to be happy with the Eagleburger instructions; they had suggested the idea to him in the first place. The issue was raised at a January 1990 dinner meeting attended by Eagleburger and a number of defense industry executives, including Don Fuqua, a former congressman from Florida who now serves as president of the Aerospace Industries Association. "We encouraged Eagleburger to do that, and he said he would be glad to do that," bragged Fuqua. Conflict of interest questions were raised by the presence at the dinner meeting of D. Travis Engen, the CEO of ITT's defense unit, whose board Eagleburger had served on for the five years prior to taking his post in the Bush administration. When investigative journalist Peter Stone raised questions about the propriety of the meeting in light of Eagleburger's pledge to recuse himself from matters involving his former companies and clients, State Department officials argued lamely that there was no conflict because ITT wasn't a "formal party" with a specific petition or official proceeding before the government. But there was no question that ITT and other defense firms stood to gain from Eagleburger's placement of the State Department's overseas personnel at their disposal as an adjunct marketing force, thus potentially improving the company's bottom line and perhaps even boosting the value of Eagleburger's pending pension from ITT.[37] This kind of conflict of interest, which might have at least caused a ripple of scandal in the early Reagan years, had become so commonplace by the time George Bush took over that it was barely commented upon in the mainstream media.

While Eagleburger and his colleagues at the State Department were busy reorganizing themselves the better to serve the needs of the arms industry, the Pentagon was undertaking its own unprecedented effort to become a virtual partner with industry in arms sales promotion. The first example of the Pentagon's new attitude came in connection with a 1989 sale of General Dynamics M-1 tanks to Saudi Arabia.

The M-1 case demonstrated how officials in Bush's Pentagon had decided early on to use arms exports as their principal economic adjustment strategy for military industry in an era of declining post–Cold War weapons budgets. The M-1 lobbying strategy began in 1989 with a series of background briefings for Congress and the press in which administration officials stressed the employment and budgetary benefits of the proposed sale of 315 of the tanks to Saudi Arabia. Administration experts argued that the sale would not only help keep General Dynamics's two main production plants, in Lima, Ohio, and Warren, Michigan, up and running, but that it would also generate billions in export income for the nation and hundreds of millions in budgetary savings for the army. In addition, administration representatives noted that beating the British to the punch on the Saudi deal could lead to cancellation of their new Chieftain II tank, clearing the way for the possible sale of six hundred M-1s to Britain.

During the November 1989 hearings on the Saudi tank deal in the House of Representatives, State Department and Pentagon officials went public with the economic arguments they had been making behind the scenes, complete with citations of state-by-state employment and revenue impacts of the Saudi sale. In the past, the etiquette of pork barrel politicking had generally called for the contractor to make these kinds of nuts and bolts economic pleas for a weapons program, not the government. But the Bush administration cast aside the normal division of labor and incorporated General Dynamics's exaggerated figures on the benefits of M-1 exports directly into the State Department's fact sheet on the Saudi sale. In all, forty states were claimed as beneficiaries of the $3 billion deal, which sailed through Congress with barely a discouraging word.[38]

The fervor of the economic appeal on behalf of M-1 sales was intensified in 1990 after Secretary of Defense Cheney announced a new round of projected Pentagon cutbacks that would result in both of General Dynamics's main tank production plants being mothballed by 1993—unless there were sufficient foreign orders to keep them open. The company rushed into print with a study singing the praises of tank exports and bemoaning the difficulties of returning the plants to full production once they have been put on inactive status. They even set a target—overseas sales of two thousand M-1s—that would need to be reached to keep the tank production lines open until the next round of army orders was scheduled to begin in 1998.[39]

The Bush administration tried to take advantage of the Persian Gulf crisis to sell another five hundred M-1s to Saudi Arabia, which would have put exports at a level well on the way toward General Dynamics's sales target for keeping its tank plants operating. But congressional resistance to the $20 billion package, of which the 500 tanks would have been a part, forced the Bush administration to cut the tank offer to 150, still a significant sale but not what General Dynamics had hoped for.

The alternative to export promotion as a means of keeping domestic weapons projects alive—converting part of the nation's bloated defense industrial base to civilian uses—was reportedly ruled out in the M-1 case by Secretary of Defense Cheney. When asked why one or both of the M-1 plants couldn't be put to work building civilian products such as heavy earth-moving machinery or railroad cars, a General Dynamics spokesperson asserted that the defense secretary had told the company that he wanted "to leave the plants [on standby] if the need arises for producing more tanks."[40]

In addition to helping apply pork barrel pressure to Congress to overcome any potential opposition to arms sales to controversial clients in volatile regions like the Middle East, the Pentagon moved to match its counterparts in the State Department in taking direct measures to assist in the overseas marketing of U.S. arms. The first initiative in this regard was the creation in February 1990 of the "Catalog of U.S. Defense Articles and Services" under the auspices of the Defense Security Assistance Agency. As mentioned in chapter 1, the catalog had been heavily plugged at the agency's July 1991 conference on "Defense Exports in the Post–Desert Storm Environment." A follow-up memo to participating firms in October 1991 indicated that the average U.S. government overseas security assistance office had a catalog of over five hundred pages on hand and encouraged arms exporting firms to send more information in order to take advantage of "an inexpensive overseas marketing tool for defense related items."

The Pentagon also took the unprecedented step of involving active-duty military personnel in the Bush administration's foreign military sales push, as evidenced by the presence of over 150 pilots and military police from Operation Desert Storm at the 1991 Paris Air Show. For the first time ever, service men and women in uniform were flown to the air show at taxpayer expense. Their "assignment" was to help U.S. defense contractors tout the performance of U.S. armaments in the Gulf War, in hopes of assisting them in landing some lucrative new clients. In addition, in keeping with a memorandum distributed by Undersecretary of Defense for Policy Paul Wolfowitz in March 1991, the Pentagon agreed to pick up the cost of transporting and displaying U.S. aircraft at international air shows. In the past, U.S. arms companies had leased aircraft from the government for use at international air shows, at a cost of up to a few hundred thousand dollars per plane. Wolfowitz's policy reversal saved defense exporting firms millions of dollars in fees and expenses, while sending a powerful signal that whatever George Bush might say about arms sales restraint, the U.S. government was putting its money and its energy behind an all-out drive for greater arms sales.[41]

These policies of using State Department, Pentagon, and active-duty military personnel as virtual sales representatives for the arms industry helped contribute to a surge in U.S. sales in 1992. Total U.S. weapons sales brokered by the Pentagon and licensed by the State Department reached nearly $20 billion, and there were deals in the pipeline that would push that figure even higher in 1993.[42] And in sales to the Third World as measured by Congressional Research Service analyst Richard Grimmett, the United States had cornered roughly 60 percent in 1992, almost three times the level of its closest competitor, France, and nearly ten times the level of sales by its traditional rival for the top position, Russia.[43] George Bush's talent for arms sales diplomacy and his systematic efforts to institutionalize government-sponsored arms sales promotion had paid off beyond the industry's wildest dreams.

8

The Permanent Arms Supply Network (I): The Corporate Arms Merchants

Gen. Howard Fish stands out among the thousands of former Pentagon officials who represent U.S. arms manufacturers in Washington, both because of his position at the center of industry lobbying efforts and because of his disarming openness about his role. He also has impeccable credentials. Before going into international marketing, first at LTV and then with the Loral Corporation, Fish served as head of the Pentagon's Defense Security Assistance Agency during the Nixon and Ford administrations.

In a 1991 visit with Fish at his LTV office suite in Crystal City, Virginia, I was struck immediately with the low-key sense of business as usual. Other than the need to indicate on the sign-in sheet whether I was there to discuss classified or unclassified matters, it was like visiting any other corporation. It just happened to be a weapons-exporting firm.

General Fish was clearly a revered figure around the office, with secretaries, drivers, and midlevel executives alike jumping to meet his every need even as they shook their heads over his grueling and at times chaotic schedule. The walls of Fish's office were filled with mementos of a life in the arms business. Autographed pictures of President Reagan and Saudi King Fahd sat side-by-side on a bookcase, affirming his personal acquaintance with two of the most important political figures in the recent history of the arms trade. Behind his desk was a picture of a younger, slimmer Fish at a meeting with former secretary of defense James Schlesinger. The general was in a particularly fine mood on this day in late February 1991, as he took a series of calls from industry contacts and Capitol Hill lobbyists seeking his views on the imminent conclusion of the Gulf War. Fish chuckled over his own foresight—he claims to have predicted both the timing of U.S. intervention and how long it would take to oust Saddam Hussein's forces from Kuwait, down to the day. He told one caller how much he was looking forward to the upcoming Paris Air Show, where he predicted that "everybody's going to be selling 'how my weapons won the Gulf War.'"

Between calls, paperwork, and scheduling his next trip, Fish took a few minutes to give me his perspective on the war and its implications for the industry. He pointed proudly to the performance of his company's systems in the Gulf, from the omnipresent "Hummer," or High Mobility Multipurpose Vehicle, which is the modern version of the standard military jeep, to the Multiple Launch Rocket System, an antitank rocket battery that Fish describes as "the Patriot of the ground war." Citing rumors of a plan to triple the size of the Saudi armed forces, he pointed to the Saudi market as the next great opportunity. And he expected most of their purchases to come from the United States, in repayment for the U.S. decision to send 550,000 troops to protect the Saudi monarchy from Saddam Hussein: "We're defending them now, so they'll be inclined to buy from us." Even as these words crossed Fish's lips, he got a call "from a gal we have watching the Hill for us," who informed him that the Pentagon's estimate of potential U.S. arms sales for the year to come was an astounding $33 billion. "There's a scoop for you," he said, smiling and animated as he passed along what was clearly one of the best pieces of news he had heard in some time.

Fish's most important service to the arms industry is carried out not in the spotlight created by high-profile events like the Gulf War but in the day-to-day battles to influence legislation and regulations that affect the industry's sales prospects. Fish serves as the chairman of the American League for Exports and Security Assistance (ALESA), the arms industry's chief lobbying group on export issues. In this capacity he spearheads industry efforts to create a legal and regulatory framework that will make it easier to sell arms abroad. One of his most important priorities is to beat back the demands for tighter controls over arms exports that invariably follow in the wake of embarrassing events such as the Iran/contra scandal or the provision of U.S. military technology to Saddam Hussein. Fish comes to these legislative battles well equipped. One of his proudest achievements during his tenure at the Pentagon was his leadership role in the fight to water down the Arms Export Control Act of 1976. He was instrumental in the Ford administration's successful effort to eliminate the proposal for a legislative ceiling on U.S. arms transfers and knock out a half dozen provisions that would have allowed Congress to veto arms sales on human rights and other nonmilitary grounds. In a phone conversation prior to our interview, Fish casually mentioned that he had recruited former Pentagon counsel Ben Forman, the man who had written Ford's veto message on the Arms Export Control Act, to work at LTV: "Ben's a good guy, so when I came over here, I hired him."

One piece of legislation that drew particularly strong fire from Fish, Forman, and ALESA in the late 1980s was the Arms Export Reform Act, a measure cosponsored by Democratic senators Joseph Biden of Delaware and Claiborne Pell of Rhode Island and Congressman Mel Levine of California. The bill would have dramatically shifted the balance of arms sales decisionmaking by requiring an affirmative vote of the Congress before major arms sales to the Third World could proceed. This would have reversed current practice, under which Congress has thirty calendar days to introduce resolutions of disapproval. If both houses of Congress fail to act within the thirty-day limit, or if they fail to pass the resolutions of disapproval with a veto-proof majority, the sale goes ahead. Forcing Congress to vote on all major sales would increase public debate and congressional accountability, neither of which would be welcomed by General Fish and his friends in the arms industry.

Led by Fish and former ALESA lobbyist Joel Johnson, the trade association pulled out all the stops to kill the Biden/Pell/Levine measure. They won the battle hands down, aided by the lack of political courage exhibited by the average member of Congress. The industry's most persuasive argument can be summarized in three words: "avoidance of controversy." This position was articulated by United Technologies president and ALESA member Harry Gray in his testimony on the bill:

> I can't understand why, from a political perspective, the Congress would want to make such a change. . . . Currently the Congress can pick its own battles. . . . Under the new system, Congress would have to make an up or down vote a number of times a year on arms transfers, and no matter how a member voted, certain constituents would be unhappy. In every foreign sale, there are jobs at stake, there are indi-

viduals who favor and dislike every foreign government, and there are people who believe that exports are intrinsically good or arms sales inherently evil.[1]

In short, the industry argued, introducing democracy into the arms sales decisionmaking process would be too messy and troublesome, because it would expose members of Congress to potential criticism—not the least of which would be the criticism orchestrated by the arms industry itself. As Joel Johnson put it, "There are a number of things that Congress must deal with in the dead of night . . . and one of those things is arms sales." He went on to underscore Harry Gray's point, noting that most members of Congress would agree that "being forced to vote 40 to 50 times a year on arms sales is a no-win proposition." On the strength of this argument, Biden/Pell/Levine dropped off the congressional agenda without ever coming to a floor vote. So much for accountability.

Another area in which Howard Fish has had a less visible but equally effective role is in his position as chairman of the Export Policy Committee of the Defense Policy Advisory Committee on Trade (DPACT). Established in 1983 as a result of an executive order by President Reagan, DPACT comprises a Who's Who of defense industry executives, including the chief executive officers of Lockheed, Northrop, Martin Marietta, McDonnell Douglas, and General Dynamics, as well as representatives of secondary suppliers like Cincinnati Milacron, a major machine tool manufacturer. The nearly three dozen private industry members of DPACT provide regular, confidential advice to the secretary of defense and the U.S. trade representative on what they describe as "defense trade and industrial base issues."[2]

While the details of DPACT's recommendations are normally carefully guarded, a November 1988 report designed to shape the policy of the incoming Bush administration gives a flavor of the kinds of suggestions Fish and his colleagues have been regularly pushing upon their counterparts in the Department of Defense behind closed doors. Among their recommendations, released under the unprepossessing title "Report Outlining U.S. Government Policy Options Affecting Defense Trade and the U.S. Industrial Base," were several that rapidly found their way into Bush administration policy. The report called for renewed U.S. embassy support for foreign sales, to the point of making it clear to embassy personnel that such support would be "a major element in the job description and a significant factor in the overall job performance" of U.S. government personnel posted overseas. DPACT got even more than it bargained for out of this suggestion, which was taken up with a vengeance by Deputy Secretary of State Lawrence Eagleburger a year later when he sent his memo to overseas embassy personnel encouraging them to help U.S. contractors promote foreign arms sales.

Other DPACT proposals are still working their way through the system, under the watchful eye of industry supporters in the executive branch and the Congress. For example, a recommendation to weaken the Arms Export Control Act and recast it in terms of "defense trade" narrowly missed being passed into law during 1992 (see further discussion below). More important, Fish and DPACT have been trying to create a new, taxpayer-supported military sales financing mechanism. The Bush administration first took up the proposal in earnest in the spring of 1991, but the $1 billion program met with stiff opposition in Congress. It would have been an addition to the $4–5 billion per year that the Pentagon was already spending to assist in the export of U.S. armaments. Despite political resistance, the plan is still being actively promoted by representatives of states with large defense industries, most notably senators Christopher Dodd of Connecticut and Christopher "Kit" Bond of Missouri. It came within one vote of passing the Senate in 1990, and the arms industry has made it a top priority ever since.

In the spring of 1993, the industry took a new tack in its quest for additional subsidies when Martin Marietta CEO Norman Augustine sent a letter to members of the House Armed Services Committee urging them to raid the Clinton administration's $20 billion defense conversion budget and put some of the money into a $5 billion weapons export loan guarantee fund. In a verbal sleight of hand, Augustine tried to equate conversion to civilian production and promotion of foreign arms sales by stressing the importance of "converting some of our nation's tax and export policies which currently discriminate against the U.S. industry and jeopardize its ability to compete in the world marketplace." Congressman Tom Andrews of Maine was adamant in his opposition to the industry's plan:

> It's wrong and crazy . . . to take precious money allocated for conversion and use it to expand our market share of arms sales. Every dollar invested in exporting is one less dollar invested in real conversion—in ports, ships, and a rail service worthy of the name.

Andrews and his colleagues in the House of Representatives rejected the proposal outright; the industry couldn't even recruit a member to sponsor an amendment on its behalf. But the arms traders weren't about to give up. In the summer of 1993, a new, $1 billion export financing plan surfaced under the sponsorship of Republican congressman Dirk Kempthorne of Idaho. In November, a House–Senate conference committee authorized the creation of Kempthorne's proposed loan guarantee program, but the Congress declined to appropriate any funds to support it.

To its credit, the Clinton administration held off industry pressure for a new arms export loan guarantee program throughout 1994, arguing that a decision on the issue should be part of its overall review of arms transfer policy (see chapter 13). The administration's ultimate decision on whether to approve this priority item on the weapons manufacturers' wish list will be a litmus test of whether Clinton policymakers have retained any serious commitment to controlling the spread of conventional armaments.[3]

The Industry Speaks: The "Real World" Perspective of Joel Johnson

As impressive as General Fish's credentials as a lobbyist are, his effective insider role is rivaled by Joel Johnson, a vice president of the Aerospace Industries Association who has spent more than a decade fighting for controversial industry-backed proposals on arms sales. When the arms industry speaks with one voice on arms transfer policy, more often than not the message is crafted by Joel Johnson.

Unlike many of his other colleagues in the business, Johnson did not come straight out of a military or Pentagon background. A former "white hat," as he puts it, Johnson worked for years as a development economist with the Treasury Department and the Senate Foreign Relations Committee before "switching sides" to go to bat for the arms industry. A fast-talking, animated conversationalist who bears a slight resemblance to David Letterman, Johnson can be surprisingly frank in his defense of the corporate arms traders.[4]

As if to underscore his argument that the weapons that he helps to sell don't really hurt anyone, Johnson's D.C. office is adorned with model aircraft, some of which are gifts from the companies he represents and some of which he built himself. A particularly smart-looking model fighter plane is perched on top of his computer in the far back corner of the office, looking as if it is ready to take off through the ceiling at any moment.

Johnson's stock in trade is transforming debates about the risks of selling arms and the consequences of using them into discussions of the business opportunities that are lost when weapons sales are stopped on arms control or human rights grounds. When I first visited him on a hot July afternoon in the summer of 1989, Johnson was thinking out loud about how to head off congressional efforts to legislate sanctions on China in the wake of the crackdown on unarmed democracy protesters at Tiananmen Square. The discussion offered a fascinating insight into the distorted worldview of the arms industry lobbyist and his ability to turn even the most unpleasant evidence of how weapons are used into a reason to sell even more.

In response to public outrage over the massacre, President Bush had issued an executive order imposing sanctions on military sales to China, but Johnson and his industry colleagues were hoping to keep the initiative in the President's hands. An executive order could be reversed at the stroke of a pen, reopening the Chinese market to U.S. arms manufacturers in relatively short order. Legislation mandating sanctions would be much more difficult to overturn, so Johnson and his colleagues wanted to make sure that didn't happen.

Johnson began by berating Congress for not understanding that "these decisions are twenty year decisions. . . . If we get cut out of the Chinese market now, we could lose out on sales well into the next century," he argued, pointing to the maintenance, repair, and follow-on orders that accompany any major weapons sale. His hardheaded economic argument seemed designed to sweep aside any moral or political concerns about the implications of arming a nation that had just turned its army on its own people. In Johnson's view, it was just another business decision.

If he had stopped there, his position would have been understandable, if a bit cold and calculating. But Johnson took the argument a step further, speculating that the deaths at Tiananmen Square meant much more to Western TV audiences than they did to the people of China: "For the Chinese, whether it was 200 or 2,000 deaths, it's just a blip on the radar screen. It's like their version of Kent State." His tone was reminiscent of Gen. William Westmoreland's infamous statement during the Vietnam War that the Vietnamese don't put the same value on human life as Americans do. But unlike Westmoreland, Johnson immediately recognized the insensitivity of his remark. He backtracked, noting that of course any loss of life was tragic, and that the real point was to learn better, less violent means of crowd control. At this point he broke into a brief discourse on the relative merits of Israeli versus South Korean methods of crowd control, applauding the Koreans for what he viewed as their less violent, more disciplined methods.

The whole interview had a surreal air about it, as if in groping for a justification of continued arms sales to an admittedly brutal regime in China, Johnson had temporarily taken leave of his better judgment. But in another sense, he was just doing his job. What I had witnessed was a sort of "rough draft" of the more refined arguments he would promote on Capitol Hill, in the State Department, and in the media to shift the focus of arms sales debates away from the human consequences in regions of conflict toward the economic payoffs in American communities. It was a sort of willful blindness that was necessary to put the best light on the weapons trading business.

Johnson revealed his underlying philosophy when he suggested that part of the problem was that people have a negative view of "arms sales" and that what U.S. industry was really engaged in was "defense trade." He noted that "the term *arms* has unpleasant associations for people." Besides, he argued, "a lot of what we sell isn't the kind of thing that goes *boom* and kills people." To remedy this "problem," Johnson had been vigorously promoting industry recommendations to change the name of the Arms Export Control Act to the Defense Trade and International Cooperation Act, in hopes of erasing any unpleasant associations members of Congress might have in signing off on major military sales to the Middle East or other volatile regions.

But whatever one chooses to call arms exports, Johnson has made it clear in interviews and public statements since the end of the Gulf War that he views the 1990s as a period of unique opportunity. He joins other industry representatives in asserting that the conflict offered a unique "showcase" for U.S. weaponry even as it downgraded the status of the Soviet systems that Iraqi personnel were using. Johnson believes that the end of the Cold War could further enhance the foreign sales potential for U.S. firms. As military budgets in the United States and Europe decline, the importance of foreign sales increases, leading to a potential "winner takes all" situation in certain lines of the weapons trade. Echoing arguments made by the Bush administration during the 1989 M-1 tank sale to Saudi Arabia, Johnson argued that "if we can knock the Brits out of the box" by locking up tank sales to Saudi Arabia, they may be forced to abandon their own tank production, "and that leaves us with no real competitor in the world tank business." Spinning out how the scenario might affect other arms products as well, Johnson predicted a potential era of U.S. hegemony in the world arms market. And he sees nothing wrong with that. In Johnson's view, weapons are just "low volume, high value capital goods, and we're good at producing that kind of thing [in the U.S.]. . . in part because we have a large domestic market." He cited other "low volume, high value" items like commercial airliners and mainframe computers where U.S. firms control 65–70 percent of the world market, and he argued that now that "artificial barriers" like Soviet military aid and Cold War alliances are dropping out of the picture "we should control a comparable percentage of the defense market."[5]

Johnson is aware that the industry's goal of establishing such overwhelming dominance of the weapons trade will cause some image problems, but he dismisses any such criticism in advance as unfair and impractical. "Does that make us arms merchant to the world?" he asks rhetorically. "Maybe it does." But Johnson sees a bright side to this development, asserting that it will "give us the opportunity to control how those weapons are used."

This leads to perhaps the most dangerous aspect of the industry's argument for unrestrained arms sales, the notion that there is no real need for government controls on weapons exports because U.S. arms suppliers can always stay one step ahead of potential U.S. adversaries. Johnson's views on this point echoed a position put forward by a marketing executive at Boeing who told me that he felt it was actually preferable for U.S. adversaries to be armed with U.S. weapons, because "that way you know what they've got." Johnson even suggested conspiratorially that some U.S. systems may soon incorporate devices that emit signals, unbeknownst to the purchasing nation, that would allow U.S. forces to track and target them if they fall into hostile hands. Just as the Star Wars missile defense program was promoted by the industry in the mid-1980s as a technical "quick fix" that would obviate the need for nuclear arms control, Johnson seemed to be suggesting that the industry could find technical solutions to the problems caused by the proliferation of advanced conventional armaments. The common thread uniting the two arguments was that the public would take all the risks, while industry would reap the profits regardless of whether its proposed scheme reduced or increased the risks of war.

Johnson's musings on the state of the world and the role of U.S. arms in it offer a capsule view of the mind-set of the industry lobbyist: sell, sell, sell, even to unstable, repressive regimes, because if we don't do it, somebody else will. Even if advanced U.S. armaments fall into the hands of a U.S. adversary, U.S. technology will keep U.S. forces one step ahead of the game. The net result of this logic would be an arms race between the United States and renegade Third World regimes like Hussein's Iraq or a radicalized Saudi Arabia in which the U.S. arms industry would in essence be supplying both sides of the conflict: an arms merchant's dream but a nightmare for U.S. security.

Job Blackmail: The Ultimate Weapon

The trump card in the arms industry's lobbying arsenal has nothing to do with security, the balance of power, or how U.S.-supplied weapons end up being used in areas of conflict. When all else fails, the most convincing argument in favor of a major sale can be stated in one word: jobs.

Jim McInerney has made a science of pork barrel lobbying on behalf of arms sales to the Middle East, first in his post as executive director of ALESA and more recently with an even larger industry lobbying group, the American Defense Preparedness Association. A friendly, soft-spoken, articulate defender of arms sales, McInerney spent twenty-three years in the army and air force and six years at McDonnell Douglas before taking over as ALESA's point man in Washington in the mid-1980s. From an office suite just down the hill from the Capitol, he served as the key organizer of several concerted industry efforts to convince members of Congress of the economic importance of arms sales—and the political dangers of voting against them.

When I spoke to him in his D.C. office in the summer of 1989, McInerney had the air of a man who was satisfied that he had by and large accomplished his mission. "In Congress, they're showing signs of understanding the world as it is," said McInerney. "Members are finding it harder and harder to say 'I don't care about jobs in my district.'" ALESA's member corporations have made it their business to make it hard for Congress to veto overseas arms sales, sponsoring a series of studies purporting to demonstrate that limiting U.S. sales of fighter planes and other advanced equipment to Arab regimes could cost the United States up to 150,000 jobs per year. McInerney is confident that this "data" has helped win Congress over to the industry's point of view, noting that "we're all singing from the same song sheet now."

ALESA's efforts have been supplemented by pork barrel lobbying by individual companies as well. General Dynamics was among the most blatant practitioners of these tactics, beginning with a 1989 joint campaign with Bush administration and Department of the Army officials to soften up Congress for a flood of new sales of the company's M-1 tank (see chapter 7).

While General Dynamics has benefited from strong executive branch support in its efforts to sell the M-1 abroad with minimal interference from Congress, Raytheon pulled an even more impressive lobbying coup on behalf of the now famous Patriot missile defense system by getting the liberal Massachusetts congressional delegation to plead its case. Congressman Joe Moakley, a progressive noted for his stands against costly weapons systems such as Star Wars and the MX missile, was instrumental in getting funding that the Pentagon had not even asked for to purchase several hundred million dollars' worth of support equipment for Patriot missiles slated for export to Italy. The funds to install the equipment were written into the Pentagon's budget before the Italian government had even made a final decision to purchase the Patriot, as a way to induce them to proceed with the deal. Moakley made no effort to justify his support for the costly equipment on strategic grounds, telling the *Wall Street Journal* that "they told me that 3,200 people were going to hit the streets if we didn't get the money."[6]

But these efforts by General Dynamics and Raytheon were small potatoes compared with the campaign sketched out by Jim McInerney and ALESA in support of the second phase of President Bush's record-breaking proposal to sell Saudi Arabia $20 billion in U.S. armaments in September 1990. The proposed sale was a potential windfall that the industry could not afford to pass up. McInerney noted that many of the items slated for sale to the Middle East were "endangered species," systems such as the F-15 aircraft, the Patriot missile, the M-1 tank, and the AWACS airplane that were scheduled for termination by the Pentagon and needed immediate foreign sales to keep production lines open.

By the end of September 1991, reeling from an unexpected move in Congress to cut Bush's Saudi package into two parts, it was time for ALESA to regroup. The coalition had mounted an initial lobbying effort on behalf of the whole $20 billion package, including a special 800 number that served as a "hotline" to send a predetermined telegram to the caller's member of Congress:

> I strongly urge you to support President Bush's proposed sale of American defense equipment to Saudi Arabia for her security needs. With the lives of American men and women at stake in the Persian Gulf, the export of American defense equipment to an important ally is clearly in our national interest. These exports are also important to our own national security. They will assist in maintaining the defense industrial base and provide thousands of American jobs.[7]

This generalized economic appeal on behalf of the sale proved too little too late to save the whole package, but McInerney and his colleagues were determined to do everything they could to get the rest of the package approved as soon as possible.

In an attempt to coordinate industry's lobbying response, McInerney formed a Middle East Action Group, comprising sixty-three lobbyists, executives, and public relations experts representing over thirty military companies, consulting groups, and industry associations, including ALESA and the Aerospace Industries Association as well as the U.S.–Arab Chamber of Commerce and the National Council on U.S.–Arab Relations. McInerney's group developed an elaborate "game plan" to block congressional opposition to the larger, second phase of Bush's $20 billion sales proposal, drawing on proposals from an outside consultant, Burdeshaw Associates, as well as materials prepared by ALESA members. While elements of the overall lobbying plan were overtaken by events, the strategy set forth by ALESA's Middle East Action Group offers a rare inside view of the industry's lobbying machine in full gear and of the tactics and techniques that are routinely used to neutralize congressional opposition to controversial foreign arms sales.

According to the briefing book that served as its basic reference point, the goal of the campaign was to "foster a political environment in Congress that is more favorable to this sale" by mustering all the D.C. lobbying muscle and national "grassroots support" of over two dozen firms with major interests in sales to the Middle East. Participants ranged from military firms like General Dynamics and LTV to major construction firms like the Bechtel Group, whose former alumni include Reagan administration secretaries of defense and state Caspar Weinberger and George Shultz. The action group was divided into three subcommittees—one on threat analysis, one on strategy, and one on public affairs. Congress was divided into seven regions, with a company representative assigned to coordinate lobbying efforts in each area.

A key element of the strategy was to involve as many trade union representatives, smaller suppliers, and subcontractors as possible to give the effort a grassroots feel, so it wouldn't appear to be just a bunch of self-interested defense contractors pushing their wares. A memo by a Raytheon executive stressed the importance of this approach, urging major contractors to ask each vendor or subcontractor to call, write, and meet with their local representatives and senators, in both their district offices and their Washington offices, to express support for the sale. In addition, each company was told to have its employees send their own letters and telegrams. As the analysis noted, "If a small business is able to persuade 20 to 40% (preferably more) of its workforce" to send personal letters to Congress, "then the effects will dramatically increase." In all, this grassroots campaign set as its goal the generation of "hundreds of thousands of letters" to Congress in support of phase II of the Saudi arms package deal.

To tailor its message, ALESA contracted with the Science Applications International Corporation, a well-known Department of Defense research contractor, to conduct a study entitled "The Domestic Economic Impact of the Prospective Sale of Selected Military Equipment to Saudi Arabia." The study, more than three hundred pages long, contains a district-by-district breakdown of alleged income and employment benefits of the entire Saudi package, estimating an immediate impact of $45 billion in new business activity and over three-quarters of a million jobs in all. The report included handy reference tables on the employment and income benefits in more than three hundred congressional districts, from a low of three jobs in Congressman John Porter's 10th District in Illinois to a high of over forty-one thousand in Congressman Jim McDermott's 6th District in Washington State.[8]

In order to deploy this information where it could do the most good, ALESA sent out a letter to major defense company CEOs with the signature of Gen. Howard Fish in which he put the case directly: "I urge you to personally become involved and to marshal the resources of your company *and* your subcontractors to support the sale." Fish appealed for a four-part strategy, including an in-house public relations campaign to "insure that the constituent members of your company, plus sub-contractors, understand the sale with emphasis on the economic benefits to their districts"; a flood of letters, phone calls, and personal visits to D.C. offices of members of Congress; meetings at district offices of key members, which Fish noted "can be most effectively accomplished by a large number of subcontractors and their unions/employees"; and a concentrated "one-on-one" approach to individual members of Congress, utilizing as many "middle managers and union representatives from your plants" as possible. ALESA provided a sample letter to Congress for distribution to company employees and subcontractors, stressing the alleged security need for the sale, then moving quickly to the billions in purported economic benefits. To drive home this point, the sample letter ended with a personalized P.S., as follows:

> P.S.,[SPACE HERE IS LEFT FOR A HANDWRITTEN MESSAGE INFORMING THE MEMBER THAT THE PERSON WRITING THIS LETTER WORKS FOR "ABC WIDGET COMPANY," FOR INSTANCE, AND THAT WHAT IS SPECIFICALLY AT STAKE FOR THE MEMBER'S DISTRICT ARE X# OF JOBS, AND X# OF DOLLARS. CLOSE WITH A VARIATION ON THE MESSAGE: 'ABC WIDGET COMPANY IS COUNTING ON YOU TO SUPPORT THIS SALE. YOUR ACTION ON BEHALF OF THIS

DISTRICT WILL BE WATCHED CLOSELY IN THE DAYS AHEAD AND LEADING UP TO ELECTION DAY. THANKS FOR YOUR SUPPORT.']

This elaborate lobbying infrastructure was geared up and ready to go by December 1990. A number of contractors, including armored-vehicle manufacturer FMC, even held their own little "pep rallies" for subcontractors to school them in how to lobby their local representatives on behalf of phase II of the Saudi deal. FMC's meeting was attended by approximately 120 subcontractors, and it included a briefing by the industry's point man in Washington, Joel Johnson. The plan was to put on a full-court press as soon as President Bush notified Congress of the sale, getting as many subcontractors, employees, union officials, and local business executives as possible to convince their member of Congress that voting against the package would be economically costly to their district (not to mention politically costly to the representative down the road). But the Gulf War changed the political climate in which the Bush administration made its decision on the Saudi sale, forcing the Middle East Action Group to adjust its lobbying tactics accordingly.

As 1991 wore on, first with the air and ground wars in the Persian Gulf and then with the postwar recriminations about whether selling more advanced weaponry to the region was a good idea, the industry's dream of a single $14 billion arms deal with the Saudis began to fade. Wary of public opposition to unrestrained arms trafficking in the wake of the Gulf War and unwilling to take on a visible public fight with congressional supporters of Israel on the eve of an election year, President Bush decided to spread out the second phase of the Saudi sale into a series of smaller sales—a few thousand tactical missiles here, a thousand bombs there, several hundred cluster bombs here. Sales of big-ticket items like the McDonnell Douglas F-15 and the Boeing AWACS were put off indefinitely.

The Bush administration's postponement of the big-ticket items in phase II of the Saudi package deal was the subject of a fair amount of behind-the-scenes grumbling by industry lobbyists at the June 1991 Paris Air Show, where several company representatives made pointed references to their urgent need to conclude major deals with the Saudis soon, to save their production lines. The most vocal complaints over Bush's decision to stretch out the package came from McDonnell Douglas. Company vice president Bob Trice gave a briefing on "Why the U.S. Should Act Now on F-15 Foreign Military Sales Programs." Trice relied on straightforward pork barrel arguments: "We have

7,000 people on that production line, and it's about to shut down if the President doesn't muster the political will to make the sale." If the F-15 sale doesn't go through soon, said Trice, "four years from now, we're going to look back and say this was a plane that shot down 36 of 41 enemy aircraft in the Gulf War, and we let the line shut down."

As for the argument that stopping the F-15 sale could form part of an overall policy of restraining the Middle East arms race, Trice took strong exception: "Multilateral controls don't work. We had the CAT talks [seeking conventional arms transfer limitations] under Carter and they were a joke." Given that history, Trice argued, "why should we be the first" to press for restraints this time around? He closed by acknowledging that "we have a vested, parochial interest, there's no denying that . . . but we also think this sale makes sense."[9]

While Trice and McDonnell Douglas may have been convinced that the summer of 1991 was the time to go ahead with an F-15 sale to Saudi Arabia, some of their allies were beginning to have their doubts. Several industry insiders were convinced that opposition from Israel and its supporters in the Congress, combined with a public mood that favored doing everything possible to promote the newly convened Mideast peace talks, made an F-15 sale to the Saudis unlikely for some time to come. The united industry front was beginning to break down. One key player that decided to strike out on its own was Raytheon. The Massachusetts-based arms producer had garnered priceless free publicity from the one-sidedly positive coverage of its Patriot air defense missile during the Gulf War, and company officials wanted to cash in on the reputation of the Patriot now, without the political complications that would come from linking it to an F-15 sale to the Saudis.

At a midafternoon meeting over drinks at Washington's Union Station in the summer of 1992, Raytheon lobbyist Jim Hickey took time out between his appointments on Capitol Hill to explain the company's strategy for selling the Saudi Patriot deal to a reluctant State Department. By the summer of 1991, the company had been in desperate need of a foreign sale to keep the Patriot production line in Andover, Massachusetts, open. "We had to break out of the $14 billion package. . . . We didn't want to be tied to the F-15 any more," Hickey said.

He went on to describe a three-step strategy that the company pursued to get a sale of Patriot missiles to Saudi Arabia approved before the end of 1991. First, the company would prevail upon the Saudis to put in a request for the Patriot earlier than they normally would have done. Second, they would urge that the Patriot sale be considered separately from the politically charged F-15 sale. Third—and this was the most creative wrinkle—they would seek to demonstrate that the sale had such overwhelming support in Congress that the State Department could proceed without fear of any serious domestic political fallout.

Step one was easily accomplished. Prompted by Raytheon, Saudi ambassador to Washington Prince Bandar bin Sultan sent a letter to Defense Secretary Dick Cheney in October 1991 indicating that his nation was interested in buying additional Patriot missile batteries. Steps two and three were then pursued in tandem, as Hickey and other Raytheon lobbyists approached key congressional opponents of arms sales to the Middle East to see if they would support the sale of purely "defensive" Patriot missiles to the Saudis as a straight deal, separate from the F-15. Raytheon began by approaching Gerry Studds, a Massachusetts liberal and member of the House Foreign Affairs Committee. To Hickey's surprise, Studds not only agreed that he wouldn't oppose the sale, he even offered to help Raytheon promote it. Studds did an informal poll of the usual critics of Mideast arms sales, such as Congressmen Mel Levine and Howard Berman of California and Foreign Affairs Committee chairman Dante Fascell of Florida—described by Hickey as "the whole crowd of AIPAC [the American Israel Public Affairs Committee] supporters on the Foreign Affairs Committee"—to see if they would support a Patriot sale to the Saudis. According to Hickey, they all bought the notion of the Patriot sale as a purely defensive export that they could support despite their traditional opposition to weapons sales to the Arab regimes of the area. But when Raytheon passed this information along to the State Department, the bureaucracy was so nervous about the possibility of congressional opposition that they asked the company to get the positions of key members in writing.

Hickey proudly informed me that what followed was "unprecedented" in the annals of arms sales lobbying. Fascell and Senate Foreign Relations Committee head Claiborne Pell each sent their own letters to Secretary of State James Baker encouraging the administration to sell Patriot missiles to Saudi Arabia without delay. Pell's letter argued that since the Patriot was "purely defensive," the administration need not fear a congressional outcry: "With regard to this particular sale, we are not aware of any serious opposition."[10]

It was one thing for Congress to roll over and approve an arms sales proposal launched by the executive branch under pressure from industry, but Hickey asserted that this was "the first time Congress had ever lobbied the administration in favor of an arms sale." Congress was notified of a $3.3 billion sale of Patriots and related support equipment to Saudi Arabia in mid-November 1991, and the deal sailed through with barely a discouraging word from the House or the Senate. Raytheon's lobbying gambit had worked. The Patriot production line—which Hickey described as "the heart of Raytheon"—would stay open for several more years, during which time the company could actively court additional foreign customers. Nations on the active list of potential clients include South Korea, Taiwan, Israel, Kuwait, Egypt, the United Arab Emirates, Italy, and the United Kingdom.

Meanwhile, back at McDonnell Douglas, company strategists were chomping at the bit, trying to figure out a way to force the Bush administration's hand and get the Saudi F-15 deal approved. Lobbyist Mark Kronenberg signaled his company's urgency about the project in September 1991 when he told me that the company would "mobilize the same coalition" that was assembled by ALESA to fight for the larger Saudi package in support of an F-15 sale standing alone. Kronenberg elaborated, asserting that "we'll use our subcontractors and our union guys to the hilt" to counter any lobbying against the sale by AIPAC and congressional supporters of Israel. In Kronenberg's view, the only thing holding up presidential notification of the sale was the wait until "after Israel gets its payoff"—the billions in housing loan guarantees from the United States that were then being held up over a U.S.–Israeli dispute over settlements in the occupied territories. Kronenberg felt that, until the loan guarantee issue was resolved, Bush would be too vulnerable to arguments by supporters of Israel: "You didn't want to give Israel money for housing because that will upset the peace process, and now you want to sell $10 billion in weapons to the Saudis and you're telling me that won't affect the peace process?" Even Kronenberg had to acknowledge that "frankly, it's a convincing argument" and that the company would probably have to bide its time until 1992, after the impasse on the housing assistance for Israel had been definitively resolved.

But this wait-and-see attitude was clearly not shared throughout McDonnell Douglas. Trice, who had come perilously close to calling George Bush a coward at the Paris Air Show in June, turned up the heat at the November 1991 Dubai Air Show when he announced that the Saudis were ready, willing, and able to buy the F-15 *now*.[11] Normally, whatever lobbying they may do behind the scenes, the weapons firms leave it up to the U.S. government to make pronouncements on the status of arms deals with major allies. By violating normal procedure, Trice was obviously hoping to pressure the Bush administration into making a deal sooner than it would otherwise have done. In response to a reporter's inquiry about why McDonnell Douglas was announcing Saudi interest in striking a deal, Trice showed a politician's flair for doubletalk:

> The announcement was not designed to put pressure on the Administration, but if the U.S. wants to retain the F-15 option, now is the time to act. . . . We understand why it has been slow going in Washington, but we're running out of time. The [F-15 production] line could die and with it the unique capabilities of the line for us and the entire American defense industry.[12]

So much for not exerting pressure.

The immediate impact of Trice's announcement on Capitol Hill was overwhelmingly negative. Sen. Howard Metzenbaum of Ohio quickly pulled together a coalition of sixty-seven senators—the same number that would be needed to override a presidential veto—to send a strongly worded letter to President Bush opposing the sale. Even some of Trice's industry colleagues questioned whether Trice had made a serious tactical blunder that would alienate the Bush administration. But the events of 1992 were to prove them wrong.

The real relationship between the administration and McDonnell Douglas over the F-15 sale was not entirely antagonistic, as Trice's remarks may have suggested—it was more of a partnership. In Congressman Berman's view, the Bush administration told McDonnell Douglas to "go out and soften up the Congress for this sale . . . and when they're soft enough, we'll submit it." Or, as an industry source put it to David Morrison of the *National Journal*, "What the Administration is saying is 'After you, Gaston.' You go out and make sure that we don't get clobbered, and then we'll send it up." In light of this division of political labor, the Metzenbaum letter was merely a benchmark of how much "softening up" of Congress McDonnell Douglas would need to do before the political climate was ripe for the F-15 sale.[13]

During the remaining weeks of 1991, company officials prepared the way for what Howard Berman has described as "the most sophisticated and far reaching campaign to promote an arms transfer that I've seen since I've been in Congress." Borrowing a page from ALESA's Middle East Action Group, McDonnell Douglas made jobs the centerpiece of its lobbying efforts on behalf of the F-15 sale. Activities on behalf of the sale were done under the umbrella of the U.S. Jobs Now coalition, which included fellow contractors United Technologies, Hughes Aircraft, Martin Marietta, Northrop, and General Electric along with unions ranging from the United Auto Workers and the International Association of Machinists to the Teamsters, carpenters, and plant guards unions. Beginning in early 1992, the McDonnell Douglas–led coalition began distributing glossy brochures promising "40,000 highly skilled jobs" as a result of a Saudi F-15 sale. The brochures were supplemented with scores of briefings of key congressional staffers and members of Congress, full-page ads in the *Washington Post* and other key outlets, and a slick, seven-minute video that attempted to imply that foregoing the sale of seventy-two advanced combat aircraft would fuel mass unemployment in the nation's industrial heartland.

This multimedia assault fueled a campaign that bombarded members of Congress with over twenty thousand letters from defense executives, union members, representatives of local chambers of commerce, and employees of the thousands of subcontractors that work on some part of the F-15. Members of Congress were repeatedly told that the F-15 had 2,070 suppliers in 345 congressional districts and 46 states, as the defense contractors and their union allies sponsored everything from mass rallies in favor of the sale to carefully targeted meetings to lobby key representatives.[14]

As hard-hitting as these initial efforts were, by the spring it still appeared that McDonnell Douglas faced an uphill battle. In April, Congressman Levine joined 235 of his House colleagues in sending a letter to President Bush that noted that Saudi Arabia had already bought nearly $15 billion in U.S. weaponry since the outbreak of the Gulf War and that "the sale of F-15 aircraft to Saudi Arabia is incompatible with any meaningful arms control policy. . . . An F-15 sale would represent a significant escalation of the regional arms race."[15] In addition to this continuing show of opposition by a majority of members of Congress, the political calendar was also working against McDonnell Douglas. Several rounds of the ongoing Mideast peace talks were scheduled to occur in Washington during the spring, and the end of May marked the first anniversary of George Bush's pledge to work toward restraining the flow of arms into the region. Moreover, Israel had elections scheduled for June, and the loan guarantee issue had yet to be settled. Announcement of a major new fighter sale to the Saudis in the midst of all this diplomatic activity and political turmoil would put the president at risk of being branded a hypocrite who was undermining the prospects for Mideast peace and jeopardizing long-term Israeli security for short-term gain.

McDonnell Douglas plowed ahead nonetheless, with the able assistance of House majority leader Dick Gephardt, whose St. Louis district includes the F-15 plant. By the end of the summer, as the economy worsened and Bush's political fortunes seemed destined to go down with it, the appeals to "Save U.S. Jobs" had more and more appeal to the president. Finally, on September 11, less than a week after he had told the American Jewish Congress that he hadn't yet made up his mind on the sale, Bush appeared in St. Louis to announce that he would be going ahead immediately with the sale of F-15s to Saudi Arabia. Potential opposition from Israel and its supporters in Congress was muted as a result of the simultaneous agreement on the long-awaited housing loan guarantees for Israel, as well as a quiet U.S. pledge to supply the Israeli armed forces with whatever aid and technology they would need to maintain their "qualitative edge" over the Saudis. Other than the criticism from consistent arms sales critics like Howard Berman, the congressional opposition that had seemed so strong only a few months earlier had evaporated under the barrage of industry propaganda about a vote against the sale meaning a vote against U.S. jobs.

While a few big-ticket items remained on hold despite the best efforts of McInerney and the Middle East Action Group, the overall prospects for the industry had brightened considerably in the wake of the Gulf War. Despite industry concerns about the viability of announcing major arms sales during an election year, 1992 looked like it might be the best year yet for the corporate arms merchants—in a one-week stretch in September alone, the Bush administration announced deals worth nearly $17 billion for sales of F-15 and F-16 aircraft to Saudi Arabia, Taiwan, and Greece.[16] Candidate Bill Clinton was quick to endorse each of the sales, thereby foreclosing the prospect of any serious national debate over the strategic dangers inherent in allowing narrow economic interests to control arms export decisionmaking (for further discussion of the role of arms sales in the 1992 campaign, see chapter 13). The industry's pork barrel lobbying efforts had paid off handsomely.

The Permanent Arms Supply Network

As impressive as the efforts of lobbyists like Howard Fish, Joel Johnson, and James McInerney are, they represent a tiny cross section of a "permanent arms supply network"—of major defense contractors, former military and intelligence operatives, foreign brokers and middlemen, and influential government officials—that is working to ensure that the United States remains the world's leading arms trafficking nation.

During the 1980s, a small army of Pentagon and State Department officials moved from arms sales and weapons procurement policymaking positions in government to jobs as lobbyists and corporate officers of the nation's largest military contractors. This revolving-door syndrome was clearly accelerated by the get-rich-quick ethos of Ronald Reagan's Washington—in the Pentagon alone, the number of individuals who moved into slots in the arms industry more than tripled from 1980 to 1985. According to the General Accounting Office, a full 20 percent (six thousand people) of the thirty thousand high-ranking military and civilian officials who left the Pentagon during 1983 and 1984 went to work for defense contractors.[17] This race through the revolving door was bolstered by a parallel increase in the number of independent consultants like former navy procurement chief Melvyn Paisley, who was at the center of a wide-ranging conspiracy to trade on inside information and stolen government documents to give specific defense contractors an edge in bidding on domestic and foreign arms contracts. The scheme, uncovered in a Justice Department investigation code-named Operation Ill Wind, has so far resulted in the conviction of sixty industry and Pentagon officials.[18] So, to get a full measure of the influence wielded by the corporate arms merchants, the impact of the more visible activities of major lobbyists like Howard Fish and Joel Johnson must be multiplied many times over to take into account thousands of their lesser known counterparts who are busily tapping their own contacts inside the government on the industry's behalf.

As we will see in chapter 13, despite the crackdown on illegal activities by industry consultants and despite Bill Clinton's promises to clean up Washington lobbying processes, there is ample evidence that the political clout of the permanent arms supply network may actually be growing rather than diminishing. But first we will examine the underside of the weapons lobby, the dealers and middlemen who facilitate the secret, often illicit, aspects of the trade.

9

The Permanent Arms Supply Network (II): Middlemen, Dealers, and the Secret Trade

On the evening of October 5, 1986, the Reagan administration got its first indication that the contra arms supply scheme was about to unravel. At 11:00 P.M., Samuel Watson, a national security aide to George Bush, received a call from Iran/contra operative Felix Rodriguez informing him that one of the network's planes was missing. The next morning, Rodriguez called back to report that the aircraft had been shot down inside Nicaragua and that one of the crew members had been captured.

The captured crew member was Eugene Hasenfus, a forty-five-year-old former marine and unemployed construction worker from Green Bay, Wisconsin. When Hasenfus's wife, Sally, was asked by reporters about her husband's activities, she pleaded ignorance: "I don't know where he is and what he's doing. I only know what I see on TV, too, and I don't know any more." His brother admitted that Eugene was the "type of guy who goes looking for adventure," but he claimed that as far as he knew he had been in Florida working for a legitimate air freight firm. A friend said that Hasenfus had told him he had a little job to do but that it was no big deal and he would be back soon to do some hunting. It ended up being a lot more complicated than that.

What happened next is well known. Through his own personal

admissions and documents found on the plane, Hasenfus was definitively linked to Richard Secord's arms enterprise. He was put on trial in Nicaragua, and within six weeks the Iran/contra scandal was front-page news.

Eugene Hasenfus was supposed to be a bit player in all of this, a hired hand who earned $3,000 a month kicking boxes of weapons out of the back of C-123 transport planes. But the interplay of personal and corporate connections that brought him to Nicaragua offered critical insights into the anatomy of the arms trade. From 1966 to 1972, Hasenfus had worked for Air America, a CIA proprietary airline that reportedly ran guns and drugs in Southeast Asia. It had been fourteen years since he had done that kind of work, but now he needed a job, and William J. Cooper, another Air America alumnus, had called him a few months earlier to offer him a position doing "the same as we were doing in Southeast Asia, different geographic location, different time period." Cooper had been the pilot of the downed C-123, and he was killed in the crash.

The aircraft had been leased from Southern Air Transport, a former CIA front company that is frequently chosen for sensitive missions. Southern Air in turn had a close working relationship with American National Management Corp., a firm that had been hired by the U.S. government to conduct covert actions from the Caribbean to the Persian Gulf. Within a few days of his capture, Hasenfus had identified his supervisor for the air drops in Nicaragua as Max Gomez, the code name for George Bush's favorite former CIA operative, Felix Rodriguez.

Because of these associations and others that were uncovered by journalists and government investigators in the months and years that followed, the crash of Eugene Hasenfus's plane did much more than blow the Reagan administration's cover story on Iran/contra. It opened up a window on an extensive underground network that has been involved in facilitating secret weapons deals for over three decades.[1]

The Permanent Arms Supply Network and the Roots of Iran/Contra

Both Ronald Reagan's vision of a massive, secret arms trafficking "enterprise" and George Bush's more recent scheme to use arms sales as the centerpiece of his war on drugs have relied heavily on the involvement of a covert subculture of militarists, mercenaries, and arms traders who have participated in a series of official and unofficial arms supply operations stretching back to President Kennedy's ill-fated 1961 Bay of Pigs invasion of Cuba. Players from the same cast of characters that ran guns to anti-Castro paramilitary forces and attempted a series of "dirty tricks" against the Cuban regime in the early and mid-1960s—including such harebrained schemes as trying to murder Fidel Castro by slipping him a poison cigar—turned up twenty-five years later with central roles in Oliver North's Iranian and Nicaraguan arms supply lines. But this time the line between government-sponsored covert actions and private profiteering was hopelessly blurred.[2]

As investigative writer Peter Maas pointed out when the Iran/contra scandal broke, one of the most incredible aspects of the whole affair was the "strange recruits" Oliver North came up with to help him run his public/private weapons pipeline. North's most intimate associates in the Iran/contra dealings—retired air force major general Richard Secord, former CIA men Theodore Shackley and Thomas Clines, and Iranian businessman and arms merchant Albert Hakim—all had close connections with former CIA agent Ed Wilson, who is serving a fifty-two-year term in a federal penitentiary for shipping plastique explosives and other tools of terrorism to Libya's Muammar Qaddafi. In a feature article in the *New York Times Magazine*, Maas, who had documented the association of these men with Wilson in his best-selling book *Manhunt*, wondered out loud about North's choice of associates: "How could he have put together this crew? Was he really that dumb?"

In fact, North's recruiting decisions were not so much an error in personal judgment as a logical outgrowth of the contacts developed over the years by Secord, the gung-ho general and former air force pilot who met North when the two men were helping to steer the $8.5 billion Saudi AWACS sale through Congress in 1981 (see chapter 5). Secord's résumé reads like a capsule history of the major U.S. covert military and weapons trafficking ventures of the past three decades. The men he chose to assist him in fulfilling North's request reflected that history.

For example, former air force colonel Robert Dutton, who helped oversee the day-to-day activities of North and Secord's secret contra arms airlift, first met Secord in the early 1960s when the two men served in an elite air force special warfare unit known as the Air Commandos, based at Hurlburt Field, Florida. Secord claims that one of his first assignments there, in 1961, was to run secret bombing missions in Vietnam when U.S. involvement was allegedly still in an advisory capacity. And during the nuclear missile crisis of October 1962,

Secord stood by with a small group of pilots from Hurlburt, poised to lead an attack against Cuba—a mission that Secord wistfully reports had to be called off when the Kennedy administration reached a last-minute accommodation with Soviet premier Nikita Khrushchev.[3]

This was only the first in a series of professional connections between Dutton and Secord that culminated in their role in the contra supply effort. In 1976, Dutton served under Secord at the U.S. Air Force's Military Assistance Advisory Group (MAAG) in Iran. Of this period in his career, culminating with his oversight of the negotiations and lobbying that led to the Saudi AWACS sale, Secord bragged in an interview that "for six straight years, I was a key figure in the military-sales business—first in Iran and then as the head for world-wide Air Force security systems. I was Jesus Christ as far as those defense contractors were concerned." Despite an environment in which Secord saw middlemen "bribing everybody, just everybody," and in which he was certain he "could have become enormously wealthy," he claimed proudly that "I didn't come out of there [Iran] with any money." The same could not be said for his role in North's Iran/contra venture, in which Secord apparently made up for whatever opportunities he may have missed during his posting to Teheran in the late 1970s.[4]

When Secord picked him to help run the contra arms network in April 1986, Dutton was back serving as deputy chief of operations for the 23rd Air Force, which oversees the Air Commando wing at Hurlburt Field. The wing became a rich source of recruits for Secord. By the time they began to collaborate on Iran/contra, Dutton and Secord already had a long history of working together in government-sanctioned arms deals.

The same was true of Clines and Shackley, former CIA men who met Secord in the late 1960s when the three men were intimately involved in carrying out the CIA's secret war in Laos. The war bore some resemblance to the contra support operations of the mid-1980s, involving the recruitment of Meo tribesmen to fight a "guerrilla war" against North Vietnamese forces who were allegedly using Laotian territory to ferry weapons to the Vietcong in South Vietnam. But this war was far bloodier than the contra campaigns—over two hundred thousand Meo tribesmen ultimately lost their lives in the secret hostilities, which were only finally abandoned in 1975, at the end of the Vietnam War. By his own account, Secord was "in charge of all the tactical air operations in support of the CIA" in Laos, including everything from dropping U.S. advisers and weaponry into war zones to deploying U.S. fighter aircraft in support of the Meo guerrillas. As CIA station chief in Laos, Shackley came to know and appreciate Se-cord's skills on a day-to-day basis. Shackley was joined in Laos by his young protégé Tom Clines, who had worked with him since the early 1960s, when Shackley was CIA station chief in Miami and Clines was an up-and-coming case officer organizing missions into Cuba by anti-Castro exiles.

The last of North's "strange recruits" to establish a connection with Secord was Iranian businessman and arms dealer Albert Hakim, who was an active presence in Iran during the period from 1975 to 1978 when Secord was heading up the U.S. Air Force's military assistance mission to the court of the shah. While the other men in the group brought important intelligence and military experience to the Iran/contra effort, it was Hakim's financial wizardry that helped pull the whole operation together.

An outsider like Peter Maas was stunned at the notion of using Secord and his colleagues for such a sensitive mission, but from the amoral, "can-do" perspective of inside players like Oliver North and CIA director William Casey, it made perfect sense to turn to these veterans of past secret wars and arms trafficking ventures to run the Iran/contra operation. But even a brief investigation of their histories should have indicated that Maas's healthy skepticism was more than justified.[5]

Well before Secord, Shackley, Clines, and Hakim teamed up to serve as the backbone of Oliver North's secret arms pipeline, they were associated with an even more dangerous operative who went even further beyond the bounds of legality—rogue CIA agent Ed Wilson. Wilson's specialty was getting weapons from one place to another. It was a trade he plied for over a decade in the CIA before going on to run covert operations for the navy's top-secret Task Force 157, which was charged with monitoring the movement of Soviet military vessels, among other tasks. Ed Wilson was a master at setting up "proprietaries"—business fronts that were financed by the intelligence community to carry out secret missions. In his case, Wilson ran the companies more for what they could do for him than for what they could do for his country's military and intelligence agencies. Despite an official government salary that never topped $25,000, Wilson had managed to purchase a mansion at Mount Airy in Virginia horse country, where he entertained an impressive roster of senators, congressmen, generals, and intelligence operatives. The funds for this ostentatious life-style had clearly come from Wilson's knack for turning proprietary enterprises into opportunities for personal profit. But by the mid-1970s, the commander of Task Force 157, Donald Nielsen, tumbled onto Wilson's game and had him run out of the navy.

At this point Wilson went totally beyond the pale, using contacts with former CIA personnel and his obvious skills at moving arms and money to set up a multimillion-dollar training and weapons operation for Libya's Muammar Qaddafi. Wilson supplied Qaddafi's regime with tens of thousands of pounds of C-4 plastique explosive, the state-of-the-art in terrorist bomb-making material, which could evade detection by most airport security devices. He also supplied guns, helicopters, and a team of former Green Berets and explosives experts to teach Libyan personnel how to use their new arsenal to the fullest. As Peter Maas pointed out, Wilson's motive in all of this was "abundantly clear": greed. He netted upwards of $10 million on the Libyan supply operation. But Wilson may have been too greedy this time: a leak by one of his operatives and a persistent campaign by a determined young U.S. attorney named Larry Barcella led to Wilson's conviction on charges of smuggling explosives to Libya, conspiracy to commit murder, and a rash of other charges.

One of the people who testified at Ed Wilson's trial was none other than Maj. Gen. Richard Secord, who was serving as a deputy assistant secretary of defense for the Near East and South Asia. Secord maintains that he was subpoenaed by both the prosecution and the defense in the Wilson case, and his testimony was confined to recounting a number of professional and social encounters with Wilson over a ten-year period. But the question remained—what was a central figure in U.S. government arms transfer policy doing as an associate of one of the most infamous arms smugglers in United States history? Ed Wilson—hardly an unimpeachable source—has provided one answer.

Wilson asserts that in addition to their social interactions, Secord, Clines, and Shackley had a business relationship with him as well. The men were also allegedly joined in the scheme by Eric Von Marbod, another Pentagon arms sales specialist. (Ironically, Von Marbod was one of the people whom Gerald Ford's secretary of defense James Schlesinger had sent to Iran in the mid-1970s to help "clean up" the corruption in the arms sales process there.) According to Wilson, the deal involved the formation of a corporation known as Egyptian-American Transport Services, Inc. (EATSCO), which was set up at Wilson's behest to ship billions in U.S. arms and support equipment to Egypt under the military assistance program Cairo had concluded with the Carter administration under the Camp David accords. Wilson claims that EATSCO was actually a secret partnership involving equal shares for Clines (the only other publicly acknowledged partner), Wilson, Shackley, Secord, and Von Marbod. Clines and Shackley had left the CIA by this point, but Secord and Von Marbod were still at the Pentagon, a flagrant conflict of interest if the charges of their role in EATSCO are true. Von Marbod, in particular, had authority to approve the EATSCO contract, and he made the unusual move of approving a large up-front payment of $71 million in advance of any actual services rendered.

Clines ultimately took the fall on EATSCO, paying a small fine under a plea bargain that brought an end to the federal investigation of the affair. Although the charges regarding his involvement in the scheme were never proven, Secord left the Pentagon under a cloud of suspicion cast by the EATSCO scandal. Von Marbod left shortly thereafter to take a job as Carlucci's executive assistant at Sears World Trade, a subsidiary of Sears, Roebuck involved in international consulting and technology brokering. In the early 1990s he turned up as a European marketing representative for the LTV Corporation.[6]

What happened next is an object lesson in the pervasiveness of the permanent arms supply network and its capacity to take care of its own while government regulators and law enforcement agencies turn a blind eye. Far from being shunned by the government in the wake of their involvement with Wilson, these men were actively sought out, as private contractors, to carry out even more secretive, more critical missions than they had been entrusted with during their tenure in government. Secord was at the center of it all, leaving the Pentagon in 1983 to go into partnership with his longtime acquaintance Albert Hakim in a firm known as the Stanford Technology Group, a company involved in exports of security systems and weaponry to governments around the world. While Secord was head of the U.S. military assistance mission in Teheran, Hakim made a multimillion-dollar sale of surveillance technology to the shah's secret police, the SAVAK, and Secord was apparently impressed enough with Hakim's ability to make the right contacts that he decided to go into business with him.[7]

Stanford Technology wasn't the only business where Secord hung his hat. He also had affiliations with American National Management Corporation, Eagle Aviation Services and Technology, and Airmach, companies set up by retired colonel Richard Gadd, another central figure in Iran/contra. According to a *Wall Street Journal* investigative report, these firms "played a role in clandestine operations far beyond shipping arms to anti-Sandinista guerrillas in Nicaragua." The companies helped the U.S. government acquire a helicopter that was used to gather intelligence prior to the 1983 invasion of Grenada, and they provided logistical support for the military's elite Delta Force commandos, best known for their failed 1979 hostage rescue mission in the Iranian desert. Secord had worked with Delta Force in planning a second hostage rescue attempt that was ultimately put on the shelf, and his contacts there no doubt helped cement this secret contract.[8]

Both Clines and Shackley were plugged into the Stanford Technology network as well. Clines was an officer of several of the companies, and Shackley was a consultant. So when Oliver North went looking for an extragovernmental network to carry out his covert plans, first to arm the contras and then to swap arms with Iran for a pledge to help release the hostages, the Secord/Hakim/Clines/Shackley operations offered a convenient, ready-made tool for evading the law. Oliver North asserts that former CIA director William Casey personally urged him to go to Secord to set up the Iran/contra enterprise. According to North, Casey had recommended Secord as "a person with a background in covert operations," someone "who got things done, and had been poorly treated."[9]

But despite Casey's glowing recommendation, Secord's and North's interests didn't coincide in all respects. Contra leader Adolfo Calero accused Secord of marking up the weapons he sold to the contras by as much as 60 percent. Secord acknowledged that "I was in the arms trade to make money" but claims his profits were "only" about 30 percent on sales to the contras.[10] With all the front companies, questionable characters, and easy money floating around, it was hard to tell how much of North's "enterprise" was motivated by misguided patriotism and how much was sheer profiteering by a band of veteran arms sales operatives who felt that the U.S. government owed them one.

Even more disturbing is that after all the Iran/contra revelations—including the congressional investigation and the mild slaps on the wrist that North and his associates received as a result of the investigation by special prosecutor Lawrence Walsh—this covert network, or one very much like it, is still operating, still selling arms, and still shaping U.S. foreign policy with little or no input from Congress or the public.

Anatomy of the Secret Arms Supply Network: Facilitators and Front Companies

The conventional wisdom on Iran/contra and other arms scandals is that they underscore the ease with which so profitable an activity as trafficking in weapons can evade the efforts of government to control it, no matter how well intentioned these efforts may be. This traditional view assumes that government authorities are trying to control the secret arms trade in the first place. In fact, a symbiotic relationship exists between the publicly acknowledged, legal arms trade carried on by government bureaucrats and executives of major corporations and the black-market trade in arms that is dominated by so-called private arms dealers. As the case of Iran/contra forcefully demonstrates, the private practitioners engaged in the secret arms trade almost invariably got their start in the business in government military or intelligence agencies. And more often than not the secret arms trade is either quietly fostered by governments seeking "deniability" for their actions or acquiesced in by government functionaries who may need to turn to a Richard Secord or an Adnan Khashoggi for a favor at some point down the road. In a discussion of the secretive, circuitous shipments that helped keep the Iran–Iraq war supplied for eight years, Hamilton Spence, managing director of British operations for Interarms, the world's largest dealer in guns and ammunition, underscored the importance of government complicity to the smooth functioning of the "private" arms markets:

> The only way it can be done on such a large scale is by going through cracks in the system of controls, which have been deliberately created by governments. A shipment of 150,000 rounds of 155mm ammunition requires a large ship and vehicles to transport it to the port. That is not something that can be done without a government noticing.[11]

The private wing of the permanent arms supply network exists on the scale that it does because governments have allowed it—indeed encouraged it—to do so.

The term *arms dealer* does not adequately capture the multiple functions performed by the denizens of the underground arms bazaar. There are at minimum four types of operatives at work: arms sales *facilitators* like Richard Secord and his colleagues in the Iran/contra supply network, a group consisting primarily of former CIA and military men in the United States and other supplying countries that serve as points of contact between weapons producers and their ultimate clients; foreign *middlemen* like Adnan Khashoggi, Manucher Ghorbanifar, and Sarkis Soghanalian, who use their contacts within weapons purchasing nations to grease the wheels for specific arms deals, enriching themselves in the process; genuine arms *dealers* like small-arms specialist Sam Cummings, who maintain stockpiles of arms at the ready for any and every occasion of conflict that demands them; and, finally, entrepreneurial arms *producers* like the late Canadian weapons expert Gerald Bull and Chilean industrialist Carlos Cardoen, who have proven willing to sell weapons know-how to literally any customer who can come up with the cash to close a deal.

The role of arms sales facilitators has been described above, in the discussion of the North/Secord network. Their essential function is to do privately what the U.S. government often prefers not to do publicly, from negotiating with foreign buyers, to arranging financing, to delivering the weapons, to teaching clients how to use them.

While the main players in Iran/contra were being pushed temporarily to the sidelines by the legal and public relations repercussions of the scandal, at least one similar quasi-covert network was operating on another front: in George Bush's highly touted "war on drugs." As noted in chapter 7, shipments of weapons and supplies to U.S. Drug Enforcement Agency personnel and local police and military forces in Peru, Colombia, and Bolivia were handed off to Corporate Jets, Inc., a firm that was staffed in part by former employees of the CIA-run air charter company Air America. Working out of a base in Opa-Locka, Florida, under the cover name National Air Transport, by mid-1990 Corporate Jets had upwards of 150 employees involved in flying and maintaining a fleet of helicopters, crop-spraying planes, and transport aircraft used to keep U.S. antidrug bases in Latin America supplied.

As in Iran/contra, the contracting out of U.S. antidrug policy to private operatives fostered an atmosphere that encouraged violations of basic legal and ethical standards. For example, the chief of aircraft operations at National Air Transport had to leave his post in early 1990 after he was indicted for smuggling drugs from Mexico to the United States prior to his employment by the State Department. A few months later, one of the company's pilots was indicted for stealing $150,000 worth of helicopter parts that had been paid for by U.S. taxpayers; another pilot was under investigation for using government funds to refurbish his private plane. In mid-1991, the parallels between Bush's drug war and Iran/contra grew even tighter when the State Department replaced Corporate Jets and gave a five-year, $100 million contract to another Florida-based firm named Dynacorp. One of Dynacorp's subcontractors was Eagle Aviation Services and Technology, the outfit run by retired colonel Richard Gadd that had figured prominently in Richard Secord's contra air supply operation in the mid-1980s.[12]

The hiring of Air America alumni to staff Bush's Latin drug wars was a logical outgrowth of the shift in the CIA's relationship to its front companies that was brought to fruition during the 1980s by Reagan administration CIA director William Casey. After harsh public and congressional criticism of the operations of Air America and other CIA proprietaries in the mid-1970s, the military and intelligence communities began to adopt a new model of operations. Rather than having the CIA own its own companies, it moved more and more toward contracting with firms that would do its bidding as needed. This was the pattern followed with Southern Air Transport—the CIA sold it off in the late 1970s, but it reemerged as a contract player in the Iran/contra scandals, ferrying hundreds of tons of U.S. weaponry to El Salvador's Ilopango air base, the way station for arms going on to the contras via North and Secord's private air-drop operation. And it was Southern Air that was contracted to ship U.S. arms to Israel for transshipment to Iran in the attempted arms-for-hostages swap that raised Iran/contra to the level of a full-blown public scandal. As noted above, one of the firms that worked with Southern Air throughout all of this was American National Management Corp., one of Richard Secord's corporate connections.[13]

In using Corporate Jets as a central tool in its Latin drug wars, the Bush administration was helping to keep alive the tradition of contracting out U.S. government arms and military training missions to private firms that by their very nature are even less accountable to Congress and the public than the government agencies they are "standing in" for. Indeed, State Department officials openly acknowledge that they hired the company to get around congressional prohibitions on involving U.S. military pilots directly in antidrug patrols or other paramilitary missions in the region. This privatization of U.S. foreign policy escalated so dramatically during William Casey's tenure at the CIA that some observers estimate that by the mid-1980s CIA contract firms were employing more people than agency "subsidiaries" like Air America had in the late 1960s and mid-1970s. If true, this would imply that the CIA may have more personnel at its disposal in "off-the-books" private firms like Southern Air Transport than it employs directly. The expansion of this practice into other agencies—from the Secord/Hakim companies that North used from the National Security Council to firms like Corporate Jets that have worked under State Department auspices—has magnified the confusion between government policy and private profiteering that ultimately ran North's Iran/contra operation aground. At a time of proposed cutbacks in intelligence agency funding, Congress and the Clinton administration should make sure that this contracting out of covert functions is also reined in.[14]

Until there is a full public accounting of the operations of these hybrid, half-public, half-private arms supply enterprises, the odds of preventing future Iran/contra scandals will be virtually nil. But these front companies are only one layer in the elaborate private arms supply network that the U.S. government has helped to nourish over the past forty years.

The Middlemen: Khashoggi, Ghorbanifar, and Soghanalian

The least trustworthy link in the secret arms trade—and the one most heavily relied upon by governments seeking to conduct deals that would be too embarrassing to carry out in the public spotlight—is the roster of seemingly independent middlemen and traders who organize, finance, and broker arms deals. A highly competitive breed, each vying with the next for recognition as the preeminent figure in their field, these free-lance arms merchants include men like the wealthy Saudi middleman Adnan Khashoggi; his rival Sarkis Soghanalian, a key arms broker for Iraq's Saddam Hussein; and Iranian go-between Manucher Ghorbanifar, a man so duplicitous that even the CIA refused to do business with him.

While government regulators frequently throw up their hands when discussing the activities of these private merchants as if nothing meaningful can be done to rein in their activities, a look at their backgrounds in the business quickly demonstrates that all of the major arms middlemen have benefited at strategic moments in their careers from government contracts, support, or, at the very least, tacit acceptance of their activities. In order to have these private dealers available to them when a secret sale is in the works, governments have been willing to look the other way when they engage in illegal activities that have served to fuel conflict and foment arms races across the globe.

If not the world's leading private arms merchant, Saudi financier and middleman Adnan Khashoggi is surely the flashiest. Until his recent financial troubles, Khashoggi was known for jaunting across the globe in a customized corporate jet and throwing parties for the rich and famous in homes on three continents. His father, Dr. Mohammed Khashoggi, was the personal physician of King Abdul Aziz, the founder of modern Saudi Arabia. Khashoggi's once-fabulous fortune, now depleted by a spectacular series of bad business deals, was literally founded on the massive U.S.–Saudi arms trade that perked up in the 1960s and reached multibillion-dollar levels in the 1970s.[15] Khashoggi urged Saudi king Fahd to commission a U.S. study of Saudi defense needs in 1964, and he made sure to get in the middle of most of the U.S.–Saudi arms deals that flowed from that arrangement. Amidst the frantic pace of arms buying sparked by the Nixon Doctrine and the oil price increases of the early 1970s, Khashoggi was raking in hundreds of millions of dollars in commissions from U.S. firms such as Lockheed, Northrop, and Raytheon. When a Senate committee revealed in 1975 that Khashoggi had been the bagman for $450,000 in bribes paid by Northrop to two Saudi generals, he laid low for a few years, focusing on his other, nonmilitary business interests.[16]

But when the Iranian arms initiative began in 1984–85, Khashoggi was back on the scene. The Saudi financier played middleman in a complex three-way game among the United States, Israel, and Iran, providing $15 million in bridge financing for the transfer of U.S. weaponry to the so-called Iranian moderates. By some accounts, the Iranian initiative was the brainchild of Khashoggi and Iranian middleman Manucher Ghorbanifar, a scheme that Oliver North could not resist.[17] Khashoggi's on-again, off-again relationship with the U.S. government and U.S. defense contractors over the span of more than twenty-five years epitomizes the role of the arms merchant in the overall weapons trade, greasing the wheels when times are good and helping make connections for secretive and unpopular sales that governments might not have the nerve to make in the cold light of day. Far from a shadowy arms dealer operating beyond the control of U.S. or other government regulators, Khashoggi has served as a sort of junior partner in major U.S. arms initiatives in the Middle East, from the decades-long Saudi military buildup to the Reagan administration's Iranian arms sales initiative.

Despite the whiff of corruption attending Khashoggi's business dealings, he has the image of a downright solid citizen compared with his cohort in the Iran/contra dealings, Manucher Ghorbanifar. Though Ghorbanifar is described variously as a "shipping executive" and a "commodities trader," his associates have confirmed that the commodity he has been most interested in trading is advanced weaponry. Prior to the 1978 Islamic revolution in Iran, Ghorbanifar reportedly had ties to the shah of Iran's secret police, the SAVAK. After the Ayatollah Khomeini took power, Ghorbanifar managed to ingratiate himself with members of the new power structure in Iran as well, allegedly by tipping off Iranian officials about a planned coup against Khomeini by Iranian air force officers loyal to the shah. Ghorbanifar was intent on parlaying his new connections into a bonanza of arms sales commissions, and he was the prime source for Oliver North's apparent belief that selling arms to Iran would strengthen "moderates" within the Islamic regime's ruling circles. It was this false assumption that opened the way for the whole Iran/contra fiasco, all based on the word of a man whose associates told *Time* magazine that he "could not tell the truth about the clothes he is wearing."[18] Even Ted Shackley, the first of the Secord network to make contact with Ghorbanifar, described him as "a wheeler dealer and [one who] could play both ends against the middle for a profit in a business deal."[19] The CIA had given up on Ghorbanifar well before he turned up in the middle of Iran/contra. After repeated instances in which the Iranian supplied them with false information, the agency went so far as to send out an official notice to other government agencies warning them to stay away from Ghorbanifar. But that didn't stop the North network from utilizing him and Khashoggi as trusted advisers and strategists.

Last but certainly not least, no survey of the current world of arms middlemen can ignore the presence of Sarkis Soghanalian, the three-hundred-pound, Turkish-born Lebanese arms dealer who made a fortune in the 1980s brokering deals for Saddam Hussein. Soghanalian, a jealous rival of Khashoggi who feels that his more glamorous Saudi counterpart gets far too much attention, has made a cottage industry out of regaling the media with tales of his prowess. For most of the 1980s Soghanalian ran his business from his own private hangar in the Miami airport.[20] Despite a 1987 indictment for trying to sell Hughes military helicopters to Iraq, Soghanalian continued to go merrily about his business with no major interference from U.S. authorities until he was finally convicted on those charges after the end of the Gulf War, in the fall of 1991.[21]

Soghanalian makes no apologies for his activities on behalf of Saddam Hussein in the United States. In fact, with respect to his most controversial sales to Iraq, he maintains that State Department and NSC officials were "in on the deal" and fully aware of what he was doing. Soghanalian claims that this was all part of the U.S. tilt toward Iraq during the Iran–Iraq war, in which first Reagan administration and then Bush administration officials encouraged sales of military technology to Hussein's regime in hopes of fostering a stalemate that would hold the Khomeini regime in check.[22] (The consequences of this policy and the details of Soghanalian's role in it will be explored in more depth in chapter 11.)

Although Khashoggi, Ghorbanifar, and Soghanalian have each recently had their own brushes with the law, the surprising thing is not that U.S. authorities finally acted to limit their more egregious activities but how freely they've been allowed to operate over the years.

The Dealer: Sam Cummings

The reigning veteran and self-proclaimed champion of private arms dealing is Sam Cummings, a Philadelphia-born British subject who runs Interarms, a firm that has quietly dominated the small-arms trade for over three decades. Cummings sells over $80 million worth of pistols, rifles, submachine guns, hand grenades, and other weaponry every year to customers ranging from Guatemala to the People's Republic of China. Unlike such middlemen as Khashoggi and Soghanalian, who acquire arms more or less on a deal-by-deal basis, Cummings has amassed what may be the world's largest stockpile of small arms, ready to ship out at a moment's notice. It is this massive investment in his weapons inventory that separates Cummings from most other arms traders.[23]

Cummings got his start in the business rounding up arms for the CIA-sponsored coup that toppled the democratically elected Arbenz government in Guatemala in 1954. He left the agency soon thereafter to become a private dealer, drawing on his intelligence contacts to build a worldwide client list that was the envy of his rivals. Among his other convenient connections, Cummings was also the brother-in-law of the late Senate Armed Services Committee chairman John Tower.[24]

One of Cummings's great professional disappointments was that the U.S. government turned to "bunglers" like Khashoggi and Ghorbanifar to organize the arms-for-hostages swap with Iran.

> It's almost a classic lesson in how not to do something. . . . Who needs Adnan Khashoggi? Who needs the Israelis? . . . If the U.S. government wanted TOW missiles moved to Iran, I would have said, move the TOWs to Interarms warehouse in London. I would notify the correct Iranian people—and these are people I know a lot better than Khashoggi does—and I would have invited them to take a look at them and inspect them.
>
> At that point, I would have said, "Send me the hostages, and once the plane lands, you can load it up with TOWs and off you go." . . . And I wouldn't have charged any multi-million dollar commissions because that would have been a service.[25]

But despite his chivalrous offer, the bulk of Cummings's trade, which he conducts out of warehouse/office complexes in London, England, and Alexandria, Virginia, involves a substantial markup. Cummings considers the Far East his most lucrative market, with sales to the Philippines, Indonesia, Malaysia, Singapore, and Thailand keeping his order books filled to capacity. While he laments the drop in the total volume of his business from his heyday of the 1950s and 1960s, he explains, with a bit of cynical personal philosophy, his continuing commitment to selling weapons: "The military market is based on human folly, not normal market precepts. Human folly goes up and down. But it always exists, and its depths have never been plumbed."[26]

The Producers: Guerin, Cardoen, and Bull

The most dangerous layer of the private arms supply network consists of the men who sell not just finished weapons systems but the know-how needed to produce armaments. Like their counterparts in other facets of the trade, these men have been helped at critical points along the way by government contracts and connections with U.S. intelligence agencies. For various reasons, they have chosen to become manufacturing mercenaries, selling their technical skills to the highest bidder. During the 1980s, the highest bidders were inevitably the most desperate and repressive regimes on earth, from Saddam Hussein's Iraq to Gen. Augusto Pinochet's regime in Chile to the apartheid regime in South Africa. Taken together, the stories of James Guerin, Carlos Cardoen, and Gerald Bull offer the ultimate cautionary tale about how U.S. government efforts to nurture the secret arms supply network can backfire when runaway arms producers take what they have learned at U.S. government expense and put it up for sale on the world market.

The least likely candidate for the role of renegade arms producer is James Guerin, a devout Christian and noted local philanthropist who built his backyard business outside of Lancaster, Pennsylvania, into a multimillion-dollar defense electronics firm known as International Signal and Control (ISC). Until 1988, when he sold his firm to British electronics giant Ferranti International, Guerin was barely known outside his adopted hometown, where he was considered a model citizen who donated millions to local charities, taught a Bible study class, and sang in his church choir. But there was another side to Guerin. Not only was he a "major league arms dealer," as one Customs Service official put it, he was also a world-class fraud.

Shortly after they purchased ISC, Ferranti executives learned that they had paid nearly $700 million for a paper empire. The books had been inflated with fake orders—for example, an alleged missile deal with Pakistan that had been "corroborated" by the word of a Pakistani general who was bribed by Guerin to give the impression that a sale was in the works. In all, Ferranti charged that Guerin had stolen nearly $200 million by loading ISC's books with bogus orders and then selling his company to the British conglomerate. It was an awesome scam, one that the *Wall Street Journal* likened to "the schemes of fugitive financier Robert Vesco."[27]

As often happens in the cutthroat world of arms dealing, it was this dispute over money between ISC and Ferranti that finally exposed the illegal nature of Guerin's business to full public view. A federal investigation of ISC's fraudulent practices revealed that not only had Guerin engaged in a pattern of financial fraud and money laundering but that he had routinely violated the international arms embargo against South Africa and smuggled hundreds of thousands of critical electronic components to Iraqi military factories. Guerin's move into the illicit arms trade dated back to the early 1970s, when his fledgling company began doing business with South Africa's state-owned arms company, ARMSCOR, and South Africa's largest multinational corporation, Barlow Rand. The U.S. government encouraged Guerin's South African connection, as part of a top-secret 1975 National Security Agency plan that called for ISC to sell South Africa the technology for intelligence "listening posts" that could be used to monitor Soviet naval activities in and around the Cape of Good Hope, at the southernmost tip of the African continent. The deal was moving along—ISC had gotten as far as setting up a front company, Gamma Associates, to handle the technology sales to South Africa—when Jimmy Carter took office in 1977 and canceled the arrangement as part of his tougher stance against the apartheid regime.[28]

But Gamma lived on, as did Guerin's ties to U.S. intelligence agencies. A joint investigation by ABC News "Nightline," the *Financial Times* of London, and the Lancaster *Intelligencer-Journal* uncovered shipping documents and other hard evidence of a steady military technology trade between ISC and South Africa during the 1980s that averaged nearly a shipment a week for five years, from 1984 through 1989. This time the technology was not just for listening posts. According to weapons proliferation expert Gary Milhollin, ISC's illicit shipments encompassed "exactly what a country would need to develop, test, and perfect long-range nuclear capable ballistic missiles"—telemetry tracking equipment, sophisticated gyroscopes, and photo-imaging equipment that can be used to analyze missile prototypes and design missile guidance systems.[29] Most of the shipments were handled by R. Clyde Ivy, a missile engineer who spent three years in South Africa in the late 1970s, on loan from ISC as a consultant for the apartheid regime's missile programs. According to court papers filed in the Ferranti/ISC case, Ivy was known within ISC as "the grandfather of South Africa's missile industry," and he used his

South African contacts to the hilt in promoting the bustling missile components trade between ISC and the Pretoria regime during the 1980s. Government sources familiar with the deal told members of the ABC News "Nightline" investigative team that the CIA was aware of ISC's illegal transfers throughout this entire period, but the agency looked the other way.[30]

As if this government-sanctioned transfer of sophisticated missile technology to one of the most abhorrent regimes on earth were not enough of a scandal in its own right, U.S. Customs officials involved in the ISC investigation determined that South Africa passed on some of this technology to Iraq, where it found its way into Iraqi howitzers, antiaircraft guns, and even Iraq's own cluster bomb factory. Confronted with this evidence of arms trafficking and intelligence activities run amok, House Foreign Affairs Committee member Howard Berman summed up its implications:

> If these reports are true, and I take it there's a great deal of evidence to suggest that they are, then we have a renegade operation on our hands for whom the rule of law means nothing . . . [over] which the elected representatives apparently have no control, have no ability to direct policy, have no ability to say what they can and cannot do.[31]

Guerin's penchant for illegality finally caught up with him in November 1991, when he was indicted by a federal grand jury in Philadelphia on multiple counts of money laundering, fraud, and violations of arms export control laws. A month later he pleaded guilty, and in June 1992 he was sentenced to fifteen years in federal prison. But by the time federal authorities took action, the damage had already been done. Not only had Guerin and his associates spent most of the 1980s helping South Africa with its ballistic missile program, they had used South Africa as a conduit for shipping sensitive military technology to Iraq.[32]

There is no question that Guerin was able to defy the law for as long as he did because of his carefully cultivated contacts with key players in U.S. intelligence and military circles. He was always telling business associates that this or that aspect of his secretive operation was being done at the behest of "Washington" or "the CIA." Former Reagan administration secretary of state Alexander Haig served as a consultant to ISC, earning nearly $600,000 in fees for tasks such as "helping sell cluster bombs to Pakistan and weapons fuses to China." But Haig has strenuously denied any involvement in Guerin's fraudulent or illegal arms deals.[33]

Another heavy hitter who helped Guerin at a key moment was Adm.

Bobby Ray Inman, the former second-in-command at the CIA who later went on to become President Clinton's short-lived selection to replace Les Aspin as Secretary of Defense. Inman sent a letter to the sentencing judge in Guerin's fraud and arms trafficking case urging leniency on the grounds that Guerin had "displayed patriotism towards our country" during his work with U.S. intelligence agencies in the 1970s. While not condoning Guerin's later role in sending missile technology to South Africa and Iraq, Inman seemed to be implying that these crimes should be mitigated because Guerin served as a covert intelligence contact during the NSA (National Security Agency) and CIA's secret campaign of cooperation with South Africa in the mid-1970s.[34] With friends like these—and the U.S. government's historically cozy relationship with arms traders of all stripes—James Guerin could easily have lived out his days in Lancaster as a pillar of the community and a prosperous weapons dealer. If he had kept better books, and if he hadn't been quite so quick to cheat a major allied defense contractor, the U.S. government's arms trade watchdogs might have steered clear of investigating his illicit dealings with South Africa and Iraq.

Another arms producer who has only recently had a scrape with the law after years of supplying U.S. military technology to outlaw regimes is Chilean arms manufacturer Carlos Cardoen. A U.S.-trained engineer who earned his degree at the University of Utah before returning to Chile in the late 1970s to set up his own arms company, Cardoen earned hundreds of millions of dollars during the 1980s selling U.S.-designed cluster bombs to nations like Iraq and Ethiopia. As was the case with Guerin, there is evidence that the CIA was aware of Cardoen's Iraqi connection all along, but federal authorities moved when it was much too late to make a difference: in April 1992 the Customs Department and the U.S. Attorney's Office in Miami seized Cardoen's Florida assets and charged his firm with money laundering and illegal shipment of weapons-grade zirconium from the United States to cluster bomb facilities in Chile and Iraq. This civil action was followed up a year later by a criminal indictment by the Clinton Justice Department that charged Cardoen and two employees of the Teledyne Wah Chang corporation with violations of U.S. export laws for unauthorized zirconium shipments to Chile and Iraq. As of this writing, Cardoen is still at large.

The last straw in Cardoen's case may have been that federal investigators uncovered evidence that he was continuing to ship cluster bomb technology to Iraq even after Iraq's August 1990 invasion of Kuwait, during the UN military embargo against Saddam Hussein's regime. Cardoen has accused the U.S. government of mistreating an old friend, charging that he had started his transfers during the period "when Iraq was considered a friend of the West who was fighting the Ayatollah." In addition, he has put forward an amoral justification that is not that far from the philosophy that motivated the Reagan/Bush arms sales policy: "Moral responsibility lies in the person who uses the weapons, not in the one who manufactures them."[35] (Evidence of U.S. government acquiescence in Cardoen's illicit arms supplies to Iraq during the 1980s and early 1990s will be discussed in chapter 11.)

Probably the most infamous "spinoff" of the U.S. policy of nurturing independent arms producers was Gerald V. Bull, the Canadian rocket scientist and artillery expert whose life was cut short by an assassin's bullet in March 1990. Although he began his career in Canada in the mid-1950s in pursuit of a new kind of gun that could launch projectiles into space, by the late 1960s the Canadian government had lost interest in Bull's pet project and he turned to the U.S. government to sustain his work.

Aided by millions of dollars in U.S. Army artillery contracts and a special bill that Sen. Barry Goldwater shepherded through Congress granting him U.S. citizenship, Bull established his own armaments company, the Space Research Corporation. The firm was situated on a unique ten-thousand-acre complex that straddled the U.S.–Canadian border outside of Burlington, Vermont. It was an ideal setup for evading customs inspectors.

By the time he started Space Research, Bull had lowered his sights a bit, following his funding base away from his "space gun" project toward more mundane products such as extended-range 155mm howitzers and artillery shells. Bull's howitzers earned Space Research most of its income throughout the 1970s. One of his biggest clients for the guns was the South African government.[36]

According to former CIA station chief for Angola John Stockwell, during the late 1970s Bull provided South Africa with tens of thousands of artillery shells and the technology to build his long-range GC-45 howitzer with the encouragement of the CIA. The CIA was backing South Africa and Jonas Savimbi's UNITA movement in the Angolan civil war, against the governing MPLA and the Cuban troops that had come to help the MPLA fight off the South Africans. Cuban artillery had been outdistancing the guns used by the South African forces, so CIA case officer John Clancy III put South African military officials in touch with Bull to help them correct their deficiency in this area. There were other telltale signs that Bull must have been getting help from the U.S. government, such as his ability to get the shell casings for South Africa built to his specifications in a U.S. Army arsenal in Scranton, Pennsylvania. Bull got approval for this unorthodox arrangement in just four days, prompting Stockwell to suggest that someone inside the U.S. government must have "concentrated on it and pushed it through."[37]

There was one small problem with all of this: it was a clear violation of U.S. law and the related UN arms embargo against South Africa. But when U.S. Customs agent Larry Curtis tried to make an arms smuggling case against Bull and Space Research, he was distressed to learn that the Justice Department had quietly offered Bull a plea bargain that resulted in a paltry four-and-a-half-month jail term. Bull served his time within the comfortable confines of Allenwood Prison, a minimum-security jail for white-collar offenders that bears the nickname "Club Fed." Curtis suspects that a deal was cut to hide the CIA's role in Bull's South African arms sales:

> I was told that the reason we never went any further was because there had been a phone call from the White House. I took that to mean there had been a phone call from the White House to Justice stating, "Don't go any further with this investigation."[38]

After Bull served his few months of penance at Allenwood in 1980 he set off for Belgium, where he established a new home base for Space Research and began hiring himself out as a weapons designer and scientific mercenary to clients ranging from the People's Republic of China to Saddam Hussein's regime in Iraq. This was all done with the blessing of the U.S. government, although Bull remained a U.S. citizen and the howitzer technology that he was selling had been developed under U.S. military contracts. The State Department's Office of Munitions Control actually gave Bull official clearance to market his weapons manufacturing skills around the globe. And in 1984, when Larry Curtis developed substantial evidence of arms export control violations by Bull in shipping U.S.-origin howitzer technology to China, the Justice Department and other federal law enforcement agents refused to pursue the case. Federal prosecutors told Bull's lawyer that they were just "going through the motions" and that his client had nothing to worry about. A year later, the reason for the government's indifferent attitude became clearer: as had happened with his 1970s shipments of howitzer technology to South Africa, Bull's illegal military transfers to China coincided with a larger, unstated policy goal of U.S. military and intelligence bureaucracies. At a summer 1985 Pentagon meeting on munitions sales to China, a decision was made to "actively" work to build up China's military and to "overlook . . . prior indiscretions by private companies." No one in the

U.S. government was going to call Bull to account for his illegal technology shipments to China now that they fit so perfectly with the U.S. government's own policy on the matter.[39]

Even in the extreme case of Bull's assistance to Saddam Hussein's military buildup, the U.S. government was well aware of Bull's activities and allowed them to continue until the eve of the Gulf War (see chapter 11).

So, first by setting Bull up in business, then by helping him find his most lucrative customer, then by offering him a cushy plea bargain when his illegal activities became public, and finally by looking the other way while he spent the 1980s hawking his U.S.-designed howitzer to Third World dictators, the U.S. government played a critical role in sustaining one of the greatest weapons proliferators of the twentieth century.

In the interests of maintaining a ready "stable" of dealers it can turn to when it wants to quietly arm a repressive regime, sponsor a coup, bolster an unpopular tyrant, or trade arms for hostages, the U.S. government has evolved an ongoing working relationship with dealers and middlemen like Cummings, Khashoggi, and Soghanalian. At this level, the U.S. role in the arms trade amounts to a sort of bargain with the devil in which the U.S. government is compromised by its long-standing relationships with these unsavory characters to the point where it is often forced to avert its glance when these same individuals engage in illicit activities like drug running or arming terrorist states. The executive branch's ongoing policy of sustaining this shadowy arms network has succeeded in keeping information about who receives U.S. military technology well beyond the reach of Congress and the public, other than on those rare occasions when enough of the details leak out to raise the visibility of these activities to the level of a full-blown scandal.

But beyond their lack of accountability, these secretive dealings are an outright threat to world peace. By one rough estimate, the worldwide growth of smuggling and off-the-books deals pushed the value of the secret arms trade to as much as $9 billion per year by the mid-1980s. And for every sale that is justified on "national security grounds"—no matter how ultimately flimsy or ill conceived—probably two or three more are concluded simply because there's money to be made. By fostering and protecting the private arms dealers in exchange for their occasional services to U.S. covert arms supply operations, the U.S. government and the governments of the other major powers have created a monster—a permanent arms supply network that has no other purpose than to sell advanced weaponry for a profit and no serious government enforcement mechanism standing in its way.

10

The Middle East: Bottomless Market, Endless War?

The nations of the Middle East and the Persian Gulf are by far the world's largest arms market, accounting for two-thirds of all arms purchases by Third World nations in the two decades since the Nixon Doctrine sparked a global weapons export boom in the early 1970s.[1] This lucrative trade has been spurred onward and upward by the Arab–Israeli conflict, which has erupted into war five times since 1948. Arms sales to the region received an added boost in the 1980s from the eight-year Iran–Iraq war, while the 1990s were ushered in with Iraq's invasion of Kuwait and the ensuing Gulf conflict. Beyond these political and military factors, the Middle East has been an arms merchant's dream because of the existence of ample oil revenues, which have allowed states such as Iran, Iraq, Saudi Arabia, Bahrain, and Kuwait and their allies to shop for the pick of the world's arsenals with little attention to cost.

British journalist Anthony Sampson has aptly described the seemingly endless arms race in the Middle East as "a croupier's table" where the major powers have "poured in arms on both sides in a succession of balances and counterbalances . . . each time raising the stakes and making arms control more difficult."[2] The military history of the Middle East provides a succinct indictment of the notion that arms sales can be carefully calibrated to maintain a balance of power that will prevent war. In the Middle East, weapons sold almost always become weapons used, and each war to date has been rapidly followed by a rush to supply even deadlier armaments to fuel the next round of conflict: The trends in U.S. weapons exports to the Middle East in the post–World War II period provide a telling synopsis of the evolution of arms sales in U.S. foreign policy, from an occasional tool to a lethal addiction. By the beginning of the 1990s, the United States had moved on from competing with the Soviets and Europeans in arming the Middle East to a position of such dominance that it was virtually competing with itself. And the web of political and strategic relationships that had grown up around arms sales to key regional allies like Saudi Arabia and Israel made it almost impossible for the executive branch or the Congress to exert meaningful control over U.S. sales to the region.

Fueling Mideast Wars

The Middle East arms race started out on a relatively small scale by the standards of the time. When Israel did battle with five Arab adversaries in the 1948 war, both sides used whatever weapons they could scrounge from the leftovers of World War II. Anthony Sampson has observed that Israel managed to scrape together "a motley arsenal of British weapons bought from the scrapheaps of Europe," along with a collection of secondhand rifles, fighter planes, and other aircraft. The Arab states went into battle with equally outdated equipment.[3]

Ironically, it was this first, relatively lightly armed Arab–Israeli war that sparked the only serious effort at controlling the flow of weaponry into the region, the 1951 Tripartite Declaration by Britain, France, and the United States. The three nations agreed to coordinate their sales to Egypt, Iraq, and Israel to maintain a "rough balance" in the region. The agreement was built upon the theory that as the major powers engaged in the Middle East, they could head off another conflict by controlling the flow of arms. But other suppliers were free to sell as they wished, and by 1953 France had broken ranks and begun to sell current-generation fighter planes to Israel (with a discrete subsidy from the United States). The breaking point for the agreement was reached in September 1955, when Egyptian leader Gamal Abdel Nasser, rebuffed in his requests for armaments from the United States and Britain, struck a deal with Czechoslovakia for Soviet fighter aircraft, bombers, tanks, antiaircraft guns, and bazookas. Czechoslovakia was widely viewed as a conduit for what was in fact the first major

Soviet arms sale outside its immediate sphere of influence, and it marked the beginning of a Soviet effort to swap arms for influence in the Middle East in the manner that had already been long practiced by its Cold War adversaries in the West. The tripartite agreement to limit transfers to the region could not withstand this new development—the flow of arms into the area jumped to over $200 million per year, five times what it had been in the early 1950s. Within a year there was another war in the region, as Britain and France intervened alongside Israel to overturn Egypt's nationalization of the Suez Canal.[4]

The 1956 war set a pattern that was to persist for the next thirty-five years, right up to the eve of the Gulf War: war, rearmament, and then another, even deadlier conflict. In addition to the tensions generated by the ongoing Arab–Israeli conflict, the Middle East was becoming a battleground of the Cold War as well, with all the dangers of escalation that it entailed. The Soviets rushed to rearm their new client, Egypt, with MiG-17 fighters, bombers, and even submarines. Israel turned to France for Mirage III fighters. An analyst at the time argued that Israel's role in testing French equipment in battle and passing on suggestions for improvements and modifications made it a virtual "branch office of the French Air Force." In an effort to maintain a favorable image with the Arab regimes of the region, U.S. transfers to Israel during this period were conducted through third parties, such as an early 1960s shipment of two hundred surplus U.S. tanks via West Germany. But when these back-door sales were exposed, the United States began to edge toward a more open posture, with direct U.S. weapons exports to Israel topping $50 million for the first time in 1965.[5]

Despite the presence of a UN peacekeeping force and a general agreement among the United States, France, and Britain to try to prevent another war, the accumulation of tensions—and armaments—led Nasser to make another military move in 1967, this time under fear of an Israeli preemptive strike. Nasser's blockade of the Straits of Tiran and his expulsion of the UN force was met by Israeli air strikes that destroyed a good portion of Egypt's air force while it was still sitting on the runways. Israel's lightning-quick victory in the Six-Day War established its military superiority over its Arab adversaries, encouraging the United States to come out into the open and play its Israeli card more forcefully. In the fall of 1968, the Johnson administration agreed to sell fifty F-4 fighter bombers to Israel, the first sale of these advanced aircraft to a non-NATO ally. Mideast analyst Joe Stork argues that the F-4 sale "defined a distinct era of U.S. policy" in the Middle East, by signaling "*military* as well as diplomatic support" for the notion that Israel should hold onto the occupied territories until the Arab nations were prepared to make peace with Israel.[6] U.S. policy had now abandoned any pretext of maintaining a balance of armaments between Israel and the Arab regimes of the region, moving instead toward open promotion of an Israeli military advantage.

The immediate result of the 1967 war was another ratcheting upward of the arms race in the area. Arms shipments reached over $600 million per year, more than triple the levels at the time of the Suez conflict. The Soviets moved into Egypt in force, providing surface-to-air missiles (SAMs), new tanks and aircraft, and thousands of advisers to reinforce Nasser's regime. U.S. sales to Israel topped $800 million for the period from 1968 to 1971, more than five times the level of arms that had been transferred in the twenty years since the founding of Israel. The Soviets also strengthened their arms and training ties to Syria and Iraq during this period, and the Arab–Israeli conflict took on the color of a U.S.–Soviet confrontation in the making. This dynamic was briefly and dramatically interrupted in 1972, two years after Nasser's death, when new Egyptian leader Anwar Sadat followed the advice of his Saudi allies and expelled all Soviet advisers from Egypt. Sadat's abrupt change in policy offered one of the most spectacular examples of why supplying arms does not necessarily lead to reliable influence over the recipient nation. But Sadat's hope that his grand gesture would win concessions from the United States in prying the occupied territories loose from Israel was soon disappointed, and he reverted to the more confrontational approach favored by his predecessor. In October 1973, Egypt and Syria launched a preemptive attack on Israel, inflicting the heaviest losses suffered by the Jewish state in any of the Arab–Israeli wars.

Once hostilities broke out, the Soviets overcame their embarrassment at having been summarily kicked out of Egypt and began arms deliveries to Egypt and Syria. Israeli air raids damaged Soviet merchant ships that were bringing weapons to Syria. By mid-October the Soviets had threatened to introduce their own forces into the conflict if the Israelis pushed on to attack Damascus or destroyed the besieged Egyptian Third Army. After some initial delays, the United States embarked on its own huge airlift to Israel; by October 24, 1973, in a clear warning to the Soviets that direct intervention in the conflict would run the risk of starting World War III, the United States put its worldwide nuclear forces on alert. As three arms control experts from the Carter administration noted in retrospect, "In 1973 routine decisions to sell arms in peacetime led gradually yet inexorably to a real risk of conflict between the United States and the Soviet Union."[7]

Far from raising doubts about the wisdom of continuing to rely on arms transfers as the principal tool of U.S. foreign policy in the Middle East, the 1973 war reinforced the resolve of President Nixon and his foreign policy czar Henry Kissinger to use weapons supplies to bolster Israel *and* to curry favor with Egypt, Saudi Arabia, and the other Arab regimes.

One pillar of the new U.S. strategy was to make Israel an exclusive arms client of the United States, with funds for the bulk of Israeli purchases coming straight out of the U.S. Treasury. This policy began even before the 1973 conflict, with an August 1971 agreement by the Nixon administration to allow Israel to use a "cash flow" method of paying for its U.S. weapons. This meant that rather than having to deposit the entire cost of a multibillion-dollar purchase in a Pentagon-controlled trust account up front, as other major U.S. arms clients generally did, Israel could pay piecemeal, on a year-by-year basis. The new arrangement was based on the tacit understanding that there would be a steady enough flow of U.S. military aid to cover payments as they came up. These favorable terms were soon exceeded in the wake of the October 1973 war, when the Nixon administration gave Israel the unprecedented sum of over $2 billion in military grants and credits, a level that has essentially been maintained ever since.[8]

The second pillar of post-1973 Middle East arms sales strategy has been discussed already: the building up of Iran and Saudi Arabia as "regional surrogates" that would police the Persian Gulf and stem the growth of radical and nationalist forces that might threaten privileged U.S. access to the region's oil resources. Iranian purchases peaked at almost $4 billion in 1974, while Saudi imports, which included a healthy dose of U.S. military construction and training along with actual weapons, hit $7.4 billion by 1976, the last year of the Ford administration.[9]

The third leg of an increasingly wobbly U.S.-built security structure in the Middle East involved the use of arms sales as political overtures to Egypt. This tactic was pioneered in Kissinger's negotiations over the 1975 accords for Israeli withdrawal from the Sinai. Kissinger's approach was expanded upon by the Carter administration in the Camp David accords, which were sealed with a $4.5 billion military aid package for Israel and Egypt, as well as a pledge to place Egypt at the center of the U.S. military aid budget for years to come. Indeed, as a result of this policy of making Egypt a close second to Israel as a recipient of U.S. military assistance, the two nations received a total of over $50 billion in U.S. security aid during the 1980s, accounting for well over half of U.S. military assistance throughout the period. The aid took the form of grants, "loans to be forgiven" (essentially a euphemism for aid), and Economic Support Funds, a flexible form of mostly cash assistance that could be used to offset the costs of arms purchases from the United States.[10]

So, the net result of the arms sales diplomacy of the 1970s was to make the United States the principal supplier both to Israel and to key Arab regimes like Saudi Arabia and Egypt. In essence the United States was racing with itself to maintain the mythical military "balance" between the parties, which in U.S. diplomatic parlance meant keeping Israel one step ahead of its Arab neighbors. In the meantime, the Soviet Union focused on large sales to Iraq, Syria, and Libya, markets it had to compete for with the French, Italians, British, and West Germans. Between the United States and its European allies, virtually every party to any potential conflict in the Middle East now had ready access to top-of-the-line Western weapons systems.

Israel's assertive use of U.S. arms to destroy Iraq's Osirak nuclear reactor in 1981 and to bombard Beirut and southern Lebanon in 1982 raised yet again the question of whether these weapons supplies were underwriting "stability" or fueling an endless round of ever more destructive conflicts. As noted in chapter 5, the Osirak bombing sparked a brief suspension of U.S. transfers to Israel during the summer of 1981 over the question of whether the Israelis had violated agreements to use U.S. weaponry only for "defensive purposes," but the overall flow of U.S. sales to Israel was barely affected. A senior Israeli official commented bluntly on why he had expected the U.S. suspension to be lifted: "We know that the U.S. is not selling us airplanes only for use for parades on Independence Day. They sell them because of the common strategic interest between our two countries. I believe the planes will be delivered." And they were. A year later, when Israel invaded Lebanon, there were no questions asked—the Reagan administration acquiesced in its ally's aggressive strategy.[11]

But even as Israel continued to benefit from consistent U.S. military supplies, the other states of the region had a much broader supplier base to turn to, due in large part to their access to billions of dollars in oil revenues. Saudi Arabia, Syria, and Iraq, as well as the smaller Gulf sheikdoms like the United Arab Emirates, Bahrain, and Kuwait, together purchased in excess of $150 billion in advanced armaments from the end of the 1973 Arab–Israeli war through 1990. While traditional suppliers like the Soviet Union, the United States, France, and Britain have led the charge to sell weapons to these Arab regimes, other suppliers entered the field in force as well—most notably, China, North Korea, Brazil, Italy, and Czechoslovakia.[12] Even before the end of the Cold War confrontation between the United States and the Soviet Union, sales to the Middle East showed no clear ideological pattern. Regimes like Syria and Iraq, which had strong anti-Israel, anti-U.S. policy orientations, were as likely to be getting their arms from a U.S. ally like France, Italy, or Britain as they were to get them from the Soviet Union.

Unquestionably the clearest example of how the Middle East arms race was bringing out the worst in the supplier nations and vastly complicating the prospects for curbing the arms trade was the Iran–Iraq war. The conflict raged on from 1980 through 1988, costing over a million casualties and hundreds of billions of dollars in damages to the combatants. Despite high-minded rhetoric about the need for "neutrality" and calls to stem the flow of arms fueling the conflict, by the end of the war each of the permanent members of the UN Security Council (the United States, the Soviet Union, France, the United Kingdom, and the People's Republic of China) had armed *both* sides in the war. And they were not alone. The Stockholm Peace Research Institute determined that fifty-three nations had provided weapons supplies for the Iran–Iraq war, with twenty-nine of them supporting both sides.[13]

Politically, there was no apparent rhyme or reason to the pattern of arms supplies to the conflict. The Soviet Union was a key supplier to Iraq, but its erstwhile allies in Syria and Libya were major suppliers to Iran. As analyst Stephen Goose observed during the conflict, the Khomeini regime received supplies from "some very strange bedfellows. . . . Iran has been supplied by both sides in other conflicts: China and Vietnam, North Korea and South Korea, Israel and Syria."[14] U.S. allies France and Great Britain became significant supporters of Iraq's war effort, with the private encouragement of the Reagan administration. And as discussed in the next chapter, not only did the United States swap arms for hostages with Iran at the same time that it was touting an international embargo of Iran, but the Reagan administration quietly signed off on U.S. financing and technology for Saddam Hussein's war machine.

The simplest explanations for this chaotic rush to arm both sides in the conflict are also by and large the correct ones: callousness and greed. Most major powers with any interest in the region saw the continuation of the war on an indefinite basis as a welcome outcome, presuming that it would simultaneously weaken Khomeini's revolutionary Islamic regime in Iran and keep Saddam Hussein's military forces tied up and out of trouble. That the people of the two nations would suffer devastating human and economic losses as a result of this cynical strategy seemed to provoke little regret in most world capitals. This "stalemate strategy" was certainly a strong motivating factor in the Reagan administration's policies toward the Persian Gulf region during this period.

But beyond any strategic calculations, however cold-blooded and ultimately misguided they may have been, the bottom line was money. Except for the Iran–Iraq war, the 1980s was a period of declining markets for armaments, primarily because of a worldwide economic recession and the huge debt problems of Third World countries that had been the fastest-growing part of the arms market. But the confrontation between Khomeini's right-wing radicalism and Saddam Hussein's megalomania was beyond such practical economic calculations: together Iran and Iraq accounted for more than half of the arms purchased by Third World nations in the mid-1980s, with total purchases in excess of $100 billion over the course of the decade. Second-tier suppliers like Brazil, North Korea, and especially the People's Republic of China made billions in new sales, allowing them to prop up their domestic arms industries and earn critically needed hard currency. France traded arms to Iraq for access to oil, and Italy and Britain saw the Iran–Iraq war as an important outlet for the production of their ailing domestic arms producers. As a result, both Iraq and Iran were able to keep fighting for years more than they could have if there had been an international embargo on exports to both combatants, and the death and destruction mounted.

Far from stabilizing the region by wearing down the two major regional powers, the strategy of encouraging Iran and Iraq to keep fighting merely set the stage for the next conflict in the Gulf. Kuwait, Saudi Arabia, and the other Gulf sheikdoms, which had financed Saddam Hussein's war with Iraq to the tune of hundreds of billions of dollars, were soon to learn that this support had bought them neither friendship nor respect. Shut out of the credit markets because of the $80 billion foreign debt Iraq had run up during the war with Iran, and with little to show from eight years of war, Hussein turned on the Gulf sheikdoms that had been his principal financial allies during the 1980s. Experts estimated that the cost of rebuilding Iraq back to prewar levels would be at least $300 billion. With no ready source of funding and hundreds of thousands of discontented young army veterans to contend with, Hussein needed a quick source of cash. When he failed in his efforts to pressure Kuwait and the United Arab Emirates to stop exceeding their OPEC quotas and allow the price of oil to rise, Hussein decided to fix his financial problems in a quicker, more brutal way: he seized Kuwait and its oil fields in one fell swoop.[15] If the international community, led by the Soviet Union, France, the Gulf sheikdoms, and the United States, had not prolonged the Iran–Iraq war by supplying Hussein with tens of billions of dollars' worth of advanced weaponry during the 1980s, he might not have had either the financial incentive or the amply equipped armed forces that emboldened him to invade Kuwait. (The role of U.S. policy in bringing on this latest step in the tragic march from conflict to conflict in the Gulf region is the subject of the next chapter.)

With arms pouring back into the region at a rapid clip in the wake of the Gulf War, the deadly logic that has seen virtually every round of rearmament in the region lead to a new, more devastating conflict could easily be played out yet again—unless forceful measures are taken to limit arms transfers to the region and scale back the existing arsenals of the key powers in the area. So far, the Middle East peace talks that began after the Gulf War have failed to stem the flow of military technology to any of the parties to the various Mideast conflicts. And the arms transfer control talks among the Big Five weapons exporting nations have been mostly that—just talk—even as U.S. sales to the region approached record levels in 1990 and 1991. The "croupier's table" of Mideast arms sales is still open for business, and the U.S. policy of accelerating exports to its long-standing clients in the region is continuing to drive the stakes higher, despite the lessons of the past four decades.

The Saudi Connection

By far the most lucrative—and controversial—Middle East market for U.S. arms traders over the past twenty years has been Saudi Arabia. The Saudi monarchy has liberally stocked its air force, navy, and national guard with U.S. weapons. And in what may rank as one of the most extensive military infrastructure programs of the post–World War II era, the Saudis have hired U.S. contractors to build bases, ports, and even entire military cities in the desert to help protect the regime from its internal and external enemies.

Beginning with the Nixon Doctrine's "twin pillar" policy of building up the Saudis and the shah of Iran as the guarantors of U.S. interests in the Persian Gulf, up through the Saudi role in "hosting" the U.S.-led multinational force that drove Saddam Hussein's forces out of Kuwait in the Gulf War, the U.S.–Saudi arms supply relationship has been a focal point of U.S. strategic initiatives in the Middle East. From 1971 through 1991, the United States sold over $50 billion in weapons and military services to the Saudis, including everything from F-15 fighters and AWACS radar planes to naval and air bases, pilot training, and advanced military communications systems.[16] For most of this period, this steady flow of military technology and training has been justified on the grounds of preventing Soviet incursions, direct or indirect, into the Persian Gulf oil states that are such valuable suppliers to the United States and its allies in Europe and Japan. Now that the former Soviet Union has been radically transformed from an outward-looking socialist regime into a fragile string of independent states absorbed with their own political and economic problems, the traditional rationales for U.S. arms sales to the Middle East ring hollow. As a stand-in for the "Soviet threat," the Pentagon's new enemy in the region is "instability," meaning essentially any government or movement that is perceived as posing a threat to Israel or to U.S. access to the region's oil resources. The Pentagon's desire to be the dominant military player in the region has not changed, and arms sales are still viewed by Pentagon planners as the royal road to access to the region's military facilities.

The end of the Cold War has had virtually no impact on the U.S. arms sales relationship with Saudi Arabia. The Saudi regime has actually experienced an increase in the pace of its arms transfers from the United States in recent years. Arms sales have served as the glue holding together a U.S.–Saudi partnership in the economic, political, and strategic realms that would have proceeded regardless of whether the Soviets had been global rivals of the United States.

Ronald Reagan offered a glimpse of the real foundation of the U.S.–Saudi relationship in October 1981 when he explicitly pledged that "Saudi Arabia . . . we will not permit to become another Iran." The comparison with Iran, where the shah was overthrown by his own people, was a revealing choice. Reagan had openly acknowledged that the real purpose of U.S. strategy was not so much to keep the Soviets out as it was to keep the Saudi royal family in—in power and in control of 25 percent of the world's known oil reserves. White House aides confirmed that Reagan made reference to the shah's fate to underscore the fact that the United States would protect the Saudi regime "from internal as well as external threats."

Reagan was even more blunt in explaining why the Saudi monarchy and other Gulf sheikdoms merited this special level of U.S. protection:

> [These nations] provide the bulk of the energy that is needed to turn the wheels of industry in the Western world. . . . There's no way that we could see that taken over by anyone that would shut off that oil.[17]

Experts on the history of U.S. oil company involvement in the region have questioned whether the issue was really access to Saudi oil or control of that precious resource on terms favorable to U.S. oil companies. Beginning with the first concession offered to Standard Oil of California by Abdul Aziz ibn Saud, the "founding father" of Saudi Arabia, in 1933, U.S. oil conglomerates have enjoyed advantageous arrangements for the exploration and marketing of Saudi oil resources, with strong backing from the U.S. government.

The Saudi concession was a mutually profitable arrangement. It provided ibn Saud with the revenue he needed to survive the worldwide economic depression and consolidate power over rival tribal leaders within Saudi Arabia, and it gave the small group of U.S. oil companies (SoCal, Esso, Texaco, and Mobil) that became partners in the newly formed Arabian American Oil Company (Aramco) free reign over what turned out to be the most productive oil lands in the world. The arrangement also marked the beginning of a symbiotic relationship among the Saudi royal family, the oil firms, and the U.S. government that continues to this day. In founding Saudi Arabia, ibn Saud created what British analyst Fred Halliday has described as "an unstable anachronism . . , the only state in the world that was titled as the property of a single dynasty [where] all power was held in the hands of the leading male members of the Saudi family." Without a steady flow of oil revenues and the military protection of the U.S. government, it is highly unlikely that this fragile, top-down ruling structure could have survived this long into the twentieth century without granting its citizens some measure of popular participation in government.[18]

The first U.S. government assistance to the House of Saud came in the form of Lend Lease funds for ibn Saud's regime that were authorized by the Roosevelt administration in 1943. The impetus for U.S. aid came from Aramco, which was looking for a way to respond to ibn Saud's urgent requests for additional royalties to cover a shortfall in oil revenues and Saudi government fees from Moslem pilgrims to the holy city of Mecca, both of which had fallen off as a result of the outbreak of World War II. As Joe Stork noted in his history of the region's oil politics, Aramco was "interested in coming up with the cash but not wishing to bear the burden alone," so company representatives "turned to Uncle Sam."[19]

The oil companies' appeal to the Roosevelt administration came at the very highest level: James Moffett, the chairman of Caltex (a partner in Aramco) and an old friend of Franklin Roosevelt's, called personally on the president to seek Lend Lease and Export-Import Bank funding for Saudi Arabia. Roosevelt suggested that the British be encouraged to "continue to take care of the King" out of a portion of their Lend Lease aid from the United States, and this arrangement was followed from late 1941 through 1943. But U.S. oil company representatives feared that funneling the aid through the British might give British firms leverage to gain their own oil concession in Saudi Arabia. In 1943 SoCal pressed once again for direct U.S. aid, arguing that "unless this is done, and done soon, this independent kingdom, and the entire Arab world, will be thrown into chaos."

The oil companies' viewpoint prevailed, and later that year Roosevelt formally declared that "the defense of Saudi Arabia is vital to the defense of the United States," clearing the way for over $17 million in Lend Lease aid to the Saudi king over the next several years.[20]

The direct financial link between the Saudi monarchy and the profits of major oil companies was only part of the "vital interest" that Roosevelt and his successors set out to defend by providing Saudi Arabia with arms and training. A State Department analysis forwarded to Pres. Harry Truman shortly after the conclusion of World War II described Saudi Arabia as a place "where the oil resources constitute a stupendous source of strategic power, and one of the greatest material prizes in world history." U.S. secretary of the navy James Forrestal had elaborated on this point in a memorandum he sent to the secretary of state during the war:

> The prestige and hence the influence of the United States is in part related to the wealth of the Government and its nationals in terms of oil resources, foreign as well as domestic. . . . The bargaining power of the United States in international conferences involving vital materials like oil and such problems as aviation, shipping, island bases, and international security arrangements relating to the disposition of armed forces and facilities, will depend in some degree upon the retention by the United States of such oil resources. . . . Under these circumstances it is patently in the Navy's interest that no part of the national wealth, as represented by the present holdings of foreign reserves by American nationals, be lost at this time. Indeed, the active expansion of such holdings is very much to be desired.[21]

Forrestal's concerns were echoed and amplified in a 1951 series in the *New York Times* that placed oil at the very center of the struggle between capitalism and communism. In a classic application of Cold War logic, the *Times* reasoned that if Middle Eastern oil resources were to fall under Soviet control, "either directly or indirectly through nationalization," the Soviet Union could combine this "abundant supply of cheap oil" with "the enormous manpower available" in communist China "to bring a virtually unbeatable military force into being." In contrast, keeping Near East oil available to Western European nations would strengthen capitalist economies there with the result that "the radical elements in Europe will be kept in check, since communism makes slow progress in prosperous areas."[22] Couched in these larger terms, the question of whether SoCal or Mobil maintained their control over Saudi oil resources was elevated from the status of a narrow economic interest to part of a global power struggle against the Soviet Union and China, a much more marketable rationale for U.S. government intervention on the oil companies' behalf. The most obvious of the many weak links in this sweeping argument was the notion that nationalization by local forces was tantamount to Soviet domination of the region's oil resources, a position that left no leeway for indigenous democratic forces to assert control over the region's principal resource on any terms other than those most favorable to U.S. companies.

Now that the defense of Saudi Arabia and mastery of its oil resources had been duly anointed as a "vital national security interest" of the United States, the question became how best to secure that interest. The first U.S. military mission came to the kingdom in the mid-1940s to train King Saud's army, and the U.S. built an airfield at Dhahran, near the oil fields. Dhahran was run as a U.S. base from the late 1940s up through 1964, when it reverted back to nominal Saudi control. The United States signed a mutual defense assistance agreement with the Saudi regime in 1951, and a formal U.S. military assistance advisory group was sent to Saudi Arabia in 1952 to replace the existing British training mission.

While this formalization of the U.S.–Saudi arms supply relationship marked an important milestone, a congressional study has observed that "the earlier years of the United States–Saudi Arabian military assistance relationship were characterized by comparatively modest shipments of unsophisticated equipment and limited training for Saudi personnel." This modest arms flow increased substantially in the mid-1960s, when the United States and the United Kingdom engaged in a joint program to substantially upgrade the Saudi armed forces under a project code-named Magic Carpet. It was this effort, which led to the purchase of advanced air defense missiles and Northrop F-5 fighter aircraft by the Saudis, that set the stage for the oil-driven arms purchasing boom of the 1970s.[23]

Once the initial strategic relationship had been solidified during the 1940s and early 1950s, a series of U.S. administrations came to rely not only on relatively cheap access to Saudi oil but also on Saudi political assistance in the Arab world and Saudi financial support for U.S. strategic and economic objectives worldwide. By the early 1970s, the balance of power within the U.S.–Saudi relationship had changed significantly, as continuing U.S. dependency on foreign oil and OPEC activism had given the Saudi regime a stronger hand to play in negotiations with its superpower ally. From helping to shore up a weak dollar in the 1970s to financing a large part of the Reagan Doctrine's covert military adventures in the 1980s, the Saudi regime had become a junior partner to the U.S. government and business elite. In return, the Saudi ruling family received an implicit U.S. commitment to do whatever was necessary to keep it in power. In blurting out his willingness to use force, if necessary, to preserve the Saudi regime, Ronald Reagan was merely stating openly a premise that has formed part of the underlying logic of U.S. policy toward Saudi Arabia for nearly six decades.

Checkbook Diplomacy: The Saudis as Surrogate Arms Financier

Saudi support for U.S. objectives has not come cheap. Although the Saudis have not been major recipients of U.S. foreign aid over the years, they have had their own asking price for cooperating with U.S. global initiatives: unimpeded access to the most advanced equipment in the U.S. arsenal. The Saudis have purchased Boeing AWACS planes; McDonnell Douglas F-15 fighter aircraft; General Dynamics M-1 tanks; FMC Corporation M-2 armored personnel carriers; and a panoply of howitzers, transport vehicles, air defense missiles, cluster bombs, and other military equipment. In return for the run of the U.S. arsenal, the Saudis have not only offered their military facilities to U.S. forces, they have also spent their extensive oil revenues on behalf of pet U.S. foreign policy projects. This implicit swap of U.S. arms for Saudi political and financial support helps explain why every president from Richard Nixon to George Bush has expended considerable political capital in promoting a series of increasingly controversial Saudi arms sales over the strenuous objections of congressional supporters of Israel.

Probably the most difficult sale of all was the 1981 AWACS aircraft sale, initiated during the Carter administration and steered through a skeptical Congress by the Reagan administration. The fierce debate over the Saudi sale and the ultimate victory of the Reagan administration's position offer a case study in the inherent weaknesses of congressional oversight procedures for major arms sales packages.

The details of the AWACS lobbying campaign have already been discussed in chapter 5, but the underlying rationales for the sale, which were never revealed to the public at the time of the sale, deserve a fuller discussion. There was a hidden dimension of the AWACS deal that helped shape the pattern of U.S. foreign policy throughout the 1980s. In a page-one piece that appeared on February 4, 1987, Jeff Gerth of the *New York Times* reported that U.S. officials had acknowledged a link between the 1981 AWACS sale and the Iran/contra scandal of the mid-1980s. Gerth's sources asserted that "King Fahd and other top Saudi Arabian officials agreed to aid anti-Communist resistance groups around the world as part of the arrangement allowing them to buy sophisticated American AWACS radar planes." The implication of the charges, made by a series of U.S. officials involved with the AWACS deal who spoke off the record, was that later "donations" by the Saudis—like the $30 million they donated to the Nicaraguan contras in 1984–85 and the nearly $500 million per year the Saudis faithfully sent to their favorite Afghan rebel factions—were in part a repayment to the Reagan administration for weathering the storm of congressional opposition to the AWACS sale.[24]

A Reagan administration official told Gerth that there was a link between AWACS and Saudi funding for secret U.S. weapons trafficking: "I recall the Saudis agreeing to fund anti-Communist groups at the time of the AWACS sale, in connection with the sale." At the time of the deal, officials familiar with the arrangement report, it was open ended, sort of a flexible "revolving fund" for the support of U.S.-designated movements. Ultimately, there was documented evidence of considerable Saudi financial support not only for the Afghan rebels and the contras but also for Jonas Savimbi's UNITA movement in Angola, all pursuant to the 1981 AWACS quid pro quo. A number of former Reagan and Carter administration officials have argued that while the Saudis may have had their own motivations for funding the Afghan rebels, the provision of funds to arm the contras and Savimbi could have come only at the behest of the United States. A California businessman offered further confirmation of the secret Saudi fund, describing a 1985 conversation with Saudi prince Bandar, the current Saudi ambassador to Washington, in which Bandar asked him to funnel some money to the contras for him. Bandar told the businessman that the deal was being conducted with the approval of the Reagan administration because "we've had similar arrangements with the U.S.

going back a long time, since I was involved in the AWACS sale."[25]

The interaction between aboveboard, publicly debated arms transfers like the AWACS sale and covert arms sales bankrolled by the Saudis raises serious questions about the accountability of the U.S. government's arms sales enterprise. The use of arms sales to leverage foreign funds for purposes the executive branch knows the Congress won't support has the potential to permanently undermine the constitutionally mandated role of the legislative branch on matters of war and peace.

The temptation to tap the Saudis' billions to run an off-the-books U.S. foreign policy was evidently irresistible. William Quandt, a former Middle East specialist on the National Security Council, bluntly summarized the advantages of this approach:

> It takes King Fahd about 10 seconds to write a check. It takes Congress weeks to debate the smallest issue of this sort. If you can get somebody else to pay for it, it's nice and convenient.

Another U.S. diplomat with years of Middle East experience underscored this point: "Any time we needed them to pay for something, we always turned to the Saudis. We viewed them as this great milk cow."[26]

But, in order to keep the "great milk cow" happy, the flow of advanced U.S. arms to the Saudis has to continue virtually uninterrupted, regardless of how these arms may ultimately be used by the Saudi sheikdom or a successor regime. Once this becomes institutionalized, the secret arms trade becomes much more than a case of the U.S. government occasionally winking at illegal activities on the part of a few anticommunist "cowboys" run amok—it becomes part and parcel of how the president makes foreign policy. These surrogate arms sales create a parallel universe in which Congress and the public are manipulated into supporting a sale like the AWACS deal for one reason, only to learn years later that it was used for an entirely different purpose.

Military Construction and Services in Saudi Arabia: Project and Defend

When George Bush sent U.S. troops to Saudi Arabia in the fall of 1990 in response to Iraq's invasion of Kuwait, the troops felt more at home than might have been expected—they were stationed at military bases and airfields that had been built to U.S. specifications. Dhahran, a relatively unknown facility that had provided access to U.S. aircraft in the region on and off for four decades, came to prominence in the Gulf War as the place where Arthur Kent and other television stalwarts did their "standups" in front of U.S. aircraft taking off for bombing missions in Iraq. But Dhahran represented only a small part of a unique history of sales of U.S. military construction services that have transformed the desert kingdom into a ready platform for U.S. military intervention in the region. In essence, the U.S. Army Corps of Engineers has served as a sort of general contractor for the effort to transform Saudi Arabia from a string of seminomadic villages into a modern nation-state.

In keeping with the overall pattern of U.S.–Saudi military transfers, early projects like the military airfield at Dhahran and a companion civil airport were built with U.S. assistance funds. But from the early 1960s on, all U.S. military construction projects in Saudi Arabia have been paid for by the Saudis. In a 1975 congressional hearing, a U.S. Army Corps of Engineers official confirmed that the group's role in Saudi Arabia is "a special deal," a deal that has been offered to no other government in the world. Under a formal 1965 "Engineer Assistance Agreement," the army corps has built civilian projects such as a radio station in Riyadh and the Saudis' national television network, as well as major military bases at Khamis Mushayt and Tabuk. In one of the largest military construction projects ever undertaken, the corps also built the fifty-thousand-person King Khalid Military City during the 1970s. This activity was in addition to work in modernizing major Saudi ports as part of the Saudi Naval Expansion Program and building a new headquarters for the Saudi Arabian national guard. In all, from the mid-1960s onward, the army corps built over $15 billion worth of military facilities in Saudi Arabia.[27]

Building a modern military infrastructure was only part of the military service provided to the Saudi regime under the U.S. foreign military sales program. The project of most direct personal interest to the royal family was the training and modernization of the Saudi Arabian national guard, an elite unit whose main job is to defend the ruling group against internal threats, whether from terrorists, potential assassins, or rival power alignments. The national guard modernization program began in the 1970s as a four-year, $275 million project designed to train and equip three mechanized infantry battalions of one thousand men each, along with a howitzer battalion of about the same size. A unique feature of the project was its reliance on a private contractor, the Los Angeles–based Vinnell Corporation. Vinnell was hired in part to take some strain off an already overtaxed U.S. military mission in Saudi Arabia and in part to avoid the domestic political repercussions within the kingdom stemming from having uniformed U.S. military personnel training Saudi internal security forces.

The Vinnell contract generated considerable controversy. In his pre-CNN days as a reporter for the *Washington Post*, Peter Arnett filed a February 1975 dispatch entitled "U.S. Vets to Train Saudis," which strongly implied that the Vinnell contract was a mercenary operation. Vinnell president John Hamill argued defensively that his company, which had built Dodger Stadium and worked on the Grand Coulee Dam, was "not a spook outfit." Hamill further claimed that his firm had "worked hard for this contract, sinking five years of effort into winning the confidence of the Persian Gulf countries." The most important bit of work done to obtain the contract was the hiring of Col. William G. Walby, former commander of the 4th Advanced Individual Brigade and Training Command at Fort Ord, California, to head up Vinnell's Saudi national guard training operation. Vinnell wasted no time in bringing the colonel on board: he was hired just three days after his retirement from active military service. Walby used his military connections to recruit several hundred former U.S. Special Forces personnel to carry out the Vinnell training mission in Saudi Arabia.

Arnett's article and a subsequent congressional hearing raised the question of whether this private training arrangement wasn't simply a new form of the time-honored practice of hiring foreign mercenaries to protect regimes whose own people could not or would not perform that function. One former U.S. Army officer involved in the mission tried to split hairs, telling Arnett that "we are not mercenaries because we are not pulling the triggers; we train people to pull the triggers." The weakness of his logic was apparent to a colleague, who laughed and said, "Maybe that makes us executive mercenaries." Terminology aside, the Saudi national guard training program is indicative of how committed the U.S. government has become to the survival of the Saudi monarchy, even if the Saudis are expected to pay generously for their U.S. protection. In June 1993, the Vinnell contract was renewed through 1998.28

This pledge of protection goes well beyond training, to a de facto commitment to send in U.S. troops, if necessary, to keep the Saudi regime firmly in power. To carry out this mission, which was an important part of the rationale for the initial U.S. involvement in the 1991 Gulf War, the Saudi–U.S. policy of building massive, modern military facilities that are compatible with U.S. equipment and communications gear has been a critical prop. (The genesis of this policy, and the role of Richard Secord in promoting this arms-for-access arrangement with the Saudis and other Gulf sheikdoms, has already been described; see chapter 7.)

Ironically, the very same weapons that have been pushed on the Saudi leadership in the name of defense may pose a threat to the survival of the Saudi regime. After the 1991 Persian Gulf War, Bush and Clinton administration officials pressured Saudi officials to maintain a rapid pace of weapons purchases from the United States, despite the fact that these deals were draining Saudi cash reserves and forcing the government to reduce its traditionally generous social benefits to citizens of the kingdom. A close adviser to the Saudi monarchy told the *New York Times* that massive U.S. weapons sales were likely to provide "ammunition" to fundamentalist opponents of the regime, implying that the resulting backlash could lead to a repeat of what happened to the Shah of Iran, the favorite U.S. weapons client of the 1970s:

> People think we have a wonderful gold mine in Saudi Arabia, that we can sell a lot of military equipment to them to create jobs, to help the defense industry's transition out of the Cold War, to improve our balance of payments, and to make Saudi Arabia safer . . . I don't think the U.S. government realizes what it is doing by shoving weapons down the Saudis' throats. They're forgetting that what they are doing is creating instability in Saudi Arabia. That could be the greatest risk to Saudi security.[29]

By the end of 1994, there were indications that the Clinton Administration may have reluctantly begun to accept the fact that the Saudis were not a bottomless market for U.S. military equipment. Administration insiders claimed that about fifteen proposals by U.S. manufacturers for new sales to the Saudis had been quietly turned down as part of an effort to reschedule outstanding Saudi payments on weapons deals that had already been struck. Assistant Secretary of Defense for International Security Affairs Joseph S. Nye asserted that "this building [the Pentagon] has acted very responsibly in seeing itself as the protector of the Saudi alliance in the long term, rather than as an arms merchant in the short term."[30] Despite Nye's assurances that the Pentagon has long-term Saudi stability as its top priority, no effort has been made to cancel any of the costly, multibillion dollar weapons export agreements that helped put the Saudis in such a precarious financial position in the first place.[31]

The U.S. and Israel: The Special Relationship

Just as arms sales to Saudi Arabia have been linked to larger political, economic, and strategic commitments that have made it very difficult for any U.S. administration to say no to Saudi arms requests, the special relationship between the United States and Israel has been firmly grounded in military aid and transfers of military technology for over two decades. By the late 1970s the U.S.–Israeli arms relationship had already reached the stage where, in the words of one Mideast analyst, "its sheer immensity made it practically impervious to decisions on specific programs or items."[32] To find out how the Israeli aid program arrived at that seeming "point of no return," it is necessary to look back to the two godfathers of the U.S. arms export boom: Richard Nixon and Henry Kissinger.

Ever since the Nixon/Kissinger policy of massive subsidies of Israeli arms purchases took hold in 1974, Israel has commanded a lion's share of the U.S. foreign aid budget. In the seventeen years following the end of the 1973 Middle East war, Israel has received almost $30 billion in U.S. aid under the Pentagon's Foreign Military Sales Financing Program. Israel's share amounted to almost one out of every two dollars distributed under this premier U.S. military aid program over the period, a sum rivaled by no other nation except Egypt in the years since Camp David enshrined it as a preferred U.S. arms customer.[33]

But the amount of U.S. aid to Israel tells only part of the story. Ever since a secret November 1971 agreement was worked out by the Nixon administration with Israel, the United States has also supplied significant technical assistance in the development of Israel's own arms industry. Unlike any other U.S. client, Israel is allowed to spend up to $300 million of its U.S. aid every year on military components built in Israel, providing an important boost to the nation's military-industrial complex. Many of Israel's indigenous weapons, from the Merkava tank to the Kfir fighter, have benefited from U.S. technology and components. This technology transfer has allowed the Israeli industry to grow to the point where it is nearly self-sufficient in everything from armored vehicles to ammunition to missiles. This U.S.-supplied technical edge has given Israel an important advantage over most of its potential military adversaries in the region, who are still much more dependent on outside suppliers.[34]

This U.S. military aid to Israel has bought more than a strong ally in an area of vital concern to U.S. strategists. In much the same way that Saudi Arabia has served as a financial surrogate for U.S. arms policies in the Middle East and beyond, Israel has played a role as a surrogate supplier of military equipment to regimes that U.S. administrations have wanted to support without being publicly associated with them. The most extreme examples of this Israeli role as a surrogate arms supplier are in Central America, where forces ranging from the Guatemalan and Salvadoran military juntas to the contras in Nicaragua have been beneficiaries of Israeli arms and training.

A former head of the foreign relations committee of the Israeli Knesset has explained the rationale behind Israel's role:

> Israel is a pariah state. When people ask us for something, we cannot afford to ask questions about ideology. The only type of regime that Israel would not aid would be one that is anti-American. Also, if we can aid a country that it may be inconvenient for the U.S. to help, we would be cutting off our nose to spite our face not to.[35]

Guatemala has certainly qualified as "a country that it may be inconvenient for the U.S. to help," given its long record of human rights abuses and military repression. Israel has gladly stepped in at strategic moments to supply the Guatemalan military when the U.S. government has been constrained from doing so because of congressional restrictions on U.S. weapons transfers to any of a series of military-dominated regimes in Guatemala.

In early 1977, just three months after Jimmy Carter took office, the State Department issued a report condemning the Guatemalan regime's "gross and consistent" violations of human rights. The Guatemalan junta protested that it would no longer accept military aid from the United States if it imposed human rights conditions, and Congress suspended U.S. military aid to Guatemala at President Carter's request. Israel quickly filled the gap, providing a comprehensive program of counterinsurgency training and arms transfers, which included outfitting the Guatemalan army with ten thousand Israeli Galil assault rifles at a cost of $6 million.

Israeli assistance took on even greater importance during the early years of the Reagan administration, when the Congress kept military aid restrictions in place despite the president's best efforts to have them removed. By 1982, Israel reportedly had over three hundred military advisers in Guatemala. The Israeli and Central American press widely reported allegations that these advisers were involved in the 1982 coup that brought right-wing, pro-U.S. general Efrain Rios Montt to power. Israeli defense minister Ariel Sharon accelerated aid to Guatemala in 1981 on the theory that "Israel could increase its leverage over Washington by performing indispensable functions for the U.S. in third countries." And there were few more important strategic locales for the Reagan foreign policy team than Central America, the place it had chosen to "draw the line" against communism, as Secretary of State Alexander Haig put it. Lt. Gen. Wallace Nutting, head of the U.S. Southern Command, had singled out Guatemala as a particularly important part of the region, noting that "the situation in Guatemala is potentially more serious than in El Salvador because the population is larger, the economy is stronger, and the geographical position is more critically located in a strategic sense." If Sharon was looking to score points with the Reagan administration, he could not have picked a better place to do so than in Guatemala, where the new administration's instincts to bolster the military against popular organizations had been at least initially thwarted by Congress.[36]

Israel's surrogate supplier role was even more pronounced in Nicaragua. During 1978, when the savagery of Nicaraguan dictator Anastasio Somoza's U.S.-trained National Guardsmen finally forced the Carter administration to cut off U.S. military supplies to Nicaragua, Israel stepped in to become Nicaragua's primary source of arms and ammunition. Carter administration officials lamely explained that they "had decided against trying to prevent Israel from supplying light arms" to Somoza's regime. As in Guatemala, the pattern in Nicaragua shifted from acquiescing in Israeli sales during the Carter administration to actively encouraging them during the Reagan era. Beginning in the summer of 1983, according to reports in the *New York Times*, "senior Reagan Administration officials" prodded Israel to "send weapons captured from the Palestine Liberation Organization to Honduras for eventual use by the Nicaraguan rebels." Taking it a step further, there have been allegations growing out of the Iran/contra affair that the Reagan administration instructed Israel to set aside a specific portion of its $2 billion in annual U.S. military aid to pass on to the contras. This startling charge received little or no follow-up from the congressional Iran/contra investigating committees, although given the level of U.S.–Israeli cooperation in the affair it seems like a plausible extension of Israel's role as a surrogate arms supplier for the United States.[37]

The most notorious Israeli client—and the one that has caused the greatest international outcry—has been the apartheid government of South Africa. Andrew and Leslie Cockburn have described the longstanding ties between the military and intelligence establishments of the two nations as a "marriage of convenience" spurred by parallel histories of political and economic isolation. Israel was one of the first nations to violate the UN embargo against South Africa when it shipped nearly three dozen tanks to the Pretoria regime in 1962. That move was reciprocated shortly thereafter when South Africa shipped ten tons of uranium to Israel for use in its military research and production reactor at Dimona. Israeli arms sales jumped in the 1970s after France curtailed its weapons shipments to South Africa, with everything from Israeli machine guns and assault rifles to fighter plane and guided missile technology finding its way into the inventory of the South African armed forces. There is circumstantial evidence to indicate that Israel and South Africa may have collaborated on a nuclear bomb test in 1979; and in 1989 the apartheid regime tested a medium-range ballistic missile whose performance characteristics bore a striking resemblance to Israel's Jericho II missile system.[38]

Since U.S. military aid accounts for the bulk of Israel's weapons development budget, much of the technology that has been making its way to South Africa via Israel over the past three decades has come from the United States. Consistent with the pattern of transfers of U.S. weaponry to other repressive regimes via Israel, there is strong reason to believe that the U.S. government had condoned, if not outright promoted, the Israeli–South African military trade. An Israeli analyst has argued that it was the result of a conscious strategy:

> Israel's main role in the relationship was as a go-between. There were countries such as . . . South Africa, that the United States wanted to assist. It was very convenient in cases such as this to give the aid via Israel, or to encourage Israel to step up its exports to these countries.[39]

The U.S. government's rationale for encouraging this Israeli–South African military relationship was grounded in a twisted Cold War logic that saw South Africa as the only reliable bulwark against a wave of Soviet-inspired communism in southern Africa. This approach completely ignored the legitimate aspirations of the people of the region to control their own affairs, free from the influence of the outmoded governing structures of the colonial era; it also vastly overstated the political influence the Soviets had over liberation movements that received arms from them. The net result of this covert U.S. policy of using Israel to bolster the South African regime was to strengthen the apartheid war machine and slow the pace of democratic change in southern Africa. Israel had its own reasons for supplying arms and training to the South Africans, not the least of which was to keep alive a healthy source of income to supplement Israel's tiny domestic market for military equipment. But the encouragement of its principal aid donor and military ally, the United States—particularly during the period of Henry Kissinger's campaign to destabilize the socialist government in Angola—reinforced Israel's resolve to do military business with South Africa despite the UN arms embargo.

Having fostered this Israeli–South African liaison during the Cold War, U.S. administrations were reluctant to exert pressure to break it off, even after there was no conceivable possibility of a "Soviet threat" to southern Africa, if there ever had been. What did develop late in the Bush administration was a kind of back-door bureaucratic infighting within the State Department, pitting supporters of Israel against officials who felt that the Jewish state had been too intransigent on issues such as settlements in Israeli-occupied territories. During 1992, information regarding Israel's arming of South Africa, China, Ethiopia, and other repressive regimes was widely released to media outlets by figures inside the Bush administration, not so much in an effort to change Israel's arms export policies as to embarrass Israel politically and use the resulting leverage to win concessions on issues such as its stance on settlements in the occupied territories. This was the apparent motivation behind a March 1992 leak to the *Wall Street Journal* of classified portions of a report by State Department inspector general Sherman Funk. Funk's report revealed details of Israeli reexports of U.S.-origin weapons systems, including air-to-air missiles to China, antitank missiles to South Africa, and cluster bombs to Ethiopia and Chile. No significant punitive action was taken against Israel for these alleged violations of U.S. law, indicating one of two possibilities: U.S. military or intelligence agencies had signed off on the sales without informing key officials at State, or Israel went beyond the kinds of sales the United States would normally have approved of but Bush administration officials were not willing to go so far as to cut off military assistance over exports that were similar in kind to ones the United States *had* approved over the years.[40]

It is not yet clear whether this new willingness to engage in selective criticism of Israeli policies on the retransfer of U.S. weapons technology will result in the Congress or the Clinton administration cracking down on Israeli arms sales to repressive regimes. But the history of the U.S.–Israeli arms sales relationship makes such a reversal of policy unlikely, unless there is considerable public pressure for change in the United States and Israel.

U.S. Policy for the Nineties: Racing with Ourselves?

The 1990s have been a confusing period for U.S. arms transfer policy toward the Middle East. First came the Gulf War, in which a U.S.-led coalition did battle with an Iraqi military force that was created with the assistance of the United States and its Western allies. Then came the political collapse of the Soviet Union, an event that eliminated a major source of subsidized weapons to aggressive regimes such as Syria and Iraq, a supply line that had been a large part of the U.S. rationale for aggressively arming its own allies in the region.

Next, with the Gulf War over and the Soviet Union out of the regional security picture, George Bush promised to seek curbs on weapons exports to the region. But the arms transfer control talks that emerged as a result of that pledge were long on rhetoric and short on action. By 1991, despite the absence of Soviet involvement and the continuing embargo on Saddam Hussein, U.S. weapons sales to the Middle East had actually increased. Even without a credible enemy to justify the billions in U.S. transfers to the region—not to mention the sorry history of the role of past U.S. sales in fueling conflicts there—U.S. sales accelerated, accounting for 72 percent of weapons deals in the region from 1990 through 1993.[41] In April 1994, the Clinton administration offered Israel twenty five top-of-the-line F-15I fighters to counterbalance the September 1992 sale of F-15s to Saudi Arabia, at a cost to the U.S. taxpayers of $2.4 billion. In all, U.S. arms sales agreements with the Middle East from the beginning of the Gulf War in August of 1990 through the summer of 1994 topped $41 billion, a pace of more than $1 billion per month.[42]

The habit of swapping arms for political favors—or selling them to shore up an oversized domestic military-industrial complex—continues to override the powerful evidence that a reduction in sales to the Middle East would best serve the interests of regional peace and U.S. security. Whereas in the 1970s and 1980s the United States, the Soviet Union, and Europe were engaged in a three-sided race to arm their favored clients in the region, by the early 1990s the United States was virtually racing with itself. In the process, the Bush administration may have thrown away a historic opportunity to use the unique leverage of the United States in the wake of the Gulf War to bring an end to the cycle of arms race, war, and rearmament in the Middle East.

Even the ongoing Middle East peace process may not be enough to slow the rate of arms flowing into the region. Despite this historic step forward, Israel has persevered with its plan to acquire dozens of new U.S. fighter aircraft, Jordan has sought hundreds of millions of dollars worth of U.S. military aid as a quid pro quo for signing a peace agreement with Israel, and none of the other nations in the area have made any explicit pledges to reduce their weapons purchases any time soon. [43]

The most infamous example of the misguided U.S. policy of relying on military technology exports as its principal foreign policy tool in this volatile region—the U.S. role in arming Iraq—is the subject of our next chapter.

11

Who Armed Iraq?

There is no greater monument to the folly of the Reagan/Bush policy of using arms and military technology as the ultimate bargaining chip in relations with other nations than the hidden history of U.S. complicity in the construction of Saddam Hussein's war machine.

Unbeknownst to most Americans, their government was hard at work supplying Iraq with billions of dollars in U.S. government financing and hundreds of millions of dollars' worth of advanced machinery and electronic equipment in the years leading up to the 1991 Gulf War. While Bush administration officials tried to downplay the importance of this assistance, there is now no question that the United States provided vital resources that were utilized in Iraqi programs for the construction of missiles, conventional bombs, and nuclear, chemical, and biological weapons.[1]

But it was only after the Gulf War that conclusive evidence emerged about the degree to which Saddam Hussein, the man George Bush denounced as the moral equivalent of Adolf Hitler, had the U.S. government to thank for critical funding and technology that helped him build one of the most powerful arsenals in the world. And if there was one individual Hussein could thank for spearheading U.S. government efforts to help him become the dominant military power in the Persian Gulf region, it was George Bush. First as Ronald Reagan's vice president and then during the first year of his own presidency, Bush intervened time and again to override objections within the U.S. government about the wisdom of providing export financing and militarily useful technology to Iraq.

How had this been allowed to happen, and why had there been so little public outcry against this policy until it was far too late—*after* U.S. troops were locked in a confrontation with Iraqi forces in the deserts of the Persian Gulf? There are two answers to this question, one rooted in politics, the other in technology. The political answer has to do with the U.S. decision to back Saddam Hussein as the "lesser of two evils" in the eight-year-long Iran–Iraq war. Reagan administration policymakers wanted to prevent a victory by the Ayatollah Khomeini's Islamic fundamentalist regime in Iran, even if it meant supporting Saddam Hussein's dictatorial regime in Iraq. It was this now infamous tilt toward Iraq that prompted U.S. officials to provide funds and technology that were put to use in Hussein's ambitious armaments programs.

The technological answer to the question of why U.S. policymakers helped arm Iraq had to do with the fact that the United States was not supplying Iraq with weapons systems—the tanks, fighter aircraft, helicopters, and other basic armaments that make up a modern army. Saddam had turned for these kinds of systems to the Soviet Union, France, Italy, and other weapons supplying nations. The most critical U.S. contribution to the Iraqi war machine was indirect—through the provision of government-guaranteed loans and "dual use" equipment such as advanced computers and machine tools that could be used either for benign commercial purposes or to build modern weapons systems.

This indirect support proved to be just as important to Hussein's grand military designs as the Soviet tanks and French fighter planes that were his most visible military imports, but these critical transfers fell into a gray area. Not only were dual-use technology exports much harder to monitor than sales of complete weapons systems, but their dangerous implications were also much easier to brush aside with the wishful thought that they would be used only for "civilian" projects. In fact, over the course of a six-year-period from 1984 to 1990, this steady flow of U.S. funds and military technology played an integral part in Iraq's weapons production program, adding up to one of the greatest arms trading scandals in U.S. history.

Act I: The Little Italian Bank

On February 28, 1991—the same day that President Bush announced the cease-fire in the Gulf War—members of the highest echelons of U.S. law enforcement gathered in Washington to announce the indictment of several officers of the Atlanta branch of the Italian-owned Banca Nazionale del Lavoro (BNL). The officials were accused of making billions of dollars' worth of illegal loans to Iraq, funds that had been used to purchase militarily useful technology. Attorney General Dick Thornburgh, joined by FBI director William Sessions, Commissioner of Customs Carol Hallett, and representatives of the Internal Revenue Service and the Federal Reserve Bank, characterized the BNL scandal as "an international white collar scam with dire global consequences." Thornburgh went on to say that "this case should serve notice . . . that law enforcement is now prepared to deal with criminals who seem to neither know, nor fear, nor respect international borders."[2]

At first the timing of Thornburgh's announcement seemed like an odd coincidence—the public disclosure of a major, U.S.-based criminal scheme to finance Iraq on the very same day that the U.S.-backed war against Iraq was coming to a halt. A suspicious mind might even wonder whether the announcement of the indictment in the BNL case had been purposely timed to come out on the last day of the Gulf War, to divert attention from the case and fend off political criticism about why it had taken the Bush administration so long to take action against Saddam Hussein's U.S.-based bankers. But the actual links between the BNL scandal and the war with Iraq turned out to be much deeper—and much more troubling—than a mere public relations gambit.

The Justice Department's version of the BNL scandal was that Christopher Drogoul, the thirty-eight-year-old manager of BNL's Atlanta branch, had single-handedly masterminded the fraudulent transfer of over $4 billion to Iraq. The indictment asserted that Drogoul had gotten away with this for years without the knowledge of the bank's New York or Rome-based management, much less Georgia bank examiners, the Federal Reserve, or even U.S. intelligence agencies, which have their own systems for monitoring international monetary transfers.[3]

Justice's version of the story was fine as far as it went, but it didn't go nearly far enough. It ignored the question of potential complicity in the scheme by BNL management in Rome and senior governmental officials in at least four countries. There was a sense from the outset that Drogoul was being made a scapegoat for a crime that had been facilitated at the highest levels of the U.S., Italian, British, and Iraqi governments. As Marvin Shoob, the federal judge who handled the BNL case, put it in an April 1992 hearing, it was simply unbelievable "that somebody who was a branch manager of a bank could move $4.5 billion in the fashion that was done without some type of participation by the people in this country and outside this country."[4]

Leaving aside for a moment the question of who aided and abetted Drogoul's fraudulent scheme, there was no question that the young bank manager had his own special talent for deception and manipulation that probably would have found some criminal outlet regardless of help from higher-ups.

Drogoul arrived quietly on Atlanta's international banking scene in the late 1970s, when he took a job at Barclay's Bank. In 1982 he took a modest step up when he became the manager of BNL-Atlanta, which one former BNL executive has described as "a little branch in the boondocks." According to federal court records, BNL-Atlanta had "no facilities for accepting deposits or conducting cash or checking transactions for individuals." It was a decidedly low-profile operation. Even seven years after the opening of BNL-Atlanta, when the Iraqi loan scandal began to surface in the business press, one member of Atlanta's international banking community told the *Financial Times* of London that "we were never quite sure what BNL was doing. We heard they were quite involved in commodity lending, but we never saw them involved in commercial credits like us." A colleague from another local bank described Christopher Drogoul as "tall and blond," with "an attractive continental flair" and "a very outgoing and charming personality," but he had no idea what he had been doing on the lending front during his tenure at BNL-Atlanta.[5]

Drogoul's minimal contact with other Atlanta-based bankers was undoubtedly by design—he had bigger fish to fry. His most important customers were based in London and Baghdad, not Atlanta. Beginning in 1985, Drogoul transformed BNL-Atlanta's "little branch in the boondocks" into the single largest source of credit for Iraq and the most important source of loans to Iraq's Ministry of Industry and Military Industrialization.

Drogoul's Iraqi connection started innocently enough in December 1984, when he met with officials of the Iraqi Central Bank and Iraq's only commercial bank, the Rafidain, to arrange BNL-Atlanta's participation in $100 million worth of U.S.-government-guaranteed loans to Iraq under the U.S. Department of Agriculture's (USDA's) Commodity Credit Corporation (CCC) program. Since the Reagan administration had first initiated its political tilt toward Iraq in 1982–83, the CCC program had been a primary tool for funneling U.S. assistance to Saddam Hussein's regime. The credits essentially functioned as U.S. government guarantees for commercial loans negotiated by the recipient country for the purchase of U.S. agricultural products—private banks supplied the loans, but the U.S. taxpayers were on the hook if a recipient nation defaulted on its payments.

On the surface, it appeared that Drogoul's loans to Iraq under the CCC program were a simple extension of the U.S. government's policy of promoting agricultural trade with Iraq. But there was more to these "agricultural loans" than met the eye. From 1985 through 1988, BNL-Atlanta became Iraq's favorite source of CCC-guaranteed loans, extending over $2 billion in credit to the Iraqi government.[6]

The CCC program whetted Drogoul's appetite for doing business with the Iraqis, in no small part because of the regular kickbacks he received for arranging the loans. These illicit funds were used for everything from renovating Drogoul's home in Atlanta, to renting a summer house for his family in Southampton, to paying his monthly Diner's Club and American Express bills. Drogoul set up an arrangement with Entrade, a Turkish trading company that handled much of BNL's agricultural trade with Iraq, in which it double-billed all of Drogoul's travel expenses to CCC-guaranteed loans. This allowed Drogoul and his coconspirator, Yavuz Tezeller, to divert at least $1 million to their own personal use. When the Iraqis made it clear that they wanted more loans than they could get under the CCC program alone, Drogoul was happy to comply.[7]

At the urging of Iraqi officials, in early 1987 Drogoul embarked on a much riskier scheme for financing Iraq. He began negotiating a series of unsecured, medium-term loans to the Iraqi government that were to total over $2 billion by April 1989. These loans had no government guarantees. Even worse, they were extended at a time when most other lenders were cutting back their exposure in Iraq because of Saddam Hussein's difficulties in paying back the $50 billion in debts he had run up during the war with Iran. The new loans might never be paid back, but from Drogoul's perspective, they had one obvious advantage: they dramatically increased his opportunities to skim funds off the top for himself.

Federal prosecutors have alleged that Drogoul did this all on his own, without the knowledge of government regulators or BNL executives in Rome or New York. The illegal medium-term loans were accounted for in a separate set of "gray books" that were kept on personal computers and in portable file boxes so that they could be moved out of the office whenever bank regulators came to visit. Drogoul and his associates at BNL-Atlanta even had a sense of humor about their scheme of double bookkeeping: they described unauthorized loans to Iraq, from which they were receiving lavish kickbacks, as

"Perugina," after the popular brand of Italian candy. Authorized loans, which presumably netted them no personal financial gain, were described as "non-Perugina."[8]

Given the importance of Drogoul's services as Iraq's personal banker, particularly during 1988 and 1989 when Saddam Hussein's regime was virtually shut out of the international market for medium-term financing, it is extremely unlikely that his activities could have gone unnoticed by other BNL executives or U.S. banking and intelligence authorities. Congressional investigations and criminal proceedings have uncovered evidence that U.S. government agencies knew what BNL-Atlanta was up to all along and chose to look the other way. Drogoul's assistant manager, Paul Von Wedel, claims that he informed an executive from BNL-Rome about BNL-Atlanta's medium-term loan agreements with Iraq during a 1988 encounter in Baghdad and sent him numerous follow-up memos. Von Wedel's memos on the subject to BNL-Rome are now in the possession of federal prosecutors in Atlanta, but no action has been taken against higher-ups in the bank thus far. Alan Friedman, the investigative journalist for the *Financial Times* of London who broke the story of BNL's illegal loans to Iraq, told producers for the Public Broadcasting System's "Frontline" program that the sheer size of the paper trail involved guaranteed that U.S. intelligence agencies would have had to be aware of what was going on.

> We're talking about letters of credit—2,500 of them—which flowed abundantly around Atlanta, Georgia, Baghdad, Iraq, and New York City. These letters of credit are not hard for the CIA and NSA [the U.S. government's National Security Agency] to track.[9]

On the same "Frontline" broadcast, former National Security Council official Norman Bailey backed up Friedman's point:

> NARRATOR: Dr. Norman Bailey created the National Security Council's program for tracing the movement of money worldwide. We asked him if there was any way the U.S. could have been ignorant of the BNL loans.
>
> NORMAN BAILEY: Well, no. I think it's entirely impossible that an operation of that size would have gone unnoticed by the headquarters of the bank itself, and also by the regulatory agencies in the United States.[10]

Finally, Judge Marvin Shoob, who heard the BNL case in Atlanta and knows more about what went on than anyone else outside the executive branch, has been emphatic in asserting that Drogoul could not have acted alone. He suggested in June 1992 that a special prosecutor might be the only way to get the whole truth about the case. But a House Judiciary Committee request for the appointment of a special prosecutor was turned down in August 1992, just a week before the Republican National Convention, allegedly on the grounds that it was a routine matter that could be handled by the Justice Department with no conflicts of interest. A second House request for an independent investigation of "Iraqgate" was rebuffed by Bush administration attorney general William Barr's handpicked investigator, former federal judge Frederick Lacey, in December 1992. Clinton administration attorney general Janet Reno has likewise opted to forgo a special prosecutor in the case, choosing instead to proceed with the narrow case against Drogoul that was put together by Bush appointees.

The Clinton administration has sent out mixed signals on the BNL case, prompting critics such as *New York Times* columnist William Safire to charge that there has been a continuing attempt to cover up the role of high-ranking U.S. and Italian government officials in the affair. In August 1993 John Hogan, a top aide to Janet Reno who was asked to review the BNL case, publicly reaffirmed the Bush administration's contention that Christopher Drogoul had acted on his own, without the knowledge of his superiors at BNL-Rome. Judge Shoob blasted Hogan's finding as "absurd," and argued that the personnel from BNL-Atlanta who had been charged in the case were merely "pawns or bit players in a far larger and wider-ranging conspiracy that involved BNL-Rome and possibly large American and foreign corporations and the governments of the United States, England, Italy, and Iraq." In September 1993, after Judge Shoob had recused himself from the case at the request of the government, Drogoul was allowed to plead guilty to reduced charges involving just three of the seventy counts of the original indictment against him.

But the BNL affair didn't end there. Ten days after Drogoul's guilty plea, Hogan announced that he would head up a new probe that would be "looking at various investigations and prosecutions around the country to see if there are common threads that reveal criminal activity in conjunction with how Iraq was armed." Shoob supported Hogan's initiative as a first step, but he argued that to really get to the bottom of the case "you still need an independent counsel, with the resources and time to fully investigate the issues." As if to prove Shoob's point about the need for an independent probe, Hogan's investigation quietly wound down over the summer of 1994 without holding a single U.S. government official accountable for the illegal financing of Iraq's military machine. In an attempt to justify the Justice Department's failure to get to the bottom of the BNL affair, a source involved in the investigation told the *American Banker* that "it's not a crime to make loans to Iraq." This perspective informed the January 1995 final report of the Justice Department's BNL Task Force, which made a narrow finding that no finished weapons systems had been supplied to Iraq and ignored the substantial contribution of U.S.-supplied dual-use technologies to the construction of the Iraqi war machine. The most interesting passage in the entire report came in the declassified annex, which revealed the CIA's continuing inability to keep track of its far-flung weapons trafficking operations: "In one instance, it took the CIA two months to identify the intended recipient country of weapons shipped at its request. Limitations on the CIA's ability to retrieve information preclude complete confidence that we have seen all relevant records." In contrast to the Justice Department's "see no evil" approach to the BNL scandal, an Italian parliamentary commission issued a report in January of 1994 asserting that government officials in Italy and the United States consciously used BNL as a mechanism for channeling military assistance to Iraq, and that "the political direction of the operation was always firmly based in Washington."[11]

However these allegations of a larger conspiracy are resolved, it is clear that the Bush administration's suggestion that it didn't realize what BNL-Atlanta was up to until the eve of the Gulf War doesn't hold up to scrutiny, particularly when one considers the types of technology transfers that were being financed by Drogoul's off-the-books operation.

Building up Saddam: Iraq's U.S. Procurement Network

One of the most amazing aspects of the BNL scandal was that not only was the bank financing Iraq out of its Atlanta branch, it was making deals for transfers of advanced military technology to Iraq from U.S.-based firms. Most of these exports were approved by the U.S. Department of Commerce. Even if U.S. authorities somehow managed to overlook the massive flow of BNL credits to Iraq, it's hard to believe that officials in the Commerce and State Departments, not to mention the Pentagon, could have missed the significance of Iraq's extensive purchases of militarily useful technology from U.S. firms.

The nerve center of Iraq's covert U.S.-based procurement network was the Solon, Ohio, facility of Matrix Churchill Corporation, a British-based machine tool company that was controlled by an Iraqi front company, the Technology Development Group (TDG) of London. TDG's chairman was Safa al Habobi, a member of Iraq's secret service and a high-ranking official in Iraq's Ministry of Industry and Military Industrialization. Habobi reported directly to Hussain Kamil, Saddam Hussein's son-in-law and the man in charge of Iraq's military buildup. Habobi, Matrix Churchill, and BNL-Atlanta were the three key players in Iraq's secretive effort to buy the best military production technology that U.S. industry had to offer: Habobi gave the orders about what equipment to go after, Matrix Churchill made the purchases from other U.S.-based companies, and BNL provided the financing.[12]

The close working relationship among Matrix Churchill, BNL, and their Iraqi overseers was illustrated by the extensive joint efforts that were undertaken to procure U.S. technology for the abortive Condor II missile project. The Condor was a combined Iraqi–Argentinian–Egyptian effort to develop a ballistic missile with a range of 500–1,000 kilometers. This strange partnership had been organized by Iraqi officials who offered to put up the financing for a longer-range version of Argentina's Condor I missile and then recruited Egyptian participation in an effort to obscure their own involvement. The new missile project had been initiated in 1984, but by 1988 the other two partners had pulled out of the deal and Iraq was proceeding on its own. The Condor was being developed at three separate sites within Iraq under the code name Project 395. The work was being supervised by the Iraqi Technical Corps for Special Projects, or TECO. Matrix Churchill served as the point of contact for all of TECO's U.S. purchases for the Condor project, and BNL provided loans to the supplying companies at favorable rates. In February 1992, U.S. House Banking Committee chairman Henry Gonzalez provided some insight into how brazenly the Iraqi procurement network operated inside the United States. Gonzalez released an August 1988 telex in which TECO ordered Matrix Churchill to set up appointments with over a dozen U.S.-based manufacturers to meet with an Iraqi procurement delegation that would be arriving in Washington later that week. The telex had a subject heading that said "Badush Project," the name of a dam that was then under construction in Iraq, but the involvement of TECO and a reference to "Project 395" made it clear that the Badush Dam was being used as a front for the purchase of equipment that would in fact be used in the construction of the Condor missile factories.

Based on shipping documents uncovered in his investigation, Congressman Gonzalez determined that over a dozen U.S. companies provided equipment to Iraq's Condor missile production sites through the efforts of Matrix Churchill, backed by BNL-Atlanta credits.[13]

Company and Location	Equipment Provided
Mack Truck, Pennsylvania	Tractors, trucks, and trailers
Lincoln Electric, Ohio	Welding machines and supplies
Rotec Industries, Illinois	Cement handling equipment
Hewlett Packard, California	Computer systems
EMCO Engineering, Massachusetts	Water treatment facility
IONICS, Massachusetts	Water demineralization plants and water pumping systems
Dresser Construction, Illinois	Construction equipment
Mundratech, Ltd., Illinois	Dump trucks
Caterpillar Tractor, Illinois	Tractors/earth movers
Grove Manufacturing, Pennsylvania	Truck-mounted cranes
Ingersoll Rand Co., New Jersey	Cement compacting machines
Liebherr-America, Virginia	Liebherr cement mixers on Mack truck chassis
Mannesmann Demag, Illinois	Heavy-construction equipment

Part of the difficulty in uncovering the Iraqi procurement efforts in the United States was evident from reviewing the list of equipment provided for the Condor project: it was mostly generic machinery that could have been used to build almost anything. And it is conceivable that many of the companies supplying the technology could have believed the cover story concocted by Matrix Churchill and the Iraqis, that it was all destined for a civilian dam. The Gulf War broke out before Saddam could finish the Condor project, so the missiles did not figure directly in the conflict. But there were plenty of other cases that weren't so innocent on their face, some of which contributed to weapons systems that were used directly against U.S. and allied troops in the Gulf War.

For example, XYZ Options of Tuscaloosa, Alabama, received a $14 million BNL-financed contract to build a plant that produced tungsten carbide machine tool bits for Iraq's Ministry of Industry and Military Industrialization. True to form for Iraq's clandestine procurement effort, XYZ was recruited by Matrix Churchill. XYZ president Bill Muscarella, a thirty-year veteran of the machine tool industry, was asked not only to send teams to Iraq to supervise construction of the plant but also to train Iraqi workers in Alabama. Muscarella's firm was

also asked to enter into direct contracts with over two dozen U.S. firms to purchase additional equipment needed for the project. In essence, XYZ was being used as a front for a front, to disguise the extent of Matrix Churchill's technology purchases in the United States.

Iraq claimed that the carbide tool bits would be used for the production of commercial trucks and truck engines, but Muscarella told journalist Kenneth Timmerman that the tools "could be used for just about anything, including weapons." The suspicion of military use deepened once one considered the destination of the items: the Huteen State Establishment. This sprawling complex to the south of Baghdad was an integral part of Hussein's arms production network, with facilities for manufacturing everything from cluster bombs to rocket propellant. Stephen Bryen, the former director of the Pentagon's Defense Technology Security Agency (DTSA), theorized that the Iraqis may have wanted XYZ to give them the capability to make their own tungsten carbide tool bits so that they could use them to make special artillery shells from depleted uranium. The shells, which are used by advanced tanks like the M-1, have greater armor-piercing capabilities than regular artillery shells. But the depleted uranium is very hard, and it requires extremely durable drill bits to mold it into shells.

Whatever the ultimate purpose of the carbide tool plant, its completion was cut short by the war. Ten XYZ employees were still in Iraq in August 1990 when Saddam Hussein invaded Kuwait, but they quickly fled the country.[14]

The most telling indication of how far the Bush administration's arms transfer and military technology policies had gone astray was an export that never made it to Iraq. In mid-1990, CONSARC, a New Jersey–based firm, received a license from the Commerce Department to provide "skull furnaces" to Iraq. The Iraqis claimed that they needed the high-temperature furnaces to make artificial limbs for wounded veterans of the Iran–Iraq war. Although the furnaces could be used for this purpose, they rarely were, and it seemed strange that Iraq would be seeking them nearly two years after the war with Iran had been concluded. Even the company had its doubts. In February 1989 CONSARC president Raymond Roberts warned a Commerce Department representative that the furnaces could be used in the production of nuclear weapons components. A week later another CONSARC official told Commerce Department engineer Alan Stoddard that the furnaces could be used in the production of atom bomb parts "without modification." Nonproliferation expert Gary Milhollin later described the CONSARC furnaces as the foundation for "a Cadillac production line for atomic bomb and ballistic missile parts, even better than the facilities at American nuclear weapons labs."[15]

Despite these warning signals, Stoddard and his colleagues at Commerce continued to encourage CONSARC to make the sale to Iraq, grasping at Saddam's claim that he planned to use these dangerous machines to make state-of-the-art artificial limbs. If it hadn't been for a timely political intervention from outside the Bush administration, the skull furnace sale would have gone through and Saddam Hussein's nuclear and missile programs would have been blessed with the best production line money could buy. In June 1990, Stephen Bryen received a tip about the pending deal from a reporter at the *Philadelphia Inquirer*. Bryen passed the information along to his former colleagues at the Pentagon's Defense Technology Security Agency (DTSA), who had never been informed of the proposed export by the Commerce Department despite its obvious strategic implications. DTSA chief William Rudman immediately dismissed the notion that "Saddam is so caring of his own people that they're all going to go around wearing high tech wooden legs" and declared that "the end use . . . is clearly nuclear." Commerce persisted in defending the sale even after Rudman's assistant tried to get the U.S. Customs Service to stop the export of the furnaces. It was only after this bureaucratic tug-of-war was written up in the *Philadelphia Inquirer*—and a bipartisan group of eight senators led by Republican Jesse Helms of North Carolina and Democrat Jeff Bingaman of New Mexico wrote to President Bush about it—that the Commerce Department's position was finally overturned by the National Security Council. The decision was made on July 19, 1992, just one day before the furnaces were set to leave the Port of Baltimore bound for Iraq and less than two weeks before Iraq's invasion of Kuwait.[16]

The CONSARC case underscores the pivotal role of the Commerce Department in deciding who should receive dual-use technology from U.S. companies. Dual-use items, such as advanced computers, machine tools, electronic components, and various measuring and testing devices, can be used for either military or civilian purposes. In theory, the Commerce Department is supposed to serve as the lead agency on the licensing of dual-use exports, seeking input from experts in the Pentagon, State Department, Department of Energy, and other federal agencies on cases that raise weapons proliferation concerns. But under the leadership of Bush's chief campaign fundraiser, Robert Mosbacher, promoting exports had become the top priority of the Commerce Department. Dennis Kloske, the head of the agency's Bureau of Export Administration, apparently took his cues from the top, pushing exports to Iraq based almost entirely on the expected economic return to U.S. companies, frequently neglecting to involve the Pentagon and other agencies in decisions about dual-use licenses. In the fall of 1990, after months of congressional pressure and scrutiny spearheaded by Congressman Douglas Barnard of Georgia, it was finally revealed just how misguided this approach had been. Between 1985 and 1990, the Commerce Department licensed 771 militarily useful technology exports to Iraq, worth $1.5 billion. Nearly half of this equipment had already been turned over to Iraq by the time President Bush imposed sanctions in August 1990.[17]

But Barnard and his colleagues didn't stop there. They wanted public disclosure of precisely what had been licensed for export to Iraq and which companies had been involved. Finally, after Barnard's subcommittee threatened to vote to force Commerce to release the information, the Bush administration relented and released a list of dual-use export licenses to Iraq in March 1990.

If the sheer volume of items licensed for sale to Iraq had been a shock, the list of what was cleared for export was even more devastating. Approved licenses included several for "computing equipment, electronic" for Saad 16, the notorious Iraqi missile production site; "navigation equipment" for the Iraqi air force; oscilloscopes for the Iraqi Council for Scientific Research, an agency that was a major participant in the development of the Iraqi war machine; "bacteria, fungi, and protozoa" for the Iraqi Atomic Energy Agency (raising the specter of possible use in development of biological weaponry); and "computing equipment" for the Ministry of Industry and Minerals. Since Iraq had no Ministry of Industry and Minerals, it was believed that this listing was a clumsy attempt to hide a transfer to the Ministry of Industry and Military Industrialization.

On page after page, the hefty list of approved licenses gave one example after another of exports with obvious military potential, either because of the technology being transferred or because the recipient agency was an active participant in the Iraqi military buildup. In an attempt to share the blame for this record of support for Iraqi military efforts, the Commerce Department released a chart along with the list of approved exports that implicated other executive branch agencies in the licensing fiasco. The chart demonstrated that more than half of the licenses that Commerce considered were also referred to the Department of Defense and that that agency approved the licenses it reviewed at a slightly higher rate than Commerce had approved the larger number of licenses that it considered (69 percent for Defense; 68 percent for Commerce). Commerce was taking great pains to demonstrate that to the extent that it approved militarily useful exports to Iraq, it was not simply out of blind bureaucratic support for exports at any cost but as part of a larger administration policy. There was a significant grain of truth in Commerce's position, as became evident in reviewing the role of the State Department, the CIA, and the Department of Justice in several cases in which items that could only have been for military use were blithely cleared for export to Iraq.[18]

One of the most damaging leaks of advanced U.S. arms technology to Iraq involved the supply of cluster bombs and the technology for producing them to Baghdad via the notorious Chilean arms dealer Carlos Cardoen. Cluster bombs are an advanced conventional explosive composed of scores of tiny "bomblets" that are capable of blanketing a large area with fire and shrapnel. They are a U.S.-designed weapon that was used to devastating effect by U.S. forces in Vietnam and by the Israeli air force during the 1982 invasion of Lebanon. Cardoen acquired his cluster bomb technology in an illicit partnership with James Guerin of International Signal and Control (see chapter 9).

According to Nasser Beydoun, a Lebanese-born arms dealer who serves as Cardoen's U.S. representative, Cardoen and Guerin cut a deal in early 1983 to "divide the world cluster bomb market in half," with Cardoen supplying Latin America and proscribed destinations like South Africa and Iraq, while Guerin targeted Asia and U.S. allies in the Middle East. As part of this deal, Guerin gave Cardoen the know-how to make the fuzes for cluster bombs, by far the most difficult component to produce. Both Beydoun and Guerin assert that the CIA was aware of the illegal transfer of U.S. cluster bomb technology to Iraq via Cardoen; they allege that the CIA "looked the other way" on the sales to Iraq because it had an interest in a covert operation that Guerin and Cardoen were helping out with, a scheme to transfer missile technology to South Africa—in violation of U.S. and UN sanctions against the apartheid regime—in exchange for military intelligence and cooperation from the South African regime. As a result, Cardoen was allowed to sell Iraq $400 million worth of cluster bombs and the technology to build its own cluster bomb factory without interference by any U.S. government agency. CIA officials tried to brush off the allegations of their complicity in the scheme when they were aired on a May 23, 1991, broadcast of ABC News "Nightline," but as host Ted Koppel pointed out, they never directly denied them.[19]

The CIA was not the only agency that should have done something about the illegal transfer of U.S. cluster bomb technology to Iraq. In 1986, Cardoen applied to the U.S. Patent Office for a patent on his own version of the cluster bomb, incorporating several modifications of the original U.S. design for the system. Although Chile was not allowed to receive U.S. cluster bombs at the time and the CIA and other government agencies were already well aware that Cardoen was the principal supplier of cluster bombs to Iraq, Cardoen's patent was approved with no questions asked. The final irony in this long tale of covert wheeling, dealing, and bureaucratic bumbling came in January 1991. The air forces of the anti-Iraq coalition were given the Saad 38 factory south of Baghdad as one of their first targets, because the plant was producing U.S.-style cluster bombs with the technology that had been supplied to Iraq by the Guerin/Cardoen/South African alliance—all with a nod and a wink from U.S. intelligence agencies.[20]

Another gaping "oversight" that allowed advanced U.S.-designed military systems to flow into Iraq by way of intermediary firms in South Africa, Austria, and China was the U.S. government's lax treatment of Canadian-born artillery specialist Gerald V. Bull. As noted in chapter 9, at strategic points in his career Bull received assistance from the Pentagon, the State Department, and the CIA. This history of support for Bull began to backfire in 1987 when the Chinese government moved to sell some of its Bull-designed howitzers to Iraq. This wasn't the only example of how the U.S. government's on-again, off-again relationship with Gerald Bull redounded to the detriment of U.S. security. In the mid-1980s, Iraq also received one hundred of Bull's "G-5" long-range 155mm guns from South Africa. South Africa's state-run armaments agency, ARMSCOR, had received the technology for building the guns from Bull in the late 1970s, with the knowledge and support of the CIA. Rounding out Saddam Hussein's collection of Bull-designed guns, Iraq purchased a few hundred more from the Austrian firm of Voest-Alpine in 1981, with the acquiescence of U.S. embassy officials who were aware of the transfer and gave it their tacit support as long as the Austrians agreed to cut off transfers of similar guns to Iran.[21]

In the case of Iraq, the long-term consequences of the policy of turning a blind eye to the operations of international arms merchants like Bull were nearly disastrous. Bull's most ambitious Iraqi project—a "supergun" with the capability to send warheads thousands of miles—was ultimately stopped not by any action on the part of U.S. enforcement authorities but by an assassin's bullet that ended Bull's life in March 1990 (most probably fired by someone in the employ of Israeli intelligence). Even without the supergun, Bull's U.S.-designed technology gave Iraqi forces some of the most capable and far-ranging artillery pieces in the world.[22]

When he became aware of the full history of U.S. government acquiescence in Bull's illicit arms trading, Congressman Howard Wolpe of Michigan was angered:

> The bottom line here is that because we have been so lax in our enforcement of American laws we are now finding American-made technology in the hands of the Iraqi forces that are pointing their cannons at American soldiers. That's outrageous.[23]

One final example of U.S. government complicity in the arming of Saddam Hussein is the strange case of Sarkis Soghanalian, who for years operated as an arms dealer for Iraq out of the Miami airport. Soghanalian has historic ties to the CIA, serving as a contract agent and middleman in deals to arm such Cold War U.S. allies as Anastasio Somoza of Nicaragua and Ferdinand Marcos of the Philippines. Soghanalian's U.S.-based arms deals with Iraq included brokering a proposed sale of Romanian-produced uniforms to the Iraqi army and exporting twenty-six Hughes MD-50 helicopters, which were sold as "civilian" aircraft and then armed with machine guns once they reached Iraq. His partners in these two deals were former Nixon administration attorney general John Mitchell (now deceased), former Nixon vice president Spiro Agnew, and former Nixon military aide Col. Jack Brennan, who later went on to take a job in the Bush White House.

Mitchell, Agnew, and Brennan worked with Soghanalian through the Washington office of their firm, Global Research International. They even enlisted Nixon's assistance in the proposed uniform sale, in the form of a personal letter from the former president to his old friend Romanian dictator Nicolae Ceau escu. Nixon's letter vouched for the "integrity" of Mitchell and his company and urged Ceau escu to help them consummate the $181 million deal that would provide Romanian-produced uniforms to the Iraqi armed forces.[24]

The sheer volume of U.S. military technology transfers to Iraq during the period leading up to the Gulf War—from machine tools and computers to howitzers and cluster bombs—was simply too extensive and well known to pertinent U.S. government agencies to be explained away as a result of "oversights," "bureaucratic infighting," or the exploitation of "loopholes" in the export laws, as the Bush administration attempted to do. Perhaps the most damning evidence of all that the arming of Iraq was a conscious policy of the Reagan and Bush administrations was the role of key administration personnel in lobbying for U.S. government credits to Iraq long after the end of the

Iran–Iraq war, and long after it was clear that Saddam Hussein was using these credits to buy military technology.

The Credits

As noted above, U.S. financing was at least as important to Saddam Hussein's military complex as was U.S. technology, and many of the loans were U.S.-government guaranteed. The Reagan administration's initial logic for providing credits to Iraq was set out in an October 31, 1983, State Department cable that was unearthed by congressional investigators working with Congressman Henry Gonzalez:

> In considering ways to build international confidence in Iraq's economic and financial future we should give serious thought to offering Eximbank [Export-Import Bank of the United States] credits. New U.S. credits in combination with our CCC credits would demonstrate U.S. confidence in the Iraqi economy. This in turn would encourage other countries to provide similar assistance. Such concrete demonstrations of support could ease pressure on Iraq.[25]

The CCC program, an agricultural loan guarantee program that was virtually unknown among most members of Congress, much less the public, was an even more convenient route than the Eximbank for funneling first hundreds of millions and then billions of dollars in U.S. support to Saddam Hussein's regime. Iraq became eligible for the program in 1983 after the Reagan administration removed it from the list of terrorist-supporting nations, despite evidence of ongoing Iraqi support for terrorist organizations. The United States immediately provided $364 million in CCC credits to Baghdad, in the hopes of staving off food riots against Saddam Hussein's government stemming from the shortages induced by his ongoing war with Iran. Iraq quickly grew to become the largest recipient of CCC guarantees, garnering 20 percent of all guarantees granted under the program between 1984 and 1989. Henry Gonzalez pointed out that the Reagan and Bush administrations had basically "used the CCC program for Iraq as a back door means of achieving its foreign policy agenda."[26]

The CCC credits, which reached $5.5 billion by 1989, were extremely valuable to Iraq because they freed up scarce hard currency, which could then be devoted instead to Saddam's relentless military buildup. This was no small matter, particularly from 1988 through 1990, when Iraq's flow of aid from the Gulf sheikdoms that had helped finance its war with Iran began to dry up. During this period, while Hussein's debt-ridden economy was shut out of private markets for anything but limited and costly short-term credits, the CCC program gave the Iraqi dictator some critical breathing space that he used to bolster his military forces and plot his next move. But it did much more than that.

As CNN investigative reporter Mark Feldstein has revealed, during the last few years of the Iran–Iraq war, Iraqi trade officials routinely asked for kickbacks on agricultural contracts financed under the CCC program. American corporations were pressed "to throw in free trucks, cranes, cash, and military supplies in exchange for multimillion dollar contracts for rice, grains and other products." These extra items—euphemistically referred to as "after sales services" by participants in the CCC program—included military spare parts, tires for military vehicles, and even trucks and cranes that may have been used in the launching of Iraqi Scud missiles during the Gulf War. There were even some reports that grain purchased by the Iraqis was delivered instead to Eastern Europe, where it was bartered for arms that were sent on to Baghdad. The Agriculture Department's approach was so lax, anything seemed possible—no participant in the entire history of the CCC program had ever been barred from the program for breaking the rules. A USDA bureaucrat shrugged off the problem, asserting that "if someone wants to commit fraud, [he's] going to do it." North Carolina Congressman Charlie Rose argued that the CCC fiasco was a direct outgrowth of the tilt toward Iraq:

> I think our government wanted to be good to Saddam Hussein and to help him as quietly as they could. They didn't want to *directly* ship military systems to Iraq [emphasis added]. They didn't want to excite Israel. They didn't want to directly offer foreign aid or military sales credit. So they told USDA to be as generous as [it could] with agricultural credits.[27]

Iraqi officials clearly understood that the CCC credits were a political favor from the Bush administration to the regime of Saddam Hussein, not a carefully considered commercial decision. When a USDA official asked Iraqi agriculture minister Hassan Ali for an accounting of Iraq's finances in January 1985, Ali refused to do so. Ali implied that the credits would keep flowing regardless of whether Iraq was a responsible borrower: "The U.S. did not make such credit available because of Iraq's 'lovely brown eyes.'"[28]

Not everyone in the U.S. government was sold on the idea of providing unlimited credit to Saddam Hussein. There were serious doubts about Iraq's ability or willingness to repay the loans, particularly on the part of analysts at the Export-Import Bank, which had entered into $300 million in credits with Iraq between 1984 and 1989. In 1986 and 1987, Eximbank had suspended Iraq from receiving further loans altogether because of its late repayment of existing credits. Between 1986 and 1989, Eximbank's country risk analyses for Iraq repeatedly cited the ways in which Iraqi officials manipulated foreign credits to meet spending targets for "advanced military technologies," including chemical and biological warfare agents and nuclear weapons projects. Eximbank's wariness was unfortunately not shared by officials at the White House or the State Department, who repeatedly moved to override their concerns. George Bush was a central figure in the campaign to pressure Eximbank to put aside its doubts.[29]

Bush's first intervention with Eximbank officials on Iraq's behalf came in 1984, in connection with a $484 million loan for the Bechtel Corporation to build an underground pipeline from the Iraqi oil fields to the Jordanian port of Aqaba. Eximbank analysts had opposed the loan on the grounds that "there would not be reasonable assurance of repayment for any medium-term and long-term transactions" given the state of Iraq's war-ravaged economy. At the urging of the State Department, which saw Eximbank credits in general and the pipeline project in particular as important tools in the strategy of bolstering Iraq in its war with Iran, Bush called Eximbank chairman William Draper. According to the "talking points" that were prepared for the call, Bush argued that "Eximbank could play a crucial role in our efforts in the region. Early and favorable action on applications would be clear and very welcome evidence of U.S. commitment to these objectives." Shortly after Bush's call, the Eximbank board ignored the assessment of its own financial experts and approved the credits for the pipeline project. The project was later shelved by the Iraqis, but the pattern of George Bush coming to Iraq's rescue whenever it got into trouble with Eximbank had been set.[30]

In February 1987, Iraq was seeking a $200 million short-term credit from Eximbank, although it had been suspended for nonpayment of its outstanding Eximbank loans for over a year at that point. Bush called the new Eximbank chairman, John Bohn, and made the case that new loans for Iraq would send an important signal of U.S. support to Saddam Hussein's regime. Bohn buckled under Bush's pressure, and the loan was made, again despite grave reservations from Eximbank's own analysts. Bush went on to dutifully report his actions to Iraqi ambassador Nizar Hamdoon. Talking points prepared for a March 2, 1987, meeting between the two men urged Bush to play up his successful lobbying of the Eximbank chairman and to sympathize with Iraq's concerns over the Pentagon's attempts to hold up licenses for high-tech exports to Iraq. On the licensing issue, Bush was instructed to tell Hamdoon about upcoming revisions in licensing procedures that would make it easier to buy dual-use items from U.S. firms. "In the meantime," the memo continued, "we can point to progress on a few specific cases. After extensive discussions with State and DOD [the Department of Defense], Commerce has issued long-pending licenses for two high priority scientific projects, including one at the Iraqi Space and Astronomical Research Center."

Bush's efforts on Iraq's behalf came back to haunt the United States later, as the export credits he lobbied so vigorously for contributed to the Iraqi war effort. Adding insult to injury, Iraq never repaid the $200 million in credits, sticking the U.S. taxpayers with the bill—just as the Eximbank experts had predicted.[31]

But Bush saved his most decisive efforts on Iraq's behalf for the fall of 1989, during his first year as president. Although the Iran–Iraq war had ended over a year earlier, the State Department was proceeding full-speed ahead with its policy of trying to win over Saddam Hussein by plying him with credits and military technology. But an August 4, 1989, FBI raid on the BNL-Atlanta office put a crimp in the State Department's strategy. There was now no denying that illicit loans and military technology were flowing to Iraq from U.S. sources and that some of this activity had been supported by U.S.-government-guaranteed loans. Despite this evidence, and although officials at Eximbank, the Federal Reserve, and the Office of Management and Budget (OMB) all felt that Iraq was a bad credit risk, Iraq's "Republican guards" at the State Department continued to lobby vigorously for $1 billion in new CCC credits to Iraq. At an October 4, 1989, meeting of the National Advisory Council, an interagency council that makes policy decisions on U.S. credit programs, agreement was finally reached on a compromise that would have offered $400 million in credits to Iraq for the year to come.[32]

State Department representatives tried to make light of the concerns of its fellow agencies with respect to Iraq's creditworthiness, complaining that the Office of Management and Budget was "taking its role as a 'watchdog against scandal'" too seriously! Iraqi officials rejected the $400 million offer as "insultingly low," and Iraqi foreign minister Tariq Aziz pressed U.S. secretary of state James Baker to seek a reversal of the decision. One of Baker's State Department aides urged him to overlook the BNL scandal even though it "may involve several high Iraqi officials." The aide instead pointed out that "Iraq is now our ninth largest customer for agricultural commodities. . . . Our ability to influence Iraqi policies in areas important to us, from Lebanon to the Middle East peace process, will be heavily influenced by the CCC negotiations."[33]

Baker took his assistant's advice to heart, but first he got a giant boost from his boss, George Bush. During that same month of October 1989, Bush signed National Security Directive 26 (NSD-26), which called for "pursuit of improved economic and political ties with Iraq." Baker made reference to these new marching orders in a phone call to Agriculture Secretary Clayton Yeutter in which he pressed him to increase Iraq's CCC credits to $1 billion. Deputy Secretary of State Lawrence Eagleburger played the same card in memos to OMB and the Treasury Department, arguing that "the CCC program is important to our efforts to improve and expand our relationship with Iraq, as ordered by the President in NSD-26."[34]

The combined efforts of Baker and Bush paid off. At its November 8, 1989, meeting, the National Advisory Council reversed its position on CCC credits and approved the full $1 billion that Iraq was seeking. However, according to a confidential memo on the meeting that was uncovered by Congressman Gonzales and his investigators, Treasury Department, Federal Reserve, and OMB representatives were still wary of the move. One official worried that "allegations of Iraqi wrongdoing in the BNL case, though not backed by evidence at this time, could eventually embarrass the administration." As for their concerns about Iraq's creditworthiness, they, too, proved prophetic: Hussein ultimately reneged on $2 billion in CCC loans, which had to be paid off by the U.S. taxpayer.[35]

This wasn't the end of the extraordinary administration campaign to finance and provision Saddam Hussein's regime, come hell or high water. In November 1989, Congress passed legislation imposing sanctions on Iraq for its human rights abuses against its own citizens. The law specifically prohibited further Eximbank financing to Baghdad unless there was a presidential waiver. The State Department quickly wrote up just such a waiver for Bush's signature, and on January 17, 1990, Bush cleared Eximbank credits for Iraq on the grounds that they were "in the national interest of the United States." Bush continued to block congressional attempts to impose meaningful sanctions on Iraq right up until the eve of Hussein's August 2, 1990, invasion of Kuwait.[36]

The Cover-up

Henry B. Gonzalez of Texas is a congressman from the old school. The seventy-six-year-old House banking committee chairman lacks the blow-dried, made-for-TV look of his fellow members who came to Congress in the wake of the Watergate scandal. But he retains a firm belief in the role of the legislative branch as a check on abuses of executive power, which has outlasted the ephemeral commitments to reform and accountability espoused by many of his younger colleagues. It is because of Gonzalez's determination to get to the bottom of the BNL scandal that the Reagan/Bush policy of providing Iraq with financial, technological, and intelligence aid during the 1980s finally saw the light of public debate and discussion. One of the most intriguing findings of Gonzalez's three-year investigation was the revelation of the lengths to which members of the Bush administration were willing to go to cover up their aid to Iraq's military machine.

If it had been up to the Bush administration, Henry Gonzalez wouldn't have held hearings on the BNL scandal in the first place. When Gonzalez first announced his intention to look into the matter in the fall of 1990, he received a letter from Bush's attorney general, Dick Thornburgh, urging him to call off the hearings because "this is a sensitive case with national security concerns." Thornburgh also argued that a decision by Gonzalez to proceed with interviews of individuals and witnesses involved in the BNL investigation would "significantly diminish the Department's ability to prosecute this matter." Gonzalez fired back a letter underscoring his committee's legitimate investigative interest in the case and asserting that the Justice Department had offered no credible proof that his proposed hearings would in any way jeopardize the BNL prosecution.[37]

In fact, as Gonzalez discovered almost two years later, it was the White House, the State Department, and the Justice Department in Washington that were the principal impediments to the BNL prosecution, not the congressional inquiry into the affair. One of the most tantalizing bits of evidence involved the Justice Department's attempt to hide its original plan to hand down an indictment in February 1990, not February 1991. After months of wrangling with federal agencies over pertinent documents, banking committee investigators uncovered a January 9, 1990, letter to officials of the Federal Reserve Bank from Robert Barr, the U.S. attorney from Atlanta, and Gale McKenzie, the chief prosecutor on the BNL case. The letter referred to assistance they would need from Federal Reserve personnel "prior to an indictment early next month." This section had been blacked out in the original version supplied to Gonzalez, allegedly on national security grounds.[38]

Gonzalez got a fairly good indication why the BNL indictment was delayed. He found documentation of a phone call from a staff member of White House counsel Boyden Gray to BNL prosecutor McKenzie in which he informed her that it was a "potentially embarrassing case" for the president. Shortly after this call was placed, Justice Department officials in Washington, working in consultation with the State Department, moved to deny the Atlanta-based BNL investigators funds they needed for traveling to Europe and the Middle East to interview key witnesses in the case. Banking committee staffers also turned up a copy of an April 1990 memo by a Federal Reserve investigator familiar with the case that referred to perceptions among law enforcement officials that the BNL case had been hampered by "interference from the Justice Department in Washington."[39]

Executive branch interference in the BNL case didn't stop there. In February 1991, shortly before the Justice Department's indictment in the case was finally handed down, State Department officials moved to limit its scope. In a series of memos to Justice Department staffers, State Department officials attempted to protect both the Central Bank of Iraq and Wafaj Dajani, an influential Jordanian with close ties to King Hussein. Justice Department investigators had been adamant about the need to indict Iraq's Central Bank, because it held $1 billion in U.S. assets that could be seized for fines. But they yielded to State Department arguments that indicting the Central Bank would "set a bad precedent" by exposing U.S. government agencies to similar suits on the part of foreign law enforcement authorities. As for Mr. Dajani, officials at State pointed out that his brother was a former minister of the interior in Jordan and that "Wafaj himself is considered well connected to the King and to U.S. grain exporters." The memo went on to note that "his indictment would be seen as a further U.S. attempt to 'punish' Jordan" for its support of Iraq during the Gulf War. A few days after State raised these points, the Central Bank of Iraq and Wafaj Dajani were removed from the indictment and listed instead as "unindicted co-conspirators."[40]

This delay and manipulation of the BNL indictment was part of a larger pattern of activities designed to keep the Reagan and Bush administrations' true role in creating Saddam Hussein's arsenal from the public and the Congress. One of the most audacious aspects of the cover-up was the submission of a doctored list of export licenses to the Congress. A report by the Commerce Department's own inspector general indicated that at least sixty-eight of the licenses for technology transfers to Iraq that were disclosed to Congress had the designation "military truck" removed before the report was sent to Capitol Hill. And while Commerce officials tried to blame the changes on former undersecretary of commerce for export administration Dennis Kloske, Henry Gonzalez unearthed several memos indicating that the changes were overseen directly by officials in the president's National Security Council. Gonzalez immediately understood why the NSC took such a strong interest in this list of export licenses:

> Given that the NSC was instrumental in setting export policy toward Iraq, it had a strong political motive to mislead the Congress as to the military nature of goods sent to Iraq. It did not want the public to know that the White House had provided aid to the Iraqi war machine.[41]

In perhaps his most interesting discovery of all, Gonzalez found direct evidence of how the Bush administration organized a comprehensive effort to cover up its financing and military technology assistance to Saddam Hussein, under the direction of Nicholas Rostow, the general counsel to the National Security Council. The "Rostow gang," as Gonzalez called it, consisted of lawyers from NSC, along with the Departments of Justice, Defense, State, Treasury, Commerce, Agriculture, and Energy and the CIA. The team of administration lawyers adopted a three-pronged strategy to obstruct congressional investigators: (1) review all document requests at the outset to determine which ones can be denied on grounds of "executive privilege"; (2) whenever possible, offer an oral briefing to members of Congress or their staffs rather than providing actual documents; and (3) if documents must be shown to members of Congress, attempt to limit access by permitting documents to be viewed but not copied; and try to stamp any notes taken during the viewing as classified. When all else failed, the lawyers were to pass along only those documents specifically requested by congressional investigators, preferably in the form of limited summaries of the original.

Gonzalez described how the process worked in the case of the doctored list of Commerce Department export licenses. Internal department memos indicated that they were supplying "a summary reference document" that had been cleared with the "fifth floor"—Secretary Mosbacher's office—not the full licensing list. It was further noted that Commerce personnel were following "guidance and requests from the State Department and the National Security Council . . . that no additional information be provided that does not directly access the committee's request." Gonzalez charged that this manipulation of the data supplied to Congress was designed to hide "the true responsibility for the transfer of United States technology to the Iraqi war machine," which lies "with the White House and the State Department, because they set technology transfer policy. . . . They need[ed] U.S. high technology transfer as an inducement to gain favor with Saddam Hussein." According to Gonzalez, the cover-up mechanism was devised by the White House and the National Security Council for one simple purpose: "to mislead the Congress and the public . . . about the military nature of the transfers to Iraq."[42]

The final issue raised by the Gonzalez investigation was the remarkable extent to which conflicts of interest played a role in shaping Bush administration policy toward credits and technology transfer to Iraq. When he worked for Kissinger Associates, Bush national security adviser Brent Scowcroft had Banca Nazionale del Lavoro as one of his clients—he even briefed the BNL board in Rome for a fee during his tenure with Kissinger. Deputy Secretary of State Lawrence Eagleburger, another Kissinger Associates alumni, was instrumental in getting the Yugoslavian bank LBS set up to do business in the United States; LBS had significant financial ties to BNL. In fact, on August 8, 1990, Bush granted special "conflict of interest waivers" for eleven cabinet-level officials involved in making policy relating to the Gulf War, including his chief of staff, John Sununu, and the heads of the departments of Defense, State, Commerce, Agriculture, and Energy and the CIA. Bush noted that a number of these top aides had "quite substantial interests in industries that might be affected . . . by the resolution of situations that may arise" out of the Gulf conflict.[43]

Far from learning its lesson from the consequences of dual-use exports to Iraq, during 1991 and 1992 the Bush administration proceeded to use a similar strategy in providing militarily useful technology to Syria and Iran, with a similar aim of exerting influence that had originally prompted administration officials to open the technology spigots for Saddam Hussein. A policy shift initiated in the fall of 1991, after the Gulf War, allowed sales of sensitive items such as computer-controlled machine tools and sophisticated measurement devices that can be used in the development of missile guidance systems to Iran and Syria on a case-by-case basis, as long as "assurances" were provided that the materials were being used for civilian projects. Of course, Saddam Hussein had provided similar assurances when he claimed that equipment for the Condor missile program was intended for the "Badush dam" project.[44]

The fruits of the U.S. government's latest foray into trading arms technology for influence remain to be seen. In 1991 alone, Iran received $60 million in militarily useful exports as a result of this shift.[45] A year later, in the fall of 1992, the Bush administration reversed field and began urging its allies to restrict certain high-tech exports to Iran on the grounds that it had aggressive plans to become a dominant military force in the Persian Gulf. But, as with the on-again, off-again position on limiting military transfers to Iraq, Bush officials seemed to be pursuing an ad hoc policy: because Iran was being elevated to the status of the new U.S. "enemy" in the region, the United States wanted its allies to abruptly cut back high-tech trade with Iran. But the administration's political zigzagging did not appear to be grounded in any larger overall effort at limiting the transfer of technologies that pose proliferation risks to a broader range of countries, not just the designated U.S. enemy of the moment. What is clear from the experience with Iraq is that U.S. government officials learned next to nothing from their disastrous role in building up Saddam Hussein's arsenal and that it is entirely possible that they will make the same mistakes again with other aggressive regional powers.

The bureaucratic conflicts between the potential economic benefits and the possible security risks posed by dual-use exports appear to have carried over from the Bush administration into the Clinton era. On the one hand, the new administration is seriously concerned about the possible spread of weapons of mass destruction, as evidenced by the shuttle diplomacy engaged in by Pentagon and State Department officials to press for an end to nuclear deployments and programs in Ukraine and North Korea. A logical outgrowth of this concern should be a tighter rein on technology exports, but in September 1993 the Clinton administration announced a new export promotion plan that would allow dual-use items to go to most destinations without a license. This announcement was followed in April 1994 by a move to terminate the Coordinating Committee for Multilateral Strategic Export Controls (COCOM), a Cold War era regime designed to keep Western military technology out of the hands of Soviet, East European, and Chinese military industries. Pointing to the possibility that these relaxed rules could spur an accelerated third-party trade through Eastern Europe to Third World nations seeking to build nuclear weapons, nonproliferation expert Gary Milhollin asserted that "they have not learned from Iraq."[46]

12

Selling Out: The Korean Connection and the New Dynamics of the Arms Trade

The arming of Iraq was carried out using back-door methods and secretive channels precisely because Reagan and Bush administration officials knew that it would cause a domestic political uproar if the policy was made public. Yet for nearly twenty-five years, stretching back to the earliest days of the Nixon Doctrine, U.S. weapons manufacturers have been openly and aggressively marketing arms production know-how to dozens of other Third World regimes through licensing and coproduction agreements. These arrangements can involve anything from fabricating components of a U.S. weapon in the purchasing nation to providing the technical data and equipment needed to build a complete system. This wholesale transfer of weapons production capabilities to nations such as South Korea, Taiwan, Egypt, and Indonesia has become a routine practice, provoking little of the public debate or scrutiny that was generated by the revelations of military technology shipments to Iraq.[1]

Government policymakers have traditionally rationalized this dangerous shift from the proliferation of individual weapons systems to the proliferation of entire weapons production complexes on the grounds that it has served to strengthen key anticommunist allies. This argument may have had some superficial plausibility during the Cold War. But in a post–Cold War environment where stemming the proliferation of armaments should be the number one priority of U.S. policymakers, continuing to sell production technology as a means of "closing the deal" with Third World buyers is tantamount to selling out long-term U.S. security interests for short-term gains.

Arms manufacturers have a familiar rationale for selling arms-making capabilities to Third World nations, the same one they cite for selling arms in the first place: if they don't do it, they will simply lose market share to British, French, or German firms that are more than willing to do so. But even from the perspective of the U.S. arms industry's ultimate interests, it makes little sense to spread the techniques for building top-of-the-line weapons systems to every corner of the globe. The willingness of U.S. military firms to sell production technology to nations that could become competitors five or ten years down the road is just one more indication of how desperate such firms are to make foreign sales to boost their flagging profit margins during the post–Cold War Pentagon spending crunch. The question is whether the U.S. government will continue to facilitate and subsidize these questionable arrangements now that they are so clearly contrary to the national interest.

In addition to the issues of proliferation and economic competitiveness that are at stake, coproduction and the related practice of providing industrial "offsets" to arms customers have opened up new possibilities for corruption and influence peddling in foreign weapons sales on a scale not seen since the bribery scandals of the mid-1970s. Offsets basically represent a pledge by the exporting firm to help "offset" the cost of the sale by steering business to firms in the purchasing nation. Offsets are part of an all-encompassing concept that includes anything from a deal to produce certain weapons components in the purchasing country (coproduction), to providing the blueprints for another nation to produce a U.S.-designed system (licensing), to entering into agreements to make specified commercial investments in the purchasing country (indirect offsets). The offset commitment is a technique for channeling some of the billions of dollars spent on the purchase of a major system like an F-16 fighter or an M-1 tank back into the economy of the recipient country. Depending on who gets the offset business, it can also be an extremely effective way to disguise improper lobbying expenses and outright bribes.

Perhaps nowhere is the volatile mix of economic and security issues raised by the issue of coproduction and offsets more vividly illustrated than in the arms sales relationship between the United States and South Korea. The alliance is a microcosm of the new dynamics of the arms trade, an indicator of how much it has changed—and how much it has remained the same—since Richard Nixon and Henry Kissinger helped inaugurate the worldwide weapons export boom twenty-five years ago.

The Korean Connection and the Rise of Coproduction and Licensing

The U.S.–South Korean alliance is firmly rooted in the logic of the Cold War. The U.S. intervention on the side of the South during the Korean War was the most visible example of the post–World War II strategy of containment of communism. Beyond that, U.S. mobilization for that conflict did more than any other single event to revive a large and permanent military-industrial complex in the United States after the substantial cutbacks that were implemented in the first few years after World War II. The South Korean regime continued to play a pivotal role in U.S. security strategy in Southeast Asia after the Korean War by providing bases for U.S. troops, sending Korean forces to fight alongside U.S. forces in Vietnam, and serving as one of the most visible beneficiaries of the Nixon Doctrine's policy of stepping up U.S. arms transfers to anticommunist allies.[2]

While it has clearly shaped U.S. military planning and strategy, the U.S.–Korean defense relationship has had an even more profound impact on Korean society. Forty years after the Korean War, there are still forty thousand U.S. troops and scores of U.S. military bases in South Korea, and U.S. involvement in Korea's internal affairs has been a focal point for periodic mass protests since the late 1970s. In addition to its direct political support for a series of authoritarian governments, the United States has been instrumental in fostering a powerful military-industrial complex in Korea that has served as an impediment to democratic reform.

From the Korean War through the end of the 1960s, Korea's defense requirements were met through a combination of a heavy U.S. troop presence and ample quantities of second-hand military equipment provided free of charge under U.S. aid programs. Korea's own military industry didn't really get off the ground until the late 1960s with the enunciation of the Nixon Doctrine, which called for U.S. regional allies to promote U.S. military objectives with more arms assistance and less reliance on U.S. troops. Because of its direct assistance to the U.S. war effort in Vietnam and its long-standing importance to the U.S. containment strategy in Asia, Korea was a favored recipient of the U.S. military aid and technology that accompanied the Nixon Doctrine.[3]

This new U.S. strategy neatly coincided with the wishes of South Korean dictator Park Chung Hee and his successors to develop a degree of self-sufficiency in weapons production as a counterweight to North Korea's Soviet-supported military buildup. Beginning in the early 1970s, South Korean industry received approval to produce all or part of more than two dozen U.S.-designed weapons, from machine guns and ammunition to fighter aircraft and surface-to-surface missiles. By the 1980s, Korea had parlayed this imported expertise into a position as a significant producer of armaments, both for its own forces and for export. In its peak sales year, 1982, Korea racked up close to $1 billion in foreign arms sales, ranking it fifth among Third World arms exporting nations.[4] But the success of the Korean military industry masked underlying tensions with the United States over how the Seoul regime was putting its U.S.-supplied technology to work. One of the most serious problems arose with the first U.S. system that Korea produced under license: the M-16 rifle.

The M-16 affair demonstrates how easily U.S. control of arms making technology can be lost once the equipment has been transferred to another nation. In theory, the 1971 arrangement providing Korea with a complete factory to build Colt Industries M-16 rifles contained strict controls. South Korea agreed to observe specific limits, both on the total number of rifles it would produce and on sales of Korean-built M-16s to third countries—no sales were to be made to other countries without explicit U.S. approval.

Total Korean M-16 production was originally fixed at six hundred thousand rifles, but by the mid-1980s it was clear that Korea had exceeded those levels and was selling the rifle to foreign buyers without the required approval. This state of affairs was not discovered by an official of the U.S. government but rather revealed by a Colt Industries executive who witnessed Korean marketing efforts for the M-16 in Singapore and complained that Colt was being cheated out of its $7-per-rifle royalty payment. The violation of the agreement coincided with the Korean government's transfer of the M-16 factory to a private firm, Daewoo Precision Industries, a company that now figures prominently in Korean efforts to coproduce U.S. fighter aircraft.

The M-16 affair raised serious questions about the U.S. government's commitment to monitoring the uses recipient nations make of U.S.-supplied arms technology. Both the Pentagon and the State Department told investigators from the General Accounting Office that it wasn't their job to monitor overproduction or third-country sales of the M-16. In fact, it appeared that no one in the U.S. government was keeping tabs on the rifle factory. As a result, Korea was able to make illegal exports of M-16s for over four years without being detected. Colt Industries officials estimate that South Korea may have illegally produced between 140,000 and 300,000 M-16s for export, enough to outfit several small armies.[5] During a May 1988 hearing on the matter, Republican Congressman Larry Hopkins of Kentucky blasted both South Korea and the U.S. government for their roles in the fiasco, in terms resembling later criticisms of the U.S. role in arming Iraq:

> This ally has not only ripped up and ignored the agreement allowing them to build this weapon, but it is now beating us over the head with it in the world marketplace. . . . We are not dealing with sewing machines or sides of beef; we are dealing with military weapons which can turn the balance of power in certain regions and could end up being used against American citizens.[6]

Hopkins's warning went largely unheeded. A year later, a General Accounting Office review of U.S. coproduction programs found that out of eighteen projects surveyed, nearly one-third had experienced unauthorized transfers of U.S.-designed weapons or weapons components to third countries.[7] And as another South Korean example was to make painfully clear, these illicit transfers could involve far more than rifles.

Korea's pursuit of ballistic missiles shows how hard it is to put the genie back in the bottle once the United States has transferred military technology to a regime that is determined to put it to its own uses. During the 1970s, one of Korean dictator Park Chung Hee's top priorities was to develop a ballistic missile that could reach the North Korean capital of Pyongyang. When Korea tested its first surface-to-surface missile in 1978, it was a modified version of the U.S. Nike Hercules, a system that Korea's Agency for Defense Development had become intimately familiar with as a result of a maintenance contract it had entered into with the United States back in 1972.

The Carter administration issued several diplomatic protests over this clear misappropriation of U.S. technology, but administration policymakers ultimately decided not to punish Korea. Instead, they decided to *upgrade* the technology of the U.S.-made Nike and Honest John missiles already in Korea's inventory, under the dubious theory that access to this additional technology would convince Korea to put aside its drive to develop its own long-range missiles. Missile proliferation expert Janne Nolan has argued that the technology upgrade not only "proved of benefit to Korean military industry" but, "left to its own resources, Korea might have failed in its indigenous effort." Instead, with U.S. help, Korea was able to develop the basis for what one expert has described as a "fine tactical nuclear weapon."[8]

The most significant U.S. military technology transfers to Korea are yet to come, as part of the Korean Fighter Program, a crash effort by the Seoul government to produce an indigenous Korean fighter aircraft. The battle among U.S. aerospace giants to sell fighter planes to South Korea demonstrates how two problems—proliferation of arms technology and corruption in foreign arms sales—have become closely intertwined. Both trends are signs of how the decisions over whom the United States should arm and what technology should be sold have come to be dominated by private, commercial interests in a process that is unaccountable to the Congress or the public.

The New Face of Corruption: The Korean Fighter Wars

The official story regarding bribery and corruption in the marketing of U.S. weapons systems is that it has been reined by the reforms that were enacted after the foreign payment scandals of the mid-1970s (see chapter 6). In fact, there is growing evidence that far from abandoning corrupt practices, U.S. arms makers have simply adopted more sophisticated techniques. Some of the strongest indications that corruption is alive and well in the weapons trade come from the decade-long battle among Northrop, General Dynamics, and McDonnell Douglas to sell advanced fighter aircraft to South Korea. The Korean fighter wars are a prime example of how the dependency of U.S. military contractors on foreign sales has driven them to the point that they will do almost anything to close a major deal, regardless of the legal niceties or larger national interests involved.

Just as Northrop served as a model for the industry's corrupt business practices of the 1960s and 1970s, the company was at the forefront of the new influence peddling scandals of the 1980s. Ironically, the most instructive example of Northrop's "innovative" marketing procedures emerged from a deal that fell through: the failed campaign to sell the firm's F-20 Tigershark to South Korea. The rise and fall of the F-20 is first and foremost the story of the U.S. aerospace industry's premier arms salesman of the Cold War era, former Northrop chairman and CEO Tom Jones.

Tom Jones is no ordinary aerospace executive. His rapid rise and glamorous life-style have earned him near-legendary status in the defense industry. After getting his engineering degree from Stanford and working at Douglas Aircraft during World War II, Jones spent four years in Brazil helping to set up that nation's aerospace industry. From Brazil Jones went to the Rand Corporation, where he wrote a landmark study on the economics of commercial airliners. Then it was on to Northrop, where his genius for conceptualizing and marketing new weapons vaulted the struggling firm into the top ranks of the aerospace industry and made him the youngest chairman in company history at age forty. During the 1950s he made his mark as the consummate arms salesman, spending up to three hundred days a year on the road hawking prototypes of Northrop's F-5 Tiger Jet, the predecessor to the F-20. Up to that point, U.S. policy had focused on giving away secondhand fighter planes, not on selling new ones. Jones was the first aerospace executive to see the potential for selling a capable, relatively affordable fighter in the Third World. And he made a hell of a sales pitch. His mastery of technical and economic issues was matched by a knack for striking up friendships with wealthy foreign customers like the shah of Iran and King Fahd of Saudi Arabia. One of Jones's prized possessions is a Persian rug that he received as a personal gift from the shah.[9]

Jones's talent for making powerful friends paid off handsomely for himself and for Northrop, transforming the F-5 into the most successful export fighter in the history of the industry, not to mention Northrop's main source of income for more than fifteen years. His successful salesmanship won Tom Jones accolades well beyond the aerospace industry. In 1961, a front-page article in *Time* called Jones a "visionary." Two years later *Newsweek* touted Jones as a "Renaissance Executive—a man who blends business leadership with extracurricular breadth and tempers the profit motive with a social conscience." These were certainly rave reviews for a man who made his living as an arms merchant.[10]

A former U.S. government official has described Tom Jones as "the most personally involved CEO that I've come across."[11] And there is no question that Jones dominated Northrop's day-to-day operations in his three decades at the helm. He managed to make himself a wealthy man in the process: by the time Jones retired in 1991, his Northrop shares alone were worth over $50 million.[12] But beyond the money, Jones was motivated by the excitement of getting a risky new project off the ground. The F-20 was just such a program—Jones was so confident that he could sell it that he financed the plane's development entirely out of the company's own funds, a practice almost unheard of in the cozy world of military contracting. Selling the Tigershark was soon to become Tom Jones's obsession.

By the early 1980s, it was clear to Jones that without a victory in the upcoming competition to sell new fighter aircraft to South Korea, the F-20 would have to be canceled. Tom Jones was in an uphill battle against his larger and more politically influential rivals General Dynamics and McDonnell Douglas, whose candidates for the Korean sale were already well established in the inventories of U.S. and foreign armed forces. No nation, including the United States, had ever purchased an F-20. But Jones was determined to make this sale. If that meant cutting deals with a few shady characters, so be it. As a friend and former Northrop executive put it, "Tom gets a big kick out of getting into trouble and then getting out. It is ingrained in his personality."[13]

Jones had taken more than his share of risks in his thirty years at Northrop, and he ran into more than his share of trouble along the way. In the mid-1970s, a series of government investigations revealed that Tom Jones had been the architect of an elaborate secret network of influential "sales agents" who had been making millions of dollars in illegal payments to grease the wheels for Northrop business at home and abroad. The linchpin of Jones's covert money laundering apparatus was a Paris-based lawyer named Bill Savy, whose trademark was a double-lined raincoat specially designed to conceal the huge stacks of cash he routinely handed out as bribes. Jones himself was convicted for making illegal contributions to Nixon's 1972 reelection campaign—in his typical hands-on style, he made the final payment personally, in cash, to Nixon lawyer Herbert Kalmbach. Jones also faced sanctions from the SEC for distributing over $30 million in "improper" foreign payments through such diverse intermediaries as Prince Bernhard of Holland and Saudi arms broker Adnan Khashoggi.[14]

Unlike many of his industry colleagues, who were demoted or fired or, in several cases, even committed suicide in response to the revelations in the foreign bribery scandals, Jones weathered the storm. He was forced to step down as Northrop's chairman in 1975, but he returned six months later under a government-imposed agreement requiring him to report to an executive committee of the Northrop board of directors that had been created specifically to keep an eye on Jones and his overseas dealings. The board had considered firing Jones in the wake of the scandals, but it made a business judgment that his value to the company's bottom line outweighed his habit of "cutting a few corners ethically," as one Northrop official euphemistically described it.[15]

If he was shaken by the scandals, Jones certainly didn't show it. He barely skipped a beat before launching a new "export only" fighter, the

F-5G. The project, later renamed the F-20, was devised in response to the Carter administration's policy of restricting the sale of advanced fighter planes to the Third World in favor of less capable, more affordable aircraft. But the prospects for the new plane soon turned sour when Jones's old California friend Ronald Reagan took office in 1981. Reagan's aggressive arms sales policy was great for the arms industry in general, but it was bad for Northrop and the F-20 in particular. With the blessing of Reagan policymakers, potential F-20 customers like Venezuela, Pakistan, and Indonesia began purchasing the top-of-the-line General Dynamics F-16 fighter—the same plane used by the U.S. Air Force. The market for the Tigershark was evaporating before Jones's eyes.[16]

Left in the lurch by Reagan's policy shift, Jones realized that the last chance to save the Tigershark was the upcoming competition to sell advanced fighters to Korea, a deal worth several billion dollars. The Korean contract would be enough to keep the F-20 program afloat until additional sales to the U.S. or foreign governments could be secured. It was a long shot, but Korea's air force had been built around the Northrop F-5 in the 1960s and 1970s. Jones felt that if there was one place the Tigershark could win a competition against the F-16, it was South Korea. It was time for Tom Jones to gear up Northrop's marketing machine for one more sales pitch.

Cutting the Deal

At first glance, Jimmy Shin seemed like a strange choice to run Northrop's Korean sales campaign for the F-20 fighter. A wiry, flamboyant man-about-town who was frequently seen driving around Honolulu in his Rolls-Royce Silver Shadow, Shin had credentials for his new position that were questionable at best. After a brief stint in the South Korean marines in the mid-1960s, he had gone on to run an ice cream parlor and two nightclubs, one in Saigon at the height of the Vietnam War and one in Honolulu. Perpetually in debt and frequently at odds with the law, Shin was forced to temporarily shut down his Honolulu club in a gambling raid, and he had to sell his ice cream stand to raise cash for one of his four divorce settlements. To round out Shin's résumé, his partner in the S Club, Book Sook Park, was a known hoodlum and organized crime figure in Korea. When an investigator for the Honolulu Liquor Commission later learned of Northrop's relationship with Shin, he said: "Gee, they should have checked out his credentials. Old Jimmy Shin was a real wheeler-dealer."

Despite (or maybe because of) all of this, Shin was the man Northrop hired in March 1983 for $102,000 per year—plus expenses—to promote its business interests in South Korea, the most pressing of which was touting the California aircraft maker's troubled fighter plane, the F-20.[17]

It soon became clear that Jim Dorsey, Northrop's vice president for Pacific marketing, hadn't signed Shin to this lucrative consulting arrangement for his business sense or his moral integrity. He hired Jimmy Shin because Shin knew the right people in Korea. Shin's most influential Korean connection was C.K. "Pistol" Park, who ran a bar in downtown Seoul and was a former member of the Korean National Assembly and former bodyguard to Korean dictator Park Chung Hee. Pistol Park, once the second most powerful man in Korea, maintained his wide-ranging contacts in Korean business and government circles after Park Chung Hee's assassination in 1979. He was a lifelong friend and mentor of Korean president Chun Doo Hwan, who had appointed Park to the coveted job of directing the organizing committee for the 1988 Summer Olympics in Seoul.

Pistol Park's bar, a garish night spot called the Safari Club, was best known for its red felt-covered walls, private blackjack room, and a special, secluded lounge where foreign businessmen could meet high-priced call girls. The club was a gathering place for a colorful clientele that included international arms merchants and high rollers the likes of Pistol Park's friend and occasional business associate Adnan Khashoggi. On quiet nights, Park would liven up the proceedings by taking out his gun and shooting out the mirrors behind the bar.

Pistol Park was soon to become Northrop's "man in Korea," secretly running a multimillion-dollar lobbying effort through a complex network of shell companies that stretched across Asia. Jimmy Shin would serve as his junior partner. Park would deal with high-level officials; Shin would handle mid- and lower-level officials.[18]

The hiring of Shin and Park seemed particularly surprising given Northrop's strict regulations against hiring foreign agents who have a "reputation for activities which are either illegal or improper or are likely to embarrass the company." This corporate policy had been imposed upon Northrop by the Securities and Exchange Commission after the firm was implicated in the foreign bribery scandals of the mid-1970s. But Tom Jones wasn't about to let an SEC decree stand between him and the sale of his pet fighter plane to South Korea.[19]

The F-20 lobbying campaign began in Honolulu, where James Dorsey ran Northrop's Pacific marketing headquarters out of an office suite at the Hilton Hawaiian Resort at Waikiki Beach. Since the mid-

1970s, Dorsey had been friendly with Jimmy Shin, a Korean businessman who also had offices at the resort complex. Dorsey informally asked Shin if he had any useful contacts in South Korea, and after Shin made a few introductions for him Dorsey decided to sign his Korean acquaintance on as a consultant for the Tigershark sales campaign.

Shin began earning his keep immediately, setting up a series of meetings between Northrop executives and Korean military and government officials. He also took the initial steps toward bringing Pistol Park on board.

Shin's first contact with Park came through O.H. Kang, a frequent visitor to Shin's Honolulu nightclub who was known in Korea as "Wheelchair Kang." Kang had earned the nickname after being shot in the back in a "business dispute" that had left him confined to a wheelchair. A grossly obese man who was fond of wearing bizarre ensembles like a tuxedo crowned with an electric-green bow tie, Kang might have been an object of ridicule if he was not also a leader of one of Korea's most feared organized crime syndicates. More important, Kang was a close associate of Pistol Park.[20]

Park agreed to serve as Northrop's front man in Korea, but it was going to cost the company. He demanded that Northrop sign a sales representation agreement with Dong Yang Express (DYE), a company that was run by his brother-in-law Lee Min Ha but secretly controlled by Park. DYE, a bus company with no experience in the aerospace business, was to be Northrop's sales agent in Korea, earning a commission of up to $55 million if the F-20 sale went through. This was a phenomenal sum, more than ten times the amount Northrop had spent for any other commission agreement and nearly twice the total sum of the questionable foreign payments that had caused Northrop so much trouble in the 1970s.[21]

But the sales representation agreement was just the first part of Pistol Park's strategy. Park told Northrop executives James Dorsey and Welko Gasich, the head of Northrop's Seoul office, that he would also need $5 million in cash up front that he could use to wine, dine, and—if necessary—bribe Korean officials to convince them to buy the F-20. Since entertainment was part and parcel of his approach to doing business, Park made his pitch to Northrop executives for what he called his "sales promotion fund" at a two-day meeting in his suite at the Tokyo Prince Hotel in March 1984. Pistol Park, Wheelchair Kang, Jimmy Shin, James Dorsey, and Welko Gasich all attended, along with a number of Park's other associates who were prospective partners in the F-20 marketing deal. Shin later told Northrop's lawyers that he had been staggered by the cost of the affair, which included a visit to a hostess club at the Rapongi Private Members Club that cost nearly $1,000 per person. Park picked up the tab, which he viewed as a minor expense compared with the resources Northrop was about to put at his disposal.[22]

Dorsey and Gasich were initially resistant to Park's request for cash, not because they objected to what he planned to do with it but because they thought it might look bad. They asked him to come up with an alternative. This prompted Park to devise an ingenious scheme that he promised would "guarantee" Northrop the sale.

This was where the most innovative wrinkle in Northrop's lobbying campaign came into play, a technique that is apparently serving as a model for other U.S. arms firms in their dealings with foreign governments. Park proposed that Northrop invest $6.25 million in a joint venture called the Asia Culture Travel Development Group, yet another company controlled by Park and run by his relatives and associates. The alleged purpose of the partnership would be to build a conference center and hotel complex in Seoul as part of the offset package that would be offered to Korea in conjunction with the F-20 sale. Offsets—agreements to make a specified level of investments or buy certain products from the nation purchasing a major weapons system—had become standard practice in the arms trade. As an arms industry insider explains it, "These countries can't justify spending billions of dollars on a foreign system unless they can show some kind of economic benefit coming back." But in this instance, the purpose of the hotel project wasn't to help Korea's economy, it was to provide Northrop with a conduit to launder the money it would be providing for Pistol Park's sales promotion fund. If any questions arose about the large sums of cash they were giving to their Korean lobbyists, Jones and his marketing men could just claim that it was part of a complex, innovative offset investment.

But an investment of this magnitude couldn't be made without the approval of Northrop's board of directors. While Dorsey and Gasich had been doing the legwork so far, getting this deal past the board was a job for Tom Jones.

On July 18, 1984, at Jones's behest, William McGagh, Northrop's chief financial officer, made a presentation on the Seoul hotel venture to the board of directors. The board members had plenty of questions: about the value of the property the Koreans were putting up as their part of the joint venture; about the backgrounds of the Korean partners; about what kind of representation Northrop would have on the board of the joint venture company; and about whether the Korean government would give Northrop credit for the hotel investment in tallying up the company's offsets for the F-20 sale. Jones spoke up at this point, promising to personally check out the Korean partners and all the other aspects of the deal.

Jones and McGagh agreed to report back to the board. On September 19 McGagh told the executive committee that the majority of their concerns had been addressed and that the others would be taken care of shortly. What he didn't tell them was that the entire $6.25 million had already been sent to Pistol Park almost six weeks earlier, on August 8. Nor did he mention that the funds weren't sent to South Korea but to the personal Hong Kong bank account of a woman named Milli Kim, a friend of Pistol Park. Evidently McGagh and Jones gave masterful performances: their charade of seeking approval for a done deal didn't raise any eyebrows.[23]

Steering the hotel plan past his fellow board members whetted Jones's appetite for intrigue, but he couldn't leave it at that. He wanted to play a hands-on role, as he had done during the glory days of the F-5 program. Jones set up a one-on-one meeting with Pistol Park at the 1984 Summer Olympics in Los Angeles. There is no record of what was said, but it is clear that they didn't spend the whole time talking sports. This was apparently when Jones first asked Park to arrange an audience for him with the one man who could make or break the F-20 sale: Korean president Chun Doo Hwan.[24]

But there were complications along the way. Since the Tigershark had no track record, Pistol Park arranged a test flight of the aircraft for Korean government and military officials at Suwon Air Force Base in October 1984. This golden opportunity to show off the plane quickly became a public relations nightmare when it crashed during the demonstration; Northrop's chief test pilot, Darrell Cornell, was killed in the accident. Northrop officials and Park tried to convince Korean officials that the crash was a result of pilot error, not a malfunction of the aircraft, but it was still a stunning setback.[25]

In the months leading up to the crash, Park had shifted his Korean lobbying machine into high gear, meeting with generals, government ministers, and Pres. Chun Doo Hwan himself to convince them to give the Northrop plane a chance. Throughout the summer and fall of 1984, Park and Shin entertained Korean officials at a furious pace, racking up $90,000 a month in expenses. Now was the time for Park to draw upon the reservoir of goodwill he had built up in these frantic social rounds. In December, Park wrote an encouraging letter to Tom Jones on his International Olympic Committee stationery. Park described a number of his discussions with generals and cabinet ministers and told Jones that, despite the crash, he had "the continued assurance of President Chun Doo Hwan that the F-20 program is 'Go.'" Park closed by saying that he had "guaranteed support where it counts most."[26]

The face-to-face meeting between Jones and Chun took on even greater importance in the wake of the failed test flight. It was finally arranged for May 1985, in Honolulu. Jones and Chun stayed at separate hotels to avoid suspicion, and they reportedly met and talked for over half an hour about what Northrop could do to help Korea—and President Chun.

Jimmy Shin claims that Jones was told flat out at the Hawaii meeting that he should make an $8 million payment to Chun in exchange for his approval of the F-20 contract. This was one of a host of corruption charges involving Chun and his relatives that were to haunt him even after he relinquished the Korean presidency to his handpicked successor, Roh Tae Woo, in 1989. But Korean authorities were never able to verify whether the F-20 payment had actually been solicited—or received. Some Korean analysts have charged that Pres. Roh Tae Woo put a stop to the probe. "My reading is, the president doesn't want to see his old friend dragged into a public forum" over the F-20 charges, said Daryl Plunk, a Washington consultant with frequent business dealings in Korea. Instead of prosecuting his predecessor, Roh cut a deal in which Chun agreed to return $25 million in personal cash, political funds, and real estate accumulated during his rule and make a televised apology to the nation in lieu of fully disclosing how he had raised and disbursed these huge sums of money. The full story of Chun's role in the Korean fighter deal may still be uncovered, but it has yet to be revealed as part of the across-the-board probe of Korean weapons procurement programs that was set in motion by Korea's newly elected president, Kim Young Sam, in early 1993.[27]

Chun's troubles came well after his 1985 meeting with Jones. From Jones's perspective at the time, the Hawaii meeting had been a success; he felt reassured that Pistol Park's impressive connections and relentless lobbying might just save the day for Northrop.

Park's persistence on Northrop's behalf was not going unnoticed, or unrewarded. Around the time of his meeting with Jones at the Los Angeles Olympics, Park was signed to a direct consulting deal for $75,000 per year plus expenses. Unlike Shin's deal, which called for monthly written reports and documentation of expenses, Park's deal called only for him to consult orally with James Dorsey from time to time. Then, in 1985, around the time of the Jones/Chun meeting, Northrop invested $900,000 in another of Pistol Park's business schemes, a Hong Kong trading company called Bancaborro, which would allegedly be used to help secure additional offset deals in connection with the F-20 sale.[28]

Unaware of all these behind-the-scenes machinations, by early 1985 Northrop's board members had the general feeling that the F-20 deal was in the bag. Despite their obligation under the 1975 consent decree to scrutinize the work of Jones and his marketing men, the board had fallen into the old pattern of trusting Jones to do what was best for the company, with few questions asked.

The Deal Unravels

The board's optimism was jolted in July 1985 when an F-20 bound for a demonstration at the Paris Air Show crashed in Labrador, Canada. The chances for a Korean sale were destroyed once and for all in December, when Pistol Park died of liver cancer at the age of fifty-five. The whole elaborate architecture of shell companies and concealed funds that Park had constructed on Northrop's behalf was next to useless without his personal clout. Tom Jones had been fighting against tough odds from the start, and the death of Pistol Park was the final blow for the Korean sale and for the F-20 program. General Dynamics won a contract to supply thirty-six F-16s to South Korea, and Northrop canceled the Tigershark in mid-1986, taking a $1.2 billion write-off in the process.[29]

If Tom Jones had been lucky, that would have been the end of it. But Park's death sparked a scramble among his relatives and business partners to make one last stab at getting more money out of Northrop—hush money. Wheelchair Kang sent Dorsey a letter asking for a $16.5 million cancellation payment on the consulting contract with Dong Yang Express, threatening to "publish all facts that I know" about Northrop if the company didn't pay up. The typewritten letter was weak on syntax but clear in its demands, complaining that Northrop's refusal to deal with Kang "was utterly unreasonable and made me annoyed very much. I have consequently determined to find out the way of self-help to get paid for what I have done until now for Northrop." Simultaneously, Pistol Park's brother-in-law Lee Min Ha was submitting a "bill" for the $16.5 million to Donald Foulds, Northrop's vice president in charge of offset agreements, listing expenses on entertainment and chauffeur-driven limousines in Panama, Singapore, and Indonesia, as well as South Korea and Japan. Seven months after receiving Kang's letter, Northrop settled with Dong Yang for $1.5 million, although the original contract called for no cancellation fee and Northrop had never paid one before on any of its foreign commission agreements. Wheelchair Kang's blackmail tactics had paid off.[30]

At the same time that Kang and Lee Min Ha were staking their claim, Jimmy Shin was writing to Jones asking to be reimbursed for the "long arduous hours" he spent "promoting the F-20 in Korea." Shin's complaints soon drew the attention of the Northrop board, which launched an internal investigation headed up by Vice Chairman of the Board Frank Lynch. In hopes of getting one last payment out of Northrop, Shin laid bare the whole F-20 scheme in a two-day interview in Honolulu with representatives of the company's law firm, Jones, Day, Reavis and Pogue.[31]

The revelations by Northrop's erstwhile Korean partners also caught the attention of congressional staffers working for Congressman John Dingell of Michigan. One of their sources from a prior investigation told them that Northrop had paid hush money to its Korean consultants, piquing their curiosity about the whole F-20 sales effort.

In early 1988, when congressional investigators began asking questions about the Korean F-20 campaign, the company began a determined effort to stall the inquiry by withholding documents, putting off interviews, and canceling scheduled appointments to testify about the deal. After six months of playing cat and mouse with Northrop, Dingell finally decided he had had enough. On September 28, 1988, the Oversight and Investigations Subcommittee of his House Committee on Energy and Commerce held public hearings on the F-20 scandal. Chief investigator Bruce Chafin laid out the details of the Northrop scheme, based on interviews with Korean contacts, a leaked copy of Shin's conversations with Northrop's lawyers, and the few documents that had been grudgingly supplied by Northrop. The hearings provided a devastating portrait of Northrop's top management and Tom Jones's role in the scandal. Chafin raised a host of questions about the F-20 campaign and the phony hotel deal that Northrop could not or would not answer. Why had the money for the alleged hotel gone to Hong Kong, even after Northrop's lawyers told them about the Korean government's strict legal requirement that all foreign investment funds be deposited directly in Korea? Why had Northrop forwarded the full $6.25 million to Park and his associates almost a year *before* there were any permits, plans, or approvals for building a hotel? Why had Park, Lee Min Ha, and Jimmy Shin immediately divvied up $5 million of the alleged "investment fund" within two weeks of its arrival in Hong Kong? And why hadn't Northrop

asked any questions about where its money was going until *after* the F-20 sale had fallen through?[32]

Northrop's management was either incredibly devious or unbelievably incompetent. Chafin made his position on this point clear—he believed that Northrop had purposely set up a shoddy deal with minimal accountability as a way to establish "plausible deniability" if the firm was ever accused of making illegal payoffs. Jones may have been pulling the strings, but the board had allowed him to do so by abdicating its responsibility for keeping an eye on him. The findings of Dingell's subcommittee prompted civil and criminal investigations into the Korean sale by the Justice Department, the U.S. attorney's offices in Los Angeles and Honolulu, the IRS, the SEC, and the Korean government. As of this writing, other than a conviction of one of Park's Korean associates on a minor charge, no one has been called to account in the scandal.

For public relations purposes, Northrop continued to claim that it had been cheated by "clever Korean con men" and that it had always planned to build the hotel. To prove that it was all just an unfortunate mistake, Northrop took legal action in Korea to recoup the $6.25 million "hotel investment" from Lee Min Ha and Park's widow. A source familiar with Northrop's decision asserted that the move to recover the funds was part of an elaborate charade calculated to make the firm appear innocent: "Otherwise, it would look like they intended it as a lobbying fund all along."[33]

Much to Northrop's chagrin, a Korean arbitration panel ruled against the company, despite what one source described as the "planeloads of lawyers" Northrop had sent to Korea to plead its case. The panel charged that there had never been a serious plan to build a hotel and that Northrop officials were well aware of this fact. In the meantime, Lee Min Ha was arrested, tried, and sentenced to six months in jail for violations of Korea's foreign exchange laws in connection with his laundering of Northrop's money for the phony hotel deal. But the arbitrators were silent on the crucial question of what they thought Northrop had actually intended to do with the funds.

Northrop spokesperson Tony Cantafio—the only Northrop official allowed to speak publicly about the F-20 scandal—wrote off the Korean arbitrators as "biased." The company brought in another, international, arbitrator—Wolfgang Kuhn of the International Chamber of Commerce—whom Northrop claimed would set the record straight. Unfortunately for Tom Jones and Northrop, Kuhn did exactly that. He ruled that not only was the hotel venture bogus but that top Northrop officials—up to and including Tom Jones—had always intended the $6.25 million to be used as a lobbying slush fund. In its most telling phrase, the arbitrator's report charged that "this was not a situation where low-level employees colluded to defraud Northrop, but instead Northrop was acting through its highest level of management in violation of the law."[34]

Even Tom Jones was having a hard time wriggling out of this one. On September 19, 1990, the same day that the international arbitrator's report was made public, Jones announced his resignation as chairman of the board of Northrop. He had already stepped down as Northrop's president and CEO earlier in the year, a move that many industry analysts had speculated was a direct result of the emerging F-20 scandal. It was widely believed that the bribery allegations, on top of a parallel conviction on seventeen counts of criminal fraud in the company's nuclear weapons programs, had been the last straw. Although Northrop has denied that Jones's resignation was related to the scandals, a former Northrop executive asserts that Jones saw the handwriting on the wall: "It was a situation where Jones himself recognized that it was time to leave. There were people in Washington, in the Air Force, and at the Pentagon, who let it be known that they would not be unhappy if he retired."[35]

Lessons of the F-20 Scandal

On the surface, the F-20 story might seem like a cautionary tale against the use of bribes and influence peddling in foreign arms sales. After all, didn't Northrop lose the sale? And although Tom Jones was never prosecuted for wrongdoing, didn't he step down in disgrace once the Korean scandal hit the light of day? Not exactly.

First of all, Northrop didn't lose the sale because of influence peddling. It lost because it didn't do it skillfully enough. Jones and his men picked unreliable partners for the Korean end of the deal—people close to the investigation agree that if Jimmy Shin and Wheelchair Kang hadn't been so greedy and "told all" after the deal fell through, Northrop might never have been caught. And the paperwork on the phony hotel plan was just too sloppy to withstand even minimal scrutiny.

Jones's competitors fared better on the influence peddling front. General Dynamics, which won the first phase of the Korean fighter competition, hired retired Korean Air Force general E.Y. Yoon's firm, Buyeon—which means "quick riches" in Korean—to funnel cash to key Korean officials to induce them to buy the F-16. Investigators are convinced that General Dynamics used Buyeon as an intermediary to make bribes, but a congressional inquiry into the payments was stopped dead when the Reagan Justice Department refused to seek access to the records of Yoon's Paris bank account.[36]

Northrop's rival McDonnell Douglas went after even bigger game in a second, larger phase of the Korean fighter competition, hiring former head of the U.S. Pacific Fleet Adm. James "Ace" Lyons as its chief lobbyist in its drive to sell the firm's F/A-18 fighter to Korea. The company may have improperly approached Lyons for his help before he left the navy, but the details were placed under seal in a federal district court in St. Louis as a result of dogged litigation on the part of McDonnell Douglas. The company's exercise in revolving-door diplomacy appeared to have paid off in December 1989, when McDonnell won a $6 billion deal to send Korea 120 F/A-18 fighters along with the blueprints and production technology to build its own planes.[37]

But the deal slowly but steadily fell apart as McDonnell Douglas officials haggled with their Korean counterparts over the price of coproducing components of the plane in Korea. Shortly after the 1991 Gulf War, the Korean Air Force reversed field and opted for the less expensive, single-engine F-16, which was produced by General Dynamics. Company vice president A. Dwain Mayfield asserted that the selection of the F-16 was based entirely on its lower cost and the plane's performance in the Gulf conflict, but a number of sources close to the deal expressed suspicions that General Dynamics may have engaged in improper lobbying to encourage the Korean government to switch to the F-16 from the F-18. At the end of 1992, the Korean F-16 project was taken over by Lockheed as part of its purchase of the General Dynamics fighter division, but the doubts about the legitimacy of the deal remain.

Kang Chang Sun, a former Korean army general who now serves in the national legislature, has asserted that millions of dollars in bribe money were paid to secure the shift to the F-16. By the summer of 1993, questions raised by the F-16 deal had prompted a Korean government investigation of corruption in its entire weapons purchasing system that resulted in the firing of over thirty top military officials and the arrest of two former defense ministers. As of this writing, there have been no arrests directly linked to the F-16 sale, but several officials were accused of taking payoffs in connection with the sale of another Lockheed aircraft, the P-3C antisubmarine warfare plane. It was unclear whether the probe would delay the F-16 project or implicate U.S. industry officials directly, but the *Wall Street Journal* summed up the industry's perspective on the mounting scandal when it noted that "all this comes at a bad time for U.S. defense companies, which are counting on foreign markets to help offset declining sales at home."[38]

What is clear is that barring a complete reversal of the F-16 deal, which seems unlikely at this point, it will now be Lockheed's job to "help South Korea build an aeronautics industry." Ultimately, it was this pledge to help develop Korea's aerospace industry that was a more powerful lever in convincing Korean officials to buy the F-16 than any bribe could ever be. General Dynamics had agreed to roughly the same coproduction and offset terms that McDonnell Douglas had already negotiated with Korean defense officials: the first 12 of the 120 aircraft will be produced in the United States, with the next 36 assembled in South Korea and the final 72 produced there under license. In addition, General Dynamics promised to help its Korean partners develop an indigenous Korean trainer aircraft and to funnel billions of dollars of related business to Korean aerospace firms. Lockheed took on these same commitments when it took over the project at the end of 1992.[39]

An executive of Samsung, one of the Korean partners in the F-16 coproduction deal, described the arrangement as "the first step in building up the [Korean] aerospace industry." An official of the Korean Ministry of Trade put this observation in a broader context when he told the *Wall Street Journal* that South Korea would "rather have the power to manufacture our own aircraft [because] we have a strong wish to become a manufacturing center of the world." The result could be that ten or fifteen years down the road the same kind of problems that cropped up in controlling Korea's export of U.S.-origin M-16 rifles could turn up in the F-16 program, with far more serious consequences.[40]

While coproduction has been a good deal for corporate executives and well-paid lobbyists here and abroad, it has been a raw deal for workers in U.S. defense plants whose jobs are exported overseas as part of the bargain. In the Korean fighter deal, for example, General Dynamics agreed not only to have significant parts of the F-16 aircraft produced in South Korea, but it even attempted to enlist workers from its Fort Worth, Texas, factory to teach Korean workers how to do their jobs. On June 25, 1992, thousands of workers from the General Dynamics Fort Worth plant staged a protest over management's attempt to add insult to injury. George Kourpias, the international president of the International Association of Machinists, told the rallying workers that "we are here to protest the government's indifference to communities like Fort Worth, which will face certain devastation unless an economic conversion program is put in place." But Kourpias saved his strongest rhetorical fire for the F-16 coproduction scheme:

> You all know that this company... originally wanted to bring 500 Korean workers here .... Right here to Fort Worth and have you, their employees, train them. So they could take away your jobs.
>
> That is like the warden asking the prisoner on death row to chip in to pay the electric bill so they can electrocute him quicker. And they thought we would smile and do what the big master said.
>
> Can you imagine the arrogance?[41]

As a result of the protests, General Dynamics was forced to shelve its plan to train Korean workers at its Fort Worth plant. But the exporting of jobs will continue—a backup plan has been instituted under which a small contingent of managers from the facility (which is now controlled by Lockheed) will train Korean workers in Korea and another group of Korean workers will receive hands-on experience at a U.S.-backed F-16 factory in Turkey. The Korean fighter sale is a clear contradiction of the arms industry's constant refrain that management and labor benefit equally from weapons exports.

As for Tom Jones, the aerospace executive par excellence, far from being scarred by his final scandal, he received high praise from his colleagues in the arms industry. In December 1989, a year and a half after the Korean F-20 scandal was first revealed, Jones was given the prestigious Wright Brothers Award at a black-tie banquet in Washington attended by eight hundred of his peers. Jones was selected in recognition of "public service of enduring value to the aerospace industry" and "creative and innovative contributions to the competitiveness of the United States aerospace industry."[42]

Those among Tom Jones's peers who had any qualms about the Korean bribery allegations evidently shared the view of John Bennett, a Washington-based lobbyist:

> The whole thing just smells to high heaven. But when you're selling military hardware, what can you do? Payments are an ancient and honorable tradition in the aircraft industry, and they were desperate to sell that plane.[43]

While presumably Jones's colleagues were not honoring him for his innovations in the field of foreign payoffs, they clearly learned a great deal from his Korean scheme. An investigator involved in the F-20 probe reports that Northrop's approach of using investment projects as the cover for bribes and entertainment funds is the new, state-of-the-art industry lobbying tactic: "No one gives straight bribes any more. They're all doing it through offsets now." A congressional source adds that this new method is even harder to track down than the old approach of passing on some cash in an envelope:

> [It is] almost impossible to trace the money flow. How are you going to figure out if some general's sister-in-law in Turkey or South Korea owns a title company that's getting an inflated fee for doing the paperwork on some real estate project that's part of an offset deal?

Northrop's problem was that Jones and his sales team just didn't cover their tracks well enough on the F-20 deal, but their industry colleagues are apparently learning from that mistake.

If there is a moral to the F-20 story and the whole push to sell advanced fighter planes to Korea, it is that the pressure to sell at all costs has fostered a pervasive culture of corruption among the corporate arms merchants, as sophisticated forms of bribery and influence peddling become routine, unquestioned "costs of doing business." But even more disturbing than the payoffs and political manipulation that have become the arms merchants' stock-in-trade is the relentless drive to export that lies behind these tactics. The question of whether the United States should be supplying its most advanced arms and arms production technologies to virtually any regime willing to pay for them is being pushed aside in the scramble to make bigger, more lucrative arms deals. Unfortunately, Korea is far from the only Third World regime that has benefited from U.S. contractors' practice of selling arms production know-how.

Coproduction and Offsets: Creating the Competition

The Korean fighter sale is only the most prominent of literally scores of coproduction and licensing deals engaged in by U.S. firms with the blessing of the U.S. government. From 1960 through 1988, the United States led all nations in fostering the spread of arms production capabilities: over the past three decades, at least 140 U.S. weapons designs have been produced under license by foreign firms. Most of these deals were with U.S. allies in industrialized nations like Japan and Europe. But a significant number of the licenses—forty in all—went to support weapons production in developing nations. The

closest competitor in this race to help create new arms industries is France, but as of 1991 French firms had fewer than half as many systems under licensed production worldwide as their U.S. counterparts. These arrangements may be good for the balance sheets of Western defense firms, but they pose serious risks of proliferation of advanced armaments.[44]

The majority of the newly developing arms exporting nations owe their tremendous progress in weapons production over the past three decades to technology transfers from the United States or its European allies. Israel, Egypt, South Korea, Taiwan, Brazil, and Indonesia are all significant second-tier arms suppliers, and all of them are also at the top of the list of nations receiving arms technology from the United States and Europe under coproduction and licensing agreements. If this trend continues unchecked, some time early in the twenty-first century there could be as many as two dozen major arms producing and exporting nations, instead of the current half dozen or so that dominate the trade. The result will be devastating to any hopes of reining in weapons proliferation—the chances of getting agreement from two dozen major exporters are far more difficult than the prospects of getting five or six nations to join in an arms transfer control accord. Ironically, the spread of weapons know-how could also eventually cut deeply into the market shares of U.S. and European weapons producers, particularly in the manufacture of low-to-medium-technology weapons systems in which nations like Indonesia and Singapore can exploit their cheaper labor costs to offer substantially lower prices.

As a study by the congressional Office of Technology Assistance (OTA) has pointed out, the United States has a pivotal role to play in determining whether this proliferation of arms industries continues at its current pace. A 1991 OTA report asserted that "in the absence of foreign assistance, the indigenous defense industrial capability of most of the developing nations would cease to expand and might even collapse." The study went on to recommend that the United States take the lead in resolving the problem of defense "collaboration" and the transfer of arms manufacturing capabilities:

> As the largest and most advanced producer of defense systems in the West, a U.S.-led diplomatic initiative to restrict collaboration might slow the pace of defense industrial and technological dispersion. It would also place the United States in a position to exert diplomatic pressure on its NATO allies and the [states of the former] Soviet Union. Working together, the NATO countries and the [states of the

former] Soviet Union could stem the vast majority, perhaps as much as 90 percent, of technology transferred in international defense trade.[45]

While congressional analysts rightly suggest that if the U.S. government is serious about stopping proliferation of advanced armaments it must take the lead in promoting a "concerted multilateral effort" to limit transfers of arms making technology, U.S. arms industry executives are dead set against any such reform. They see technology transfers as a necessary evil in an international buyer's market for arms, and they are loathe to give up any potential inducement that they can utilize to edge out the competition.

For all their apparent realism about the need to give importing nations a "piece of the action" if they are going to win foreign weapons contracts, arms industry lobbyists are reluctant to acknowledge their most closely guarded secret regarding coproduction and offset arrangements—that they involve shipping tens of thousands of U.S. jobs overseas. Most major U.S. arms sales now entail offset commitments worth 50 to 100 percent of the value of the original deal, meaning that U.S.-based firms must pledge to steer hundreds of millions, or even billions, of dollars worth of business to the purchasing nation.

Some major export deals actually provide the majority of jobs for foreign workers, with only a tiny fraction of the work being performed in the United States. For example, when Egypt "bought" forty F-16 fighter aircraft from the United States at the end of the 1991 Persian Gulf War, the $1.6 billion they spent on the planes came not from Egypt, but from a U.S. government grant. To add insult to injury, the bulk of the production work on the planes is being done at F-16 plants in Turkey that were set up as part of a U.S. coproduction arrangement with that nation. As a result, 100 percent of this major "arms sale" is being paid for by U.S. taxpayers, while the associated jobs and technology transfers are benefitting the Turkish economy, not the U.S. economy. Unfortunately, this is not an isolated case. A June 1994 General Accounting Office (GAO) report examined four dozen cases in which the U.S. government provided $11.6 billion worth of U.S. weaponry to Israel, Egypt, Turkey, and Greece. The GAO found that despite the fact that these systems were being provided under Pentagon aid programs, the recipient countries negotiated offset deals that resulted in an additional $4.7 billion in production and related investments being sent their way. As Rep. Cardiss Collins summed up this practice, "American taxpayers are actually paying to move defense-related production, and American jobs, to foreign countries."[46]

Even when U.S. government assistance is not involved, offsets can drain jobs away from the United States toward foreign countries. In early 1993, Sen. Russ Feingold was approached by a Wisconsin company that was competing to sell $50 million worth of equipment to a major paper manufacturing company. The company claimed that *another* U.S. company, the Northrop Corporation, had offered the paper manufacturer a payment of over $1 million if it would buy its equipment from a company based in Finland, in preference to the Wisconsin firm. When Feingold's office contacted Northrop to ask them why they were spending money to send business from the United States to Finland, a Northrop official explained that this "incentive payment" was part of an offset arrangement with Finland that was concluded as part of a sale of F-18 fighters to that nation. Feingold was stunned to learn that these kinds of payments were perfectly legal, and he has since spearheaded a drive to force U.S. arms manufacturers to reveal more of the details of their offset agreements with their foreign clients.[47]

It is far from clear that the Clinton administration is prepared to confront the arms lobby on the sensitive issue of coproduction and offsets. But it is equally clear that if something isn't done to curb this practice, the prospects for cleaning up corruption in foreign arms sales or stemming the tide of weapons proliferation in the Third World will be drastically reduced. The question is whether a world torn by ethnic, religious, territorial, and economic conflicts can afford to allow multinational arms exporting firms to indiscriminately spread weapons manufacturing know-how to every corner of the globe.

The issue of how to forge a new direction for U.S. policies on the transfer of arms and military technology for the post–Cold War era is the subject of our final chapter.

13

The Clinton Policy: Arms Control or Business as Usual?

The few short years since 1989 have witnessed the greatest transformation of the world political landscape since the end of World War II. The fall of the Berlin Wall, the breakup of the Soviet Union, the beginnings of economic integration in Western Europe, and the tentative political settlements of long-standing civil wars in Nicaragua, Afghanistan, and Cambodia are all signs that the Cold War is over. A new, uncertain era is beginning to take shape.

On the positive side, the prospects of an all-out nuclear war have been drastically reduced, and military budgets are going down in Russia and Europe and modestly in the United States. More ominously, the 1990s have already been marked by the deadliest military conflict in Europe since World War II (the civil war in the former Yugoslavia); the most extensive international military confrontation in the Middle East in decades (the Gulf War); devastating famines and civil wars in Sudan and Somalia; and an explosive acceleration of religious, ethnic, and territorial conflicts in regions from the Balkans to the former Soviet Union to the Indian subcontinent. This volatile new security environment calls for a radical reevaluation of the assumptions that shaped U.S. foreign and military policies during the Cold War, especially in the realm of arms sales policy. With nations breaking up and governments being replaced at a breathtaking pace, this is no time for the U.S. government to be handing out arms indiscriminately, as if they were some sort of post–Cold War party favor. Unfortunately, that is exactly what the Bush administration was doing from the end of the Gulf War right up to the eve of the 1992 presidential election. With a few exceptions, this runaway arms sales policy was carried out with the support of the Clinton campaign and the Democratic leadership in the Congress. And at least so far, there is no clear indication that President Clinton intends to depart significantly from the Bush policy on arms sales now that he is in the White House.

It has been suggested that George Bush was the last Cold War president. This was certainly the case when it came to arms sales policy: Bush carried on arms sales diplomacy as if the Cold War had never ended. Up to the bitter end, the Bush administration maintained a business-as-usual approach to arms sales, employing them as an all-purpose economic and foreign policy tool to win friends, intimidate adversaries, and bolster U.S. exports. Even as sweeping global political changes created new opportunities for bringing an end to runaway arms trafficking, Bush policymakers continued to aggressively push U.S. arms in the Middle East and Asia. Administration officials from George Bush on down counseled restraint in weapons exports, but their actions made it abundantly clear that the U.S. government's real priority was to do everything in its power to help U.S. firms get an "edge" in the post–Cold War arms market—regardless of the potential for fueling regional arms races entailed in such a policy.

Now that the Cold War is over, what are the prospects for developing a new approach to arms sales policy that is more accountable to the American people and more in tune with the dynamics of a rapidly changing world political system? Judging by the first two years of the Clinton administration, America's arms sales addiction is alive and well. Bill Clinton's status quo stance on arms sales policy is rooted in commitments he made during the 1992 presidential campaign. A change in policy is still possible, but it is not going to happen unless the public demands it, loudly and clearly.

Arms Sales Follies of 1992: Selling Arms on the Campaign Trail

According to Bill Clinton, the 1992 presidential campaign was supposed to be about change. But as far as arms sales policy was concerned, the only change brought by the campaign was a change for the worse. In the nine weeks from September 1992 until election day, the Bush administration announced over $20 billion in new overseas arms deals.[1] In just two months, George Bush rushed through the equivalent of a year's worth of weapons exports.

This reckless exercise in "pork barrel proliferation" should have been an inviting target for the Clinton/Gore campaign, which could have legitimately charged that President Bush was risking the nation's long-term national security interests for partisan political gain. Unfortunately, that debate never happened. Not only did Bill Clinton fail to challenge Bush's election-year arms binge, he openly supported the most controversial sale of all—the export of seventy-two F-15 fighter planes to Saudi Arabia.

Aside from a few side arguments about George Bush's role in Iran/contra and the arming of Iraq, there was no real debate on arms sales policy in the 1992 campaign: George Bush would simply announce another multibillion-dollar deal, and Bill Clinton would either quietly accept it or endorse it outright.

As late as the spring of 1992, the conventional wisdom in Washington, even among arms industry lobbyists, was that George Bush was unlikely to put forward any major arms sales during an election year. The consensus view was that if Bush did decide to go ahead with a politically unpopular deal like the Saudi F-15 sale, he would avoid doing so during the height of the fall election campaign. Unfortunately for the cause of arms sales restraint, in 1992 this bit of conventional wisdom was dead wrong.

As the summer dragged on and Bill Clinton surged in the polls, the Bush administration's political calculus regarding the wisdom of announcing major arms sales at the height of the campaign underwent a radical shift. Somewhere between the Republican convention in mid-August and Labor Day weekend, the Bush camp decided that openly pushing weapons might actually be a political plus, particularly in key battleground states like Texas, Missouri, Michigan, and Ohio, all of which were home to large military production plants and tens of thousands of defense-related jobs.

Surprisingly, it wasn't the long-awaited Saudi F-15 deal that broke the ice. It was a sale that was much closer to home for Bush, or at least to his adopted home. Two days before the start of the Labor Day weekend, Bush told a group of cheering, flag-waving defense workers at the General Dynamics plant in Fort Worth, Texas, that he had approved a $6 billion sale of 150 F-16 fighter planes to Taiwan. Standing in front of two F-16s and a banner with the words "Jobs for America—Thanks Mr. President," Bush told the General Dynamics employees that "the military technology you produce is the finest in the world." He went on to proudly proclaim his decision to break a

U.S. pledge to limit arms transfers to Taiwan that had been made during Ronald Reagan's first term.[2]

This was no ordinary arms sale. While incumbent presidents frequently use Pentagon weapons contracts or decisions about military bases to score points with key electoral constituencies, George Bush's appearance at Fort Worth to brag about an arms export was virtually unprecedented in the annals of election-year pork barrel politicking. To the extent that the American voting public thinks about arms sales and military aid, they tend to have negative opinions about them. In addition to this generalized opposition, specific constituencies are often strongly opposed to a particular sale: supporters of Israel oppose major sales of U.S. arms to Israel's Arab adversaries; peace and arms control advocates oppose sales to the Third World on the grounds that they fuel regional arms races; and human rights advocates oppose exports to repressive regimes. With all of these potential negatives to consider, normal political etiquette would have led Bush to hold off on a major arms sale to a Third World nation like Taiwan until it could be consummated quietly, outside the glare of the campaign spotlight. But George Bush's desperate need to show that he could do something—anything—to spur the economy convinced him to cast aside this traditional approach and try instead to promote arms sales as a job-creation program.

If Bush had deliberately set out to pick the best example to demonstrate that he was intent on casting aside strategic and arms control concerns in the name of pure pork barrel politics, he couldn't have chosen a better deal than the F-16 sale to Taiwan. As vice president, he had been directly involved in negotiating an agreement between the United States and the People's Republic of China in which the United States pledged "not to exceed" previous U.S. transfers to Taiwan "either in qualitative or quantitative terms." The most politically significant symbol of the U.S. commitment to limit arms sales to Taiwan had been the repeated refusals of the Reagan and Bush administrations to sell F-16s or other advanced fighter aircraft to the Taiwanese Air Force.

With Ross Perot breathing down his neck in the polls in Texas and Bill Clinton beginning to gather momentum in nationwide surveys, it didn't take George Bush long to decide that the commitment to limit arms sales to Taiwan would have to be "reinterpreted," and the sooner the better. With a little push from General Dynamics, along with a coalition of representatives from Texas that included Republican congressman Joe Barton and Democratic senator Lloyd Bentsen, Bush administration policymakers discarded the ten-year-old pledge to curb weapons exports to Taiwan over a six-week period in the summer of 1992.

Joe Barton started the ball rolling in mid-July, after a two-hour briefing by General Dynamics officials. Company representatives pleaded for his help in gaining approval of the sale, in order to preserve three thousand jobs at the company's Fort Worth assembly plant and to keep the F-16 production line running for a few more years. Barton obliged by placing a call to White House deputy chief of staff W. Henson Moore. According to Barton, White House and National Security Council staffers immediately did a "quick and dirty" review of policy on U.S. arms sales to Taiwan and decided that the F-16 sale "had a lot of merit." With that presumption in favor of the sale already in place, the issue was then farmed out to the State and Defense Departments for review. By the end of August, the defense and foreign policy bureaucracies had signed onto the plan to violate the 1982 communiqué, and George Bush was free to stage his campaign photo opportunity at the F-16 plant in Fort Worth. The push to sell F-16s to Taiwan was by no means a partisan Republican effort—one of the strongest advocates of the deal was Senator Lloyd Bentsen, a Texas Democrat who went on to become the Secretary of the Treasury in the Clinton adminstration.

While administration officials tried to paper over their opportunistic policy reversal with arguments about changes in the strategic situation in Asia, an official close to the deal acknowledged that "the driver of this is the politics and economics of it, not the national security issue." In protest, China immediately denounced the deal and threatened to withdraw from the ongoing "Big Five" talks on limiting arms sales to the Middle East. Morton Abramovitz, the president of the Carnegie Endowment for International Peace, was quick to point out the negative implications of the Taiwan deal, both for U.S. credibility and for future arms control efforts: "For a President who was establishing a new world order to massively violate a written agreement is hardly conducive to world order."[3]

While Bush's decision to go ahead with the sale of F-16s to Taiwan broke faith with a well-established international agreement, his decision ten days later to proceed with a sale of seventy-two F-15s to Saudi Arabia violated a major domestic understanding—the arrangement between the executive branch and Congress about how Capitol Hill should be notified of major arms sales. The normal procedure, grounded in the Arms Export Control Act and long-established custom, had been for members of Congress to learn of significant weapons export proposals via a three-step process: (1) informal discussions with staff members of key committees; (2) an informal, twenty-day "prenotification" to Congress that the deal was on its way; and (3) a thirty-day formal notification period, during which time the House and Senate can pass resolutions disapproving the sale if they so choose. For well over a decade, with a handful of exceptions, this had been the process through which the president consulted with Congress regarding a pending arms sale. But the Saudi F-15 sale was carried out under different rules, because it was a rush job with a tight political timetable.[4]

As late as mid-August, Pentagon and State Department officials were telling staff members on the House Foreign Affairs Committee that it was highly unlikely that an F-15 sale to the Saudis would be forwarded to the Congress in 1992. By the end of August there were some rumors circulating that the administration might reverse field. But the first official indication that the deal was going forward came on September 11, when President Bush told a rally of thousands of McDonnell Douglas employees in St. Louis that he was "delighted" to announce that he would be notifying the Congress of his decision to sell seventy-two F-15s to Saudi Arabia. Bush was trying to take advantage of the occasion to project a message that he had been having great difficulty getting across during the campaign—that he cared about the difficulties facing working men and women.

> I'm . . . aware that the past few years have been difficult for this company, for a lot of Americans, as Americans have had to adjust to the reality of a new and more peaceful world. And I know that many of you have been anxious about what the future will bring and especially about the status of the Eagle, about the F-15. And I have been sensitive to the impact of this contract on your production line, your jobs.[5]

The president went on to present the F-15 sale as a symbol of a larger commitment to working people, asserting that "in these times of economic transition, I want to do everything I can to keep Americans at work." But critics in Congress and the media charged that the most important job Bush was trying to save when he approved the F-15 sale was his own. Or, as a reporter for the St. Louis *Post-Dispatch* put it, "whether Saudi Arabia is permitted to buy some of the world's most advanced fighter planes may come down to something as simple as the number 11—the number of presidential electoral votes in Missouri, the state with the single largest stake in the F-15 sale and the one that is expected to be a key battleground between Clinton and Bush."[6]

That Bush had taken the unusual step of announcing a major

weapons sale at a staged media event before making even an informal notification of the sale to Capitol Hill angered congressional critics. Congressman Mel Levine of California, a long-standing opponent of arms transfers to Saudi Arabia and other potential adversaries of Israel, was blunt in his assessment of the reasons for the Bush administration's sudden "urgency" in rushing the Saudi F-15 sale through Congress:

> Frankly, the way in which this sale has been advanced smacks, in every possible regard, of election year politics.
>
> We've been through many arms sales before. The President of the United States has not gone to the plant . . . that will be the principal beneficiary of the sale to announce it before. It's not been done in the context of a campaign rally. And frankly, among the range of issues that I find disturbing and unfortunate about this sale, that ranks . . . near the top of the list because it undermines the basis upon which arms sales are theoretically predicated.[7]

Levine went on to argue that Bush's pork barrel logic violated the spirit of the Arms Export Control Act, which "spells out in specific statutory language the reason for arms sales—stability, regional stability, arms control.

"As important as jobs are," Levine continued, "the statute certainly didn't contemplate that these sales would be jobs programs, particularly in election years." But the drafters of the Arms Export Control Act probably didn't envision an incumbent president like George Bush who would pledge to do "whatever it takes" to get reelected; if that meant undermining the prospects for controlling the international arms trade just to win a few votes, so be it.[8]

It was bad enough that the Bush foreign policy team was letting narrow electoral concerns determine the timing and content of major arms sales proposals to Asia and the Middle East. But it was equally troubling to discover that the administration's strategic rationales for the F-15 sale to Saudi Arabia were straight out of the Cold War: bolstering a loyal ally to create that ever elusive "balance of power" against potentially threatening neighbors; swapping advanced arms for access to military bases that U.S. troops could use if the president decided to intervene in the region; fostering "interoperability" between U.S. and Saudi forces in case they had to fight together again in a rerun of Operation Desert Storm; and buying influence with the Saudi ruling clique over issues relating to the price and availability of oil. In short, arms sales were once again being treated as the linchpin of the entire U.S. political and security strategy in the Persian Gulf region and as a symbol of the de facto U.S.–Saudi alliance that had been nurtured with regular, massive infusions of U.S. weapons and training since the early days of the Nixon administration. The Bush administration's position on the F-15 sale was grounded in the increasingly dubious assumption that selling more U.S. arms to a "responsible" ally like Saudi Arabia would make another war less likely. The evidence of six major wars in the region since World War II—each fueled by the arms supplied by the United States and other major suppliers in the name of "stability" and preserving the balance of power—was studiously ignored by State Department and Pentagon officials who argued that *this* cycle of rearmament would be different. At a September 1992 congressional hearing, Levine questioned the Bush administration's suggestion that somehow selling more top-of-the-line arms to the Saudis would create a military balance in the region that would preclude the need to send U.S. troops there in the future: "Prior to the [Gulf] war we sold very large quantities to Saudi Arabia over a period of years, and when the war actually came . . . they were not able to defend themselves for five minutes. . . . If we sell these new airplanes to the Saudis, are they going to be able to defend themselves?" The Pentagon witness, Undersecretary of Defense Carl Ford, acknowledged that the answer to Levine's question was no, "not for an extended period of time against a major attack by an aggressive country like Iran or Iraq." Levine's question had uncovered the underlying premise of the sale—the politically unattractive notion that the U.S. military would be committed to defending the Saudi monarchy indefinitely and that a few more F-15s might give the Saudis a better capability to hold off a determined adversary until U.S. reinforcements could arrive on the scene.[9]

The Pentagon's indication that the Saudi sale was serving as a reinforcement—not a replacement—for future U.S. intervention in the Persian Gulf was amplified by the witness from the State Department. Frank Wisner, the undersecretary of state for international security affairs, revealed that fully one-third of the $9 billion F-15 package was set aside for technical and logistics services, personnel training, and the design and construction of supporting infrastructure. This was a roundabout way of saying that the United States would be building additional basing facilities that would be available to U.S. forces in the event of a future intervention in the Gulf. Wisner's colleague Carl Ford noted that this was consistent with the pattern of past U.S. arms sales to Saudi Arabia, in which "many of the infrastructure developments that have occurred in the facilities, air bases, were done with an eye to the possibility that the U.S. Air Force . . . might have to come into Saudi Arabia at some point, and this was a very important part of our Desert Storm/Desert Shield operations." The spirit of the 1981 AWACS deal—which entailed the use of arms sales as building blocks for a tacit U.S. military alliance with the Saudi regime—was alive and well in the 1992 F-15 sale. But just as in 1981, hardly anyone asked the fundamental question: did it make sense for the United States to use arms sales to expand its defense commitment to one of the most undemocratic regimes in the world?[10]

One congressman who did take serious exception to the Saudi F-15 deal was Larry Smith of Florida. He argued that "by making this sale, the United States will send a message that it supports the legitimacy and political judgment of the Saudi ruling group." Smith added that considering "the track record and make-up of the Saudi regime, I am not at all certain that we should be giving such an imprimatur." He noted that it was the Saudi royal family that had helped persuade the Reagan and Bush administrations to tilt toward Saddam Hussein during the Iran–Iraq war, then turned around and called in U.S. troops to bail them out when Saddam turned his military muscle southward in the Gulf War. Smith pointed out that despite the democratic revolution sweeping large parts of the world, the Saudi regime remained a "tribal enterprise, operated by a royal family that brooks no opposition." He clinched his case against the sale on the basis of what it would mean for the future of democracy in the region:

> Saudi Arabia is a textbook example of the failure of democratic development in the Middle East. By selling our most advanced weapons to such a regime, we will send an unambiguous signal of America's unconcern for democracy in the region. To the peoples of the Middle East, no pontifications will obscure the symbolic impact of such a transaction.[11]

But, as during the Cold War, the Bush administration was intent on bolstering pro-U.S. regimes like Saudi Arabia, both to counter the enemy of the moment and to reap short-term commercial benefits for U.S. industry. During the Cold War, this approach would have been rationalized with the obligatory argument about "curbing Soviet influence" in a critical oil-producing region, but now it was stripped of its anticommunist trappings. The only arguments left were those relating to maintaining close relations with the Saudi leadership. The provision of U.S. arms was now based on the notion that the Saudi regime would provide the United States with favorable access to its oil resources, spend its petrodollars in the service of the U.S. political and strategic agenda in the Third World, and do the United States the favor of allowing U.S. troops to defend it. With these outmoded policy assumptions firmly in place, Larry Smith's appeal to consider the antidemocratic implications of the Saudi F-15 sale was ignored by Bush administration policymakers.

If concerns about democracy wouldn't get the administration to reconsider the sale, what about pragmatic military concerns? Did it really make sense to sell the Saudis the most advanced fighter planes ever introduced into the Middle East when the likely result would be to stimulate new arms purchases by Israel, Iraq, Iran, and other potential Saudi adversaries? If the United States was committed to defending the Saudi regime, wouldn't it make more sense to take steps to reduce the level of armaments in the region? Levine raised precisely this point in his questioning of Undersecretary of State Wisner. After noting that the Saudi sale was directly linked to a U.S. pledge to provide a new military aid package to Israel that would preserve its "qualitative edge" over Saudi Arabia and the other Arab states of the region, Levine went on to question whether a strategy under which the United States was in essence racing with itself to arm the Middle East really made sense at this point in history:

> Wouldn't it make sense, when we are engaged in potentially pathbreaking arms control talks in the region, to put those two items [the Saudi F-15 sale and the new Israeli military aid package] on the shelf until we see whether some progress can be made with regard to arms control rather than injecting a new spiralling round of an arms race into the region. . . ? Wouldn't it make more sense to see how these arms control talks progress rather than to put the cart before the horse . . . by talking about a new set of arms to both Saudi Arabia and Israel before we see where these arms control talks go?

Wisner's response was emblematic of the entire Bush policy on arms transfer controls, which was reminiscent of an alcoholic who wants one more drink for the road. In theory, members of the Bush team favored controls, but in practice they could never find a particular sale that they would be willing to do without. Wisner's response to Levine's question demonstrated that the Bush administration retained its penchant for seeing only the benefits of any proposed arms sale, never the dangers: "Congressman, I understand your preoccupation, but I do not believe the sale will impede arms control discussions in the Middle East."[12] Wisner's views on these matters will carry weight within the Clinton administration as well, now that he has moved over to join Les Aspin at the Pentagon as the undersecretary of defense for policy.

The Clinton Promise

Foreign policy was a secondary issue in Bill Clinton's campaign for the presidency, to put it mildly. Outside of a handful of speeches and some sparring with President Bush over relations with China, loans and technology transfers to Iraq, and the Iran/contra scandal, Clinton staked his campaign almost entirely on the issue of who had the best plan for reviving the U.S. economy. Given the limited role assigned to foreign policy issues in Clinton's electoral strategy, it is not all that surprising that he failed to make a comprehensive statement on the subject of arms sales policy. In sharp contrast to Jimmy Carter, the last southern Democratic governor to ascend to the White House, Bill Clinton made no stirring promises to make human rights and arms transfer controls the centerpiece of his administration's foreign policy. And, as often seems to happen with Clinton, what little he did say about arms sales has placed him squarely on both sides of the issue.

As a lobbyist for McDonnell Douglas put it to me shortly after the election, there are really two Bill Clintons when it comes to the question of curbing the spread of armaments. On the one hand, there is the "arms control Clinton," who says "all the appropriate things" about reining in the weapons trade. On the other hand, according to this lobbyist, there is a more "pragmatic," less "idealistic" Bill Clinton that the arms industry can do business with. It was the "arms control Clinton" who ran on a Democratic platform that promised to "press for strong international limits on the dangerous and wasteful flow of weapons to troubled regions"; attacked George Bush for "coddling tyrants" like Saddam Hussein by supplying them with U.S. loans and military technology; and pledged to "review our arms sales policy and to take it up with the other major arms sellers of the world as part of a long-term effort to reduce the proliferation of weapons of destruction in the hands of people who might use them in very destructive ways."[13] Industry insiders are banking on these rhetorical pledges as strictly for public consumption, hoping that the other, more "pragmatic" side of Bill Clinton will carry the day when it comes down to setting policy.

If the 1992 presidential campaign offers any clue, Clinton's arms sales policy will be a bundle of contradictions. Candidate Clinton showed a flair for playing pork barrel politics with defense issues, a quality that doesn't bode well for the development of a consistent policy of controlling arms sales. Bill Clinton's talent for engaging in verbal gymnastics in the service of special interests in the defense industry was most clearly displayed right before the April 1992 Connecticut primary, when he suddenly came out in support of the Seawolf submarine. The Seawolf was one of the few big-ticket weapons systems that the Bush administration had actually decided to cancel, in grudging recognition that the Soviet threat it was designed to counter no longer existed. But the Seawolf was produced in Groton, Connecticut, a community that had become economically dependent on the operations of the Electric Boat submarine plant of General Dynamics. With Jerry Brown running well in Connecticut and his path to the Democratic nomination still in doubt, Bill Clinton conveniently discovered that there was now a need for the United States to produce more Seawolf submarines, a need that even the Pentagon had failed to perceive. It was a blatant appeal for votes in Connecticut, but Clinton appeared to have no problem asserting with a straight face that politics had nothing to do with it.

At another critical point, at the start of the general election campaign in August 1992, Clinton engaged in a similar pork barrel maneuver. This time his position was in direct contradiction to his platform pledge to press for limits on conventional arms sales. At an August 25th "town hall" meeting in Dallas that was broadcast live to audiences in St. Louis, Missouri, and several other cities, a St. Louis TV reporter asked Clinton whether he would support the sale of F-15s to Saudi Arabia. The reporter introduced his question by noting that "thousands of McDonnell Douglas workers here are waiting for President Bush to authorize the sale." Clinton replied without hesitation that he would support the sale "under the right circumstances." The main "circumstance" Clinton had in mind was making sure that the version of the F-15 provided to the Saudis was not a top-of-the-line ground attack model that might pose "a serious threat to Israel." To underscore that this was more than just a throwaway answer to a question that had taken Clinton off guard, the next morning the Clinton/Gore campaign issued a press release headlined "Governor Clinton Supports F-15 Sale to Saudi Arabia." This was a full two and a half weeks before President Bush announced that he would go ahead with the sale. In fact, a number of observers believe that Clinton's early support was an important factor in Bush's decision to press forward with the deal in the middle of an election campaign.[14]

What had prompted Clinton to endorse the most controversial Mideast arms sale since the Gulf War? To paraphrase McDonnell

Douglas, Clinton was undoubtedly motivated by "jobs, jobs, jobs." Clinton was afraid that opposing the sale in the middle of a recession would give a signal that he didn't care about America's battered manufacturing industries. The industrial states of the Midwest were shaping up as the battleground where the Clinton campaign felt the election would be won or lost; and the quest to win back the conservative, blue-collar "Reagan Democrats" who had abandoned the party's presidential ticket in every election since 1980 was at the center of the Clinton strategy for winning the Midwest. Downtown St. Louis had been the last stop on the first Clinton/Gore bus tour—and Clinton had no doubt gotten an earful about the "need" for the Saudi F-15 sale during his St. Louis visit from Missouri congressman Dick Gephardt, who had been spearheading efforts in the House on behalf of the deal.

Clinton's willingness to promote McDonnell Douglas's interests by supporting the Saudi F-15 deal went beyond just a short-term gesture toward a company in a key electoral state. Will Marshall, the executive director of the Washington-based Progressive Policy Institute, had been putting out the word since the Democratic convention in July that Clinton's arms sales policy would not differ in its essentials from the approach taken by George Bush. The institute is the think tank of the moderate Democratic Leadership Council, the political vehicle that Clinton used to catapult himself to national prominence by building up his image as a tough-minded, conservative, "new look" Democrat. One of the members of the Progressive Policy Institute's board of directors is the head of McDonnell Douglas's Washington office. No wonder the McDonnell lobbyist I spoke to after the election felt so confident that his firm could "do business" with President Clinton: they had already been doing so for years, through a direct connection with the political organization that, more than any other, helped transform Bill Clinton from the reasonably successful governor of a small state into the president of the United States.[15]

After his first year in office, it was still not clear which Clinton would predominate in the shaping of arms transfer policy—the "arms control" Clinton or the proindustry Clinton. During his first appearances before Congress, Secretary of State Warren Christopher—Clinton's principal foreign policy adviser and confidant—pledged to pursue "an *activist* diplomacy that puts a premium on timely prevention" of conflicts, and he indicated that a "comprehensive strategy" to halt the proliferation of nuclear and conventional armaments would be a central element in the administration's foreign policy. Christopher's position was reiterated by his undersecretary of state for international security affairs, Lynn Davis, both in her confirmation hearings and subsequent congressional testimonies. This potentially promising start was reinforced by Undersecretary of Defense William Perry's decision to limit Pentagon involvement in arms sales promotion at the 1993 Paris Air Show, even though the administration was reluctant to portray this move as an arms control measure (see chapter 1). In addition, the early word from administration insiders was that an options paper setting out Clinton's approach to curbing international arms sales might be ready by as early as the summer of 1993. It was hardly the kind of rousing start that Jimmy Carter had made on the arms sales issue, but the Clinton team's first few months in office offered some hope that it would adopt a serious long-term approach toward limiting weapons transfers.[16]

By the spring of 1993, there were already signs that this early promise was beginning to fade. The policy review on conventional arms sales was postponed indefinitely, and Lynn Davis had told an informal gathering of Washington policy experts that the administration might not even make a statement of its position on conventional arms transfers until well into 1994. Her own discussions of the subject in congressional hearings spoke of the need to deal with controversial arms sales on a "case-by-case" basis, a sure prescription for continuing with a policy of unrestrained transfers of advanced weaponry. After all, it was the case-by-case method that had made the United States the world's leading arms merchant in the first place, as successive administrations and members of Congress always managed to find reasons why the next sale on the agenda, in and of itself, posed no great threat to peace or regional stability. At the Pentagon, William Perry underscored that a traditionalist view on arms sales was rapidly reasserting itself when he told a group of industry representatives that he didn't really see weapons transfers as a major strategic issue, because he could not imagine a scenario in which any coalition of Third World powers armed with conventional armaments could possibly present a threat to the United States. Perry's position ignored the growing risks posed to U.S. forces by the weapons being sold by the United States and other major suppliers in the developing world, both in peacekeeping missions like Somalia and in full-scale interventions like the 1991 Gulf War.[17]

This myopic strategic thinking on arms sales was paralleled by a growing attachment to the economic benefits of weapons exports on the part of key players within the administration. An official closely involved with the development of the Clinton arms transfer policy told me point blank that "our first concern is to level the playing field. . . . We're not about to entertain any proposal [on limiting conventional arms sales] that would disadvantage our manufacturers." Since the United States now controls over two-thirds of the Third World arms market, and any cutback in U.S. sales might at least initially elicit sales activity by other suppliers, this position implies that no serious proposal for limiting the arms trade will be considered, because it might temporarily hurt the bottom line of a few U.S. weapons exporting firms. This "economics-first" approach to arms sales has been championed most forcefully by Clinton's secretary of commerce, Ron Brown, whose energetic promotional activities on behalf of U.S. companies have included attendance at international trade shows and direct personal pitches to foreign government officials for U.S. weapons systems (see chapter 1). During his confirmation hearings, Clinton's first Defense Secretary, Les Aspin, foreshadowed the role that economic considerations would play in frustrating progress toward controlling the arms trade.

> I do not think that we're ever going to deal adequately with the question of arms sales until you take care of the political pressure to make those arms sales, and I'm talking about domestic political pressure by people who are otherwise going to be out of work. As long as that pressure exists, I think any other review by any other group and whatever are not going to be very successful.[18]

Aspin has since left the Clinton administration, but his observations about the pivotal role of pork barrel politics in shaping arms transfer policy have proven to be prophetic. The administration's policy review—known formally as Presidential Decision Directive 41—was repeatedly delayed as Clinton policymakers have slowly but surely sacrificed the President's original commitment to arms transfer restraint on the altar of economic expediency. By early 1994, advocates of arms transfer controls within the administration were clearly on the defensive; one official described an interagency meeting at which he was reduced to making the case for restraint on public relations grounds, asserting that after such an extended internal review "we have to at least look like we're doing something different." This emphasis on spin control over substantive change was further revealed in the summer of 1994 when a Defense Department source told the industry newsletter *Inside the Pentagon* that the administration was considering the unprecedented step of *classifying* the new policy directive so that it could "characterize the plan any way [it pleases] without being faced with the text of the policy by [the press]." The source also noted that this was the first presidential review he had been involved

with that had a special "public presentation working group" charged with developing "strategies for explaining the policy to different groups, including the press."[19] The classification proposal was ultimately been shelved.

While the administration resisted putting its views down on paper throughout 1993 and 1994, a full-scale tilt toward industry has emerged as Clinton's de facto policy on arms sales. During the break at a November 1993 congressional hearing on arms sales issues, Joel Johnson of the Aerospace Industries Association observed that "so far we've gotten everything we've wanted from this administration." Johnson pointed to the administration's decision to introduce legislation to repeal "recoupment fees" on foreign military sales as a case in point. The fees are added to the price of major foreign sales as a way to recover part of the cost of taxpayer funded research and development for U.S. weapons systems. This seemingly arcane reform has been sought by the industry for years as a way to make their products cheaper to foreign clients, theoretically boosting U.S. market share in the process. So far this proposal has been blocked in Congress, but the Clinton administration continues to support it.[20]

In a much more visible shift, the Pentagon announced in January of 1994 that it would return to the Bush administration's policy of direct participation in international arms bazaars, sending U.S. equipment and troops to these exhibitions at taxpayer expense. The memo justifying the move cited the need to help U.S. industry, which "faces formidable competition from other nations who are actively marketing their equipment globally." Under this rationale, the Pentagon sent pilots and weapons systems to shows in Singapore, Paris, Farnborough (England), and Abu Dhabi (in the Persian Gulf) during 1994, at a cost of roughly $1.5 million. In addition to providing an unnecessary subsidy to arms manufacturers at a time of stringent budgets for domestic programs, the new Clinton air and trade show policy has given palpable form to its pro-industry stance by reintroducing the spectacle of U.S. government personnel standing shoulder to shoulder with industry representatives promoting weapons sales. A U.S. pilot who participated in the June 1994 Eurosatory exhibit in Paris regaled Ed Bradley of CBS's *60 Minutes* with tales of the performance of his helicopter in the Gulf War, but he tried to split hairs when Bradley asked whether his role at the show was to help the arms industry sell its wares to foreign military officials: "No sir, I'm not here to sell the aircraft, I'm here to tell them everything they need to know about the aircraft." But an executive from a firm that specializes in selling night vision devices confirmed that the Pentagon's marketing assistance was greatly appreciated:

> In the past, the U.S. military in particular had to keep kind of an arms length from the manufacturers, and so when we would go to an international exhibit we'd be pretty much on our own. And now, of course, we're working let's say as a team.[21]

By the end of 1994, even the pretense that the Clinton administration had any intention of curbing the weapons trade was being abandoned. In response to a direct question about whether the administration's proposed guidelines would have stopped any arms sale that the U.S. has made over the past fifteen years, an official involved in the policy review said "no." It's hard to imagine a more precise definition of a business as usual policy. Clinton policymakers began to leak information to the press, warning people not to expect a "radical departure" from the policies of the Reagan and Bush years, and a Pentagon spokesperson confirmed that the health of the defense industry and the "defense industrial base" would become explicit factors in deciding which exports to approve. This emphasis was confirmed in an October 1994 briefing to the House Foreign Affairs Committee by Undersecretary of State Lynn Davis. "Sustaining the defense industrial base" was cited by Davis as one of the top five reasons for selling U.S. weaponry, and she warned that any new initiatives to control the trade would be carefully focused toward limiting transfers to so-called "rogue states" like Iran, Libya, and North Korea—nations that are already barred from receiving U.S. arms. This narrow focus carried the day when President Clinton finally released the results of his policy review in February 1995. As if to signal that nothing of substance was going to change, the official White House fact sheet on the new policy noted that "given the complexities of arms transfer decisions and the multiple U.S. interests involved . . . decisions will continue to be made on a case-by case-basis."[22]

While the Clinton administration has been busy abandoning its commitment to restraint, the public and the Congress have been speaking out more loudly and clearly on this issue than at any time since the mid-seventies. During the summer of 1993, Congressman Howard Berman of California organized a letter to President Clinton from 111 members of the House of Representatives, urging him to take the lead in developing an international agreement to restrain weapons exports. In the fall of 1993, Senator Patrick Leahy of Vermont and Congress-

man Lane Evans of Illinois won a three-year extension of a moratorium on the export of anti-personnel land mines from the United States, as a first step toward pressing for an international ban on this whole class of conventional weaponry. And in November of 1993, Senator Mark Hatfield of Oregon and Congresswoman Cynthia McKinney of Georgia introduced legislation that would create a Code of Conduct for U.S. arms transfers. Under the code, nations that abuse the human rights of their citizens, engage in aggression against their neighbors, violate fundamental principles of democracy, or ignore international arms accords would be ineligible to receive U.S. weaponry without a presidential waiver affirmed by a vote of the Congress. The Code of Conduct bill is supported by the Arms Transfer Working Group, a coalition of religious, human rights, arms control, and international development groups. As of the end of 1994, the bill had 100 cosponsors in the house, and it had been endorsed by 200 national and local organizations. The vast majority of the bill's co-sponsors were re-elected in November of 1994, and Senator Hatfield intends to use his new, more powerful position as prospective chair of the Senate Appropriations Committee as leverage to gain more support for the bill in the Senate. The bill was reintroduced in February 1995, and both Congresswoman McKinney and Senator Hatfield have vowed to actively press for a vote on the measure in their respective houses of Congress.[23]

A New Policy?

As the 1992 presidential campaign and the first two years of the Clinton administration have made painfully clear, the first step toward implementing a consistent policy of arms sales restraint must be to break this nation's economic dependence on weapons exports.

The economics of arms sales is a paradox. For all the hue and cry that goes up every time the president or the Congress even consider postponing a major arms sale, weapons exports in fact support a tiny fraction of the nation's working population. A 1992 Congressional Budget Office study estimated that a substantial cut in U.S. arms sales to the Middle East would affect less than 2 percent of all defense workers and less than one-tenth of 1 percent of the nation's total work force.[24] This is hardly a large enough figure to cause serious damage to the nation's overall economic prospects, particularly if reductions in weapons exports are counterbalanced by increased efforts to develop commercial products and markets. In fact, once one takes into account the substantial hidden costs of the arms trade, the positive effects of weapons exports on the U.S. economy are marginal at best. Government subsidies alone—including Pentagon grants and loans, government personnel involved in brokering and promoting arms sales, Pentagon involvement in arms bazaars, and government publications devoted to marketing U.S. weaponry abroad—average roughly $7 billion per year. Corporate offset commitments, which amount to legalized kickbacks to weapons purchasing countries, steer billions of additional dollars worth of business from U.S. firms to foreign companies. Regional arms races in the Middle East and Asia, which are in part stimulated by massive U.S. sales, add tens of billions of dollars to the U.S. defense budget every year to prepare for military contingencies in these areas. And pushing weapons on Third World countries slows their economic growth, shrinking potential markets for U.S. civilian products in the process. The International Monetary Fund has estimated that a 20 percent coordinated reduction in military spending worldwide could create new consumer markets worth up to $190 billion over the long term, a figure four to five times greater than the entire value of the international weapons market. Even as a strict economic proposition, government sponsored weapons trafficking is no bargain.[25] Nevertheless, most political leaders from presidential candidates on down to mayors and local legislators have repeatedly caved into the arms industry's claim that reining in the arms trade at a time of reductions in Pentagon spending will have a devastating impact on the economy. What accounts for this contradiction?

Part of the answer has to do with the nature of defense jobs. They are highly visible, with major concentrations of high-paying jobs at large factories like the McDonnell Douglas plant in St. Louis, the Lockheed F-16 plant in Fort Worth, Texas, the Boeing plant in Seattle, Washington, and the immense complex of weapons plants that have made the Los Angeles area the defense industrial capital of the world. Defense jobs tend to be unionized jobs, and both the defense contractors and their unions make a point of reminding their elected leaders of their political importance. Finally, unlike many other kinds of jobs that are affected by a wide array of complex economic factors, defense jobs are closely tied to the political process: if a member of Congress votes down an arms sale or a weapons program, there is an immediate impact in the form of reduced jobs. And the defense contractors will make doubly sure that every voter knows exactly where those jobs were located—and which representatives voted for or against them. As a result, decisions about military spending and arms sales have a political impact far beyond what would be warranted by looking at their economic effects alone.

In addition to their direct impact on jobs, military spending and arms sales have also been used throughout the Cold War era as a means of running a covert industrial policy. Under the guise of ensuring national security, the U.S. government has provided production contracts, research and development subsidies, and even outright grants of plants and equipment to firms in high-tech sectors such as electronics and aerospace. This Pentagon largess has aided the growth of these industries, but at a tremendous cost. Many critics see these military subsidies as an incredibly inefficient way to help U.S. industry. But in the absence of a conscious policy of government support for high-tech sectors on grounds of commercial competitiveness, the use of military spending and arms exports to provide indirect support has formed the basis of an unstated industrial policy that the United States has used to counter the explicit, commercially oriented industrial strategies of economic rivals like Germany and Japan.[26]

Breaking the nation's economic addiction to arms sales requires a two-pronged strategy for converting the skills and resources that have been devoted to military purposes during the Cold War to meeting the pressing needs of the civilian economy. Shortly after he took office, Bill Clinton outlined a five-year, $20 billion program that could have gone a significant way toward reducing America's economic dependency on arms sales—if it was vigorously implemented. The plan called for more government support for civilian research and development; investment of funds, cut from defense, in infrastructure and cutting-edge commercial products; industrial extension centers to help small and medium-sized defense suppliers adjust from defense to commercial markets; and programs to retrain and reemploy defense industry workers. In practice, the plan has relied far too heavily on funding research into so-called "dual use" technologies with civilian and military applications.

Further steps must be taken, the most important of which is to put the whole conversion program in the hands of an independent agency—no bureaucracy can be expected to voluntarily reduce its own power and influence, and putting the Pentagon in charge of conversion is like putting the fox in charge of the chicken coop. In addition, the Clinton conversion program should promote alternative, government-supported commercial markets in areas of national need such as housing, environmental protection, transportation, and health care to replace the government-subsidized military market that has sustained significant sectors of the U.S. economy for more than four decades.[27]And Clinton policymakers must resist the arms industry's desperate attempts to "redefine" conversion to include government financing for weapons exports (see chapter 8).

Breaking the economic stranglehold of the arms export lobby will also require political reforms. Because their fortunes depend almost entirely on actions taken by the government, military contractors should be banned outright from making Political Action Committee (PAC) contributions. To cite just one example of the negative consequences of this tool of influence, the eight-company team that lobbied for the F-15 sale to Saudi Arabia made over $4 million in PAC contributions to members of Congress and presidential candidates in the runup to the 1992 election, a campaign year that was marked by an unprecedented $20 billion in new arms sales offers in the two months prior to the presidential vote. That's an excellent return on their political investment for the defense contractors, but it comes at great cost to the future security of the nation and the world. Partial figures for the 1994 Congressional elections indicate that the top ten Pentagon contractors had already spent $2.5 million on House and Senate races by August of 1994, before the usual fall funding surge.[28]

In addition to stemming the flow of money from contractors to politicians, breaking the power of the arms lobby will require stronger controls on the flow of bureaucrats back and forth between the government and the military contractors. Current restrictions are so loose that only those individuals who worked directly on a specific matter while in government are barred from lobbying on that same matter when they leave government. These regulations have left a gaping loophole for the arms export lobby, and they have taken full advantage of it. When it comes time to push for looser arms export regulations, the defense companies have literally thousands of former generals and admirals, Pentagon and State Department officials, and members of Congress and congressional staffers at their disposal to help them make their case.

The lobbying reforms put forward by President Clinton in early 1993 will only marginally slow down the revolving door between defense and foreign policymaking jobs in the federal government and lobbying positions in the arms industry that has shut ordinary citizens out of the arms sales decisionmaking process. Arms export policy is at the center of U.S. national security policy for the post–Cold War era, and we can't afford to let policy in this area continue to be corrupted by influence peddling and revolving-door politics. Bill Clinton should slap sharp limits on the postgovernment activities of all officials who play a role in shaping arms sales decisions in the executive branch or the Congress, including a lifetime ban on lobbying the U.S. government on any matter dealing with policies on the transfer of arms and military technology. The arms companies will still have more money and a

larger Washington presence than the advocates of arms transfer restraint, but these limits should at least begin to level the political playing field on proliferation issues to the point where the national interest has a fighting chance to win out over private commercial interests.[29]

In addition to moving to break the nation's economic addiction to arms exports, it will be necessary for the Executive Branch to wean itself from the political addiction to weapons trafficking that has afflicted every president since Richard Nixon. On the face of it, trading arms for political and strategic influence seems like an attractive policy option, because it appears to be relatively risk free. Selling arms requires passage of no special legislation; it doesn't involve a commitment of U.S. troops (at least initially); and, more often than not, the money is supplied by the purchasing nation, not the U.S. taxpayer. What could be easier from the president's perspective?

But the absence of short-term costs should not be allowed to blind the executive branch to the long-term negative consequences of using arms sales as a pillar of U.S. foreign policy. These consequences include the use of arms sales to build entangling military alliances with undemocratic regimes like Kuwait and Saudi Arabia—alliances that could end up costing tens of thousands of U.S. lives in some future crisis; the proliferation of U.S.-supplied military technology to potential adversaries, as happened in Iran in the 1970s and Iraq in the 1980s; the militarization of Third World societies, which has brought many of them to the brink of political and economic collapse, with immense costs for the world's economic and political system; and the stifling of open public debate about what role the United States should play in a changing world order that has resulted from the use of arms sales as tools of covert diplomacy.

Simply put, carrying on America's arms sales habit is a threat to peace and a threat to democracy, around the world and right here in the United States. If there is to be any hope of forging a more peaceful era in the wake of the Cold War, the United States must develop new, less dangerous tools for exerting strategic and political influence in the world community.

Obviously, the United States cannot put a lid on the global arms trade all by itself. Even though the United States did account for 57 percent of all arms sold to the Third World in 1992, there is still plenty of underutilized arms production capacity in Western Europe, Russia, China, and a half dozen other smaller arms supplying nations to fill the gap that would be left if the United States were to cut back its arms sales unilaterally.[30] But as the world's leading arms trafficking nation and the dominant military power of the post–Cold War era, the

United States has tremendous leverage over what happens in the international arms trade—*if* President Clinton chooses to use that leverage. The United States should take the lead in crafting a system of multilateral restraints on sales of arms and military technology. The Clinton administration should begin by reviving the "Big Five" arms transfer talks (among the United States, the United Kingdom, Russia, France, and China) that were initiated in the wake of the Gulf War, with the goal of eventually expanding the talks to include other significant suppliers such as Germany and Italy. When they were on a regular schedule during 1991 and 1992, these talks were all rhetoric and no action. Even worse, the United States has been selling weapons to the Middle East at a near record clip from the beginning of the Gulf War right up to the present, leading the other participants in the process to grumble that the United States was using the talks as a political smokescreen to put its competitors off guard and deflect political criticism while it went on its own arms sales binge.

To restore U.S. credibility on the arms sales issue, the Clinton administration should propose a moratorium on all new sales to regions of potential conflict like the Middle East and Asia, which the United States would agree to observe for as long as the other major suppliers follow suit. Then U.S. representatives to a new set of arms transfer control talks should put concrete proposals on the table. These proposals should include an outright prohibition on the sale of inhumane weapons like cluster bombs, napalm, land mines, and other systems that cause indiscriminate damage to civilian populations; strict limits on the sale of offensive weaponry like deep-strike combat aircraft, ballistic missiles, and main battle tanks; mandatory embargoes on all arms sales to regions of active conflict; and restrictions on transfers of military production technology via licensing agreements or sales of dual-use equipment.[31]

Efforts must be made to provide economic as well as political incentives for countries to participate in a new international arms transfer control regime. Nations that agree to phase out weapons exports should be given access to a special international economic conversion fund, which could be funded initially from the monies freed up by phasing out all government subsidies of arms exports. In an effort to reduce the demand for arms, access to bilateral and multilateral loans should take into account a nation's level of military spending, with nations that spend excessive amounts on armaments receiving less favorable treatment.[32]

Finally—and most important of all—the United States should take the lead in encouraging the major military powers to reduce their military spending, with an ultimate goal of cutting worldwide military spending in half by the year 2000. The funds freed up as a result of these coordinated arms reductions can be put to good use in educating and feeding the world's children, building modern infrastructure and communications networks, and creating technologies that can promote sustainable development without destroying the natural environment. Cutting arms sales can serve as a cornerstone of the larger process of demilitarization and democratization that is a prerequisite for a peaceful world in the post–Cold War era.

Reining in the arms trade will be a tall order, but the consequences of putting off a change in policy are simply unacceptable. Whether any president will have the political courage and the staying power to take on the permanent arms sales establishment that has shaped U.S. policy for the past twenty-five years will depend in large measure on how much pressure he or she gets from the American people. Without an aroused public and an active, pro-arms-control Congress, America's arms sales addiction is likely to continue, with increasingly tragic consequences for America and the world.

Epilogue

The Republican sweep of the November 1994 Congressional elections could radically alter the prospects for implementing significant reforms in U.S. foreign policy. Although the arms trade was not a high profile electoral issue, the "Contract with America" which served as the platform for Republican candidates for the House of Representatives was generally sympathetic toward the defense industry, calling for increases in Pentagon spending and a resurrection of the "Star Wars" anti-ballistic missile program. As for President Clinton, the political fallout from the election could make him even more reluctant to take on a major lobby like the defense industry in the name of controlling the weapons trade—a commitment he had been steadily abandoning in any case.

The only good news for advocates of arms sales restraint to come out of the 1994 elections was the defeat of Oliver North, covert arms dealer extraordinaire and newfound darling of the religious right, in his campaign for the U.S. Senate in Virginia. Despite earning millions of dollars in speaking and writing fees since the Iran/contra affair gave him national exposure, and raising over $17 million for his campaign through a direct mail campaign targeting right-wing supporters nationwide, North's drive to defeat incumbent Chuck Robb fell short. A post-election analysis by the *New York Times* indicated that while nearly half of Virginia voters disapproved of how President Clinton was doing his job, "an even greater number spoke of their disgust with Mr. North for his role in the Iran-contra affair." On the last day of the campaign, Robb aroused himself from what had been a fairly lack-luster effort to denounce North as a "document-shredding, Constitution-trashing, Commander-in-Chief-bashing, uniform-shaming, Ayatollah-loving, arms-dealing, criminal-protecting, resume-enhancing, Noriega-coddling, Social Security-threatening, public school-denigrating, Swiss-banking-law-breaking, letter-faking, self-serving, election-losing, snake-oil salesman who can't tell the difference between the truth and a lie." North lost the election by 3 percent of the vote, but he has vowed to run again.[1]

Meanwhile, back at the Pentagon, the spirit of North's Iran/contra enterprise lives on in a new Air Force proposal to sell over 300 upgraded F-16 fighter planes from its own stocks to countries like Morocco, Tunisia, and Singapore, then take the proceeds and plough them back into the Air Force budget to buy new F-16s. This "diversion" of arms sales revenues to buy new weaponry would warm Ollie North's heart; the only difference between this plan and the covert Iran/contra deals is that this is a public proposal that requires Congressional approval. The principal beneficiary of the plan would be the Lockheed Corporation, which would stand to profit twice: first when the planes are modernized, and second when the proceeds from foreign sales are given back to them in the form of contracts to build new aircraft. Not surprisingly, a Lockheed official has voiced strong support, calling it a "very creative approach" that "opens up the market for Third World countries that don't have tremendous resources." The author of the plan, Air Force vice chief of staff Gen. Michael Carns, has discussed extending it to include sales of surplus Lockheed C-130 transport aircraft, Boeing KC-135 tanker airplanes, Grumman/Fairchild A-10 attack planes, and even an occasional McDonnell Douglas F-15. In Febraury of 1995, President Clinton nominated Carns to head the CIA—hardly an agency that should be out looking for bright new ideas on how to sell weapons.[2]

As if this "double-dipping" weren't enough, there is a third way that Lockheed stands to benefit from the Pentagon's proposed F-16 "fire sale": by pumping up the very threats that it is using to justify spending billions of dollars on the next generation of Air Force fighters. In the company's brochure for its new F-22 combat aircraft—the most expensive fighter plane ever built—Lockheed gives as its principal rationale the fact that it is a "dangerous world" in which "sophisticated fighters and air defense systems are being sold." The centerpiece of the brochure is a foldout map of "Foreign Countries with Advanced Fighter Aircraft," the clear implication being that the U.S. needs the F-22 to outgun these potential future adversaries. On closer examination, it ends up that half of the 48 nations listed on the map received their "advanced fighter aircraft" from the United States, and that most of them are F-16s! Even allowing for some marketing hype —among the countries listed is Denmark, an unlikely prospect to ever turn its Air Force against the United States—Lockheed's marketing strategy inadvertently reveals a sort of confidence game that is at the center of current U.S. arms policies. Rather than promoting regional arms restraint, reducing potential threats to the United States, and cutting future military outlays in the process, the Pentagon and the U.S. defense industry think they have a better idea: selling advanced weaponry with relative abandon and then buying new, improved U.S. systems to stay one step ahead of the competition.[3]

If Congress and the Clinton administration are truly committed to cutting pork barrel projects and streamlining government, these new arms financing schemes should be summarily rejected; but stopping them will undoubtedly be an uphill battle. By virtue of its pending merger with Martin Marietta, Lockheed will solidify its position in front of McDonnell Douglas as the nation's largest defense contractor; the combined Political Action Committees of the two firms spent close to $1 million in the run-up to the 1994 congressional elections. And as if Lockheed didn't have enough powerful friends in Washington already, it ends up that Newt Gingrich, the new speaker of the House of Representatives, has more than a passing interest in the company's fortunes. Lockheed's Marietta, Georgia, facility, which produces both the F-22 fighter plane and the C-130 transport plane, falls just outside his jurisdiction, and according to a spokesperson at the facility "a majority of our workers live in Newt Gingrich's district." Lockheed has already made an investment in its powerful new friend, funneling Gingrich $5,000 in the waning weeks of the 1994 campaign and providing $10,000 to support Gingrich's satellite-TV lecture series, "Renewing American Civilization."[4]

For all of its advantages in terms of money and influence, the arms industry should not assume that its pro-export agenda will automatically carry the day. As of this writing, the Clinton administration was still resisting a longstanding industry request for a $1 billion arms export loan guarantee fund that would supplement the billions of dollars that the Pentagon already spends for this purpose. If Clinton reverses field and signs off on the plan, it could become a lightning rod for a populist campaign against subsidies to the weapons industry at a time of drastic cutbacks in domestic programs. Republican Senator Mark Hatfield, the heir apparent to take over the Senate Appropriations Committee, is a stalwart critic of weapons trafficking who will oppose any move to increase government largesse targeted toward arms exporting firms.

Most importantly, the public is overwhelmingly opposed to government-sponsored weapons trading: a January 1994 poll found that *96%* of Americans believe that "the United States should *not* sell or give tanks, fighter airplanes, guns or other conventional weapons to dictators or undemocratic governments." With a client list that includes Indonesia, Saudi Arabia, Taiwan, and a number of other undemocratic governments, the Clinton administration is vulnerable to a campaign of public pressure aimed at cutting off routine supplies of U.S. weapons to repressive regimes. And as the spectacle of U.S. troops in Haiti going into harm's way to disarm military and paramilitary forces that have historically been armed by the U.S. government underscores the dangerous and unpredictable ways that weapons trafficking can backfire, there is bound to be a public backlash at some point. In addition to the campaign to impose a "Code of Conduct" on U.S. weapons transfers (see chapter 13), a nascent movement against arms-related violence is beginning to bring together individuals and organizations concerned about everything from the spread of nuclear weapons to foreign arms sales to gun deaths on the streets of America. In April of 1995, at the time of the United Nations review conference for the Nuclear Non-Proliferation Treaty, this potentially powerful new coalition will come together in New York City for an "International Citizens' Assembly Against the Spread of Weapons." The success of their efforts and the work of other concerned citizens' groups will determine whether the people of the United States finally begin to make their voices heard in the debates over which nations and groups receive U.S. weaponry, or whether these life-and-death decisions remain the preserve of a small, self-interested elite.[5]

Notes

Chapter 1. The $134 Billion Question

1. George Esper, "Marine Killed in Somali Firefight," *Washington Post*, January 13, 1993; John Lancaster, "Mogadishu Ambush Leaves Marines on Edge," *Washington Post*, January 14, 1993; "The Ultimate Sacrifice," *Los Angeles Times*, January 15, 1993; and Bruce Frankel, "Marine 'Wanted to Help,'" *USA Today*, January 14, 1993.

2. Statistics and background on U.S. arms sales to Somalia during the 1980s are from U.S. Department of State and U.S. Department of Defense, *Congressional Presentation for Security Assistance Programs*, fiscal 1981–1990; and William D. Hartung, "Somalia and the Cycle of Arms Sales," *Christian Science Monitor*, February 22, 1993.

3. U.S. Department of State and U.S. Department of Defense, *Congressional Presentation*, fiscal 1994; U.S. Department of Defense, Defense Security Assistance Agency (DSAA), *Foreign Military Sales, Foreign Military Construction Sales, and Foreign Military Assistance Facts as of September 30, 1993* (Washington, D.C.: U.S. Government Printing Office, 1994); David Binder and Barbara Crossette, "As Ethnic Wars Multiply, U.S. Strives for a Policy," *New York Times*, February 7, 1993; and remarks by Lt. Gen. Thomas G. Rhame, Director, Defense Security Assistance Agency, at a conference on "Defense Exports in the Post–Cold War Environment," Tysons Corner, Virginia, October 5, 1993.

4. David Rogers, "U.S. to Buy Back Some of Missiles Held by Afghans," *Wall Street Journal*, January 15, 1993; Tim Weiner, "U.S. Will Try to Buy Antiaircraft Missiles Back from Afghans," *New York Times*, July 24, 1993; and William D. Hartung, "Proliferation's Profiteers," *CEO/International Strategies*, February/March 1993.

5. Weiner, "U.S. to Buy Missiles Back"; Jim Hoagland, "No More Frankensteins," *Washington Post*, July 13, 1993; Caryle Murphy, "U.S. Policies Trouble Egypt," *Washington Post*, August 1, 1993; and Douglas Jehl, "CIA Officers Played Role in Sheik Visas," *New York Times*, July 22, 1993.

6. Paul Taylor, "Key Angolan City Falls to Rebels," *Washington Post*, March 9, 1993; Paul Beaver, "UNITA Rebels Resume Fighting After Election Defeat," *Jane's Defense Weekly*, February 6, 1993; Paula R. Newberg, "Pakistan: At the Edge of Democracy," *World Policy Journal*, Summer 1989; and Marcus W. Brauchli, "India and Pakistan Feed Old Animosities," *Wall Street Journal*, April 20, 1993. For further background on the role of U.S. arms in these conflicts, see chapters 6 and 7; for details on U.S. coproduction arrangements with developing nations, see chapter 12.

7. The description of the Paris Air Show is based on observations and interviews by the author and on William D. Hartung, "The Boom at the Arms Bazaar," *Bulletin of the Atomic Scientists*, October 1991.

8. Presentation by Sinclair S. Martel, deputy assistant secretary of state for regional affairs, at a conference on "Defense Exports in the Post–Desert Storm Environment," cosponsored by the U.S. Department of Defense, DSAA, and the American Defense Preparedness Association, July 17–18, 1991, reprinted in the *DISAM Journal of International Security Assistance Management*, vol. 13, no. 4, Summer 1991. Other quotes in this section are from contemporaneous notes taken by the author while attending the conference.

9. David Silverberg, "Pentagon Ban of Personnel at Air Show Rankles Industry," *Defense News*, April 26–May 2, 1993; "Pentagon Reverses Trend Toward More Support for Air and Trade Shows," *Aerospace Daily*, April 23, 1993; and "Pentagon Air Show Decision Is An Anti-Arms Proliferation Policy—Sort Of," *Aerospace Daily*, April 30, 1993.

10. Unless otherwise noted, quotes and descriptions in this section are based on observations and interviews conducted by the author at the Paris Air Show, June 10–16, 1993.

See also William D. Hartung, "Welcome to the U.S. Arms Superstore," *Bulletin of the Atomic Scientists*, September 1993.

11. Brian Coleman, "Brown Says U.S. to Maintain Forceful Aerospace Policy," *Wall Street Journal Europe*, June 14, 1993; and "Commerce Chief Blasts Subsidies," *Aviation Week and Space Technology*, June 21, 1993.

12. U.S. Department of State and U.S. Department of Defense, *Congressional Presentation*, fiscal 1981–1990; U.S. Department of Defense, DSAA, *Foreign Military Sales, Foreign Military Construction Sales, and Military Assistance Facts as of September 30, 1990* (Washington, D.C.: U.S. Government Printing Office, 1991).

13. Richard F. Grimmett, *Conventional Arms Transfers to the Third World, 1986–1993* (Washington, D.C.: Congressional Research Service, 1994).

14. The figures on the dependence of the U.S. economy on arms sales are calculated by the author using data from the following sources: Congressional Budget Office, *Limiting Conventional Arms Exports to the Middle East* (Washington, D.C.: U.S. Government Printing Office, 1992); Congressional Budget Office, *The Economic Effects of Reduced Defense Spending* (Washington, D.C.: U.S. Government Printing Office, 1992); U.S. Arms Control and Disarmament Agency, *World Military Expenditures and Arms Transfers, 1990* (Washington, D.C.: U.S. Government Printing Office, 1992); and Investor Responsibility Research Center, "Foreign Military Sales: Summary of the Background Report," March 18, 1993.

Chapter 2. The Nixon Doctrine: Roots of the Arms Sales Addiction

1. For the best description of the immediate background to the announcement of the Nixon Doctrine, see Tad Szulc, *The Illusion of Peace: Foreign Policy in the Nixon Years* (New York: Viking Press, 1978), pp. 124–129; for the hyperbolic Nixon quotes, see "Urrah Neekson," *Newsweek*, August 11, 1969.

2. Szulc, *Illusion of Peace*, pp. 125–127; and Richard Nixon, "Informal Remarks in Guam with Newsmen," July 25, 1969, in *Public Papers of the Presidents of the United States—Richard Nixon, 1969* (Washington, D.C.: U.S. Government Printing Office, 1971), pp. 544–549.

3. Szulc, *Illusion of Peace*, p. 125.

4. Robert S. Litwak, *Détente and the Nixon Doctrine: American Foreign Policy and the Pursuit of Stability 1969–1976* (Cambridge: Cambridge University Press, 1984), pp. 48–51.

5. Henry Kissinger, *White House Years* (Boston: Little, Brown and Company, 1979), pp. 222–224.

6. Robert Keatley, "Nixon Feels He Has Cut Involvement in Asia; Others Fear U.S. May Get into Wider War," *Wall Street Journal*, January 29, 1971. For a slightly different formulation of the Kissinger quote on the Nixon Doctrine, see William Safire, *Before the Fall: An Inside View of the Pre-Watergate White House* (New York: Belmont Tower Books, 1975), p. 187, in which Kissinger is quoted as saying, "We wrote the goddamn Doctrine, we can change it."

7. Richard M. Nixon, "Asia After Vietnam," *Foreign Affairs*, vol. 46, no. 1, October 1967, pp. 113–114.

8. For an overview of this shift from aid to sales, see "The Evolution of Doctrine: U.S. Arms Export Policy from Kennedy to Reagan," chap. 3 in Michael T. Klare, *American Arms Supermarket* (Austin, Tex.: University of Texas Press, 1984). For the quote on the Nixon Doctrine as a gamble, see Anthony Sampson, *The Arms Bazaar: From Lebanon to Lockheed* (New York: Viking Press, 1977), p. 243.

9. Richard M. Nixon, *The Real War* (New York: Random House, 1980), p. 197.

10. Author's calculations, drawing upon U.S. Department of Defense, DSAA, *Fiscal Year Series as of September 1981* (Washington, D.C.: Data Management Division, Comptroller, Defense Security Assistance Agency, 1982).

11. For the best analysis of the U.S. arms supply relationship with the shah, see Michael T. Klare, *American Arms Supermarket* (Austin, Tex.: University of Texas Press, 1984), chap. 6.

12. The earliest documentation of the May 1972 meeting in which Nixon and Kissinger gave the shah a "blank check" to purchase U.S. arms is in Senate Foreign Relations Committee, Subcommittee on Foreign Assistance, "U.S. Military Sales to Iran" (Washington, D.C.: U.S. Government Printing Office, July 1976). For other accounts, see Gary Sick, *All Fall Down* (New York: Random House, 1985), pp. 13–15 (this is the source of the "protect me" quote); William Shawcross, *The Shah's Last Ride* (New York: Simon and Schuster, 1988), pp. 155–163; and James A. Bill, *The Eagle and the Lion: The Tragedy of American–Iranian Relations* (New Haven, Conn.: Yale University Press, 1988), pp. 200–202.

13. Shawcross, *Shah's Last Ride*, p. 164.

14. Arnaud de Borchgrave, "Colossus of the Oil Lanes," *Newsweek*, May 21, 1973; and "Policeman of the Persian Gulf," *Time*, August 6, 1973.

15. William D. Hartung, "Breaking the Arms-Sales Addiction: New Directions for U.S. Policy," *World Policy Journal*, Winter 1990–91, pp. 1–26; William D. Hartung, *Weapons for the World 1982 Update: The U.S. Corporate Role in International Arms Transfers* (New York: Council on Economic Priorities, 1982); and Paul Ferrari, Jeffrey W. Knopf, and Raul Madrid, *U.S. Arms Exports: Policies and Contractors* (Washington, D.C.: Investor Responsibility Research Center, 1987).

16. For an overview of the economic and employment impacts of the early stages of cutbacks in spending on Vietnam, see U.S. Senate, Committee on Labor and Public Welfare, "Postwar Economic Conversion" (Washington, D.C.: U.S. Government Printing Office, 1970).

17. On the impetus to sell arms to Iran to recycle petrodollars, see Klare, *American Arms Supermarket*, pp. 118–121. For the quote "Arabs . . . get control of our economy," see Michael Klare, "The Political Economy of Arms Sales," *Society*, September/October 1974.

18. For details of the charges by James Akins that Kissinger actually encouraged the shah to raise oil prices so that Iran could buy more U.S. weaponry, see CBS News, "The Kissinger–Shah Connection," transcript, "60 Minutes," vol. 12, no. 34, May 4, 1980.

19. Fred Halliday, *Iran: Dictatorship and Development* (New York: Penguin Books, 1979), p. 91; Sick, *All Fall Down*, pp. 5–7; and Kermit Roosevelt, *Countercoup: The Struggle for the Control of Iran* (New York: McGraw-Hill, 1979).

20. On the celebration at Persepolis, see Shawcross, *Shah's Last Ride*, pp. 38–48; Bill, *Eagle and the Lion*, pp. 183–185; George Ball, *The Past Has Another Pattern* (New York: W.W. Norton and Company, 1982), pp. 434–435; "Iran: The Show of Shows," *Time*, October 25, 1971; and Loren Jenkins, "Iran's Birthday Party," *Newsweek*, October 25, 1971.

21. Cited in Bill, *Eagle and the Lion*, p. 185.

22. Jenkins, "Iran's Birthday Party."

23. On the importance of the event at Persepolis in galvanizing opposition to the shah, see Shawcross, *Shah's Last Ride*, p. 47. On Khomeini's reaction, see Bill, *Eagle and the Lion*, p. 185.

24. Jenkins, "Iran's Birthday Party."

25. The "it is inevitable" quote is from "Policeman of the Persian Gulf." On the shah's ambitions to outstrip Germany and other European powers, see Louis Kraar, "The Shah Drives to Build a New Persian Empire," *Fortune*, October 1974.

26. Halliday, *Iran*, p. 272. Halliday's observation refers to the period from the 1960s through the late 1970s.

27. The Kissinger quote is from William Safire, "Son of Secret Sellout," *New York Times*, February 12, 1976.

28. For the "our liberals' griping" quote, see Shawcross, *Shah's Last Ride*, p. 163. For the Amnesty International statement, see Halliday, *Iran*, p. 85.

29. Nixon, *Real War*, p. 273; and Kissinger, *White House Years*, pp. 222–225.

30. Senate Foreign Relations Committee, "U.S. Military Sales to Iran," pp. 44–45.

31. Shawcross, *Shah's Last Ride*, p. 166.

32. Ibid., p. 168.

33. On the Kissinger/Schlesinger bureaucratic battles over arming Iran, see Sick, *All Fall Down*, pp. 13–18.

34. Senate Foreign Relations Committee, "U.S. Military Sales to Iran," pp. ix–xiii.

35. Ibid., p. 43.

36. Ibid., pp. 17–24; Klare, *American Arms Supermarket*, pp. 109, 117–118; and Sampson, *Arms Bazaar*, pp. 258–259.

37. Sampson, *Arms Bazaar*, p. 247.

38. Barry Rubin, *Paved with Good Intentions: The American Experience and Iran* (New York: Oxford University Press, 1980), pp. 161–165.

39. Klare, *American Arms Supermarket*, pp. 64–67; and Sampson, *Arms Bazaar*, pp. 133–140, 222–240.

40. Rubin, *Paved with Good Intentions*, p. 165; and Senate Foreign Relations Committee, "U.S. Military Sales to Iran," pp. 44–48.

41. Sampson, *Arms Bazaar*, p. 254.

42. Senate Foreign Relations Committee, Subcommittee on Multinational Corporations, "Multinational Corporations and United States Foreign Policy," vol. 17, August 9 and September 10, 13, 15, and 27, 1976 (Washington, D.C.: U.S. Government Printing Office, 1977), pp. 2–9.

43. Ibid., pp. 98–105; and Sampson, *Arms Bazaar*, pp. 250–251.

44. Ball, *Past Has Another Pattern*, pp. 454–455.

45. Shawcross, *Shah's Last Ride*, p. 173.

46. Kraar, "Shah Drives to Build New Empire," p. 149.

47. Statistics calculated by the author from U.S. Department of Defense, DSAA, *Fiscal Year Series as of September 1981*.

Chapter 3. Congress Steps In

1. See, for example, the speech by Sen. Gaylord Nelson in the *Congressional Record*, September 25, 1974, pp. 32532–32533.

2. Congressional Research Service, "Changing Perspectives on U.S. Arms Transfer Policy," report prepared for the House Foreign Affairs Committee, Subcommittee on International Security and Scientific Affairs (Washington, D.C.: U.S. Government Printing Office, 1981), p. 4.

3. Interview by the author with Congressman Bill Richardson, May 7, 1991.

4. Henry Kissinger, *Years of Upheaval* (New York: Little Brown and Co., 1982), pp. 337–339.

5. Nelson, *Congressional Record*, p. 32532.

6. Richard Grimmett, *Executive-Legislative Consultation on U.S. Arms Sales* (Washington, D.C.: U.S. Government Printing Office, December 1982).

7. "Foreign Assistance Authorization: Arms Sales Issues," hearings before the Committee on Foreign Relations, U.S. Senate, Ninety-fourth Congress, First Session, on S. 795, S. 854, S. 1816, S. 2662, and S. Con. Res. 21, June 17–18, November 19, 21, and December 4–5, 1975 (Washington, D.C.: U.S. Government Printing Office, 1976), pp. 51–62.

8. For background on the passage of the legislative veto, see Richard F. Grimmett, *The Legislative Veto and U.S. Arms Sales* (Washington, D.C.: Congressional Research Service, September 24, 1979).

9. *Congressional Record*, December 4, 1973, pp. 38072–38077.

10. House Foreign Affairs Committee, Conference Report on S. 3394, Foreign Assistance Act of 1961 (Washington, D.C.: U.S. Government Printing Office, 1975), pp. 40850–40852.

11. Klare, *American Arms Supermarket*, pp. 54–76.

12. Andrew Hamilton, "Uncle Sam, Arms Dealer," *Washington Post*, August 11, 1974.

13. Grimmett, *Executive-Legislative Consultation*, p. 5.

14. For background on covert U.S. involvement in the Angolan civil war, see John Prados, *President's Secret Wars: CIA and Pentagon Covert Operations Since World War II* (New York: William Morrow and Company, 1986), pp. 337–350; and John Stockwell, *In Search of Enemies: A CIA Story* (New York: W.W. Norton and Company, 1978), pp. 43–155.

15. Stockwell, *In Search of Enemies*, p. 229.

16. Prados, *President's Secret Wars*, p. 346.

17. Ibid., pp. 347–348; and Gerald Ford, "Statement by the President Upon Signing the Bill into Law [Department of Defense Authorization Act of 1976] While Expressing Certain Reservations About Certain of Its Provisions," February 10, 1976, in *Presidential Documents—Gerald R. Ford, 1976*, Vol. 12, Number 19 (Washington, D.C.: U.S. Government Printing Office, 1977), pp. 828–830.

18. Bill Boyarsky, "Humphrey Plays an Active Waiting Game," *Los Angeles Times*, December 15, 1975. For other profiles of Humphrey and his legislative style, see Martin Schram, "He's a Rare Sort of Person: Even His Enemies Are His Friends," *Los Angeles Times*, September 2, 1977; Tom Matthews, "Hubert's Last Hurrah?" *Newsweek*, January 10, 1977; and "From Defeat Rises a Free Spirit," *Time*, August 18, 1975.

19. "Foreign Assistance Authorization," p. 13.

20. Ibid., pp. 275–276.

21. Ibid., pp. 280–281.

22. For details on the original provisions of the Arms Export Control Act, see "Foreign Assistance Authorization"; U.S. House of Representatives, Report on the International Security Assistance and Arms Export Control Act of 1976, no. 94-114 (Washington, D.C.: Government Printing Office, 1976); and Congressional Research Service, "Changing Perspectives on U.S. Arms Transfer Policy," pp. 3–9.

23. Laurence Stern, "Arms Sales Bill Opposed," *Washington Post*, February 1, 1976.

24. Ibid.

25. Senate Foreign Relations Committee, "Multinational Corporations," pp. 64–80, 152–159.

26. For background on the origins and intent of the Arms Export Control Act, see Klare, *American Arms Supermarket*; Grimmett, *Executive-Legislative Consultation;* and Kevin Nealer, Richard McCall, and Richard D'Amato, *An Unconventional Arms Policy: Selling Ourselves Short* (Washington, D.C.: Democratic Policy Committee, 1983).

27. Gerald Ford, veto message on S. 2662, reprinted in *Congressional Record* (Senate), May 10, 1976, pp. 13053–13055.

28. "Foreign Assistance Authorization," pp. 499–503.

29. Hubert H. Humphrey, *Education of a Public Man* (Garden City, N.Y.: Doubleday, 1976), chap. 19.

Chapter 4. The Carter Policy: Why Not Restraint?

1. Klare, *American Arms Supermarket*, pp. 42–43; and Committee on Administration, U.S. House of Representatives, *The Presidential Campaign, 1976. Part 1: Jimmy Carter* (Washington, D.C.: U.S. Government Printing Office, 1978), pp. 266–275.

2. Sidney Kraus, ed., *The Great Debates: Carter vs. Ford, 1976* (Bloomington, Ind.: Indiana University Press, 1979), pp. 476–497; the "breadbasket" quote appears on p. 489.

3. Interview by the author with James McInerney, American League for Exports and Security Assistance, July 12, 1989.

4. Barry M. Blechman and Janne E. Nolan, *The U.S.–Soviet Arms Transfer Negotiations*, FPI Case Studies no. 3, Foreign Policy Institute, School of Advanced International Studies, Johns Hopkins University, Washington, D.C., January 1987.

5. Transcript of press conference by Carter, from *Public Papers of the Presidents of the United States: Jimmy Carter* (Washington, D.C.: U.S. Government Printing Office, 1977), p. 289.

6. Blechman and Nolan, *Arms Transfer Negotiations*, p. 7.

7. Office of the White House Press Secretary, "Statement of the President on Conventional Arms Transfer Policy," May 19, 1977.

8. Ibid.

9. The quoted portions of the six points of the Carter policy are from White House Press Secretary, "Statement of President on Arms Transfer Policy."

10. Address by Carter at commencement exercises at Notre Dame, May 22, 1977, in *Public Papers of the Presidents: Jimmy Carter*, pp. 954–960.

11. Statistics calculated by the author from U.S. Department of Defense, DSAA, *Fiscal Year Series as of September 1981*. Quotes from former Carter administration officials are from interviews conducted by the author.

12. Blechman and Nolan, *Arms Transfer Negotiations*, p. 5; and "Adam Smith's 'Money World,'" transcript 719, "Are We Arming the Next Iraq?" March 29, 1991, p. 3.

13. Blechman and Nolan, *Arms Transfer Negotiations*, pp. 18–19.

14. Brzezinski's role is sketched out in Blechman and Nolan, *Arms Transfer Negotiations;* the discussion here is also based on interviews with former Carter administration officials conducted by the author. For further evidence of the priority Brzezinski gave to Cold War geopolitics over arms transfer controls, see Zbigniew Brzezinski, *Power and Principle: Memoirs of the National Security Advisor 1977–1981* (New York: Farrar Straus Giroux, 1985), pp. 42–55, 247–249.

15. Blechman and Nolan, *Arms Transfer Negotiations*, pp. 21–27; and author interviews with participants in the talks. See also the chapter by Janne Nolan in Andrew Pierre, ed., *Cascade of Arms: Arms Proliferation Challenges of the 1990s* (forthcoming).

16. Blechman and Nolan, *Arms Transfer Negotiations;* and author interviews with Leslie Gelb, April 25, 1991, and Barry Blechman, May 29, 1991, as well as other participants in the CAT talks.

17. On this point, see William D. Hartung, "Why Sell Arms: Lessons from the Carter Years," *World Policy Journal*, Spring 1993.

18. Sick, *All Fall Down*, pp. 24–25.

19. Ibid., pp. 24–29.

20. Ibid. See also Grimmett, *Executive-Legislative Consultation*, pp. 13–15.

21. Grimmett, *Executive-Legislative Consultation*, p. 14.

22. Ibid., p. 15.

23. Ibid., pp. 16–21; and Klare, *American Arms Supermarket*, pp. 45–46, 54–55.

24. Grimmett, *Executive-Legislative Consultation*, pp. 16–21.

25. Robert G. Kaiser, "Senate Approves Mideast Jet Sales, 54-44," *Washington Post*, May 16, 1978; and Don Oberdorfer, "Oil and the New Realities," *Washington Post*, May 16, 1978.

26. On this point, see Hartung, "Breaking the Arms-Sales Addiction"; Klare, *American Arms Supermarket*, pp. 144–146, 150; and the front-page articles by Don Oberdorfer and Edward Walsh in the *Washington Post*, January 24, 1980.

27. Klare, *American Arms Supermarket*, p. 46; and author interview with Ernest Graves, July 12, 1989.

Chapter 5. Reagan's Supply Side Foreign Policy

1. Lou Cannon, "Reagan: TV News Hurts Economic Recovery," *Washington Post*, March 18, 1982.

2. U.S. Department of State, "Communist Interference in El Salvador," Special Report 80, February 23, 1981.

3. See Raymond Bonner, *Weakness and Deceit: U.S. Policy and El Salvador* (New York: Times Books, 1984), pp. 108–134.

4. Jonathan Kwitny, "Tarnished Report?—Apparent Errors Cloud U.S. 'White Paper' on Reds in El Salvador," *Wall Street Journal*, June 8, 1981. See also Robert Kaiser, "White Paper on El Salvador Is Faulty," *Washington Post*, June 9, 1981; and James Petras, "Blots on the White Paper: The Reappearance of the Red Menace," *The Nation*, March 28, 1981, reprinted in Marvin E. Gettleman, Patrick Lacefield, Louis Menashe, and David Mermelstein, eds., *El Salvador: Central America in the New Cold War* (New York: Grove Press, 1986), pp. 324–335.

5. Raymond Bonner, "Major Massacre Is Reported in Salvadoran Village," *New York*

Times, January 27, 1982; Philip Berryman, *What's Wrong in Central America, and What to Do About It* (Philadelphia, Pa.: American Friends Service Committee, 1983), p. 6. For more recent documentation of the El Mozote massacre in particular and the record of human rights abuses by Salvadoran forces in general, see Tim Golden, "Salvador Skeletons Confirm Reports of Massacre in 1981," *New York Times*, October 22, 1992; Mike Hoyt, "The Mozote Massacre," *Columbia Journalism Review*, January/February 1993; Julia Preston, "War Report Accuses Salvadorans," *Washington Post*, March 15, 1993; Tim Golden, "Salvador Officers Named as Killers in U.N. Report," *New York Times*, March 15, 1993; and Mark Danner, "The Truth of El Mozote," *The New Yorker*, December 6, 1993.

6. Bonner, *Weakness and Deceit*, pp. 178–179, 217–227; and Gettleman et al., *El Salvador*, pp. 131–135, 245–286.

7. Bonner, *Weakness and Deceit*, pp. 349–360.

8. All quotes from Buckley in this section are from the reprint of his speech, U.S. Department of State, Current Policy 279, "Arms Transfers and the National Interest," May 21, 1981.

9. Office of the White House Press Secretary, "Text of President Ronald Reagan's July 8, 1981, Arms Transfer Policy Directive," July 9, 1981.

10. For further documentation of the changes introduced by Reagan, see William D. Hartung, "The Reagan Revival of Arms Deals," *Bulletin of the Atomic Scientists*, July/August 1987.

11. Statement of Jonathan Bingham in "Proposed Sale of Airborne Warning and Control Systems (AWACS) and F-15 Enhancements to Saudi Arabia," Hearings and Markup Before the Committee on Foreign Affairs and Its Subcommittees on International Security and Scientific Affairs and on Europe and the Middle East, U.S. House of Representatives, Ninety-seventh Congress, First Session, September 28, October 1, 6, 7, 1981 (Washington, D.C.: U.S. Government Printing Office, 1981), p. 2.

12. Statement of James Buckley in "Proposed Sale of AWACS . . . to Saudi Arabia," p. 39; and Alexander Haig, "Dangerous Illusions and Real Choices on AWACS," U.S. Department of State Current Policy 324, October 5, 1981.

13. Statement of Fred Ikle in "Proposed Sale of AWACS . . . to Saudi Arabia," p. 44.

14. Steven Emerson, *The American House of Saud* (New York: Franklin Watts, 1985), pp. 195–196, 204–207. The final vote in favor of the AWACS sale was 52–48, so Henry Heinz's pledge to deliver his son's vote was never put to the test.

15. Statement of Charles Percy in Senate Foreign Relations Committee, Hearings on "Arms Sale Package to Saudi Arabia," October 1, 5, 6, 14, 15, 1981 (Washington, D.C.: U.S. Government Printing Office, 1981), p. 61.

16. The characterization of the lifting of barriers to arms sales by the Reagan administration is drawn from Hartung, "Reagan Revival of Arms Deals."

17. "Pakistan Leads U.S. into Conflict of Policies," *Congressional Quarterly*, October 31, 1987, pp. 2667–2669; and "Knocking at the Nuclear Door," *Time*, March 30, 1987.

18. Hartung, "Reagan Revival of Arms Deals."

19. Steven R. Weisman, "Reagan Ends Ban on Sending Israel 16 Jet Warplanes," *New York Times*, August 18, 1981; and Lee Lescaze, "Reagan Lifts Ban on Delivery of 16 Jets to Israel," *Washington Post*, August 18, 1981.

20. George M. Houser, "Blood on the Sahara: America Is Fighting King Hassan's War," *The Progressive*, December 1980; Edward Cody, "Morocco Seeks U.S. Arms for Sahara Warfare," *Washington Post*, November 5, 1981; Daniel Volman, "Saharan Freeze," *The Nation*, November 24, 1979; Bernard Gwertzman, "U.S. Drops Sahara Issue in Arms Sales to Morocco," *New York Times*, March 26, 1981; James F. Clarity, "Morocco Emerging as Closest Arab Ally," *New York Times*, February 1, 1983; and Tony Hodges, "Western Sahara: The Second Decade of War," *Africa Report*, March–April 1986.

21. William D. Hartung, *Weapons for the World 1982 Update*.

22. Ibid. See also Hartung, "Breaking the Arms-Sales Addiction," pp. 1–26; and Ferrari, Knopf, and Madrid, *U.S. Arms Exports*.

Chapter 6. The Reagan Doctrine: Arming Anticommunist Rebels

1. Peter Kornbluh, "President Reagan's Dangerous Doctrine," *Newsday*, February 8, 1985; and transcript of the president's State of the Union address to Congress, *New York Times*, February 7, 1985.

2. The background and quotes on Reagan's long-standing anticommunist beliefs are from Ronnie Dugger, *On Reagan: The Man and His Presidency* (New York: McGraw-Hill, 1983), chap. 19, pp. 350–354; and Karen Elliott House, "Republicans Stress Arms Buildup, A Firm Line to Soviets," *Wall Street Journal*, June 3, 1980.

3. Jeane Kirkpatrick, "Dictatorships and Double Standards," *Commentary*, November 1979, pp. 34–45. For a critique of Kirkpatrick's analysis, see Michael Walzer, "Totalitarianism versus Authoritarianism," *The New Republic*, July 4, 11, 1981, pp. 21–25. Both of these articles are reprinted in Gettleman et al., *El Salvador*.

4. Roy Gutman, *Banana Diplomacy* (New York: Simon and Schuster, 1988), pp. 19–22.

5. Peter Kornbluh, *The Price of Intervention: Washington's War Against Nicaragua* (Washington, D.C.: Institute for Policy Studies, 1987), pp. 19–24.

6. Holly Sklar, *Washington's War on Nicaragua* (Boston: South End Press, 1988), pp. 87–89.

7. Ibid., p. 88.

8. Gutman, *Banana Diplomacy*, p. 57.

9. Theodore Draper, *A Very Thin Line: The Iran-Contra Affairs* (New York: Hill and Wang, 1991), pp. 18–19; and Sklar, *Washington's War*, p. 131.

10. "The Old Republic and Edward P. Boland," in Sidney Blumenthal, *Our Long National Daydream* (New York: Harper and Row, 1988), p. 272.

11. Draper, *Very Thin Line*, p. 24.

12. David Fanning, producer, Bill Moyers, correspondent, "High Crimes and Misdemeanors," "Frontline," transcript (Boston: WGBH-TV, November 27, 1990), p. 6.

13. Joel Brinkley and Stephen Engelberg, eds., *Report of the Congressional Committees Investigating the Iran-Contra Affair with the Minority View* (abr. ed.) (New York: Times Books, 1988), pp. 114–115.

14. Jeff Gerth, "Help for Rebels for U.S. Arms," *New York Times*, February 4, 1987.

15. Fanning and Moyers, "High Crimes," pp. 9–10.

16. Ibid., pp. 12–13.

17. Oliver L. North (with William Novak), *Under Fire: An American Story* (New York: HarperCollins, 1991), pp. 260–261.

18. Glen Craney, "After Delay of Six Months, Senate Confirms Gregg," *Congressional Quarterly Weekly Report*, September 16, 1989.

19. George Shultz, *Turmoil and Triumph: My Years as Secretary of State* (New York: Charles Scribners, 1993), p. 789.

20. *Taking the Stand: The Testimony of Lieutenant Colonel Oliver L. North* (New York: Pocket Books, 1987), pp. xii–xiii, 166–167; and Peter Maas, *Manhunt: The Incredible Pursuit of a CIA Agent Turned Terrorist* (New York: Random House, 1986), pp. 278–279, 287–288. For Richard Secord's version of these events, see Richard Se-cord (with Jay Wurts), *Honored and Betrayed: Irangate, Covert Affairs, and the Secret War in Laos* (New York: John Wiley and Sons, 1992), pp. 184–195.

21. Draper, *Very Thin Line*, pp. 272–275.

22. Brinkley and Engelberg, *Report of the Congressional Committees*, p. 225.

23. Ibid., pp. 292–293.

24. Fanning and Moyers, "High Crimes and Misdemeanors," pp. 26–27.

25. Ibid., p. 27.

26. Pamela Fessler, "Senate Clears Retooled Measure Strengthening Congressional Oversight," *Congressional Quarterly Weekly Report*, August 3, 1991.

27. Sklar, *Washington's War*, pp. 168–170.

28. U.S. Congress, Arms Control and Foreign Policy Caucus, *Who Are the Contras?—An Analysis of the Makeup of the Military Leadership of the Rebel Forces, and of the Nature of the*

Private American Groups Providing Them Financial and Material Support (Washington, D.C.: Arms Control and Foreign Policy Caucus, April 18, 1985).

29. Americas Watch, *Human Rights in Nicaragua 1985–1986* (New York: Americas Watch Committee, 1986), p. 86.

30. Robert Pear, "30 Afghan Rebels Slain by Rival Band," *New York Times*, July 18, 1989; Clifford Krauss, "Congress May Cut Afghan Rebel Aid," *New York Times*, September 30, 1990; and Jim Hoagland, "Afghan Endgame," *Washington Post*, April 27, 1992.

31. Paula Newberg, "Pakistan's Troubled Landscape," *World Policy Journal*, vol. 5, no. 2, Spring 1987.

32. John Bussey, "To the Feuds, Malaise and Guns of Pakistan Comes the Free Market," *Wall Street Journal*, July 31, 1991.

33. See chapter 3 for earlier text on Savimbi's opportunism.

34. Philip Shenon, "Khmer Rouge Violence Said to Signal Goals," *New York Times*, August 4, 1993.

35. Paul Mann and James K. Gordon, "Iran Secures Operational Gains from U.S.-Backed Military Aid," *Aviation Week and Space Technology*, November 17, 1986.

36. Edward Cody, "Iran Deploys a U.S.-Style Naval Force," *Washington Post*, August 20, 1987.

37. David Johnston, "U.S. Aide Defends Lockerbie Stand," *New York Times*, November 21, 1991; Ronald J. Ostrow, "Libya Implicated in Pan Am Bomb Indictments," *Los Angeles Times*, November 22, 1991; and William M. Carley, "Iran's Revenge: The Lockerbie Bombing," *Wall Street Journal*, April 23, 1990.

38. Steve Levine, "U.S. Trying to Pull Out Rebels' Stingers," *Newsday*, January 2, 1992; and Dennis DeConcini, "U.S.-Made Stingers Can Sting Us Back," *Wall Street Journal*, October 28, 1987.

39. Anthony H. Cordesman, "U.S. Force Planning and Small Nuclear Forces in the Middle East and South Asia," in Rodney W. Jones, ed., *Small Nuclear Forces and U.S. Security Policy* (Lexington, Mass.: Lexington Books, 1984), pp. 214, 220. This reference is cited in Selig Harrison's excellent analysis of the implications of the Afghan conflict, "Afghanistan: Soviet Intervention, Afghan Resistance, and the American Role," in Michael T. Klare and Peter Kornbluh, eds., *Low Intensity Warfare: Counterinsurgency, Proinsurgency, and Antiterrorism in the Eighties* (New York: Pantheon, 1988).

40. *Taking the Stand*, p. 12.

41. Cited in Klare and Kornbluh, *Low Intensity Warfare*, p. 19.

42. *Taking the Stand*, Introduction by Daniel Schorr, p. xii.

Chapter 7. Bush Policy: Institutionalizing Arms Sales Promotion

1. David Hoffman, "Questions Dog Vice President: Bush Yet to Provide Full Account on Iran," *Washington Post*, January 7, 1988.

2. Bill Peterson and David Hoffman, "Bush Assails Criticism of His Iran Role: Issue Subsides During Iowa Debate," *Washington Post*, January 9, 1988.

3. "Text of Dan Rather's Interview with George Bush," *Washington Post*, January 27, 1988.

4. Tom Shales, "Rather, Bush, and the Nine Minute War," and "Verdict from the Veep," *Washington Post*, January 26, 1988; David Hoffman, "Vice President Set for 'Combat' Amid Confusion on Iran Role," *Washington Post*, January 27, 1988; and Phil McCombs, "In the Studio, Countdown Towards an Explosion," *Washington Post*, January 27, 1988. McCombs refers specifically to the role of Roger Ailes in preparing Bush for the confrontation: "White House sources said yesterday that Roger Ailes, Bush's media consultant, had advised the vice president on how to deal with Iran/contra questions, and had furnished him with the rejoinder about Rather's absence from the air for several minutes during a newscast last year." Ailes refused to comment when McCombs asked him directly about his role in the Bush/Rather flap.

5. Richard Morris, "Iran-Contra Affair Dogs Vice President in Polls," *Washington Post*,

March 17, 1988; and David Hoffman, "Vice President Ribbed for Misnaming Koppel," *Washington Post*, June 11, 1988.

6. Charles Babcock and Bob Woodward, "Tower: The Consultant as Advocate—Duties Were Vague in High Fee Arrangements with Contractors," *Washington Post*, February 13, 1989.

7. Gerald F. Seib, "Bush to Send Military Gear, Technicians to Colombia, Set Strategy to Fight Drugs," *Wall Street Journal*, August 28, 1989; and Molly Moore, "Aid Shipment to Arrive in Colombia Sunday," *Washington Post*, September 2, 1989.

8. Prepared statement of Melvyn Levitsky, assistant secretary of state for international narcotics matters, to the Subcommittee on Western Hemisphere Affairs, Committee on Foreign Affairs, U.S. House of Representatives, June 20, 1990; and Office of National Drug Control Strategy, budget documents for fiscal year 1990.

9. Moore, "Aid Shipment to Arrive in Colombia"; and Douglas Farah, "More Ranches, Houses Seized," *Washington Post*, September 10, 1989.

10. Testimony of Alexander Wilde, executive director, Washington Office on Latin America, to the Subcommittee on Western Hemisphere Affairs, Committee on Foreign Affairs, U.S. House of Representatives, June 6, 1990.

11. Opening statement of Peter Kostmayer, Hearings on the Andean Initiative (II), Subcommittee on Western Hemisphere Affairs, Committee on Foreign Affairs, U.S. House of Representatives, June 20, 1990.

12. Prepared statement of Levitsky to Subcommittee on Western Hemisphere Affairs, June 20, 1990.

13. Jeff Gerth, "Management Woes Hobble U.S. Air Fleet in Drug War," *New York Times*, June 13, 1990.

14. See series by Andrew Schneider and Peter Copeland, "The Drug Warriors: Americans on the Front Lines," Scripps Howard News Service, June 28–July 1, 1992. The quote on the "biggest U.S. operation ever in Latin America" is from the first article in the series, "Waging a War Without Direction: It Can't Be Won, But Can Be Lost," June 28, 1992.

15. "Arms Makers Find New War to Help Win," *Philadelphia Inquirer*, January 21, 1990.

16. Cited in David Corn, "Beltway Bandits," *The Nation*, September 24, 1990.

17. Scott Armstrong, "Saudi's AWACS Just the Beginning of a New Strategy," *Washington Post*, November 1, 1981.

18. Frank Greve, "Secord Helped Secure Secret Deals," Glen Falls (N.Y.) *Post-Star*, August 23, 1990.

19. Eric Schmitt, "U.S. to Sell Saudis $20 Billion in Arms; Weapons Deal Is Largest in History," *New York Times*, September 15, 1990.

20. Senators Daniel Patrick Moynihan, Claiborne Pell, Terry Sanford, Bob Packwood, and Paul Simon, "Dear Colleague" letter on arms sale to Saudi Arabia, September 21, 1990.

21. Walter S. Mossberg, "Bush Expected to Ask Congress to Clear $7.5 Billion Arms Sales to Saudi Arabia," *Wall Street Journal*, September 27, 1990; and Andrew Rosenthal, "Bush to Revise Proposal to Sell Arms to Saudis," September 22, 1990.

22. John Kifner, "Israelis, Irked by Arms Sale to Saudis, Ask More of U.S.," *New York Times*, September 17, 1990; William D. Hartung, "Relighting the Mideast Fuse," *New York Times*, September 20, 1991; and Lee Feinstein, *U.S. Arms Transfers to the Middle East Since the Invasion of Kuwait* (Washington, D.C.: Arms Control Association, February 11, 1992).

23. Clyde H. Farnsworth, "Egypt's 'Reward': Forgiven Debt," *New York Times*, April 10, 1991; Ann Devroy, "President to Propose Mideast Arms Limits," *Washington Post*, April 27, 1991; and Patrick E. Tyler, "As the Dust Settles, Attention Turns to New Arms Sales," *New York Times*, March 24, 1991.

24. R. Jeffrey Smith, "Administration Proposes Arms Package for Saudis," *Washington Post*, July 30, 1991; and David C. Morrison, "Still Open for Business," *National Journal*, April 13, 1991.

25. Michael Wines, "U.S. Aid Helped Hussein's Climb; Now, Critics Say, the Bill Is

Due," *New York Times*, August 13, 1990; and Lee Feinstein, "Gulf Crisis Impact on Arms Progress: Less Peace Dividend, Slower Disarmament," *Christian Science Monitor*, September 5, 1990.

26. Thomas L. Friedman, "Goodwill Goals in Mideast Cited as Baker Sets Out," *New York Times*, March 8, 1991; William D. Hartung, "Time to Curb the Weapon Makers," *New York Times*, March 18, 1991; and Hartung, "Relighting the Mideast Fuse."

27. Patrick E. Tyler, "Cheney Wants No Limit on Arms for Gulf Allies," *New York Times*, March 20, 1991; Carroll J. Doherty, "The Dilemma of Mideast Arms Sales," *Congressional Quarterly Weekly Report*, March 9, 1991; and Clyde H. Farnsworth, "White House Seeks to Revive Credits for Arms Exports," *New York Times*, March 18, 1991.

28. Ann Devroy, "President Proposes Mideast Arms Curbs," *Washington Post*, May 30, 1991; and George Bush, commencement address at the U.S. Air Force Academy, Colorado Springs, Colo., May 29, 1991.

29. Eric Schmitt, "Cheney Says U.S. Plans New Arms Sale to the Mideast," *New York Times*, June 5, 1991; and Hartung, "Boom at Arms Bazaar."

30. Lee Feinstein, "New World Orders: U.S. Arms Transfer Policy and the Middle East," prepared for the International Working Conference on the Arms Trade, November 1–2, 1991 (Washington, D.C.: Arms Control Association); and Smith, "Administration Proposes Arms Package."

31. Peter H. Stone, "Defense Exporters' Secret Weapons: How Top Administration Officials Help Boost Foreign Arms Sales: Did Eagelburger Cross the Line?" *Legal Times*, February 25, 1991.

32. U.S. Department of State, Bureau of Politico-Military Affairs, "Defense Trade Priority at State: New Leadership Addressed Problems Early On," in *Defense Trade News: The Bulletin of the Center for Defense Trade*, vol. 1, no. 1, March 1990, pp. 4–5.

33. "George Bush, in the Arms Bazaar," *New York Times*, June 6, 1992.

34. U.S. Department of State, "Defense Trade Priority," p. 4.

35. Text of Ronald Reagan's July 8, 1981, Arms Transfer Policy Directive, Office of the White House Press Secretary, July 9, 1981.

36. Stone, "Defense Exporters' Secret Weapons"; and U.S. Department of State, *Defense Trade News*, various issues, 1991, 1992.

37. Stone, "Defense Exporters' Secret Weapons."

38. Peter Grier, "Bush Pushing Tank Sale to Saudis," *Christian Science Monitor*, October 23, 1989; and "Proposed Tank Sale to Saudi Arabia," hearing before the Subcommittees on Arms Control, International Security, and Science and Europe and the Middle East, Committee on Foreign Affairs, U.S. House of Representatives, November 7, 1989 (Washington, D.C.: U.S. Government Printing Office, 1990), pp. 69–91.

39. David Silverberg, "Report: International Sales Vital to Health of U.S. Tank Industry," *Defense News*, April 16, 1990.

40. William Flannery, "Politics, Foreign Sales May Yet Save General Dynamics' Tanks," *St. Louis Post-Dispatch*, February 5, 1990.

41. U.S. Department of Defense, DSAA, memorandum on the "Catalog of U.S. Defense Articles and Services," February 20, 1990; and "U.S. Defense Articles and Services Catalog," *DISAM Journal*, vol. 14, no. 1, Fall 1991 (Dayton, Ohio: Defense Institute of Security Assistance Management, 1991), pp. 99–100.

42. Richard H. P. Sia, "U.S. Helps Firms to Exhibit at Paris Show," *Baltimore Sun*, April 14, 1991; and Hartung, "Boom at Arms Bazaar."

43. Grimmett, *Conventional Arms Transfers*.

Chapter 8. The Permanent Arms Supply Network (I): The Corporate Arms Merchants

1. Statement of Harry J. Gray on behalf of the American League for Exports and Security Assistance to the House Foreign Affairs Committee, Subcommittee on Arms Control, International Security, and Science, on "U.S. Exports and Competitiveness: A Private Sector Appraisal," March 5, 1987, p. 9.

2. Defense Policy Advisory Committee on Trade, *Report Outlining U.S. Government Policy Options Affecting Defense Trade and the U.S. Industrial Base* (Washington, D.C.: DPACT, November 1988); and Office of Private Sector Liaison, Office of the U.S. Trade Representative, Private Sector Advisory Committee, "Membership Report by Committee, DPACT: Defense Policy Advisory Committee on Trade."

3. Letter from Norman R. Augustine, CEO, Martin Marietta Corporation, to Thomas H. Andrews, April 28, 1993; Bob Young, "What Peace Dividend?" *Casco Bay News*, June 24, 1993; Philip Finnegan, "U.S. Senate Panel Proposes Export Guarantee Plan," *Defense News*, July 26–August 1, 1993; and Lisa Burgess, "Congress Backs Loan Guarantees," *Defense News*, November 8–14, 1993.

4. David Morrison, "Joel J. Johnson, Former 'White Hat' in the Arms Bazaar," *National Journal*, September 26, 1987.

5. Joel Johnson, "Conventional Arms Transfer Policy: An Industry Perspective," testimony before a joint hearing of the Committee on Foreign Affairs, U.S. House of Representatives, Subcommittees on Arms Control, International Security, and Science and on the Middle East, May 27, 1992.

6. Andy Pasztor and Gary Putka, "Raytheon Wins Army Contract of $414 Million," *Wall Street Journal*, May 22, 1990; and David Rogers, "Raytheon's Help from Massachusetts Lawmakers Is Study of Arms Politics in Post–Cold War World," *Wall Street Journal*, June 28, 1990.

7. Middle East Action Group Briefing Book, December 3, 1990, p. 6.

8. Middle East Action Group Briefing Book; and David J. Louscher and William Bajusz, "The Domestic Economic Impact of the Prospective Sale of Selected Military Equipment to Saudi Arabia" (Science Applications International Corporation, February 8, 1991), pp. 66–67.

9. Hartung, "Boom at Arms Bazaar."

10. Senators Jesse Helms and Claiborne Pell, letter to James Baker, November 21, 1991, reprinted in *Congressional Record–Senate*, November 22, 1991, p. S17578.

11. "Saudis Ask for 72 More F-15s, Could Extend MDC's Line: Trice," *Aerospace Daily*, November 6, 1991.

12. "Saudi F-15 Deal Mixes Old-New Requests Says McDonnell Official," *Defense Daily*, November 8, 1991.

13. Statement by Howard Berman at a briefing on the proposed sale of F-15s to Saudi Arabia sponsored by the Project on Demilitarization and Democracy and the National Commission on Economic Conversion and Disarmament, Washington, D.C., July 8, 1992; and David C. Morrison, "Saudi F-15 Sale: Jobs, Jobs and Jobs?" *National Journal*, April 18, 1992.

14. Morrison, "Saudi F-15 Sale"; and "F-15 for the Defense of Saudi Arabia," McDonnell Douglas promotional brochure, 1992.

15. Mel Levine et al. (235 cosigners), letter to President Bush regarding proposed Saudi F-15 sale, April 9, 1992.

16. On this point, see William D. Hartung, "Arms Sales Win Votes and Little Else," *New York Times*, October 25, 1992.

17. Philip J. Simon, *Top Guns: A Common Cause Guide to Defense Contractor Lobbying* (Washington, D.C.: Common Cause, 1987), pp. 22–25.

18. Peter Adams, "Ill Wind Results in Guilty Plea," *Defense News*, January 17, 1991; and author interview with Assistant U.S. Attorney Joseph Aronica, U.S. Attorney's Office for the Eastern District of Virginia, August 9, 1993.

Chapter 9. The Permanent Arms Supply Network (II): Middlemen, Dealers, and the Secret Trade

1. Gaylord Shaw and Dan Moran, "3 Lived, Flew, Crashed in Violent Shadow World," *Los Angeles Times*, October 12, 1986; "Shultz Denies U.S. Link to Plane Downed

in Nicaragua," *Los Angeles Times*, October 7, 1986; Doyle McManus, "Elaborate System Supplies Contras—Downed Plane Was Part of Secret Network, U.S. and Rebel Officials Say," *Los Angeles Times*, October 9, 1986; William B. Long, "Air Cargo Firm Had Ties to 2 Killed in Nicaragua," *Los Angeles Times*, October 9, 1986; and Marjorie Miller, "Political Theater of Hasenfus Trial Fills the Bill Until Soviet Circus Comes to Town," *Los Angeles Times*, November 2, 1986.

2. *Taking the Stand*, Introduction by Daniel Schorr, p. xiv; and Peter Maas, "Oliver North's Strange Recruits," *New York Times Magazine*, January 18, 1987.

3. Joe Pichirallo and Dan Morgan, "Comrades-in-Arms Who Linked Iran and the Contras," *Washington Post Weekly*, February 2, 1987; and Morgan Strong, interview with Richard Secord, *Playboy*, October 1987, pp. 59–79.

4. Strong interview with Secord, *Playboy*, pp. 59–79.

5. Maas, "Oliver North's Strange Recruits." For a detailed history of Theodore Shackley's career as a covert operator, see David Corn, *Blond Ghost: Ted Shackley and the CIA's Crusades* (New York: Simon & Schuster, 1994).

6. Maas, *Manhunt*, pp. 49–57, 138–141, 163–164, 247–249, 284–285; and Jonathan Kwitny, "New NSC Chief's Ties to Men Cited in Iran Crisis, Illegal Arms Deal May Cloud Housekeeping Task," *Wall Street Journal*, January 9, 1987.

7. Deposition of Richard Secord, in U.S. Senate Select Committee on Secret Military Assistance to Iran and the Nicaraguan Opposition and U.S. House of Representatives Select Committee to Investigate Covert Arms Transactions with Iran, *Report of the Congressional Committees Investigating the Iran-Contra Affair*, app. B, vol. 24 (Washington, D.C.: U.S. Government Printing Office, 1988).

8. David Rogers, "Network of Ex-Officers Tied to Iran-Contra Affair Had Role in Other Secret Operations, Sources Say," *Wall Street Journal*, February 13, 1987.

9. *Taking the Stand*, pp. 166–167.

10. Draper, *Very Thin Line*, pp. 37–39, 91–93, 347; Brinkley and Engelberg, *Report of the Congressional Committees*, pp. 289–317; and "Testimony of Richard Secord at Joint Hearings Before the House Select Committee to Investigate Covert Arms Transactions with Iran and the Senate Select Committee on Secret Military Assistance to Iran and the Nicaraguan Opposition" (Washington, D.C.: U.S. Government Printing Office, 1987), vol. 100-1.

11. "How the World Keeps the Iran-Iraq War Going," *Business Week*, December 29, 1986.

12. Gerth, "Management Woes"; and Corn, "Beltway Bandits."

13. Rogers, "Network of Ex-Officers"; and Clyde H. Farnsworth, "'The Company' as Big Business," *New York Times*, January 4, 1987, business section.

14. Gerth, "Management Woes"; and Farnsworth, "'The Company' as Big Business."

15. George J. Church, Ron Ben-Yishai, and Raji Samghabadi, "The Murky World of Weapons Dealers: How Arms Traders Bartered with U.S. Policy," *Time*, January 19, 1987.

16. Anthony Sampson, *The Arms Bazaar: From Lebanon to Lockheed* (New York: Viking Press, 1977), pp. 192–202.

17. Draper, *Very Thin Line*, pp. 272–275.

18. Church, Ben-Yishai, and Samghabadi, "Murky World of Weapons Dealers."

19. Draper, *Very Thin Line*, p. 126.

20. Murray Waas, "What We Gave Saddam for Christmas: The Secret History of How the United States and Its Allies Armed Iraq," *Village Voice*, December 18, 1990; and Michael Sullivan and Jim Gilmore, "The Arming of Iraq," "Frontline," transcript (Boston: WGBH-TV, September 11, 1990).

21. Sullivan and Gilmore, "Arming of Iraq"; Waas, "What We Gave Saddam"; Hartung, "Time to Curb Weapon Makers"; "Arms Dealer Indicted in Copter Sale to Iraq," *New York Times*, December 4, 1987; and Mike Clary, "Arms Dealer Found Guilty in Plot to Sell Helicopters to Iraq Regime," *Los Angeles Times*, October 22, 1991.

22. Sullivan and Gilmore, "Arming of Iraq."

23. Sampson, *Arms Bazaar*, pp. 24–32; Michael Isikoff, "Need Firepower?—Just Call Sam Cummings," *Washington Post Weekly*, January 12, 1987; and Patrick Brogan and Albert

Zarca, *Deadly Business: Sam Cummings, Interarms, and the Arms Trade* (New York: W.W. Norton, 1983).

24. Isikoff, "Need Firepower?"

25. Ibid.

26. Ibid. See also Sampson, *Arms Bazaar*, p. 25, in which the author quotes an earlier, similar remark by Cummings: "The arms business . . . is founded on human folly. That is why its depths will never be plumbed, and why it will go on forever."

27. Andy Pasztor, "Investigators Say Chilean Dealer Smuggled U.S. Weapons to Iraq," *Wall Street Journal*, November 20, 1991; Edward T. Pound and Andy Pasztor, "American Arms Dealer Was Amazing Success, or So Ferranti Believed," *Wall Street Journal*, January 23, 1990; and Roderick Oram, "Local Hero Started in Chicken House and Ended in Doghouse," *Financial Times*, September 20, 1989. For the most detailed coverage on James Guerin and ISC, see also the series of articles by Thomas L. Flannery in the Lancaster (Pa.) *Intelligencer-Journal*, January 1990–December 1991.

28. ABC News "Nightline," "*Financial Times* Arms Sales Report," show 2609, transcript, May 23, 1991.

29. Ibid.

30. Ibid. See also "Civil Action No. EC90-2535, Robert Clyde Ivy and Irene Ivy v. Ferranti International," U.S. District Court for the Eastern District of Pennsylvania, September 17, 1990, pp. 11–12.

31. ABC News, "Financial Times Arms Sales Report."

32. "James Guerin Pleads Guilty to International Arms Scam," *Wall Street Journal*, December 6, 1991; and Alan Friedman and Tom Flannery, "Ex-Ferranti Deputy Chairman Given 15-Year Jail Sentence," *Financial Times*, June 11, 1992.

33. Pound and Pasztor, "American Arms Dealer."

34. Alan Friedman and Tom Flannery, "Bush Adviser Seeks Clemency for Former Ferranti Executive," *Financial Times*, June 8, 1992.

35. Pasztor, "Chilean Dealer Smuggled Weapons"; Thomas L. Flannery, "Jacobson's Flight to Chile Was Another Link in Arms Business," Lancaster (Pa.) *Intelligencer-Journal*, July 25, 1990; Michael S. Serrill, "Of Cluster Bombs and Kiwis," *Time*, December 10, 1990; "From Chile to Miami, Miami to Baghdad," *Newsweek*, April 8, 1991; William Booth, "U.S. Accuses Chilean of Iraqi Arms Deal," *Washington Post*, April 7, 1992; Kenneth R. Timmerman, *The Death Lobby: How the West Armed Iraq* (New York: Houghton Mifflin, 1991), pp. 166–170; Michael Isikoff, "Two Accused of Selling Arms Material to Iraq," *Washington Post*, May 27, 1993; and "Carlos Cardoen, Teledyne Indicted Over Arms Exports," *Wall Street Journal*, May 27, 1993.

36. "The Man Who Made the Supergun," "Frontline," transcript (Boston: WGBH-TV, February 12, 1991); and James Adams, *Bull's Eye: The Assassination and Life of Supergun Inventor Gerald Bull* (New York: Times Books, 1992), chaps. 1–11.

37. "Man Who Made Supergun"; and Stockwell, *In Search of Enemies*.

38. As quoted in "Man Who Made Supergun."

39. Ibid. See also William Scott Malone, David Halevy, and Scott Hemingway, "The Guns We May Face in the Gulf Will Be Our Own: The Misguided Career of Gerald V. Bull," *Washington Post Weekly*, February 18–24, 1991.

Chapter 10. The Middle East: Bottomless Market, Endless War?

1. Author's calculation from Stockholm International Peace Research Institute, *SIPRI Yearbook: World Armaments and Disarmament* (New York: Oxford University Press, various years); and Grimmett, *Conventional Arms Transfers*.

2. Sampson, *Arms Bazaar*, p. 171

3. Ibid., p. 172.

4. Ibid., pp. 172–173. See also Michael T. Klare, "Gaining Control: Building a Comprehensive Arms Restraint System," *Arms Control Today*, June 1991, pp. 9–13.

5. Sampson, *Arms Bazaar*, pp. 176–177.

6. Joe Stork, "Israel as a Strategic Asset," *MERIP Reports*, Washington, D.C., Middle East Research and Information Project, May 1982, p. 4.

7. Stork, "Israel as Strategic Asset," pp. 3–13; Sampson, *Arms Bazaar*, pp. 171–175; and Barry M. Blechman, Janne E. Nolan, and Alan Platt, "Pushing Arms," *Foreign Policy*, no. 46, Spring 1982, pp. 138–154.

8. Stork, "Israel as Strategic Asset," pp. 4–5; and U.S. Department of Defense, DSAA, *Fiscal Year Series as of September 1981*, p. 88.

9. U.S. Department of Defense, DSAA, *Fiscal Year Series as of September 1981*, pp. 84–85, 108–109.

10. Author's calculations, using data from U.S. Department of Defense and U.S. Department of State, *Congressional Presentation*, fiscal years 1981–1992; and U.S. Department of Defense, DSAA, *Foreign Military Sales...*, fiscal years 1981–1992.

11. "Reagan Halts F-16s for Israel; Haig Cites New Violence," *Washington Post*, July 21, 1981; Lescaze, "Reagan Lifts Ban"; and Weisman, "Reagan Ends Ban."

12. *SIPRI Yearbook* (various years).

13. Thomas Ohlson and Elisabeth Skons, "The Trade in Major Conventional Weapons," in Stockholm International Peace Research Institute, *SIPRI Yearbook 1987: World Armaments and Disarmament* (New York: Oxford University Press, 1988).

14. Stephen D. Goose, "Armed Conflicts in 1986, and the Iraq-Iran War," in *SIPRI Yearbook 1987*, p. 306.

15. Timmerman, *Death Lobby*, pp. 227–229, 373–374; Geraldine Brooks, "Hussein Threatens Use of Force to Hold Oil-Output Quotas," *Wall Street Journal*, July 18, 1990; Karen Elliott House, "Iraqi President Hussein Sees New Mideast War Unless America Acts," *Wall Street Journal*, June 28, 1990; and Congressman Henry Gonzalez, "Introduction to the BNL Scandal—Is This Iraqgate?" undated speech, U.S. House of Representatives, Washington, D.C., 1991.

16. Author's calculation from U.S. Department of Defense, DSAA, *Foreign Military Sales...*, fiscal years 1981–1992.

17. Steven R. Weisman, "Reagan Says U.S. Would Bar a Takeover in Saudi Arabia That Imperiled Flow of Oil: Rules Out 'An Iran,'" *New York Times*, October 2, 1981.

18. Fred Halliday, *Arabia without Sultans* (New York: Vintage Books, 1975), pp. 59–61.

19. Joe Stork, *Middle East Oil and the Energy Crisis* (New York: Monthly Review Press, 1975), pp. 29–32.

20. Stork, *Middle East Oil*, pp. 31–32; and Halliday, *Arabia without Sultans*, p. 62.

21. Stork, *Middle East Oil*, p. 36.

22. *New York Times*, May 17, 1951, cited in Stork, *Middle East Oil*, p. 52.

23. "Saudi Arabia and the United States: The New Context in an Evolving 'Special Relationship,'" report prepared for the Subcommittee on Europe and the Middle East, Committee on Foreign Affairs, U.S. House of Representatives, by the Foreign Affairs and National Defense Division, Congressional Research Service, Library of Congress (Washington, D.C.: U.S. Government Printing Office, 1981), p. 47.

24. Gerth, "Help for Rebels."

25. Ibid. See also Neil A. Lewis, "Saudi Linked to Donations to Angola Rebels," *New York Times*, July 2, 1987.

26. Steven V. Roberts, Stephen Engelberg, and Jeff Gerth, "Prop for U.S. Policy: Secret Saudi Funds," *New York Times*, June 21, 1987.

27. U.S. House of Representatives, Committee on International Relations, Subcommittee on International Political and Military Affairs, "Military Sales to Saudi Arabia—1975" (Washington, D.C.: U.S. Government Printing Office, 1976), pp. 2–13; U.S. Department of Defense, DSAA, *Foreign Military Sales....*

28. Peter Arnett, "U.S. Vets to Train Saudis," *Washington Post*, February 9, 1975; and U.S. House of Representatives, Committee on International Relations, Subcommittee on International Political and Military Affairs, "U.S. Defense Contractors' Training of Foreign Military Forces," hearings, March 20, 1975 (Washington, D.C.: U.S. Government Printing Office, 1976).

29. Stephen Engelberg, Jeff Gerth, and Tim Weiner, "U.S.-Saudi Deals in 90's Shifting Away from Cash Toward Credit," *New York Times*, August 23, 1993.

30. Elaine Sciolino and Eric Schmitt, "Saudi Arabia, Its Purse Thinner, Learns How to Say 'No' to U.S.," *New York Times*, November 4, 1994.

31. For more on Saudi financial and political troubles, see Clay Chandler, "Desert Shock: Saudis Are Cash-Poor," *Washington Post*, October 28, 1994; and Geraldine Brooks, "Saudi Arabia Is Facing Debts and Defections that Strain U.S. Ties," *Wall Street Journal*, October 25, 1994.

32. Stork, "Israel as Strategic Asset," p. 5.

33. U.S. Department of Defense, DSAA, *Foreign Military Sales. . .*, various years.

34. Stork, "Israel as Strategic Asset."

35. Milton Jamail and Margo Gutierrez, "Israel in Central America: Nicaragua, Honduras, El Salvador, Costa Rica," *Middle East Report*, May–June 1986, pp. 26–30; Cheryl A. Rubenberg, "Israel and Guatemala: Arms, Advice, and Counterinsurgency," *Middle East Report*, May–June 1986, pp. 16–22.

36. Rubenberg, "Israel and Guatemala," p. 20; and Berryman, *What's Wrong in Central America*, p. 25.

37. Andrew and Leslie Cockburn, *Dangerous Liaison: The Inside Story of the U.S.–Israel Covert Relationship* (New York: HarperCollins, 1991), pp. 255–257; Jonathan Marshall, Peter Dale Scott, and Jane Hunter, *The Iran-Contra Connection: Secret Teams and Covert Operations in the Reagan Era* (Boston: South End Press, 1987), pp. 13–15; Sklar, *Washington's War*, pp. 133, 223–225; and Jamail and Gutierrez, "Israel in Central America," p. 28.

38. Andrew and Leslie Cockburn, *Dangerous Liaison*, pp. 282–283.

39. Matti Golan, *The Road to Peace: A Biography of Shimon Peres* (New York: Warner Books, 1989), p. 119, as cited in Andrew and Leslie Cockburn, *Dangerous Liaison*, p. 292.

40. Edward T. Pound, "Inquiry on Alleged Israeli Resales Finds U.S. Vulnerable to Other Arms Diversions," *Wall Street Journal*, March 16, 1992; Thomas L. Friedman, "Arms Export Reports Further Strain U.S.-Israeli Ties," *New York Times*, March 15, 1992; Norman Kempster, "Defiant Arens Defends Israeli Weapons Sales," *Los Angeles Times*, March 15, 1992; and William Safire, "Bandarbush," *New York Times*, April 20, 1992.

41. Grimmett, *Conventional Arms Transfers*, p. 52.

42. "U.S. Arms Transfers to the Midle East Since the Invasion of Kuwait," Washington D.C., The Arms Control Association, June 21, 1994.

43. John Mintz, "Despite Peace, Israel Plans Major U.S. Aircraft Purchase," *Washington Post*, September 11, 1993; David Evans, "Despite Accord, Mideast Arms Race in High Gear," *Chicago Tribune*, September 21, 1993; and Philip Finnegan and Barbara Opall, "U.S. May Give Jordan Billions in Military Aid," *Defense News*, November 7–13, 1994.

Chapter 11. Who Armed Iraq?

1. For the best accounting to date of how the United States and its allies helped build Saddam Hussein's war machine, see Timmerman, *Death Lobby*; and Alan Friedman, *Spider's Web: The Secret History of How the White House Armed Iraq* (New York: Bantam Books, 1993).

2. U.S. Department of Justice, "Officers of Italian Bank in Atlanta Charged with Making Fraudulent Loans to Iraq Totaling More than $4 Billion," press release, February 28, 1991.

3. Ibid. See also *United States of America v. Christopher P. Drogoul, Therese Marcelle Barden, Amedeo Carollis, Entrade International, Yavuz Tezeller, Rafidain Bank, Sadik Hasson Taha Abdul Munim Rasheed, Raja Hassan Ali, and Safa Haji Al-Habobi*, criminal indictment 91-78, February 28, 1991.

4. George Lardner, Jr., "Ex-Official of Italian Bank to Enter Plea in Iraq Loans," *Washington Post*, May 29, 1992.

5. U.S. Department of Justice, *United States v. Christopher Drogoul, et al.*, p. 3; and Roderick Oram, "Atlanta's Bankers Wonder About the Quiet Italian," *Financial Times*, September 8, 1989.

6. "BNL, Iraq, and the CCC Program: Statement of The Honorable Henry B. Gonzalez, Chairman, Committee on Banking, Finance, and Urban Affairs," 1992; and Henry B. Gonzalez, "Introduction to the BNL Scandal—Is This Iraqgate?" unpublished statements, 1992.

7. U.S. Department of Justice, *United States v. Christopher Drogoul et al.*, pp. 88–98; and Timmerman, *Death Lobby*, pp. 225–228.

8. U.S. Department of Justice, *United States v. Christopher Drogoul et al.*, pp. 18–21.

9. Sullivan and Gilmore, "Arming of Iraq."

10. Ibid; and Friedman, *Spider's Web*, pp. 110–111.

11. Sharon LaFraniere and Jeffrey R. Smith, "BNL Special Counsel Unneeded, Report Says," *Washington Post*, December 10, 1992; Peter Mantius, "Reno Names Ex-Aide to Head Task Force in BNL Loan Scandal," *Atlanta Constitution*, July 4, 1993; William Safire, "Is the Fix In?" *New York Times*, September 9, 1993; Kenneth H. Bacon, "Ex-Official in BNL Case Pleads Guilty; Decision May Fuel Charges of Coverup," *Wall Street Journal*, September 3, 1993; "U.S. Renews Probe into Iraqi Weapons Buildup," *Baltimore Sun*, September 13, 1993; Joe Davidson, "Defendants in BNL Case Get Probation for Involvement in Sales to Iraq," *Wall Street Journal*, August 25, 1993; "Report Says Governments Knew of BNL Loans to Iraq," *Wall Street Journal*, January 27, 1994; Kenneth Cline, "Guilty Pleas Fail to Clear Up Mystery Shrouding Lavoro," *American Banker*, January 7, 1994; and Kenneth Cline, "Troubled Lavoro Closing Its Branch in Atlanta As U.S. Probe Winds Up," *American Banker*, July 25, 1994; and U.S. Department of Justice, Addendum to the BNL Task Force Final Report," January 17, 1995.

12. Sullivan and Gilmore, "Arming of Iraq"; and Timmerman, *Death Lobby*, pp. 286–287.

13. "How Iraq Built Its War Machine Through U.S. Sources," statement of Henry Gonzalez, Chairman, Committee on Banking, Finance, and Urban Affairs, U.S. House of Representatives, February 3, 1992.

14. Timmerman, *Death Lobby*, pp. 311–313.

15. Testimony of Gary Milhollin, Director, Wisconsin Project on Nuclear Arms Control, and Stephen Bryen, Delta Tech Corp., at hearings on "U.S. Government Controls on Sales to Iraq," U.S. House of Representatives, Committee on Government Operations, Subcommittee on Commerce, Consumer, and Monetary Affairs, September 27, 1990 (Washington, D.C.: U.S. Government Printing Office, 1991), pp. 17–20, 34–37; Kenneth Timmerman, "Surprise! We Gave Hussein the Bomb," *New York Times*, October 25, 1991; and Sam Fulwood III, "2 Ex-Officials Assail U.S. Policy on Past Technology Sales to Iraq," *Los Angeles Times*, September 28, 1990.

16. Testimony of Bryen at hearings on "U.S. Government Controls"; and Timmerman, *Death Lobby*, pp. 386–388.

17. U.S. Department of Commerce, "Fact Sheet on Export Licensing for Iraq," with attached computer printout, March 1991; and Michael Wines, "U.S. Tells of Prewar Technology Sales to Iraq Worth $500 Million," *New York Times*, March 12, 1991.

18. U.S. Department of Commerce, "Fact Sheet."

19. Pasztor, "Chilean Dealer Smuggled Weapons"; and ABC News, Nightline/Financial Times Arms Sales Report, show 2609, transcript, May 23, 1991.

20. Timmerman, *Death Lobby*, pp. 167–170, 250; and ABC News, *20/20*, "Made in the U.S.A.," February 1, 1991.

21. "Man Who Made Supergun"; Adams, *Bull's Eye*, pp. 10–12, 274–278; and Malone, Halevy, and Hemingway, "Guns We May Face."

22. Sullivan and Gilmore, "Arming of Iraq"; and Waas, "What We Gave Saddam."

23. "Man Who Made Supergun."

24. Sullivan and Gilmore, "Arming of Iraq."

25. "BNL, Iraq, and CCC Program," p. 3.

26. Statement of Henry Gonzalez, Chairman, Committee on Banking, Finance, and Urban Affairs, U.S. House of Representatives, at Hearings Before the Committee on the Judiciary, U.S. House of Representatives, on the Issue of Appointing an Independent Counsel on Matters Related to Iraq, June 2, 1992, p. 7.

27. Mark Feldstein, "AGSCAM: The New World Money Order," *Washington Monthly*, April 1991.

28. "BNL, Iraq, and CCC Program," p. 9.

29. Guy Gugliotta, "Bush, Others Said to Have Repeatedly Pressed Bank to Aid Iraq," *Washington Post*, February 25, 1992; and Murray Waas and Douglas Frantz, "Bush Had Long History of Support for Iraq Aid," *Los Angeles Times*, February 24, 1992.

30. Waas and Frantz, "Bush Had Long History."

31. Ibid.

32. George Lardner, "Gonzalez Iraq Exposé," *Washington Post*, March 22, 1992; and Mark A. Siegel, "Saddam Hussein's Other Republican Guards," *Wall Street Journal*, March 21, 1991.

33. "BNL, Iraq, and CCC Program," pp. 15–16 and attachments.

34. Douglas Frantz and Murray Waas, "U.S. Loans Indirectly Financed Iraq Military," *Los Angeles Times*, February 25, 1992.

35. "BNL, Iraq, and CCC Program," attachment.

36. Frantz and Waas, "U.S. Loans"; and Lardner, "Gonzalez Iraq Exposé."

37. Committee on Banking, Finance, and Urban Affairs, U.S. House of Representatives, "Banca Nazionale del Lavoro Affair and Regulation and Supervision of U.S. Branches and Agencies of Foreign Banks," October 16, 1990 (Washington, D.C.: U.S. Government Printing Office, 1991), pp. 238–241.

38. See note 26 above; attached letter from Robert L. Barr and Gale McKenzie to the Atlanta Federal Reserve, January 9, 1990; and John J. Fialka and Peter Truell, "As 'Iraqgate' Unfolds, New Evidence Raises Questions of a Cover-Up," *Wall Street Journal*, October 9, 1992.

39. Internal Federal Reserve memorandum, included in Gonzalez, op. cit., note 26; *Congressional Record*, March 30, 1992, pp. H2005–H2014; Dean Baquet, "Investigators Say U.S. Shielded Iraqis from Bank Inquiry," *New York Times*, March 20, 1992; and Jack Newfield, "Baghdad Blunder," *New York Post*, June 9, 1992.

40. Fialka and Truell, "As 'Iraqgate' Unfolds"; and list of unindicted coconspirators in the BNL case reviewed by the author in U.S. District Court, Northern District of Georgia.

41. See note 26 above; and *Congressional Record*, March 16, 1992, pp. H1274–H1282.

42. *Congressional Record*, March 16, 1992.

43. See note 26 above; and attachments on Bush's conflict of interest waivers.

44. Douglas Frantz and Murray Waas, "U.S. to OK High-Tech Sales to Iran and Syria," *Los Angeles Times*, February 13, 1992.

45. "Data Show U.S. Approved $60 Million in Sales to Iran," *Washington Post*, January 30, 1992.

46. Lora Lumpe, "COCOM To Be Disbanded: Regime on Conventional Arms Being Cobbled Together," *Arms Sales Monitor*, No. 24, March 15, 1994; and Keith Bradsher, "U.S. Plans More Aid to Exports," *New York Times*, September 30, 1993.

Chapter 12. Selling Out: The Korean Connection and the New Dynamics of the Arms Trade

1. U.S. Congress, Office of Technology Assessment, *The Global Arms Industry* (Washington, D.C.: U.S. Government Printing Office, 1992).

2. William D. Hartung, "F/A-18 Deal Boosts Global Arms Trade," *Bulletin of the Atomic Scientists*, November 1990.

3. Chung-in Moon, "South Korea: Between Security and Vulnerability," in James Everett Katz, ed., *The Implications of Third World Industrialization* (Lexington, Mass.: D.C. Heath, 1986).

4. U.S. Arms Control and Disarmament Agency, *World Military Expenditures and Arms Transfers, 1988* (Washington, D.C.: U.S. Government Printing Office, 1990); and Thomas Ohlson and Elisabeth Skons, "The Trade in Major Conventional Weapons," *SIPRI Yearbook 1987: World Armaments and Disarmament 1987* (New York: Oxford University Press, 1987).

5. "Examination of the M-16 Coproduction Agreement Between the United States and South Korea," hearing before the Subcommittee on Investigations, Committee on Armed Services, U.S. House of Representatives, May 5, 1988.

6. Hartung, "F/A-18 Deal."

7. U.S. General Accounting Office, *Military Coproduction: U.S. Management of Programs Worldwide* (Washington, D.C.: U.S. General Accounting Office, 1989).

8. Janne E. Nolan, *Military Industry in Taiwan and South Korea* (New York: St. Martin's Press, 1986), pp. 69, 78.

9. Sampson, *Arms Bazaar*, pp. 141–145, 246; and "Thomas Jones—Life of a Salesman," in Ralph Nader and William Taylor, *The Big Boys: Power and Position in American Business* (New York: Pantheon, 1986).

10. "The World of the 'Renaissance Executive,'" *Newsweek*, November 18, 1963; and Nader and Taylor, *Big Boys*, p. 380.

11. Nader and Taylor, *Big Boys*, p. 357.

12. John Hanrahan, "The Devil and Mr. Jones," *Common Cause*, November/December 1990.

13. Ralph Vartabedian, "Era Ends as Jones Exits Top Post at Northrop," *Los Angeles Times*, January 1, 1990.

14. Sampson, *Arms Bazaar*, pp. 141–143; and Hanrahan, "Devil and Mr. Jones," pp. 16–17.

15. Nader and Taylor, *Big Boys*, p. 373; and David Pauly, John Barnes, and Lloyd H. Norman, "The Comeback of Tom Jones," *Newsweek*, January 31, 1977.

16. William D. Hartung, *Weapons for the World Update 1982: The U.S. Corporate Role in Foreign Arms Transfers*, Council on Economic Priorities publication N81-7 (New York: Council on Economic Priorities, 1982); Nader and Taylor, *Big Boys*, pp. 382–394; and Anthony F. Jurkus, "Requiem for a Lightweight: The Northrop F-20 Strategic Initiative," *Strategic Management Journal*, vol. 11, 1990, pp. 59–68.

17. Ralph Vartabedian, "Northrop's $102,000-a-Year Korean Connection," *Los Angeles Times*, June 17, 1988.

18. Eileen White Read and Joseph P. Manguno, "Seoul Brother: Northrop Signed on Secret Lobbyist to Try to Sell F-20 to Korea," *Wall Street Journal*, June 5, 1988.

19. "Northrop Corp. Investigation," hearing before the Subcommittee on Oversight and Investigations of the Committee on Energy and Commerce, U.S. House of Representatives, One-hundredth Congress, Second Session, September 28, 1988 (Washington, D.C.: U.S. Government Printing Office, 1989), pp. 5, 47; and Ralph Vartabedian, "Northrop Deals with South Korea Pursued Despite Officers' Doubts," *Los Angeles Times*, June 3, 1988.

20. Ralph Vartabedian, "Letter Suggests Extortion of Northrop in Korea Deals," *Los Angeles Times*, November 3, 1989.

21. "Northrop Corp. Investigation," testimony of Bruce Chafin, pp. 25–33, 108.

22. Ralph Vartabedian, "Consultants for Northrop Were Big Spenders," *Los Angeles Times*, August 15, 1988.

23. "Northrop Corp. Investigation," Chafin testimony, pp. 25–33.

24. Read and Manguno, "Seoul Brother."

25. Ibid.

26. International Court of Arbitration, International Chamber of Commerce, Final Award in *Northrop-Korea Investments v. Jong Hun Lee et al.*, September 4, 1990, p. 25; and Ralph Vartabedian, "Consultants Were Big Spenders."

27. "Northrop Corp. Investigation," pp. 67–107; and Read and Manguno, "Seoul Brother."

28. Ralph Vartabedian, "Letter Suggests Extortion of Northrop in Korea Deals," *Los Angeles Times*, November 3, 1989.

29. Bruce A. Smith, "Northrop Closing Out F-20 Fighter Project," *Aviation Week and Space Technology*, November 24, 1986.

30. Vartabedian, "Letter Suggests Extortion."

31. "Northrop Corp. Investigation," pp. 67–107.

32. "Northrop Corp. Investigation," Chafin testimony.

33. "Northrop Sues Ex-Aide Over S. Korean Deals," *Los Angeles Times*, February 15, 1989.

34. Ralph Vartabedian, "Northrop Claim in S. Korea Case Rejected by Arbitrator," *Los Angeles Times*, July 18, 1990; and International Court of Arbitration, Final Award in Northrop-Korea Investments.

35. Rick Wartzman and Roy J. Harris, Jr., "Northrop Draws Panel's Rebuke; Chairman Quits," *Wall Street Journal*, September 20, 1990; and Ralph Vartabedian, "Era Ends as Jones Exits Top Post at Northrop," *Los Angeles Times*, January 1, 1990.

36. "Federal Securities Laws and Defense Contracting—Part 3," hearings before the Subcommittee on Oversight and Investigations, Committee on Energy and Commerce, U.S. House of Representatives, Ninety-ninth Congress, First Session (Washington, D.C.: U.S. Government Printing Office, 1986), pp. 181–291.

37. "McDonnell Payments Described," *St. Louis Post-Dispatch*, June 23, 1988; Robert L. Koenig, "Switzerland Requests Data on Defense-Fraud Inquiry," *St. Louis Post-Dispatch*, June 25, 1988; and Hartung, "F/A-18 Deal."

38. John Mintz and Jaehoon Ahn, "South Korea Targets Military Contracts: General Dynamics' Fighter Is Among Those Being Probed for Possible Bribes," *Washington Post*, May 22, 1993; South Korea's Kim Fires General Tied to Scandal," *Wall Street Journal*, July 15, 1993; and Steve Glain, "New Arrests Made in Probe of South Korea's Weapons Deals," *Wall Street Journal*, July 19, 1993.

39. Damon Darlin, "McDonnell Douglas Picked for Seoul Fighter Project," *Wall Street Journal*, December 21, 1989; Ralph Vartabedian, "S. Korea Dumps McDonnell Jets for General Dynamics"' *Los Angeles Times*, March 29, 1991; Adam Goodman, "Korea Drops Hornets," *St. Louis Post-Dispatch*, March 29, 1991; and David Silverberg, "U.S., Korea Take Next Step Toward Completion of F-16 Sale," *Defense News*, June 10, 1991.

40. Damon Darlin, "Korea Feels Heat from Japan FSX Deal," *Wall Street Journal*, June 7, 1989; and John D. Morrocco, "FX Fighter Program to Set Stage for Air Force Modernization Plan" and "Samsung Keys Future Growth to FX Fighter Program," *Aviation Week and Space Technology*, June 12, 1989.

41. Notes for remarks by George J. Kourpias, International President, International Association of Machinists and Aerospace Workers, General Dynamics "Fairness" Rally, Fort Worth, Tex., June 25, 1992.

42. Hanrahan, "Devil and Mr. Jones."

43. Read and Manguno, "Seoul Brother."

44. U.S. Congress, Office of Technology Assessment, *Global Arms Industry*, pp. 6, 8–9.

45. Ibid, p. 27.

46. U.S. General Accounting Office, *Military Exports: Concerns Over Offsets Generated With U.S. Foreign Military Financing Funds* (Washington, DC: U.S. GAO, 1994); Lora Lumpe, "GAO Urges Banning Offsets on FMF-financed Arms Sales," *Arms Sales Monitor*, No. 26, July 30, 1994; William D. Hartung, *Conflicting Values, Diminishing Returns: The Hidden Costs of the Arms Trade* (New York: World Policy Institute, 1994).

47. "Feingold Launches Investigation into Arms Sale Payoff Offer," Press Release, Office of Senator Russ Feingold, March 2, 1993; and correspondence from Senator Feingold to the Department of Defense, U.S. Trade Representative, and other relevant agencies regarding this issue; and Lora Lumpe, "Sweet Deals and Low Politics: Offsets in the Arms Market," *F.A.S. Public Interest Report*, Vol. 47, No. 1, Washington, DC, Federation of American Scientists, January/February 1994.

Chapter 13. The Clinton Policy: Arms Control or Business as Usual?

1. Hartung, "Arms Sales Win Votes."

2. "Bush Offers $2 Billion in Farm Aid," *Rocky Mountain News*, September 3, 1992; Michael Wines, "$8 Billion Directed to Wheat Farmers and Arms Workers," *New York*

Times, September 3, 1992; and Lee Feinstein, "Administration to Sell Advanced F-16 Fighters to Taiwan," *Arms Control Today*, September 1992.

3. Don Oberdorfer, "1982 Arms Policy with China Victim of Bush Campaign, Texas Lobbying," *Washington Post*, September 4, 1992.

4. "Hearings on Proposed Sale of F-15 Aircraft to Saudi Arabia and U.S.-Saudi Commercial Disputes," Committee on Foreign Affairs, U.S. House of Representatives, Subcommittee on Arms Control and Subcommittee on Europe and the Middle East, September 23, 1992, Federal News Service Transcript, pp. 30–31.

5. George Bush, address to McDonnell Douglas employees, Lambert Field, St. Louis, Missouri, September 11, 1992; and Martin Kasindorf, "Bush: Let's Make a (Jet) Deal," *New York Newsday*, September 12, 1992.

6. Jon Sawyer, "Chances Improve for F-15 Sale to Saudi Arabia," *St. Louis Post-Dispatch*, August 30, 1992.

7. "Hearings on Proposed F-15 Sale," p. 38.

8. Ibid., p. 39.

9. Ibid., pp. 31–35.

10. Ibid., p. 28.

11. Testimony of Congressman Lawrence J. Smith before the House Foreign Affairs Committee, September 23, 1992.

12. "Hearings on Proposed F-15 Sale," p. 43.

13. "Excerpts from Clinton's News Conference at the Capitol," *Washington Post*, November 20, 1992; and "Party Statement of Policies Mirrors Clinton's Goals" (reprint of the text of the Democratic platform), *Congressional Quarterly Weekly Report*, July 18, 1992, p. 2112.

14. "Governor Clinton Supports F-15 Sale to Saudi Arabia," Clinton/Gore Campaign press release, August 26, 1992.

15. Caleb Rossiter and Anne Detrick, "Are Weapons Makers Sold on Clinton?" *St. Louis Post-Dispatch*, August 2, 1992.

16. See, for example, statement by Warren Christopher before the Senate Appropriations Committee, Subcommittee on Foreign Operations, March 30, 1993; and testimony of Lynn E. Davis, Senate Foreign Relations Committee, March 17, 1993.

17. Testimony of Davis, Senate Foreign Relations Committee; William J. Perry, "Desert Storm and Deterrence," *Foreign Affairs*, Fall 1991, pp. 66–82.

18. Testimony of Les Aspin before the Senate Armed Services Committee, January 7, 1993.

19. "Administration May Classify Conventional Arms Transfer Policy," *Inside the Pentagon*, August 18, 1994; and John Tirpak, "Clinton Defense Export Policy to Be Delayed; Draft Favors Industry," *Aerospace Daily*, July 22, 1994.

20. Joel Johnson quote is from a discussion with the author, November 9, 1993; for information on the Clinton administration's decision to support industry's request to eliminate R&D recoupment fees, see Lora Lumpe, "Admin. Seeks Repeal of FMS Recoupment Fees," *Arms Sales Monitor*, No. 22, September 30, 1994.

21. Information on shift in Clinton air show policy from Lora Lumpe, *Arms Sales Monitor*, No. 24, March 15, 1994, and various other issues from 1994; quotes from *60 Minutes* are from Ed Bradley (correspondent) and John Hamlin (producer), "Arms Supermarket," CBS News *60 Minutes*, November 27, 1994.

22. Barbara Opall, "Arms Transfer Proposal to Mimic Reagan, Bush Policy," *Defense News*, September 5–11, 1994; Tony Capaccio, "No Radical Change in Conventional Weapons Policy," *Defense Week*, October 31, 1994; Ralph Vartabedian and John M. Broder, "U.S. Weighs New Arms Sales Policy," *Los Angeles Times*, November 15, 1994; Eric Schmitt, "Clinton Devises New Guidelines on Arms Sales," *New York Times*, November 16, 1994; and White House Press Office, "Fact Sheet: Conventional Arms Transfer Policy," February 17, 1995.

23. For background on the Code of Conduct campaign, see testimony of Dr. Caleb S. Rossiter, director of the Project on Demilitarization and Democracy, before the Subcom-

mittee on International Security, International Organizations, and Human Rights and the Subcommittee on International Operations of the House Committee on Foreign Affairs, November 9, 1993.

24. Congressional Budget Office, *Limiting Conventional Arms Exports to the Middle East* (Washington, D.C.: U.S. Government Printing Office, 1992), pp. 57–65.

25. William D. Hartung, *Conflicting Values, Diminishing Returns*, op. cit.; and William D. Hartung, "The Phantom Profits of the War Trade," *New York Times*, March 6, 1994.

26. On this point, see Ann Markusen and Joel Yudken, *Dismantling the Cold War Economy* (New York: Basic Books, 1992).

27. Ibid.

28. Figures for the 1992 elections are from the Federal Election Commission, as cited by Caleb Rossiter, Project on Demilitarization and Democracy, at a Capitol Hill briefing on alternatives to arms exports cosponsored by Peace Action and the National Commission on Economic Conversion and Disarmament, June 24, 1993 figures for the 1994 elections are from Philip Finnegan, "PACs Cast a Powerful Vote," *Defense News*, November 7–13, 1994.

29. Sheila Kaplan, "The Revolving Door Still Spins—The Cash-Filled Holes in Clinton's Ethics Policy," *Washington Post*, January 31, 1993.

30. Grimmett, *Conventional Arms Transfers*.

31. See William D. Hartung, "Curbing the Arms Trade: From Rhetoric to Restraint," *World Policy Journal*, vol. 9, no. 3, Spring 1992, pp. 219–247.

32. On this point, see Nicole Ball, *Pressing for Peace: Can Aid Induce Reform?* (Washington, D.C.: Overseas Development Council, 1992).

Epilogue

1. Kent Jenkins, Jr. "North Makes a Big Profit Off Iran-Contra, Report Says," *Washington Post*, October 10, 1993; Michael Janofsky, "Harsh Words in Final Day of Campaign for the Senate," *New York Times*, November 8, 1994; and state-by-state election wrap-up, *New York Times*, November 10, 1994, p. B10.

2. Thomas E. Ricks, "Pentagon Considers Selling Overseas a Large Part of High-Tech Weaponry," *Wall Street Journal*, February 14, 1994; Douglas Barrie and Graham Warwick, "F-16 Swap Plan Could Lead to Export Boom," *Flight International*, January 26–February 1, 1994; David A. Fulghum, "Surplus Sales Seen Funding New Buys," *Aviation Week and Space Technology*, February 14, 1994; and "Lockheed Supports Air Force Proposal to Sell Inventory F-16s," *Inside the Air Force*, January 21, 1994.

3. "The F-22 Air Superiority Fighter: Peace Through Conventional Deterrence," Lockheed Corporation brochure, March 1994; and David Evans, "Catch F-22," *In These Times*, July 11, 1994.

4. Amy Borrus, "This Is Going to Be the Biggest Kahuna Around—Rivals Are Reeling in the Wake of Martin Marietta/Lockheed Merger," *Business Week*, September 12, 1994; Philip Finnegan, "Lockheed Leapfrogs McDonnell—Acquisitions Make Firm No. 1 Defense Company," *Defense News*, July 18–24, 1994; Philip Finnegan, "PACs Cast a Powerful Vote: Defense Mergers Yield Fat Political War Chests," *Defense News*, November 7–13, 1994; interview by the author with Jeff Rhodes, communications department, Lockheed Corporation, Marietta, Georgia, November 30, 1994; and William D. Hartung, "The Speaker from Lockheed?", *The Nation*, January 30, 1995.

5. The poll on public opposition to arming dictators was commissioned by the National Security News Service, and was conducted by ICR Survey Research Group of Media, Pennsylvania between January 14th and 18th of 1994; the margin of error was plus or minus 1.9%, and it was based on a survey of 1,003 Americans.

Index